OXFORD HISTORICAL MONOGRAPHS

MEN VERSUS THE STATE

Herbert Spencer and
Late Victorian Individualism

M. W. TAYLOR

CLARENDON PRESS · OXFORD
1992

Oxford University Press, Walton Street, Oxford OX2 6DP

Oxford New York Toronto
Delhi Bombay Calcutta Madras Karachi
Petaling Jaya Singapore Hong Kong Tokyo
Nairobi Dar es Salaam Cape Town
Melbourne Auckland
and associated companies in
Berlin Ibadan

Oxford is a trade mark of Oxford University Press

Published in the United States
by Oxford University Press. New York

British Library Cataloguing in Publication Data
Data available

Library of Congress Cataloging in Publication Data
Taylor, M. W. (Michael W.)
Men versus the state : Herbert Spencer and late Victorian
individualism / M. W. Taylor.
p. cm. — (Oxford historical monographs)
Includes bibliographical references and index.
1. Spencer, Herbert, 1820–1903—Contributions in political
science. 2. Individualism—Great Britain—History—19th century.
I. Title. II. Series.
JC223.S662T39 1992
320.5′12—dc20 91-24172
ISBN 0-19-820239-3

Typeset by Rowland Phototypesetting Ltd
Bury St Edmunds, Suffolk
Printed and bound in
Great Britain by Bookcraft Ltd,
Midsomer Norton, Bath

TO
MY PARENTS

PREFACE

It is customary to begin a study of Herbert Spencer with the lamentation that his work has been unjustly neglected by social scientists and historians of political thought. That his philosophy has been neglected since his death in 1903 is undoubted; whether or not that neglect is unjust is something that each reader must judge for him- or herself. This book is not intended to defend Spencer's political theory, but in it I have endeavoured to present him as a much more complex and subtle thinker than have the standard textbook accounts.

Spencer's complexity as a thinker is in large measure due to his philosophical ambitions, which were pre-eminently synthetic: the theory of evolution was to be used as a tool with which to reconcile the chief conflicting theories or modes of thought of the Victorian age. His standing as a philosopher must, therefore, depend in large measure on his success in realizing these ambitions, and, as I suggest, there remain many unresolved tensions in Spencer's thought.

Nevertheless, it would be mistaken to ascribe the subsequent neglect of Spencer to his deficiencies as a philosopher. According to a view of intellectual progress modelled on the natural sciences, each generation makes its advances by overcoming the errors and misconceptions of the past. But such a view is singularly inappropriate for the human sciences: while nothing can be more comprehensively discredited than a disproved scientific theory like Phlogiston, past political theories have a stronger capacity for survival, and exhibit a tendency of returning to haunt later generations. Furthermore, this explanation of Spencer's neglect falls foul of the observation that, not merely many members of the Victorian lay reading public, but philosophers of the calibre of Mill and Sidgwick considered him to be among the leading thinkers of the day, and regarded him as sufficiently their equal to devote considerable resources to engaging him in debate. Are we so very much cleverer than these Victorians that we are able to detect a second-rate autodidact where they saw an intellectual giant?

The reasons for Spencer's neglect must be sought elsewhere. Doubtless such an explanation will consist of a series of overlapping and mutually reinforcing factors, but it would seem worth stressing two considerations which are particularly pertinent to the argument of the present work. In the first place, unlike T. H. Green, Spencer was never a member of a university, and thus failed to spawn an intellectual progeny who would be able to continue and defend his ideas into the twentieth century. Although in the closing decades of his life Spencer did not lack for admirers, and there were plenty of political theorists who were ready to invoke his authority, they did not see the Synthetic Philosophy as constituting a project which required further development and elaboration; for the Individualists, Spencer had discovered a body of 'scientific' truth which required only repeated assertion to gain ascendency in the public mind. In contrast to Green's students, many of whom became important philosophical figures in their own right, Spencer's disciples contented themselves with producing 'Introductions', 'Expositions', and even an 'Epitome', of their master's work. Indeed, it was one of the great ironies of intellectual history that Spencer's chief theoretical innovations were more clearly appreciated by those who found his politics uncongenial, and both J. A. Hobson and L. T. Hobhouse readily acknowledged the considerable debt which they owed to his work.

Perhaps the most important reason for Spencer's neglect, however, is that for most of his mature years he was engaged in elaborating a defence of a social and economic order which was already in the process of passing away. Individualism was rooted in a set of ideals appropriate to a rapidly industrializing society rather than a society, like that of late nineteenth-century Britain, which was confronting the problems and tensions caused by a maturing industrialism. The Individualists never succeeded in comprehending the social changes which were rapidly making their ideas obsolete, and the counterpart of this was their failure fully to comprehend the enemy with which they were engaged. Their criticisms of 'socialism', while often telling, were directed at an imaginary social system which apparently had more in common with the unlamented regimes of Eastern Europe than it did with the policies of the New Radicals or with the demands of organized labour. The fact was that the mid-Victorian society to which the Individualists nostalgically harked back was being replaced by another which was, in their terms, neither 'Individualist' nor 'Socialist', a form of social organization which persists to this day. Hence not merely their ideals, but even the categories with which they thought about politics, were being surpassed by events.

Individualism was thus a political theory which remained deeply rooted in the ideas and assumptions of the mid-Victorian era, and even to its contemporary critics it appeared curiously outmoded and distant from the leading intellectual currents of the day. The Individualists all belonged to a particular generation of liberal thinkers who had, on the whole, achieved their majority in the years immediately preceding the Second Reform Act, and their doctrine was shaped by the ideals they had imbued in their youth. By the end of the first decade of the twentieth century, most of these thinkers had reached the end of their natural lives, and consequently their doctrine abandoned the scene with them; with the death of his disciples, Spencer's reputation also waned.

The conclusion that Individualism was the exclusive preserve of a particular generation of liberal intellectuals conflicts with the hypothesis with which this project was initially undertaken. It had been my intention to trace the intellectual origins of 'the New Right', a political movement which sprang to prominence in the 1970s, from the point at which the doctrine of the limited state and free market ceased to be a radical creed and became instead an instrument for the defence of the status quo. While the significance of Individualism in the history of liberal political thought is that it does, indeed, represent the first occurrence of *laissez-faire* as a conservative doctrine, there is also little evidence to support the hypothesis of an Apostolic Succession of free-market conservatives from Spencer and the Liberty and Property Defence League to Hayek and the Adam Smith Institute. Although there are important parallels both in terms of structure and detail of the arguments employed by Spencer and Hayek (an issue which is beyond the scope of the present work, although it has yet to be explored), there is no evidence of direct influence being exerted on the latter by the former, and this accords with the conclusion that Individualism had ceased to be a significant political or intellectual force by the outbreak of the First World War. The point may be best expressed by saying that although the Individualists were the precursors of the free marketeers of the 1970s and 1980s, they did not provide the inspiration for New Right theorists. The New Right independently discovered arguments which had once been the stock-in-trade of Individualism.

In thus situating Individualism so firmly in its historical context, it may appear that it is my intention to endorse the theories of those historians of ideas who regard historical texts as a complex of linguistic actions and who regard the interpreter's task as being to recover what the author was doing in writing it—the text's 'point' or 'force'. However, this work has not been inspired by the desire to vindicate a particular methodology in the history of ideas, and in so far as it rests on an explicit methodological presupposition, it is that we should aim to understand past political debates in terms which the protagonists themselves might have recognized, that we should accord significance to what for them had significance. This belief stems not from an a priori conception of the kind of knowledge or understanding uniquely available to the historian of ideas, but rather from the prosaic observation that, unless we make this effort, we have not understood the issues at stake between the protagonists in a past political debate.

I am not aware that the analogy between a book and a biological organism ever occurred to Spencer, but if it had he would no doubt have regarded it as further evidence for his view of evolution: both undergo a process of increasing complexity, increasing mass, and increasing heterogeneity (the chapters become more clearly demarcated, for example), and both adapt themselves to their environment. In the case of this book, which began life as a D.Phil. thesis at the University of Oxford, an important contribution to that environment was made by the constant support and encouragement of my supervisor Michael Freeden, who placed at my disposal his considerable knowledge of late nineteenth-century political thought. My examiners Andrew Vincent and Mark Philp made many valuable criticisms, not all of which I have successfully answered, while Jerry Cohen forced me to clarify my ideas on a number of important points. Colin Matthew also provided much sound guidance, and has prevented me from committing numerous historical blunders; those that remain are despite his best endeavours. I also owe a considerable debt of gratitude to James Meadowcroft, Fred Bartol, and Ewen Green, with whom I have had many valuable discussions on the subject of this work.

My initial year of research was conducted at Nuffield College, Oxford, and was supported by an Economic and Social Research Council grant; I am grateful to both institutions for their generous assistance. The chief work on the thesis was undertaken concurrently with my tenure of the Lecturership in Political Theory at Lincoln College, and I would like to thank my former students for tolerating a tutor who often must have seemed distracted by the demands of his own work. Thanks are also due to the Librarians of Nuffield and Lincoln Colleges, and to the staff of the Bodleian Library, the British Library of Political and Economic Science, and the London Library in St James's Square.

M.W.T.

Hoddesdon Herts

CONTENTS

INTRODUCTION

THE PARADISE LOST OF LIBERALISM

> Among the faithless, faithful only hee;
> Among innumerable false, unmov'd,
> Unshak'n, unseduc'd, unterrifi'd
> His Loyaltie he kept, his Love, his Zeale.

I. Individualism in its Political Context

Writing in the *Fabian Essays in Socialism*, Sidney Webb saw fit to berate 'Mr Herbert Spencer and those who agree in his worship of Individualism' for wanting to 'bring back the legal position which made possible the "white slavery" of which the "sins of legislators" have deprived us.'[1] Despite the fact that the writings of Fabians, New Liberals, and even Conservative Tariff Reformers abound with disparaging references to 'Individualism'', this political theory has been hitherto neglected by historians of late Victorian and Edwardian political thought. In the absence of a sustained examination, the doctrines of the Individualists, like those of the sophists, stand in danger of being known only through the mouths of their partisan critics. It is the objective of the present work to remedy this deficiency and to demonstrate the importance of Individualism for an adequate understanding, not only of the nature of late Victorian political argument, but of the transformation of the doctrine of the limited State and free market from a radical creed into one which became an instrument of the defenders of the status quo.

Like many of the leading ideas and principles of modern British political thought, Individualism had its genesis in the *fin de siècle* crisis of liberalism caused by a society experiencing profound social, economic, and political dislocation. The Great Depression, increased labour unrest and the rise of the New Unionism, the increasing awareness on

---

[1] S. Webb, 'The Basis of Socialism: Historic', in G. B. Shaw (ed.), *Fabian Essays in Socialism* (London, 1889), 40–1.

the part of the political élite of the widespread poverty and unemploy-
ment euphemistically referred to as the 'Social Problem', and the
advance of democracy brought about by the extensions of the franchise
in 1867 and 1884 gave rise to the expectation that the new century would
be characterized by a new type of politics aimed at securing the welfare
of the mass of the population. In response to these challenges the
political theorists of the New Liberalism developed liberal ideology into
a justification for an interventionist State, which accepted a positive
obligation to promote social justice, and which established the intellectual foundations for the mixed economy and Welfare State of the
twentieth century.

The New Liberalism required the abandonment, or at least the
redefinition, of many of the key tenets of the mid-Victorian ideology,
and for an older generation of politicians and political theorists reared
on the doctrines of Cobden and the Philosophic Radicals the identification of their creed with an expanded sphere of State action was
anathema. In response to what they saw as the New Liberals' 'socialistic'
perversion of the liberal tradition, the Individualists argued in defence
of the actual distribution of property and power in late Victorian
Britain.[2] As this work will argue, however, there was a fundamental
conflict between their defence of the status quo and their professions of
doctrinal purity.

Many different meanings may be attached to the term 'individualism',[3] but in the relevant sense it 'was not generally used before the
1880s, had a mainly historical reference after 1918, and is rarely used in
its pure form today.'[4] Before the 1880s, 'individualism' had been a
pejorative term used to describe the allegedly egoistical and atomistic

---

[2] The claim that there was an extended debate between Individualists and New
Liberals is not to endorse the frequent suggestion that the late Victorian 'disagreement
over the role of the state was conceptualized in terms of the opposition between
Individualism and Collectivism' (S. Collini, *Liberalism and Sociology: L. T. Hobhouse and
Political Argument in England 1880–1914* (Cambridge, 1978), 14–15. For a similar claim
see W. H. Greenleaf, *The British Political Tradition*, ii. *The Ideological Heritage* (London,
1983, 15). The fact that a group of political theorists shared sufficient common ground to
be prepared to describe themselves as Individualists does not necessarily imply that their
opponents formed a similarly coherent group who can be classified as Collectivists. Rather
than attempting to force late Victorian political debate into this dichotomous framework—
the Westminster Model of political argument—it would more accurate to regard Individualism as an entrenched position being assailed by a variety of loosely associated guerrilla
bands—including not only New Liberals, but also Idealists, socialists (Christian, Fabian,
and Marxian), and others—who were united in their opposition to Individualism but were
also often divided against each other.   [3] Cf. S. Lukes, *Individualism* (Oxford, 1973).
        [4] Collini, *Liberalism and Sociology*, 16.

social theory of liberalism, and shades of this meaning persisted throughout the period under review.[5] However, when the older generation of Radicals began to describe themselves as 'Individualists' they attempted to reverse its initially pejorative connotations. In the sense in which it was used by these political thinkers 'Individualism' (almost always spelt with a capital 'I') referred to

> that condition in which a man is free to make the most and best of his individual talents, energies, and opportunities, without being checked or fettered by the State in those directions where he does not interfere with the liberty and possessions of other people.[6]

This definition of Individualism already implies the principle which was effectively its cardinal doctrine, the Law of Equal Freedom, which stated that 'every man may claim the fullest liberty to exercise his faculties compatible with the possession of like liberty by every other man.'[7] Although this principle was first formulated by Herbert Spencer as early as 1851, it was not until the closing decades of the century that it acquired widespread use by political theorists who described themselves as Individualists. It was claimed, for example, that Individualism 'really implies the limitation of the rights of each individual by those of every other'[8] and that justice meant the 'freedom to do as one wishes; freedom from restraint—subject to the same or equal freedom in our fellows.'[9] Similarly, another writer declared that 'so long as I do no harm to my neighbour, and use my rights so as not to harm him, or infringe his right of equal liberty, so long he has no just claim to impose on me State restrictions of any kind.'[10] According to this conception, the primary function assigned to the State was that of upholding justice in the sense of ensuring that each individual's exercise of the right to liberty did not infringe the similar right of other individuals. 'It may be fairly said that

---

[5] Even in 1895 e.g. Goldwin Smith could pose the question: 'What is Individualism, against which there is now such an outcry . . . ? Does it mean self-exertion and self-reliance, or does it mean selfish isolation?' His answer was to argue that the defence of individual liberty did not entail 'selfish isolation' since 'freedom does not preclude voluntary association, which may co-exist with it to any extent.' ('The Manchester School', *Contemporary Review*, 67 (1895), 386.)

[6] G. Brooks, *Industry and Property* (London, 1895), 236–7.

[7] H. Spencer, *Social Statics* (1851; 2nd edn., London, 1868), 94.

[8] J. H. Levy, 'Individualism', in E. B. Bax and J. H. Levy, *Socialism and Individualism* (London, n.d. [1904]), 150.

[9] [A.] B. Smith, *Liberty and Liberalism* (London, 1887), 221.

[10] E. Pleydell-Bouverie, *The Province of Government* (London, 1884), 12–3.

the end of government is to promote liberty, so far as governmental coercion prevents worse coercion by private individuals.'[11]

So widespread was the use of the 'equal liberties' formula by the Individualists that it could almost constitute the defining criterion of Individualism. Furthermore, this principle gave rise to a number of subsidiary principles which were also characteristic of Individualist thought. Among these may be included *laissez-faire*, 'the principle which regards the free play of individual liberty as the best security for the good of society, and State intervention as an evil only to be justified by extreme necessity', and the principle of proprietary right which condemned legislative restrictions on property 'not only as inexpedient, but as unjust'. To these principles a third might also be added, namely that competition 'is the soundest mainspring of human progress, and the best regulator of social life.'[12]

The chief document of Individualism was Herbert Spencer's book *The Man versus the State*, first published as a series of articles in the *Contemporary Review* between February and July 1884, which represented the distillate of arguments Spencer had expounded in his System of Synthetic Philosophy over the course of twenty years. In so far as historians of political thought have taken notice of this work, they have tended to make two assumptions which it is the intention of this study to challenge. First of all, it is generally believed that *The Man versus the State* was the isolated protest of a political thinker whose leading doctrines were already intellectually 'discredited'.[13] Yet, as the present work will demonstrate, in the closing decades of the nineteenth century Spencer did not lack for admirers, and there were plenty of political theorists who were ready to invoke his authority for their opposition to any policy which undermined 'liberty and property'. Spencer was simply the leading philosophical spokesman for a significant and influential late nineteenth-century political ideology which, in contrast to the New Liberalism, has received only the slightest attention from historians of political thought.[14]

[11] H. Sidgwick, *The Elements of Politics* (London, 1891), 46.

[12] G. C. Brodrick, 'The Socialistic Tendencies of Modern Democracy', in id., *Literary Fragments* (London, 1891), 214.

[13] A. Bullock and M. Shock, *The Liberal Tradition from Fox to Keynes* (London, 1956), p. xlii; Greenleaf, *Ideological Heritage*, 81; G. Hawthorn, *Enlightenment and Despair* (2nd edn., Cambridge, 1987), 91.

[14] Among examples of the literature on the New Liberalism may be cited P. F. Clarke, *Liberals and Social Democrats* (Cambridge, 1978); Collini, *Liberalism and Sociology*; M. S. Freeden, *The New Liberalism: An Ideology of Social Reform* (Oxford, 1978); H. C. G. Matthew, *The Liberal Imperialists* (Oxford, 1973); M. Richter, *The Politics of Conscience:*

The second assumption which this work proposes to challenge is the widespread belief that the political theory expounded by Spencer is identical to the doctrines of the 'Manchester School' of mid-Victorian Radicals, and that Spencer 'remained a philosophical radical after philosophical radicalism had been obsolete for a generation.'[15] It is certainly true that the Individualists themselves wished to make this identification.[16] Nevertheless, it will be argued that Individualism represented in its own way as much a modification of the creed of the older radicalism as did the New Liberalism. Whereas the latter transformed liberalism into a theory of an activist State, the former transformed the theory of the free market and minimal State from a radical creed into one which provided a dialectical prop for the status quo, including the actual distribution of property and power prevailing in late Victorian society. Philosophic Radicalism had been what the Constitutional lawyer A. V. Dicey was to call a 'militant' creed, which had demanded of existing institutions that they justify themselves before the tribunal of utility.[17] By contrast, Individualism was a defensive creed which regarded the existence of an institution as constituting a presumption in favour of its utility. The change could not be effected without a significant theoretical reorientation.

In order to understand the process by which Individualism emerged out of the late Victorian crisis of liberalism, it is necessary to begin by examining the condition and prospects of liberalism in the mid–Victorian era. For the Individualists this period represented what Fitzjames Stephen was to call in another context 'the Paradise Lost

---

T. H. Green and his Age (London, 1964); A. W. Vincent and R. Plant, *Philosophy, Politics and Citizenship: The Life and Thought of the British Idealists* (Oxford, 1984); P. Weiler, *The New Liberalism* (New York, 1982). By contrast cursory sketches of Individualist thought are to be found in Greenleaf, *Ideological Heritage*, 82 ff., and R. Barker, *Political Ideas in Modern Britain* (London, 1978), 50 ff.

[15] G. H. Sabine and T. L. Thorson, *A History of Political Theory* (4th edn., Hinsdale, Ill., 1973), 654. The claim that Spencer represented 'Liberalism of the Manchester School' is made by Greenleaf, *Ideological Heritage*, 48, and Bullock and Shock, *Liberal Tradition*, p. xli f.

[16] See e.g. the favourable references to Cobden contained in G. Smith, 'Manchester School', 378; M. E. Grant Duff's Address to the Liberty and Property Defence League, in *Report of Proceedings and Speeches of the Twelfth Annual Meeting* (London, 1894), 13; T. D. Mackay, 'Empiricism in Politics', *National Review*, 25 (1895), 794. It is also noteworthy that about this time the collected papers of Sir Lewis Mallet, who had remained throughout his life a devotee of Cobdenite policies, were posthumously published under the title of *Free Exchange* (London, 1891).

[17] A. V. Dicey, *Lectures on the Relation of Law and Public Opinion in England during the Nineteenth Century* (London, 1905), 148.

of Liberalism', since they believed that it was characterized by the triumphant ascendancy of the doctrine of *laissez-faire*.[18] Indeed, it is unquestionable that at the beginning of Gladstone's premiership in 1868 much already had been accomplished by the party of progress. As Colin Matthew has written:

No industrial economy can have existed in which the State played a smaller role than that of the United Kingdom in the 1860s. Government had appeared to forswear responsibility for fiscal and economic management and it had abolished virtually all tariffs, save those non-protective duties required for revenue purposes. As yet, government responsibility for education existed only through its relationship with the Established Church and its schools and universities, and through small grants to non-established denominations. Government involvement in industrial relations and legislation was largely confined to labour relations in the royal dockyards and to the inspectorate created by the Factory Acts. The concept of social welfare in the twentieth-century sense did not exist. Government grudgingly accepted a 'last resort' responsibility in the specific areas of public health and pauperism, but this was a responsibility to prevent disease in the first case and death in the second, not a responsibility for any positive concern in the welfare of individuals.[19]

Nevertheless, this State structure was largely the creation of Peelites and Whigs; for the Radicals, the successors of Cobden and the Benthamites, much remained to be done. In the view of the generation of men who attained their majority in the 1850s and '60s, the future direction for radicalism resided in the further liberation of the individual from restraints imposed by the remnants of the aristocratic State. Before the advent of the Liberal government of 1868, the absence of secret ballots maintained the political influence of the landed class; while the new suffrage of 1867 went only a little way towards realizing the ultimate goal of granting 'the full rights of citizens to all persons', an objective

---

[18] This view was epitomized by Dicey, *Law and Public Opinion*, in which it was claimed that 'Individualism' was the dominant legislative tendency of the forty years after 1830. Dicey's analysis has been much criticized by historians of public policy, who have claimed that the alleged period of pure 'Individualism' or *laissez-faire* is a myth. See e.g. J. B. Brebner, 'Laissez Faire and State Intervention in Nineteenth Century Britain', *Journal of Economic History*, suppl. 8 (1948), 59–73, and, for an attempt to defend Dicey, H. Parris, 'The Nineteenth Century Revolution in Government: A Reappraisal Reappraised', *Historical Journal*, 3 (1960), 17–37. However, the importance of Dicey's account is that it indicates the existence of a body of late Victorian opinion which believed that the mid-cent. had witnessed the ascendency of *laissez-faire*. The question of whether or not this alleged paradise was a myth is no more pertinent than the demonstration of the literal truth of the Bible would be for a study of Christian fundamentalism.

[19] H. C. G. Matthew, *Gladstone, 1809–1874* (Oxford, 1986), 169.

promoted by the Philosophic Radicals and repeated by A. V. Dicey in his contribution to the *Essays on Reform* in 1867.[20] The institutional embodiment of the power of the landed aristocracy, the House of Lords, was also in need of abolition, and the monarchy was not immune from Radical criticisms. Disabilities imposed by religious affiliation remained in the form of University Tests, as did the privileged position of the Anglican Church; disestablishment and the abolition of Church rates were key Radical demands. In addition, freedom of contract was thought to be in need of extension in a variety of spheres of economic activity, especially in terms of the ownership of the land. In the wake of the Anti-Corn Law League, 'a second free trade campaign arose which for twenty years reduced agrarian reform in England to advocacy of a single principle: the abolition of obstacles to land alienation such as family settlements (at the level of the landlord) or customary tenant rights (at the level of the tenant).'[21]

For some of the extreme Radicals, like Herbert Spencer, even these policies did not go far enough. The power of the aristocracy was to be broken by the nationalization of the land, a policy for which he argued with great eloquence in his *Social Statics* of 1851.[22] Moreover, he regarded the mid-Victorian State as merely a staging-post on the way to a much more limited sphere of government in which it would cease to perform even the industrial and social functions described above; ultimately even the Factory Acts and the 1834 Poor Law were to be abolished. Although Peel's Bank Charter Act of 1844, which had lodged the monopoly of note issue with the Bank of England, had been criticized by the Radicals on a variety of grounds, Spencer was also virtually alone in opposing the very idea of a monopolistic central bank. Since all monopolies, especially State-sponsored ones, were inherently

---

[20] A. V. Dicey, 'The Balance of Classes', in *Essays in Reform* (London, 1867).

[21] Clive Dewey, 'Celtic Agrarian Legislation and the Celtic Revival: Historicist Implications of Gladstone's Irish and Scottish Land Acts 1870–1886', *Past and Present*, 64 (1974), 32.

[22] A failure to understand the nature of mid-19th-cent. radicalism has led to a number of misinterpretations of Spencer's thought. The most glaring example is the suggestion by M. Francis that only after 1884 'could [Spencer] be described as a laissez faire theorist.' ('Herbert Spencer and the Myth of Laissez Faire', *Journal of the History of Ideas*, 39 (1978), 328.) Not least of the many misunderstandings contained in Francis's article is a failure to grasp that in 1850 the land-nationalization scheme was a radical, *laissez-faire* proposal. Further, he misreads the 1860 essay on 'The Social Organism' as advocating collectivism (p. 327). It will be shown in Ch. 4 that this was the complete reverse of Spencer's intention.

corrupt, the issue of the currency should be left to the mechanism of the free market.[23]

Nevertheless, the Radicals were united in their belief that the freedom of the individual was to be secured by the further abolition of privileges and disabilities based on birth, creed, or station, and their policies aimed to 'provide for all men a chance of rising by their own exertions.'[24] This type of 'abolitionist' Radical 'only interfered to prevent interference. He would put restraint on no man in doing anything that did not directly check the free dealing of some one in something else.' The tendency of the legislative movement represented by mid-Victorian radicalism was towards the 'realisation of complete freedom of contract' and to 'set men at liberty to dispose of what they had made their own.'[25]

In certain respects the Gladstone government of 1868–74 did not disappoint the expectations of the Radicals. G. J. Goschen, who in 1863 had entered Parliament committed to the ballot and the abolition of religious disabilities and Church rates, reflected on the achievements of the first Gladstone ministry a decade after its fall:

> The chief characteristic of the legislation of 1869–74, which almost cleared the old Liberal programme, was the desire to remove privileges and inequalities. The main feature of its great Acts was abolition. We abolished the prerogative of the Church at the Universities, and in other spheres of education; we abolished the privileged position of the creed of a minority in Ireland; we abolished the power of the purse in the army; we abolished by the Ballot Act the undue influence of wealth and social position, of employers and landowners, at elections.[26]

While most Radicals would have disputed Goschen's contention that these Acts had almost completed the task of liberalism, they would have agreed with his overall assessment of them. The Gladstone administration might not have moved swiftly enough, but at least its general tendency had been in the right direction.

Nevertheless, with the advent of the second Gladstone ministry in

[23] For an excellent historical survey of free banking theories see Vera Smith, *The Rationale of Central Banking* (London, 1936). Although the idea had been a popular one in 1820s and earlier, Spencer was one of the last proponents of the theory in Britain in the 19th cent.; see ibid. 117.

[24] E. Dicey, MP, 'The Plea of a Malcontent Liberal', *Fortnightly Review*, 44 (1885), 465. The brother of A. V. Dicey, to whom he was not close, Edward Dicey became editor of the *Observer* newspaper; his pro-imperialist sentiments made him untypical of the Individualists.

[25] T. H. Green, 'Liberal Legislation and Freedom of Contract', in id., *Collected Works*, ed. R. L. Nettleship (London, 1885–8), iii. 368.

[26] G. J. Goschen, 'Since 1880', *Nineteenth Century*, 17 (1885), 723–4.

1880 radicalism showed signs of bifurcating into an 'abolitionist' and a 'constructivist' tendency. As Beatrice Webb observed with the benefit of hindsight, the first quinquennium of the decade was full of 'portents of a politics of a new type', while the second Gladstone administration 'may be fitly termed a "no man's land" between the old Radicalism and the new Socialism. For this ministry of all the talents wandered in and out of the trenches of the old individualism and the scouting parties of the new Socialists'.[27] Two major pieces of legislation from the previous Liberal government, the Irish Land Act of 1870 and the Education Act, had been straws in the wind, but they had not greatly alarmed the old Radicals (with the inevitable exception of Herbert Spencer). As Goschen remarked, the former was 'avowedly exceptional' while the latter, although introducing a 'principle of compulsion', 'was part of the old legislative scheme of the Liberal party.'[28] It was not until the development of the 'New Radicalism', embodied in legislation like the Ground Game Act, the Employers' Liability Act, and the Irish Land Act of 1881, that the Radicals of the 1860s became seriously disturbed by the direction liberalism was taking. Rather than abolishing the remaining restrictions on individual liberty, the legislative tendency of 'constructive' radicalism appeared designed to 'put restraints on the individual in doing what he will with his own.'[29] The jurist Sir Henry Maine, a moderate Liberal turned Tory, alleged that the significance of the Ground Game Act was that it furnished proof that 'Liberal–Radical politicians are departing more widely than ever from principles which were once distinctively theirs', particularly from the principle of freedom of contract.[30] The leading philosopher of the New Radicalism, the Idealist T. H. Green, acknowledged this feature of the Act, remarking that the Employers Liability Act also had been criticized for having encouraged 'the workman to look to the law for the protection which he ought to secure for himself by voluntary contract.'[31] Thus by 1885 Goschen could remark on the 'various economic principles which have

---

[27] B. Webb, *My Apprenticeship* (1926; Cambridge, 1979), 184. See also H. C. G. Matthew, introd. to *The Gladstone Diaries*, vols. x and xi (Oxford, 1990), p. lx: 'The decade of the 1880s can be seen both as the last of the old Liberal Party and the first of the new. It stands poised awkwardly between defending the achievements of the past and building upon those achievements a new structure which would recognize a fresh phase in the evolution of industrial society.'

[28] Goschen, 'Since 1880', 724.   [29] Green, 'Liberal Legislation', 365.

[30] [Sir Henry Maine], 'Hares and Rabbits', *St. James's Gazette*, 1 (1880), 76. For the attribution of Maine's unsigned articles in *St. James's Gazette*, see G. Feaver, *From Status to Contract: A Biography of Sir Henry Maine, 1822–1888* (London, 1969), 335 ff.

[31] Green, 'Liberal Legislation', 365.

died since 1880. . . . Among the most conspicuous casualties let us recall the sad fate of freedom of contract. We seem almost to have arrived at this formula—little freedom in making contracts, much freedom in breaking them.'[32] The extent to which this new legislation was perceived to have marked a break with the radicalism of the past is indicated by its being described by a 'malcontent Liberal' as involving 'direct contraventions of the principle of individual liberty, that is, of the fundamental principle of all true and sound liberalism.'[33]

The greatest contrast between the old abolitionist radicalism and its new constructive rival was to be found in the case of the 1881 Land Law Act (Ireland). The effect of the Act was, in essence, to concede the demands of the Tenant League, which the 1870 Act had scarcely addressed, for the 'Three Fs' of fixity of tenure, freedom of sale, and fair rent: it 'provided for courts to set "fair" rents and gave tenants considerable concessions on fixity of tenure and their right to sell their interest in the holding to the highest bidder.'[34] The chief feature of the Act was the Land Court, an institution avowedly intended to interfere with freedom of contract between landlord and tenant. On the view of the Act's supporters, the Irish problem could be ascribed to the attempt to impose advanced commercial law on a society not yet ripe for it, and hence the purpose of the Land Court was to protect the Irish cottiers against exploitation by their landlords by enforcing the customary rights of Celtic society.[35] The Act was defended in these terms by T. H. Green in his famous lecture 'Liberal Legislation and Freedom of Contract':

> To uphold the sanctity of contracts is undoubtedly the prime business of government, but it is no less its business to provide against contracts being made, which, from the helplessness of one of the parties to them, instead of being a security to freedom, become an instrument of disguised oppression.[36]

Moreover, to Arnold Toynbee, an Oxford economist and a disciple of Green, the Land Act marked 'not only an epoch in the history of Ireland, but also in the history of democracy.' It indicated that 'the Radical party has . . . finally accepted and recognized the fact . . . which is the fundamental principle of Socialism, that between men who are unequal in material wealth there can be no freedom of contract.'[37] Toynbee

---

[32] Goschen, 'Since 1880', 727.   [33] E. Dicey, 'Plea of a Malcontent Liberal', 466.

[34] R. Shannon, *The Crisis of Imperialism* (London, 1976), 153.

[35] Dewey, 'Agrarian Legislation and the Celtic Revival', 31 ff.

[36] Green, 'Liberal Legislation', 374.

[37] Arnold Toynbee, 'Are Radicals Socialists?', in id., *Lectures on the Industrial Revolution in England* (London, 1884), 216.

regarded this recognition as providing grounds for rejoicing, but the description of the Act as 'socialism' by its critics was not similarly approbatory.[38]

Arguments for the suspension of freedom of contract in the case of great material inequalities between the contracting parties were explicitly repudiated by the Individualists. There is a passage in Spencer's *The Principles of Ethics* in which he considered the case of a Skye crofter whose economic position was virtually identical to that of the Irish cottiers; the Crofter's Act of 1886 resembled the Irish Land Act in conceding fixity of tenure and fair rents.[39] In this case, Spencer remarked,

the making of contracts, though nominally free, is not actually free—the absence of competing landlords gives to a local landlord an unchecked power of making his own terms, and . . . the people, having little or no choice of other occupations and being too poor to emigrate, are compelled to accept the terms or starve.

Despite this recognition of the economic plight of crofters or cottiers in terms which Green himself might have used, Spencer's remedy was very different. He continued:

Here, where the conditions under which equitable exchange can be carried on are suspended, it remains for the promptings of negative beneficence to supplement those of equity, which are rendered inoperative. The landlord is called on to refrain from actions which the restraints of technically formulated justice fail to prevent.[40]

In other words, although Spencer seems to have recognized that at this point the equal liberties formula of justice broke down, the only remedy he was prepared to allow was voluntary restraint on the part of individual landlords, and he implicitly excluded the possibility of legislative, and therefore potentially coercive, redress of the kind which the Land Court represented.

Beyond their requests for voluntary restraint on the part of landlords, the Individualists could offer a very different analysis of the Irish land

---

[38] The term 'socialism', as employed by both wings of radicalism, had a much wider signification than the current meaning which attaches to the term, and was used to describe many measures which did little or nothing to transform the productive system of free-market capitalism. In general, socialism was used to describe 'any limitation of freedom of action of individuals in the interest of the community at large, that is not required to prevent interference with other individuals, or for the protection of the community against the aggression of foreigners.' (H. Sidgwick, *Elements of Politics*, 42–3). See also Freeden, *New Liberalism*, 25 ff.

[39] See Dewey, 'Agrarian Legislation and the Celtic Revival', 63 ff.

[40] H. Spencer, *The Principles of Ethics*, ii. (London, 1893), 308.

problem to that advanced by the Act's supporters. In their view, Ireland was in the throes of a Malthusian crisis caused by indiscriminate procreation and low agricultural productivity; the answer was to establish free trade in agricultural land which would redistribute it to those landlords and tenants best equipped to exploit it. If social disorder occurred during the transitional phase then it would have to be met by coercion.[41] Thus, it was argued, the supporters of the Act, basing their case on a faulty analysis of the agrarian problem, had committed themselves to interfering with freedom of contract when there was no warrant for such a course of action.

The Individualists believed that the Irish Land Act, in suspending freedom of contract, had set a precedent with momentous implications. In an address to the Eighty Club Goschen remarked that the Land Act 'embodied a principle of enormous moment, the principle of fair rents fixed by a court. The idea of abstract fairness in a bargain, outside the terms to which the parties to it may mutually agree, was an absolute innovation in modern legislation.'[42] The utilitarian philosopher Henry Sidgwick also thought that the Act was 'an attempt to introduce into a social order constructed on a competitive basis a fundamentally incompatible principle', namely the direct determination, 'by some method other than free competition', of the share of 'the appropriated product of industry' allotted to the Irish cottiers.[43] This principle was an instance of what A. V. Dicey was to describe as 'collectivism', a legislative tendency which 'curtails as surely as individualism extends the area of contractual freedom.'[44] The Land Act made 'the rights of Irish landlords and Irish tenants dependent upon status, not upon contract' and was 'the negation of free trade in land.'[45] G. C. Brodrick, a Liberal expert on land legislation, similarly condemned the Act on the grounds that it would result in 'the legislative extinction of freedom in the conduct of by far the most important industry and social relation in Ireland.'[46] In this the older generation of Radicals were at one: the

---

[41] Dewey, 'Agrarian Legislation and the Celtic Revival', 32.

[42] Goschen, 'Since 1880', 726.

[43] H. Sidgwick, 'Economic Socialism', in id., *Miscellaneous Essays and Addresses* London, 1904), 214–15.   [44] Dicey, *Lectures on Law and Public Opinion*, 263.

[45] Ibid. 263. In invoking the distinction between status and contract, Dicey intended to imply that the Land Act was a 'regression' to a more primitive type of social organization. This point is discussed in greater detail in Ch. 4.

[46] G. C. Brodrick, 'The Irish Land Act of 1881: Its Origin and Consequences', in id., *Literary Fragments* (London, 1891), 130. Significantly, perhaps, Brodrick had failed by four hours to be born an Irish landlord; for a criticism of the Act by someone whose interests were at stake see W. E. H. Lecky, *Democracy and Liberty* (London, 1896), i. 154 ff.

coercive power accorded to the Land Court was nothing less than a negation of the principles of free trade and freedom of contract which had been the pillars of their political creed.

For all that they were disturbed by the 'socialism' of the Irish Land Act, the Employers' Liability Act, and the Ground Game Act, the old Radicals also recognized that the 'greatest force of the new movement has not been seen in legislation so much as in opinion' and that the main feature of this change was 'the growing belief in the capacity of the State for direct beneficial action on the condition of individuals and classes.'[47] For example, it was claimed that 'latter-day Liberalism' had adopted the theory that 'the State is to take in hand the control of the masses and that in order to do so it is to override the rights of the individual.'[48] Another writer discerned the abandonment of the view that the function of the State was to 'protect people in their liberty and property . . . so long as they do not interfere with or injure other people' and the substitution of the theory that it was 'a great machine which is to endeavour . . . to grind out . . . a greater amount of material enjoyment and happiness for the bulk of the people'.[49] In other words, the New Radicalism had adopted the principle of which the mid-Victorian State was the negation, namely that it was the duty of government to accept responsibility for the positive welfare of its individual citizens. Although this theory of the State did not acquire a complete philosophical justification until a generation later in the work of L. T. Hobhouse and J. A. Hobson, the fact that it had been adopted in legislative practice explains the apparently disproportionate reaction of the old Radicals to measures which, from the perspective of the present century, seem comparatively minor infringements of the principle of freedom of contract.

The strength of the change in opinion on social questions could be measured by the legislative proposals which were forthcoming during the first half of the decade.[50] Foremost among these was *The Radical Programme*, which was published in instalments in the *Fortnightly Review* from the summer of 1883 to that of 1885; among its demands were free primary education, land reform and powers of compulsory purchase for local authorities for the creation of smallholdings, a moderate graduated taxation and a levy on the 'unearned' increment in land values:

[47] Goschen, 'Since 1880', 728.

[48] E. Dicey, 'Plea of a Malcontent Liberal', 466.

[49] Pleydell-Bouverie, *Province of Government*, 10. It should be noted, however, that Pleydell-Bouverie was more of a Whig than a Radical; J. S. Mill had supported Edwin Chadwick against him as MP for Kilmarnock. See *The Letters of John Stuart Mill* (London, 1910), ed. H. S. R. Elliot, ii. 128.   [50] Goschen, 'Since 1880', 727.

The socialistic measures now contemplated would preserve in their normal vigour and freshness all the individual activities of English citizenship, and would do nothing more spoilatory than tax—if and in what degree necessary— aggregations of wealth for the good of the community.[51]

The reaction of the old Radicals to these proposals was almost uniformly hostile. While they could continue to make common cause with the New Radicalism on a variety of issues, like those relating to Church disestablishment or to the reform of local government, they could find no sympathy for 'a Socialistic system of high taxation for the benefit of those who produce the least' or for a 'crusade against the property of all landowners, and all owners of houses in towns.'[52] The *Radical Programme*, Brodrick wrote, was 'largely tainted' with the 'shallow logic of Socialism' and its leading proposals were made in direct contravention of 'elementary lessons in moral philosophy and political economy.'[53] But the difference between the two wings of the radicalism was given its clearest statement by Hector Macpherson in his short introduction to Spencer's philosophy:

According to the Old Liberalism, every man has a right to his own property; according to the New Liberalism the majority have a right to encroach on other people's property in order, as Mr. Chamberlain's 'Radical Programme' puts it, to increase the comforts and multiply the luxuries of the masses.[54]

Given that the New Radicalism of the 1880s sought to extend the agency of the State to promote its 'socialistic' policies, it is not surprising that the Radicals of the 1860s despaired over the future fate of their creed and its institutional embodiment in the Liberal party. They were not the first generation of Liberals to have become disenchanted with the direction their party had taken: throughout the 1860s and 1870s liberalism had been renounced by a steady stream of intellectuals, including Matthew Arnold, Sir James Fitzjames Stephen, Sir Henry Maine, and Sir John Seeley. But unlike these thinkers, the old Radicals

[51] *The Radical Programme* (London, 1885), 13.
[52] G. Smith, 'The Organization of Democracy', *Contemporary Review*, 47 (1885), 319.
[53] G. C. Brodrick, 'The Socialistic Tendencies of Modern Democracy', in id., *Literary Fragments*, 224–5.
[54] H. Macpherson, *Herbert Spencer: The Man and his Work* (London, 1900), 161. The Individualists' hostility to Chamberlain was fully reciprocated. Beatrice Webb (*My Apprenticeship*, 123) reported his remark apropos Spencer that 'Happily, for the majority of the world, his writing is unintelligible, otherwise his life would have been spent in doing harm', while in Chamberlain's article 'The Labour Question' (*Nineteenth Century*, 32 (1892), 679) Spencer was accused of 'preaching in the wilderness'.

had no quarrel with the philosophy of mid-century liberalism; they had none of the taste for authoritarian government which Maine and Stephen had acquired from their experience of Indian administration, they preferred a Cobdenite foreign policy to that of the imperialists, and they would never have condemned liberalism for its 'petty, trivial view of life'.[55] What was distinctive about the discontent of the old Radicals was their insistence that they had not deserted the Liberal party, but rather that the Liberal party had deserted them. This theme was neatly encapsulated by the letter of resignation written by one Radical of the old school to his local Liberal association:

From the time of the first Reform Bill, the Tories have constantly played off 'Social Reform'—an alias of empirical Socialism—against Liberalism. And now Liberals are pretending, not only that they like the position into which they have been forced, but that it is the Liberal position. This is a betrayal of principle in which I can have no part . . . I leave your association, not because I have ceased to be a Liberal, but because at a time of general apostasy, I have remained one.[56]

The theme of apostasy and betrayal was a powerful one, and the old Radicals devoted hundreds of books, pamphlets, and essays to mourning 'the Paradise Lost of Liberalism'. The 'Paradise Lost' theme was echoed by Leslie Stephen when he described his lifelong friend Henry Fawcett, the Cambridge economist and Postmaster-General in Gladstone's second administration, as 'a faithful Abdiel upholding the true Radical theory, from which modern Radicals are too apt to depart.'[57] Like Abdiel, this generation of Radicals also increasingly came to perceive themselves as part of a beleaguered minority standing out against the spirit of the age. By the 1890s the New Liberalism was merely part of a much wider anti-*laissez-faire* movement and the Individualists found themselves combating not only the ideas of their fellow Liberals but also those of the Fabians, Marxists like H. M. Hyndman and E. B. Bax, and eventually even Conservative Tariff Reformers.

Therefore in the closing decades of the nineteenth century there

---

[55] Fitzjames Stephen paraphrased by J. Roach, 'Liberalism and the Victorian Intelligentsia', *Cambridge Historical Journal*, 13 (1957), 63. Unfortunately, Roach's otherwise valuable article makes no distinction between Maine and Stephen and the revolt of the old Radicals with which I am concerned.

[56] J. H. Levy quoted in S. H. Harris, *The Doctrine of Personal Right* (Barcelona, 1935), 203.

[57] L. Stephen, *The Life of Henry Fawcett* (1885; 3rd edn., London, 1886), 169. In Milton's *Paradise Lost* Abdiel was the only one of the Seraphim not to join in Satan's revolt against God.

were all the signs of a developing debate over the nature and content of the liberal ideology in which the true meaning of liberalism had itself become a matter of political dispute. To borrow a term from the genre of *Begriffsgeschichte*, the closing decades of the nineteenth century may be described as a *Sattelzeit*. According to this conception, political action normally takes place against a background of shared concepts, but there are crucial historical junctures in which the common coin of discourse itself becomes a political battlefield. In these circumstances, as the leading exponent of this theory has remarked, 'the struggle over the "correct" concepts becomes socially and politically explosive.'[58] This, I would suggest, was the form taken by the late nineteenth-century debate between the old Radicals and the new; each side claimed to be the 'true' liberals, and each condemned the other's misunderstanding (or wilful misrepresentation) of what liberalism really meant. Nor did they believe themselves to be engaged in a merely verbal dispute: the issues involved were of fundamental political importance, since they involved the legitimacy of State action over a wide range of economic, industrial, and social activities.

II. The Individualists: Biographical

By the middle of the 1880s, therefore, the old Radicals were at pains to claim for themselves the title of true liberals. Liberalism, they insisted, meant their doctrine and programme, not that of the Chamberlainites. In an elegiac essay on 'The Manchester School' Goldwin Smith, sometime Regius Professor of Modern History at Oxford, staked a claim to the Liberal title: 'The name Liberal, I submit, belongs to people of our way of thinking, not to the votaries of Socialistic interference with liberty or Socialistic confiscation.'[59] Spencer also declared himself an exponent of 'genuine Liberalism—the Liberalism which seeks to extend men's liberties, not the modern perversion of it which . . . is busily decreasing their liberties';[60] his polemic *The Man versus the State* was intended to present 'the definite conception . . . of the nature of true Liberalism for the future'.[61] It became common to draw a contrast between 'true Liberalism' which believed 'that national prosperity

---

[58] R. Koselleck, quoted in T. Ball, *Transforming Political Discourse* (Oxford, 1988), 9.
[59] G. Smith, 'Manchester School', 377.
[60] H. Spencer, *Autobiography* (London, 1904), i. 421.
[61] D. Duncan, *The Life and Letters of Herbert Spencer* (London, 1908), 243.

depends upon individual liberty and private enterprise and the security of property' and the 'Liberalism of the present day', the proponents of which were described as 'predatory pirates . . . sailing under false colours.'[62] As the Australian Bruce Smith complained, the term liberalism, which once had been synonymous with freedom, had lost its true meaning and had been perverted 'in the service of a cause the tendency of which is clearly in the direction of socialism or communism.'[63] In this he was echoed by Leslie Stephen, who thought that 'the difference between the old and modern Liberalism seems in certain directions to imply, not an evolution, but a reversal of the old theories', and he summed up the feelings of all the Individualists by remarking that 'the contrast is painful to many who recall the ideals of their youth.'[64]

The political theorists who were the self-proclaimed votaries of true liberalism were a socially and intellectually diverse group, and, as Goldwin Smith remarked apropos the Manchester School, 'there was plenty of room in that school of thought for differences of opinion on particular questions, and for varieties of degree in the application of general principles which were held in common.'[65] Nevertheless, it is possible to distinguish two broad tendencies within Individualism, the line of fissure corresponding roughly to the differences of opinion which already could be observed in the 1860s between the mainstream of radicalism, and the more extreme doctrines of Herbert Spencer. As A. V. Dicey suggested in his work on *Law and Public Opinion*, a distinction could be drawn between 'the absolute individualism of Herbert Spencer on the one hand, [and] the practical or utilitarian individualism of J. S. Mill and H. Sidgwick on the other.'[66] However, since Spencer also would have claimed to be a utilitarian, albeit of an unorthodox variety, it is perhaps more useful to distinguish between 'Spencerian' and 'empirical' Individualists.[67] The former, who took their lead from Spencer's writings, attempted to establish abstract, a priori reasons for curtailing the functions of government by deduction from 'scientific'

---

[62] F. Wemyss-Charlen's-Douglas, 9th Earl of Wemyss, Opening Address to the Liberty and Property Defence League in *Report of Proceedings and Speeches of the Twelfth Annual Meeting*, 3–4. [63] [A.] B. Smith, *Liberty and Liberalism*, p. ii.

[64] L. Stephen, 'The Good Old Cause', *Nineteenth Century*, 51 (1902), 11. For other examples of this contrast see H. S. Constable, *Radicalism and its Stupidities* (London, 1896), 5 ff., and, from a Tory political perspective, C. B. Roylance-Kent, *The English Radicals* (London, 1900), 422. [65] G. Smith, 'Manchester School', 379.

[66] A. V. Dicey, *Law and Public Opinion*, 17–18. This distinction is restated as a distinction between 'moderate' and 'absolute' Individualism by S. Collini, *Liberalism and Sociology*, 20 ff.

[67] The nature of Spencer's utilitarianism will be discussed in Ch. 1 and 6.

first principles.[68] The latter, by contrast, adopted the orthodox utilitarian position that no moral or political principle could be absolutely true since it would not maximize utility in all conceivable circumstances; hence they argued that a priori objections to State interference were unavailable. The only general principle which could be admitted was 'that the government should do what experience proves it can do efficiently', although in practice this meant leaning heavily in the direction of *laissez-faire*.[69] These two strands of Individualism were frequently at odds, with the Spencerians criticizing the empiricists for their 'indeterminism' and lack of scientific rigour, while the empiricists challenged the Spencerians' pretensions to have established an evolutionary basis for their political creed.[70]

The difference between the Spencerian and empirical Individualists was more than merely philosophical since it had ramifications for their attitudes towards such fundamental Victorian institutions as the Poor Law and the Factory Acts, which the Spencerians wished to abolish but the empiricists to maintain; it was against the former that Sidney Webb directed his scorn in the quotation with which this Introduction began. Beyond the very basic functions of military defence, the administration of justice, and the enforcement of contracts, the Spencerians held that all governmental activities were illegitimate and they even entertained fanciful conjectures about the future 'withering away' of the State. Much to the embarrassment of the empirical Individualists it was this extreme position which was most frequently identified with Individualism, especially by its critics who found valuable ammunition in some of the Spencerians' more extreme pronouncements. By contrast, the empiricists wanted to draw a distinction between legitimate governmental interference, in such areas as the Poor Law, Factory Acts, and Sanitary Acts, and the illegitimate interference which would be occasioned by the implementation of the *Radical Programme*.[71] As will be

---

[68] This generalization does not apply to Wordsworth Donisthorpe who attempted to base Individualism on the foundation of an inductive social science, deeply influenced by Spencer's sociology, which he termed 'nomology'. See Ch. 3.

[69] Stephen, *Life of Henry Fawcett*, 160. See also Fawcett's own statement of this principle in 'General Aspects of State Intervention', in id., *Essays and Lectures on Social and Political Subjects* (London, 1872), 33.

[70] Examples of the former include Mackay, 'Empiricism in Politics', and Bax and Levy, *Socialism and Individualism* (in which Levy accused Sidgwick of being 'an apostle of indeterminism'). For empiricist responses see G. Smith, 'Has Science a New Basis for Morality?', *Contemporary Review*, 41 (1882), 335–8, and H. Sidgwick's posthumously published *Lectures on the Ethics of T. H. Green, H. Spencer and J. Martineau* (London, 1902).

[71] See e.g. G. C. Brodrick, 'Democracy and Socialism', *Nineteenth Century*, 15 (1884), 627 f.

shown, this was not always an easy distinction to make on strictly utilitarian grounds.

Despite this difference of emphasis within the ranks of the Individualists, the leading theorist of their creed was unquestionably Herbert Spencer (1820–1903): not only did many of the Individualists derive direct inspiration from his work, but his standing as the greatest English philosopher in the quarter of a century after the death of Mill demanded that the empirical Individualists define their own position in relation to his. Because of the neglect which his Synthetic Philosophy has endured in our own century it is difficult to convey a sense of the pre-eminent position which it held in the thought of the late Victorian era; Spencer was too much a man of his time, too much a man of 'first principles', for his reputation to have survived, while his work lacks the pregnant ambiguity of Mill's writings which has given them their lasting appeal. Yet the appearance in 1884 of Spencer's polemic against constructive radicalism, *The Man versus The State*, coincided with 'the zenith of his world-fame as England's greatest philosopher',[72] and ten years after the book's publication it was observed that it had established his reputation as 'a safer and more consistent guide than was Mr. Mill.'[73] Moreover, although Henry George, the advocate of the 'single tax' on land, charged Spencer with intellectual prostitution for having abandoned his earlier views on land nationalization, as he also acknowledged:

[T]here can be no question that at the present time—1892—Herbert Spencer, of all his contemporaries, holds the foremost place in the intellectual world, and through a wider circle than any man now living, and perhaps than any man of our century, is regarded as a profound, original and authoritative thinker—by many indeed as the greatest thinker the world has ever seen.[74]

While Spencer's stock never stood particularly high at the Universities, especially after Idealism had established itself as the dominant paradigm of reflection, his influence on the middle-class Victorian reading public was immeasurable; William James observed that he had 'enlarged the imagination and set free the speculative mind of countless doctors, engineers and lawyers and of many physicists and chemists, and of thoughtful laymen generally.'[75] A philosopher who enjoyed such a considerable following could be expected to receive a substantial audience for this pronouncements when, in the words of the *Westminster*

[72] B. Webb, *My Apprenticeship*, 123.
[73] R. Flint, *Socialism* (London, 1894), 67.
[74] H. George, *A Perplexed Philosopher* (London, 1893), 3.
[75] W. James, 'Herbert Spencer', in id., *Memories and Studies* (London, 1912), 126.

Review, 'he steps down from the lofty heights where he walks alone amid abstract principles, and proceeds to test by these principles the soundness of current legislation.'[76] Although he lacked direct political influence, Spencer's philosophical authority did much to reinforce the general presumption against State interference.

It was not always thus: Spencer's beginnings were modest, and his life was a constant struggle against financial insecurity and a succession of nervous illnesses. Born in Derby, the son of a Unitarian schoolmaster, his education, like that of Mill, owed nothing to the public schools or to the old universities. He was educated in part by his father, but primarily by his uncle, the Reverend Thomas Spencer of Hinton Charterhouse, near Bath, who belonged to the Evangelical wing of the Established Church. Nevertheless, if Mill 'underwent too much juvenile discipline, Spencer experienced too little';[77] he would study only those subjects which interested him and consequently learned nothing of the classics, only a smattering of French, and hardly any history or literature, but a good deal of mathematics, mechanics, physics, and chemistry. This scientific background prepared him for his first career as a railway engineer, a profession which he followed intermittently until 1846. Apparently he did not find it very congenial: 'Got the sack. Very glad', he noted in his diary. The Radical journalism in which he became engaged after moving to London was apparently more to his liking. At first he was employed as sub-editor on the free-trade newspaper *The Economist*; subsequently a small legacy from his uncle and the moderate success of his first book, the *Social Statics* (1851), enabled him to set up as a freelance contributor to journals like the *Westminster Review*. During the 1850s he published another book, *The Principles of Psychology*, the first of his works to bring his name to prominence, and began to map out the project which would, almost literally, consume the rest of his life. This was the Synthetic Philosophy, which was intended to systematize or synthesize the rapidly expanding knowledge of the nineteenth century by demonstrating that the truths of each of the special sciences could be regarded as instantiations of the general law of evolution. It has been observed of this project that it 'was a greater undertaking than any of Mill's' and that 'only an intense self-will could have accomplished the task under Spencer's conditions.'[78] In many respects Spencer resembled the grammarian whose funeral was commemorated by

---

[76] Anon., 'H. Spencer's *The Man versus the State*', *Westminster Review*, 66 (1884), 553.
[77] J. M. Robertson, *Modern Humanists Reconsidered* (London, 1927), 181.
[78] Ibid. 180.

Browning; such was his intense devotion to his work that he sacrificed to it a life which, without wife or children, seems never to have afforded him any large measure of joy.[79]

The chief formative influences on Spencer's politics were those of English provincial dissenting radicalism, and he carried its political ideals with him to his grave.[80] His early radicalism was reinforced by that of his uncle, with whom he engaged in lengthy discussions of social topics, and by his involvement in railway engineering, a profession apparently inclined towards Radical politics, as might be expected of men involved in the forefront of technological innovation.[81] By the mid-1860s, Spencer had established himself in the leading literary and Radical circles of the capital: he was a close friend of the Positivists G. H. Lewes and Marian Evans (George Eliot); became acquainted with John Morley; and dined with J. S. Mill who, regarding him as 'the rising philosophical name of the present', offered financial assistance when the Synthetic Philosophy threatened to flounder through lack of funds (characteristically the offer was declined).[82] Spencer sided with Mill and the other Radicals during the Governor Eyre controversy, and approved of the extension of the franchise in 1867. Thereafter, however, Spencer and the Radicals started to drift apart both personally and intellectually; the friendship with Morley, for example, ceased as under his editorship the *Fortnightly Review* became a forum for constructive radicalism. The degree to which Spencer and the Radicals had diverged is illustrated by the hostile reception which was accorded to *The Man versus the State* by the *Westminster Review*, a journal to which Spencer had contributed thirty years earlier. By contrast, Spencer found himself 'patted on the back by the Tory papers. Had I asked in times gone by whether such a thing could have happened I should have regarded it as quite impossible.'[83] At about this time he also became

---

[79] The chief sources for Spencer's life are his posthumously published *Autobiography*, and Duncan's *Life and Letters of Herbert Spencer*. D. Wiltshire's *The Social and Political Thought of Herbert Spencer* (Oxford, 1978), contains the most comprehensive modern account of Spencer's life.

[80] J. D. Y. Peel, *Herbert Spencer: The Evolution of a Sociologist* (London, 1971), gives an excellent account of the social milieu from which Spencer's thought developed.

[81] Brunel's political views were also those of an advanced Radical. See L. T. C. Rolt, *Isambard Kingdom Brunel* (Harmondsworth, 1970), 93.

[82] Mill's estimate of Spencer is taken from *Letters of J. S. Mill*, ed. Elliot, ii. 72. For Mill's offer of financial assistance see the generous obituary tribute to Mill printed as app. G of Spencer's *Autobiography*. Mill's offer of assistance is contained in id., *Collected Works*, ed. J. M. Robson, *et al.*, xvi (Toronto, 1979), letter 916, p. 1145.

[83] Duncan, *Life and Letters of Herbert Spencer*, 243.

associated with the Liberty and Property Defence League, a loose coalition of manufacturing and agricultural interests founded in 1882 by the former Adullamite Lord Elcho, who became the Earl of Wemyss in 1883.[84] Nevertheless, the League's 'Tory' reputation precluded his formal membership; he did not want to be accused by his erstwhile Liberal allies of having 'turned tail'.[85] In any event, the Conservatives must have found Spencer an awkward ally, especially in matters of foreign policy. His final public action was to denounce the evils of jingoism, imperialism, and the Boer War, a stand which probably made a significant contribution to his already declining popularity.

A number of the political theorists who derived direct inspiration from Spencer's arguments were closely involved with the Liberty and Property Defence League. As Edward Bristow has written, despite the fact that these thinkers were 'long ago consigned to the dustheap of political ideology, they had considerable late-century reputations' and despite their often acute awareness of each others' intellectual short-comings, they provided the League with much of its theoretical justi-fication.[86] Without wanting to descend into vulgar Marxist reduc-tionism, it does seem more than merely coincidental that many of these theorists had substantial material interests at stake: among their number was included a son of a prosperous West Riding wool-merchant, a wealthy retired wine-merchant, and an Australian employer-politician.

Probably the most flamboyant and popular of the League's ideo-logists was Auberon Herbert (1838–1906), the third and youngest son of the Earl of Carnarvon, who in accordance with family tradition began his career as a Tory. As an undergraduate at St John's College, Oxford, he founded the Canning Club, and in 1865 unsuccessfully contested Newport in the Conservative interest. But he soon adopted a position of extreme radicalism, serving briefly as MP for Nottingham, and making a

---

[84] For the work and composition of the Liberty and Property Defence League see E. Bristow, 'The Liberty and Property Defence League and Individualism', *Historical Journal*, 18 (1975), 761–89 and N. C. Soldon, 'Laissez Faire as Dogma: The Liberty and Property Defence League 1882–1914', in K. D. Brown (ed.), *Essays in Anti-Labour History* (London, 1974), 208–33. See also Soldon 'Individualist Periodicals: The Crisis of Late Victorian Liberalism', *Victorian Periodicals Newsletter*, 6 (1973), 17–26.

[85] Duncan, *Life and Letters of Herbert Spencer*, 242. In fact, in the year of the publication of *The Man versus the State*, Spencer was offered the Liberal candidacy as MP for Leicester (p. 240). This had been the association to which, three years earlier, Green had delivered his famous address on *Liberal Legislation*; one can only assume that the audience had not completely digested his message.

[86] Bristow, 'Liberty and Property Defence League', 769.

strongly republican speech on the Civil List in support of Dilke.[87] He then discovered Spencer's political philosophy and underwent a conversion which, according to his biographer, resembled 'that of one of the medieval saints.'[88] After the manner of the saintly, Herbert withdrew from the affairs of the world to become 'an enthusiast, a Don Quixote of the nineteenth century' who had left 'the real battle of life to fight a strange ogre of his own imagination—an always immoral state interference.'[89] The fight was conducted from his country house, deep in the New Forest, where he and his family led a somewhat Bohemian existence far from the grooves of aristocratic custom. Herbert's chief weapon in the fight was a newspaper, the *Free Life*, in which he propagated a number of extreme Individualist policies, including a scheme for 'voluntary taxation' which prompted the remark that 'he out Herberts Mr. Herbert Spencer in his advocacy of laissez faire.'[90] Like his mentor, Herbert did not formally become a member of the Liberty and Property Defence League; he was sympathetic to many of its aims, but considered its constitution 'coercive'.[91]

Another of Spencer's followers to become involved with the League was Wordsworth Donisthorpe (1847–1914), who served on its council until breaking with Wemyss in 1888 over the latter's failure to campaign for Church disestablishment. Donisthorpe, who described himself as a 'Unionist Radical', became the League's authority on local government matters and represented it at the Fabian Society's first conference on the Nationalization of Land and Capital.[92] The only son of George Edmund Donisthorpe, a wool-merchant from Moor Allerton near Leeds, Donisthorpe was educated at Leeds Grammar School and Trinity College, Cambridge where he took a first in the moral science tripos at the same time that A. J. Balfour achieved his glittering second.

---

[87] Herbert had previously unsuccessfully contested Berkshire for the Liberals at the instigation of Goldwin Smith. S. H. Harris, *Auberon Herbert: Crusader for Liberty* (London, 1943), 84 ff.

[88] Id., *Doctrine of Personal Right*, 204. [89] B. Webb, *My Apprenticeship*, 189.

[90] D. G. Ritchie, *Principles of State Interference* (London, 1891), 57, n. 1. *The Free Life* was coedited by M. D. O'Brien, the founder of the Salford Young England and Anti-Socialist Association and author of two books, *Socialism Tested by the Facts* (London, 1893) and *The Natural Right to Freedom* (London, 1894), which were distinguished only by 'the violence of the language by which the ordinary principles of individualism are enforced.' (A. Eastwood, reviewing the second of these works in the *International Journal of Ethics*, 4 (1893–4), 412.)

[91] Bristow, 'Liberty and Property Defence League', 773.

[92] For Donisthorpe's political self-description see the letter to Rt. Hon. W. E. Gladstone dated 18 July 1888 in the Gladstone-Glynne MSS, Clwyd Record Office. I am indebted to Colin Matthew for this reference.

In 1870, a year after leaving Cambridge, he was admitted to the Inner Temple, but was not called to the Bar until nine years later. In the interim he had written *The Principles of Plutology* (1876), a doggedly orthodox treatment of economics, and was arrested in Strasburg for taking part in a republican demonstration. A man of varied interests, who practised at the Bar until his death, he attempted to construct an international language based on Latin, and projected a study (in which Spencer himself was to be a partner) of every instance of failed legislation.[93]

In 1891 the Liberty and Property Defence League published *A Plea for Liberty*, intended as its riposte to the *Fabian Essays in Socialism*.[94] It was edited by Thomas Mackay (1849–1912), a retired wine-merchant, and a permanent fixture on the council of the Charity Organisation Society, who was born in Edinburgh, the son of a colonel in the East India Company. Mackay was educated at Glenalmond, where he was a contemporary of another pillar of the Charity Organisation Society, Charles Stewart Loch, and at New College, Oxford. Although called to the Bar in 1879, Mackay believed himself unable to support a wife and family from his earnings in the legal profession, and instead went into partnership with Charles Kinloch. Mackay apparently found the wine trade uncongenial, but after only ten years he had amassed a sufficiently large fortune to enable him to retire and devote himself to the study of social problems, resulting in the *History of the Poor Law from 1834 to the Present Time*.[95]

A third Spencerian Individualist to have trained as a barrister was Arthur Bruce Smith (1851–1937), the Honorary Corresponding Secretary of the League in Australia. Born in Rotherhithe, Smith was educated at Wesley College, Melbourne and at Melbourne University, his family having emigrated to Australia when he was three years old. Smith's father, a master mariner, flourished in his new country and founded a shipping company, Howard Smith and Sons. After being called to the Bar in England, Bruce Smith practised law in Melbourne

---

[93] Bristow, 'Liberty and Property Defence League', 773; see also Soldon, 'Individualist Periodicals', 21. Another partner in this project was to have been the naval architect and Liberty and Property Defence League publicist J. C. Spence. See Spence's *The Conscience of the King* (London, 1899), pref.

[94] Bristow, 'Liberty and Property Defence League', 770. The New Liberal D. G. Ritchie referred to *A Plea for Liberty* as 'that manifesto of conflicting individualisms' (*Studies in Political and Social Ethics* (London, 1902), 27.)

[95] For biographical details see the obituary notice in the *Charity Organisation Review*, 31 (1912), 174–82.

and New South Wales, where he served in the legislative assembly, before becoming managing director of the family firm in 1884. His tenure was short-lived; four years later he quarrelled with his father, was disinherited, and left Howard Smith and Sons to resume his political career. On his return to the New South Wales Parliament he was successively Minister of Public Works and Colonial Treasurer in the Parkes ministry of 1889–91, gaining a strongly anti-Labour reputation.[96] An active advocate of Australian federation, he sat in the first Federal Parliament as a free trader and anti-socialist, campaigning for women's suffrage and against the 'White Australia' policy, but became increasingly alienated from twentieth-century politics. As the *Dictionary of Australian Biography* remarks, 'a young man of parts, Bruce Smith never lived up to his promise. In opposition most of his eighteen years in Federal Parliament, he was too doctrinaire and too quixotic, and perhaps too aware of his own intellect, to adapt to twentieth century party politics.'[97] Although Smith was the author of several books, including a volume of poetry, his political creed was stated in his first work *Liberty and Liberalism* (1887), a protest against the advances of 'State Socialism' in Victoria and New South Wales.[98]

The other Individualist pressure groups were unable to rival the Liberty and Property Defence League in terms of size, organization, or influence, but the Personal Rights Association could match it for belligerence in its polemics against State intervention. The embodiment of the Association was the editor of its journal *The Individualist*, Joseph Hiam Levy (1838–1913). Levy, who described himself as 'a Ricardian in economics and an Individualist in politics', lectured in logic and economics at the City of London College and established a considerable reputation as a debater at the Dialectical Society; his obituary in a special edition of *The Individualist* contained a glowing tribute from a one-time sparring partner named George Bernard Shaw.[99] Although a considerable Hebrew scholar, Levy left behind his Judaic upbringing to embrace a form of rationalism and became a strong supporter of Charles Bradlaugh's candidature for Northampton in 1887. His brand of

[96] The politics of this period of Australian history are examined in J. Rickard, *Class and Politics: New South Wales, Victoria, and the Early Commonwealth* (Canberra, 1976).

[97] See Martha Rutledge, 'Smith, Bruce', *Australian Dictionary of Biography*, xi (Melbourne, 1988), 639.

[98] State Socialism in Australia was discussed in C. Fairfield's contribution to T. D. Mackay (ed.), *A Plea For Liberty* (London, 1891) 145–98. Smith's book was untypical of Australian political thought of the period which was collectivist in orientation: see C. D. Goodwin, 'Evolution Theory in Australian Social Thought', *Journal of the History of Ideas*, 25 (1964), 393–416, esp. 397 ff.   [99] *The Individualist*, 328 (Nov.–Dec. 1913), 83.

Individualism was probably closest to the natural-rights-based theories of Auberon Herbert, although this did not prevent him from being an effective critic of the scheme for voluntary taxation.

The Spencerians were, on the whole, a flamboyant and colourful group; although not self-educated like their mentor, they unquestionably were not part of 'Society' or of the late Victorian *haute bourgeoisie*, and they mainly confined their political activity to pressure groups like the Personal Rights Association or the Liberty and Property Defence League. These associations notwithstanding, there was only a slight element of exaggeration in Sidney Webb's claim that the 'political influence' of the Spencerians was 'absolutely imperceptible'.[100]

By contrast, empirical Individualism was predominantly an 'Establishment' creed: it was the political theory of the University Radicals of the 1860s, modified by two decades of professional success in the form of professorships, knighthoods, honorary degrees, and decorations. The empirical Individualists served on Royal Commissions and counted Cabinet ministers among their circle of friends; many, although not all, of them became active in the Liberal Unionist associations of Oxford and Cambridge, and the literary morticians of the *Dictionary of National Biography* were on hand to record their passing. If there is an 'intellectual analogue of the Hartington–Goschen group in Parliament' it is to be found among these thinkers.[101]

While political theorists like Herbert, Donisthorpe, Smith, and Mackay derived their leading arguments directly from the work of Herbert Spencer, none of the empirical Individualists occupied a corresponding position of intellectual leadership. Nevertheless, the political writings of Henry Sidgwick (1838–1900), although not themselves the source of empirical Individualism, provided this ideology with its most carefully reasoned and philosophically sophisticated statement. In works like *The Principles of Political Economy* and *The Elements of Politics*, Sidgwick, the Knightbridge Professor of Moral Philosophy at Cambridge, offered a summation of the dilemmas confronting an orthodox utilitarian defence of *laissez-faire*. Much of Sidgwick's contribution to moral and political philosophy also reads like a dialogue with

---

[100] S. Webb, *Socialism in England*, 80.

[101] Roach, 'Liberalism and the Victorian Intellegentsia', 79, claims that 'the parallel between the Goschen–Hartington group in Parliament and the views of Maine and Stephen is very close, though the practising politicans naturally had less liberty to criticise than the independent critics.' As I have suggested, however, the empirical Individualists provide a much closer theoretical approximation to the views of the 'moderate Liberals' than do Maine and Stephen.

Spencer, whose work is subjected to a sustained and detailed critique in the firm belief that 'Individualism of the extreme kind has clearly had its day.'[102] However, Sidgwick was ill-equipped to be the founder of a school of his own: not only do his writings strive for clarity and precision at the expense of readability, but his sceptical intelligence prevented him from arriving at any unqualified or decisive conclusions. He was quick to spot the fallacies in any argument, including his own, and, as his friend James Bryce remarked, his cast of mind was 'never satisfied with the obvious view of a question, it seemed unable to acquiesce in any broad or sweeping statement. It discovered objections to every accepted doctrine, exceptions to every rule.'[103]

Born at Skipton, the son of the headmaster of the town's grammar school, Sidgwick was a contemporary of T. H. Green's at Rugby and gained a double first in classics and mathematics at Trinity College, Cambridge. Although subsequently appointed Fellow and Tutor of Classics at Trinity, Sidgwick was not destined to remain long in this capacity. The same sceptical intelligence which prevented him from becoming the founder of a 'school' made him unable to accept the Church of England's Thirty-Nine Articles and, having embraced the high-minded agnosticism so characteristic of his generation, he resigned his fellowship in 1869, a principled stand which did much to precipitate the abolition of University Tests. (In the interim, Sidgwick remained at Trinity where he had been appointed to a lectureship, a position which carried no doctrinal obligations.) But although intellectually he may have lost his faith, Sidgwick never lost his emotional need for it; he hunted ghosts on behalf of the Society for Psychical Research in the hope of discovering scientific proof of the immortality of the soul and, as his occasional golfing-partner Maynard Keynes brutally remarked, 'never did anything but wonder whether Christianity was true and prove that it wasn't and hope that it was.'

The same impression of a mind paralysed by doubt is also conveyed by Sidgwick's political commitments. By the late 1860s he had abandoned classics for the moral sciences, and had become a self-professed follower of Comte and Mill, once claiming to have read the *Considerations on Representative Government* in a single morning.[104] But he was temperamentally unsuited to be any form of Radical; as Bryce again noted,

[102] Quoted in A. S[idgwick] and E. M. S[idgwick], *Henry Sidgwick: A Memoir* (London, 1906), 399.
[103] J. Bryce, 'Henry Sidgwick', in id., *Studies in Contemporary Biography* (London, 1903), 332.   [104] A. S[idgwick] and E. M. S[idgwick], *Henry Sidgwick* 66.

'he was of all the persons I have known the least disposed to be warped by partisanship, for he examined every political issue as it arose on its own merits, apart from predilections for either party or for the view of his nearest friends.'[105] In January 1885 he spent some time at Whittinghame with A. J. Balfour, the future Conservative Prime Minister and a former student whose sister he had married in 1876. There he encountered members of his brother-in-law's Manchester Conservative association and was forced to acknowledge that 'their criticism of the present phase of Radicalism seems to be unanswerable.'[106] A year later he was also to remark 'with some alarm' on 'the extent of my alienation from current Liberalism.'[107] Throughout this period Sidgwick's political commitments fluctuated wildly until he finally broke with the Liberal party over Irish Home Rule.[108]

Many of the other empirical Individualists were to break with the Liberal party over Home Rule, and they shared in common the fact that they had been contributors to the 1867 *Essays in Reform*. Among this group may be counted Albert Venn Dicey (1835–1922), the Vinerian Professor of English Law at Oxford;[109] Goldwin Smith (1823–1910), sometime Regius Professor of Modern History at Oxford and Professor of English and Constitutional History at Cornell; and G. C. Brodrick (1831–1903), the Warden of Merton College, Oxford. Each of these theorists came from families which were pillars of Victorian respectability: Dicey, the son of the editor of the *Northampton Mercury*, was related to the Stephen clan through his mother; Goldwin Smith's father was a doctor and a director of the Great Western Railway; Brodrick, the son of an Anglican churchman who was successively Rector of Bath, Canon of Wells, and Dean of Exeter. A common pattern of public school and Oxford is also apparent in their educational background: Goldwin Smith and Brodrick were both Etonians, while Dicey was educated at King's School, London. Dicey and Brodrick were both

---

[105] Bryce, 'Henry Sidgwick', 334. Bryce's friendship with Sidgwick was tried by their differences over the Home Rule issue.

[106] A. S[idgwick] and E. M. [Sidgwick], *Henry Sidgwick*, 398.   [107] Ibid. 439.

[108] See the discussion of Sidgwick's shifting political commitments in C. Harvie, *The Lights of Liberalism: University Liberals and the Challenge of Democracy 1860–1886* (London, 1976), 225.

[109] Biographical details of Dicey are to be found in R. A. Cosgrove, *The Rule of Law: Albert Venn Dicey, Victorian Jurist* (London, 1980). Unfortunately this work does not pay sufficient heed to the ideological context of Dicey's thought. On this point see D. Sugarman, 'The Legal Boundaries of Liberty: Dicey, Liberalism and Legal Science', *Modern Law Review*, 46 (1983), 102–11.

[110] R. S. Rait, *Memorials of Albert Venn Dicey* (London, 1925), 118.

Balliol products, the former having been taught by Jowett, while Smith was an undergraduate at Christ Church and Magdalen. They rounded off their distinguished undergraduate careers (all obtained firsts) with college fellowships at Oxford—Brodrick at Merton, Smith at University, Dicey at Trinity—and became involved in journalism and Radical politics.

Dicey's early radicalism had been reinforced by an encounter with the writings of J. S. Mill. In his youth he believed passionately in individual liberty, extolled the virtues of *laissez-faire*, contributed to the *Essays in Reform*, and argued for a vigorous foreign policy on behalf of nationalist movements; although he later became a staunch Unionist, even in his seventy-sixth year he was proclaiming himself 'an old, an unconverted, and an impenitent Benthamite.'[110] In later life he was also a member of the British Constitution Association, an Individualist pressure group largely consisting of Unionist Free Traders, which was in many respects the Edwardian successor to the Liberty and Property Defence League. Indeed, a number of veterans of the League, including Herbert and Mackay, were also counted among its membership.[111]

Goldwin Smith's early politics were Peelite, but by the 1860s he had transferred his allegiance to the Radicals, supporting Mill during the Governor Eyre controversy and defending the Northern cause in the American Civil war; his views on foreign policy were strongly anti-imperialist, but in 1886 he broke with Gladstone on Home Rule. Brodrick, who has been described as 'a grotesque pedant, in whom the characteristic absurdities of the Oxford don and the *Times* leader-writer were combined' was also intensely opposed to Home Rule; his comparison of the Irish MPs to Jack the Ripper caused him to be brought before the Parnell Commission for alleged contempt of court.[112] Although Dicey and Smith may have harboured political ambitions, he was the only one of the three to stand for Parliament, contesting Woodstock in 1868 and 1874 (when he was defeated by Lord Randolph Churchill) and Monmouthshire in 1880, on each occasion as a Liberal and in each case without success.[113]

---

[111] Bristow, 'Liberty and Property Defence League', 788. Dicey's involvement with the British Constitution Association is entirely neglected by Cosgrove's biography.

[112] G. W. E. Russell, *Portraits of the Seventies* (London, 1916), 192. Brodrick escaped the direst implications of his remark by swearing an affidavit to the effect that he had been joking—an action for which, as Russell observes, he deserves to be remembered.

[113] One of the speakers in support of Brodrick's candidature for Woodstock in 1868 was T. H. Green, an interesting comment on the subsequent divisions in the ranks of the same generation of Radicals.

The political ideas of this group were characterized by a singular inflexibility: having obtained their leading principles in early manhood, they never subjected them to scrutiny or review. As the *Dictionary of National Biography* remarks of Smith, he became 'a masterly interpreter of the liberal principles of the Manchester school and of the philosophic radicalism which embodied what seemed to him to be the highest political enlightenment of his youth. His views never developed.'[114] This description was true of all these Individualists, but only Goldwin Smith could claim the singular distinction of having been described by John Ruskin as 'a goose'.[115]

A fourth contributor to the *Essays in Reform* who was later to have much ideological ground in common with the empirical Individualists was the biographer and historian of ideas, Leslie Stephen (1832–1904), now best known as the father of Virginia Woolf (who portrayed him unflatteringly as Mr Ramsay in *To the Lighthouse*). A cousin of A. V. Dicey, Stephen was educated at Eton and at Trinity Hall, Cambridge (his father apparently believed that the intellectual demands of Trinity College would be too great for his weak physical constitution), where he obtained a fellowship on graduation. Although he was ordained in 1855, his religious doubts caused him, like Sidgwick, to resign his fellowship and it was as a journalist and a man of letters that he made his reputation, his greatest achievement being the foundation of the *Dictionary of National Biography*. Although Stephen produced no single statement of his later political thought, works like *The Science of Ethics* echo many Individualist themes, while the exposition of the political philosophy of Henry Fawcett in Stephen's *Life* of his friend may be treated as an account of the author's own views.

Although empirical Individualism would thus appear to be the shared ideology of a particular generation of University Radicals as they entered late middle age, it also had an appeal beyond the ranks of former Radicals. It can be found expressed, for example, in the writings of two philosophically minded peers: George Herbert, the thirteenth Earl of Pembroke (1850–95), a Whig turned Conservative, and George Wilshere, Lord Bramwell (1808–92), of whom it has been remarked that 'he remained convinced throughout his life that the political economists had proved that the principle of freedom of contract was a

---

[114] 'Smith, Goldwin (1823–1910)', *DNB*, 2nd suppl. (London, 1912), iii. 339.
[115] Ruskin's remark is to be found in *The Collected Works of John Ruskin*, xxix *Fors Clavigera* (London, 1907), 152.

necessary part of the laws of a civilized state.'[116] Bramwell, a judge famed for his decision in the 1867 Druitt case which outlawed trade-union activity, was one of Wemyss's closest colleagues and, having joined the Liberty and Property Defence League over the Ground Game Act, remained a member of its council until his death.[117] Pembroke also served on the council of the League: an old Etonian, ill-health prevented him from attending university and cut short his political career after only one year as Under-Secretary for War in Disraeli's ministry. Instead he devoted himself to the South Wiltshire Volunteers, in which he held a commission, and to yachting, despite once having been shipwrecked in the South Pacific.[118] Empirical Individualism also best describes the political theory of William Lecky (1838–1903), the historian of the eighteenth century, Liberal Unionist MP, and Privy Councillor, who was associated with another Individualist pressure group, the Freedom of Labour Defence, which aimed to resist the regulation of female labour.[119]

III. Conclusion: A Brace of New Liberalisms

The common element underlying the often diverse views of this group of political thinkers was the claim that they represented the true principles of liberalism which the Liberal party was in the process of abandoning in its willingness to embrace 'socialism' and State intervention. Nevertheless, their claim to be the true liberals was complicated by two considerations. In the first place, those who supported the New Radicalism were equally concerned to claim for themselves the title of true liberals. Although it has been suggested that they argued for 'the modernity and innovatory nature of their proposals',[120] in fact the New

[116] P. S. Atiyah, *The Rise and Fall of Freedom of Contract* (Oxford, 1979), 375. Atiyah's work contains a concise but valuable account of Bramwell's legal career. For further biographical details see C. Fairfield, *Some Account of George William Wilshere, Baron Bramwell of Hever* (London, 1898).

[117] Bristow, 'Liberty and Property Defence League', 765.

[118] Herbert's biography is to be found in *DNB* (London, 1912) xxii (suppl.).

[119] Bristow, 'Liberty and Property Defence League', 769. Lecky belonged to the Athenaeum Club of which Spencer was also a member and they enjoyed the occasional game of billiards together. After one such occasion Lecky remarked with unconscious irony that Spencer 'has nearly finished the first volume of his "Sociology" and seems very confident that it will be a complete explanation of human life. He finds it, however, longer than he intended'. Quoted in *A Memoir of the Rt. Hon. W. E. H. Lecky by his Wife* (London, 1909), 113.   [120] Vincent and Plant, *Philosophy, Politics, and Citizenship*, 36.

Radicals went to great lengths to establish the continuity between their principles and those of the earlier Radicals. For all that the older generation claimed to be the true representatives of the liberal tradition, the New Radicals also claimed for themselves the mantle of Philosophic Radicalism, and like D. G. Ritchie, an Oxford philosopher, Fabian, and self-professed New Radical, were scathing of those

> who learn nothing from the past they profess to reverence, who build the sepulchres of those whom their fathers slew, and imitate their fathers' conduct all the while. The heroes and prophets belong not to those who invoke their names, but to the reformer who inherits their spirit by looking, as they did, to the future.[121]

Thus the New Radicals did not portray their innovations as marking a fundamental break with the radicalism of the past; rather they re-presented them as an adaptation of old principles to new conditions or the completion of the project begun by the earlier generation. As Toynbee remarked:

> We have not abandoned our old belief in liberty, justice, and self-help, but we say that under certain conditions the people cannot help themselves, and that then they should be helped by the State representing directly the whole people.[122]

The degree to which the New Radicalism formed a continuation of that of the past was stressed by Toynbee's requirement that, even when the opportunity 'of removing a great social evil' should arise, 'nothing must be done to weaken those habits of individual self-reliance and voluntary association which have built up the greatness of the English people.'[123] This substantial continuity between the old and the new radicalism is often given insufficient attention by those accounts of the transformation of the liberal ideology which overemphasize the role played by Idealist philosophy in effecting that transformation.[124]

The second factor complicating the relationship of the Individualists to their earlier radicalism is the observation that Individualism was a conservative political theory, albeit one which departed substantially from the doctrines of orthodox conservatism. It is a notoriously difficult task to establish the leading theoretical principles of conservatism, and

---

[121] Ritchie, *Principles of State Interference*, 80. Chamberlain also thought it unlikely that the 'great representatives of the older Liberalism would be content to have nothing in place of the clearance they made and the restrictions they removed.' Chamberlain, 'Labour Question', 679.
[122] Toynbee, 'Are Radicals Socialists?', 219.
[123] Ibid.   [124] On this point see Freeden, *New Liberalism*, 16 f.

any account is bound to be selective, but we may claim general acceptance for the view that conservatives adhere to the following beliefs: scepticism about the possibility of progress because of the intellectual and moral imperfections of human beings; the conviction that there is a divinely ordained order of society which is hierarchical and based on human inequality; a preference for tradition and instinct rather than reason as the guide of human life; and a commitment to order and authority rather than freedom.[125] Yet on all these measures the Individualists were not conservative theorists. The 'unreserved recognition of Progress as the appointed law of all human institutions' was part of their inheritance from mid-century radicalism, and they maintained a powerful faith in the capacity of human reason to discern the laws of social development. In addition, their agnosticism made them inclined to doubt that any social system could be divinely ordained, while they had a strong conviction in favour of human equality—not the 'social equality' of the New Radicals, but the 'civil equality' of equality before the law. Finally, they accorded paramount value not to order and authority, but to the liberty of the individual.

Nevertheless, the Individualists were conservative theorists in the sense of being defenders of the status quo. They had, of course, grown older and therefore might be expected to have become more conservative in their personal opinions; but so widespread was the Individualists' political volte-face that the difference between mid-Victorian radicalism and Individualism cannot be adequately explained by reference to merely biographical factors.[126] In 1876 Brodrick regarded the prospect of liberal principles becoming obsolete as being 'As remote as that of gravitation being superseded by some higher law of nature.' For such an eventuality to occur 'there shall be no further advance to be made, no liberties to be vindicated, no inequalities to be removed, no rights of humanity to be upheld, no wrongs to be redressed, and no private interests to be overruled for the public weal.'[127] But a mere ten years later he was more concerned with resisting the 'socialistic tendencies of modern democracy' than with redressing wrongs or upholding the rights of humanity. Similarly, a speaker at a Liberty and Property Defence League meeting told his audience that 'your work is not now to

---

[125] See e.g. F. J. C. Hearnshaw, *Conservatism in England* (London, 1933), esp. 22–3; A. M. Quinton, *The Politics of Imperfection* (London, 1978); H. Glickman, 'The Toryness of British Conservatism', *Journal of British Studies*, 1 (1961), 111–43.

[126] This is the explanation offered of Spencer's abandonment of land nationalization and universal suffrage by Wiltshire, *Social and Political Thought of Herbert Spencer*.

[127] G. C. Brodrick, 'What are Liberal Principles?', *Fortnightly Review*, 19 (1876), 193.

further useful destructive legislation but to prevent mischievious constructive legislation' since the inequalities and injustices of the past were
'dead and gone'.[128] The advanced state of liberalism had been attained,
Bruce Smith announced, and hence 'the (what I would term) aggressive
function of liberalism has been exhausted, and, with certain minor
exceptions, it only remains for it to guard over the equal liberties of
citizens generally, with a view to their preservation.'[129] Even those of
Spencer's followers who anticipated the eventual withering away of the
'compulsory co-operation' embodied in the State were inclined to view
it as the outcome of a process of slow, evolutionary growth rather than of
political action; of Spencer himself it was remarked that he was so
possessed 'by the sense of the risks of miscalculation in social or political
change that he became finally opposed to almost every legislative
proposal.'[130]

Under the pressure exerted by the New Radicalism, the Individualists
were driven to the conclusion that the existing social order, which for the
Radicals of the 1860s had been a tissue of privilege and injustice, was to
be defended at all costs, irrespective of the fact that many of the reforms
demanded by the old radicalism had not been carried into effect. Free
trade in land may not have been established, and the political power of
the landed aristocracy may not have been broken, but the rights of
property and the constitutional position of the House of Lords were to
be upheld against the challenges presented to them by the New
Radicalism. As the Fabian Sidney Ball observed in his review of *A Plea
For Liberty*, the Individualists' theories, which in the eighteenth century
would have been revolutionary, were being used in the defence of the
status quo and the book was a 'plea for "Let be" rather than "Let
go"'.[131] Similarly, in an article entitled 'Individualism and Socialism',
the author of the notorious feminist novel *The Woman who Did*, the
Canadian writer Grant Allen, argued that the Liberty and Property
Defence League would be more accurately styled the 'Confiscation and
Aristocracy Defence League'.[132] According to Allen the first postulate
of Individualism—'that all men must, to begin with, have free and equal
access to the common gifts and energies of nature'—demanded the

[128] M. E. Grant Duff, Address to the Liberty and Property Defence League, in *Report
of Proceedings and Speeches of the Twelfth Annual Meeting*, 16. Grant Duff was a former
Governor of Madras and the biographer of Sir Henry Maine.
[129] [A.] B. Smith, *Liberty and Liberalism*, 10.
[130] Robertson, *Modern Humanists Reconsidered*, 183.
[131] S. Ball, 'A Plea for Liberty: A Criticism', *Economic Review*, 1 (1891), 327–8.
[132] G. Allen, 'Individualism and Socialism', *Contemporary Review*, 55 (1889), 737.

abolition of 'all the artificial monopolies, the hereditary inequalities, the land-grabbing and coal-taxing, the ground rents and tithes.' This was similar to the position of the mid-Victorian Radicals, but, as Allen observed, the League had abandoned this postulate and he claimed that it merely represented 'Privilege tricked out under false pretences.'[133]

Thus a political theory which had once condemned the injustices of the Victorian social order was now being employed in the defence of the very privileges and inequalities it had previously condemned, and as I shall argue, this could not be accomplished without a significant theoretical reorientation. Individualism, as much as the New Radicalism, was a theoretical innovation, and the next chapter will seek to establish this point by considering the relationship between Individualism and the political thought of Bentham and Mill.

---

[133] Ibid. 738.

RIVAL CLAIMANTS TO THE
BENTHAMITE HERITAGE

I. Introduction: Individualism and Benthamism

It was argued in the Introduction that the closing decades of the late nineteenth century witnessed the emergence of a sustained debate concerning the true meaning of liberalism. The aim of the present chapter is to demonstrate that, contrary to the Individualists' own self-image as the only legitimate heirs of the Benthamites, the relationship between Individualism and the radicalism of the second quarter of the nineteenth century was more complex than the Individualists themselves believed. While it is undeniable that there were substantial theoretical continuities between Benthamite radicalism and Individualism, it will be shown that the former contained within itself a number of tensions or ambiguities which enabled the New Radicals as well as the Individualists to lay claim to the Benthamite heritage. Both parties to the dispute reconciled these tensions in contrasting ways, but the fact that they shared a common perception of their existence, and of the need to overcome them, indicates that each side was engaged in a process of theoretical revision. While the innovations produced by the Individualists were less self-conscious than those of the New Radicals, they did not simply restate the old utilitarian doctrine in the changed conditions of the late nineteenth century, but transformed it in a conservative direction.

The way in which the tensions within the Benthamite heritage were resolved by the Individualists can be illustrated by three examples. In the first place, there was a potential conflict between Benthamism as a creed of the rational reform of political institutions—which were consequently regarded as artificial structures subject to human design—and as an economic creed which preached legislative impotence by treating the system of production and distribution as a 'natural' organization, governed by laws analogous to those of physical science. Whereas the New Radicals took over and emphasized the former aspect of Benthamism, extending it into economic relations, the Individualists developed the latter aspect into a theory of society which allegedly demonstrated the futility of the radical reform of all social institutions. Secondly, the link between the economic policy of *laissez-faire* and the principle of utility had been forged by orthodox political economy. But with the waning of the authority of Ricardian economics, the New Radicals were inclined to employ utilitarian considerations to support their policies, and they could draw on a strand of the Benthamite heritage which had allowed a considerable role for the central State. By contrast, the Individualists were forced to reinterpret the principle of utility to provide a justification for their resistance to social reform. Thirdly, and perhaps the most important tension of all, the Benthamites had argued for both *laissez-faire* and democracy, but in the changed climate of the late nineteenth century these two aspirations no longer appeared to be compatible. The New Radicals adopted the democratic aspects of Benthamism and argued that their policies were the logical extension of democracy, while the Individualists preferred to defend free enterprise and the rights of property against the rights of the majority. In addition to the theoretical innovations occasioned by the necessity of reconciling these conflicts internal to the Benthamite heritage, the Individualists were also forced to accommodate intellectual developments which had taken place since the early nineteenth century, in particular the discovery of social and biological evolution, and consequently modified the older utilitarianism still further. However, before examining these theoretical innovations, the points of coincidence between Individualism and Benthamism will first be explored.

The essence of Individualism was its advocacy of a conception of man and society which, according to most historians of liberal political thought, had been abandoned by the liberal mainstream long before the end of the nineteenth century. Ernest Barker, for example, argued that by 1848 'a modification of the old [Benthamite] philosophy of social action, if not an entirely new philosophy, was an urgent necessity, if social progress was not to be checked by a social creed.'[1] On Barker's account this new philosophy was partly created by J. S. Mill, but largely 'provided by the idealist school of which Green is the greatest representative.'[2] While the importance Barker assigned to Green has been questioned by recent scholarship, the conventional interpretation has persisted in viewing the New Liberalism as the culmination of an

[1] E. Barker, *Political Thought in England 1848 to the Present Day* (London, 1915), 9.
[2] Ibid. 10–11.

inexorable process in which the liberal ideology had long since thrown off the shackles of an atomistic and hedonistic form of the utilitarian doctrine. This observation might go a long way towards explaining the otherwise unaccountable neglect of the Individualists in the standard histories of liberal political thought: if it is assumed that New Liberalism represented the culmination of a process of transformation which the liberal ideology had been undergoing throughout the entire latter half of the century, a group of late Victorian thinkers who not only opposed the New Radicalism but who even harked back to a pre-Millite form of liberalism obviously represent an embarrassing aberration in this teleological progression.[3]

In considering themselves the heirs of 'Benthamism', the Individualists had a particular interpretation of the doctrine in mind which owed more to the writings of James Mill and Ricardo, not to mention the political practice of the Philosophic Radicals, than it did to a direct acquaintance with Bentham's philosophy. It was their tendency to view Bentham through the lens of this somewhat crude and oversimplified version of the master's doctrine which made possible both Dicey's easy identification of Benthamism with Individualism and Leslie Stephen's characterization of Bentham as 'in the main an adherent of what he calls the "laissez-nous faire" principle.'[4] In the context of the late nineteenth century and the early twentieth century, this was not a particularly contentious interpretation, as Barker's remarks cited in the last paragraph make clear; it is only much more recently that scholarship has established that Bentham's own views with regard to the legitimate province of the State were complex, and often allowed for a considerable degree of governmental action. But given the prevalence of this

---

[3] This 'teleological' account of the evolution of liberal thought in the 19th cent. has also received a powerful challenge from J. C. Rees, *John Stuart Mill's On Liberty* (Oxford, 1985), ch. 3, 'On Liberty and its Early Critics'. Rees argues that far from marking a stage in the development away from the individualism of the Benthamites, Mill's social philosophy was challenged by its early critics on the grounds that it carried individualism to excess (p. 103 f.). Hence the notion of a smooth transition from Benthamism to New Liberalism via the writings of Mill is unsustainable.

[4] For A. V. Dicey, see *Lectures on the Relation between Law and Public Opinion in England during the Nineteenth Century* (London, 1905), 126 ff; for Stephen, *The English Utilitarians* (London, 1900), i. 307. Stephen recognized that 'the "individualism" of Benthamism does not necessarily coincide with an absolute restriction of government interference' but nevertheless considered 'the general tendency' to be 'in that direction; and in purely economical questions, scarcely any exception was admitted to the rule.' (p. 310.) Contrast this account with that presented by J. Steintrager, *Bentham* (London, 1977), 62 ff., and L. J. Hume, *Bentham and Bureaucracy* (Cambridge, 1983), *passim*. The re-evaluation of Bentham's attitude to *laissez-faire* owes a good deal to W. Stark's edn. of Bentham, *Economic Writings* (London, 1954).

particular interpretation of what Benthamism represented, the Individualists' claims to be the true heirs of the earlier utilitarians could enjoy a substantial degree of legitimacy, and it is unarguable that there were a number of theoretical issues on which the Individualists shared much in common with the Benthamites, or that they held in common assumptions which the more fashionable Idealist philosophy explicitly challenged.

In the first place, the utilitarian moral theory was adopted by Individualist political thinkers as different as Spencer and Sidgwick; the former combined the principle of utility with the theory of evolution, while the latter adhered to a version of the principle which appeared to be a throwback to Bentham in abandoning the qualitative distinction between pleasures introduced by J. S. Mill.[5] Indeed, Sidgwick's book *The Elements of Politics* was so far removed from the Idealist commonplaces of late Victorian Britain that Barker, while recognizing its importance, refused to discuss it in his *Political Thought in England*, believing it more appropriate to another volume in the Home University Library series which dealt with the Philosophic Radicals.[6]

Like the early utilitarians, the Individualists assumed a 'negative' definition of liberty as the absence of physical or legal restraints on an individual's actions. In its 'primary signification', the Individualists argued, liberty meant 'freedom to do as one wishes; freedom from restraint.'[7] A more precise formulation of this conception was the claim that 'when employed without qualification "freedom" signifies primarily the absence of physical coercion or confinement.'[8] Inequalities of economic power could not be regarded as a constraint on liberty, and the Individualists consequently ignored those cases

where social circumstances in general and the more or less impersonal operation of the market . . . render a man's distress so great and his bargaining power so weak that even if he knows his own interest, he may still be victimized.[9]

By contrast, however, the theorists of the New Radicalism were prepared to acknowledge this 'blind spot' of the older liberalism and argued that

---

[5] These issues are examined in greater detail in Ch. 6.

[6] Barker, *Political Thought in England*, 81 n.

[7] [A.] B. Smith, *Liberty and Liberalism* (London, 1887), 220.

[8] H. Sidgwick, *The Elements of Politics* (London, 1891), 45. For a more extensive discussion of Sidgwick's account of liberty see W. L. Weinstein, 'The Concept of Liberty in Nineteenth Century English Political Thought', *Political Studies*, 13, (1965), 145–62.

[9] Weinstein, 'Concept of Liberty', 149.

a certain degree of well-being is a necessary condition for liberty. It is a mockery to call a man free who, by labour cannot secure to himself the necessaries of existence, or to whom labour is impossible because he possesses nothing of his own, and no one will employ him![10]

Similarly the Fabian Sidney Ball argued that 'State Socialism is as much a means of individual liberty to the "have-nots" as Laissez faire is to the "haves".'[11]

An additional respect in which the Individualists were at one with the earlier utilitarians was in their belief that liberty and government were antithetic terms, and hence the less a government governed the more free were its citizens: Donisthorpe's claim that 'every extension of the law [is] a restriction of liberty' was a direct descendant, via Bentham, of Hobbes's view that liberty consisted in the silence of the law.[12] Moreover, the Individualists and the Benthamites shared the assumption that it was the extent of government rather than its form which determined whether or not a political society was free; as Spencer wrote, 'the liberty which a citizen enjoys is to be measured, not by the nature of the governmental machinery he lives under . . . but by the relative paucity of the restraints it imposes on him'.[13] This view was challenged by the Idealists who argued that, correctly understood, the State and the individual were both (to use a Hegelianism) 'Moments' of some larger organic identity. Hence power taken by the State was not necessarily power lost to the individual, and interference by the State could increase, rather than diminish, the freedom of the individual.[14]

The Individualists' conception of the common good, in a clear contrast to that of the Idealists, harked back to purely aggregative conception of the Benthamites and orthodox political economists: for the Individualists the good or welfare of the community could only be interpreted to mean 'in the last analysis, the happiness of the individual human beings who compose the community.'[15] By contrast, the Idealist view was that the common good was more than the sum of its parts and

[10] É. de Laveleye, 'The State versus the Man: A Criticism of Mr. Herbert Spencer', *Contemporary Review*, 47 (1885), 499.

[11] S. Ball, 'A Plea For Liberty: A Criticism', *Economic Review*, 1 (1891), 328.

[12] W. Donisthorpe, *Law in a Free State* (London, 1895), 22.

[13] H. Spencer, *The Man versus the State*, ed. D. G. Macrae (1884; Harmondsworth, 1969), 79.

[14] For a statement of this view see D. G. Ritchie, *Principles of State Interference* (London, 1891), 12 f. Bentham himself had, of course, contended for an extensive sphere of State action, but this was to promote the 'subsidiary ends' of legislation—security, subsistence, abundance, and equality—rather than (as the Idealists would have argued) individual liberty.　　[15] H. Sidgwick, *Elements of Politics*, 34.

T. H. Green's organic conception of the common good required the liberation of the individual to achieve self-realization in community with others:

When we measure the progress of a society by its growth in freedom, we measure it by the increasing development and exercise on the whole of those powers of contributing to social good with which we believe the members of the society to be endowed; in short, by the greater power on the part of the citizens as a body to make the most and best of themselves.[16]

The Individualists also repudiated the notion that the State might possess a corporate will or personality which could be directed towards realizing the common good. This position was defended, for example, by Sidney Ball who had argued that 'the State is not a mere means to the safe pursuit of individual purposes; it has an end, and that a moral end. It represents the total interest of humanity—the highest possible development of human power and character.'[17] Claims like these were deflated by the Individualists' crudely reductionist conception of the State. Rather than possessing a 'duty and a wisdom of its own', wrote Goldwin Smith, the State was 'nothing but the government, which can have no duties but those which the constitution assigns it, nor any wisdom but that which is infused into it by the mode of appointment or election.'[18] A. V. Dicey also compared the 'wisdom of the State' to the wisdom of the Circumlocution Office.[19]

Additional support for the Individualists' advocacy of a limited State was derived from their abiding attachment to the doctrines of orthodox political economy. The Individualists espoused the form of individualism which Steven Lukes has termed 'economic', and would have agreed with the assertion that

a spontaneous economic system, based on private property, the market, and freedom of production, contract, and exchange, and on the unfettered self-interest of individuals, tends to be more or less self-adjusting; and that it conduces to the maximum satisfaction of individuals and to (individual and social) progress.[20]

---

[16] T. H. Green, 'Liberal Legislation and Freedom of Contract', in id., *Collected Works*, ed. R. L. Nettleship (London, 1885–8) iii. 371.

[17] S. Ball, 'Plea for Liberty: A Criticism', 337.

[18] G. Smith, *Essays on Questions of the Day, Political and Social* (New York, 1893), 9. The same phraseology was used by G. C. Brodrick, 'Socialistic Tendencies of Modern Democracy', in id., *Literary Fragments* (London, 1891), 227.

[19] A. V. Dicey, 'Mill "On Liberty"', *Working Men's College Journal*, 7 (1901), 39.

[20] S. Lukes, *Individualism* (Oxford, 1973), 89.

Their authorities for this view were the early, pre-'socialist', editions of Mill's *The Principles of Political Economy*, the fount of all wisdom, and Fawcett's *Manual of Political Economy*, which was little more than water bottled at the font. The Individualists believed that the orthodox political economists had discovered economic laws analogous to the laws of physical science: 'Political economy is a science quite as much as chemistry is, and its laws . . . are quite as true in their nature, and as certain in their effects, as the laws of chemistry themselves are.'[21] Furthermore, according to the Individualists, the laws of economics were not statements of tendencies expressed in the indicative mood, but precepts expressed in the imperative.[22] The old orthodoxy might be criticized for its 'rigidity', and political economy might be 'dead in the public mind', as Bagehot put it, but its basic premisses were fundamentally correct and unchallengeable. Long after Mill had abandoned the wage-fund theory in 'Thornton on Labour and its Claims', it was still a central plank in the Individualists' case against trade-unionism: Auberon Herbert insisted that although the doctrine had been bitterly attacked, 'it has never been substantially shaken . . . the all-important fact . . . remains, that only as the methods of production are improved and more is produced at less cost, can more be divided between employer and employed.'[23] This aspect of Individualism further served both to link it with Philosophic Radicalism, and to distance it from the intellectual developments of the late nineteenth century. Most of the Individualists proceeded in blissful ignorance of the combined assault launched on the old orthodoxy by Jevons's 'marginal revolution' and economists inspired by the German Historical School, like Toynbee, William Cunningham, and W. J. Ashley; even the most sophisticated economic theorist of the group, Henry Sidgwick, belonged in substance and method to the age of Mill rather than to the age of Marshall.

[21] G. Brooks, *Industry and Property* (London, 1895), 215.

[22] During the course of the Parliamentary debates on Irish land tenure J. S. Mill had accused Robert Lowe of having confused economic laws with precepts rather than statements of tendencies: 'Political Economy in my eyes is a science by means of which we are enabled to form a judgement as to what each particular case requires; but it does not supply us with a ready-made judgement upon any case, and there can be no greater enemy to political economy than he who represents it in that light.' (Speech on the State of Ireland, 12 Mar. 1868, in id., *Collected Works*, ed. J. M. Robson *et al.*, xxviii (Toronto, 1988), 256.) Yet this was exactly the error made by the Individualists, with the honourable exception of Henry Sidgwick.

[23] A. Herbert, 'The True Line of Deliverance', in Mackay (ed.), *A Plea for Liberty*, 392. For other examples of references to the wage-fund theory by Individualists see Brooks, *Industry and Property*, 81, and L. Stephen, *The Life of Henry Fawcett*, (1885; 3rd edn., London, 1886), 155.

The nature of the Individualists' theoretical assumptions is also reflected in their attitude towards the thought of J. S. Mill, which they criticized in proportion to its departure from Benthamite ideological purity. The Mill whom the empirical Individualists had once regarded as their guide in political and economic matters was the author of *A System of Logic* and the early editions of the *Principles of Political Economy*. As Dicey remarked,

The influence of Mill at the time I was growing up was exceedingly great. Between 1848 and 1870, Mill exercised a more salutary influence than almost any other author of his time. At Oxford we swallowed Mill, rather undigested; he was our chief intellectual food until 1860.[24]

Yet as the empirical Individualists grew older, Mill appeared to have become an apostate from true liberalism. In this regard his increased willingness to employ the power of the State against the obstacles of vested interests and private property was more important than having declared himself a fellow-traveller of the Utopian socialists: the 1868 pamphlet 'England and Ireland' argued in favour of conferring on the Irish cottiers the rights to fixity of tenure which they were eventually granted by the 1881 Act, and Mill's proposals for the taxation of the 'unearned increment', the compulsory purchase of wasteland, subsidies for working-class housing, and free, secular education were all later incorporated in the *Radical Programme*.

The greater the extent of Mill's sympathy towards 'socialism', exemplified by his revisions of the later editions of the *Principles of Political Economy* and the posthumous 'Chapters on Socialism', the less did the Individualists keep faith with the demigod of their youth. Leslie Stephen dismissed the 'Chapters on Socialism' with the observation that they were 'obviously imperfect, and scarcely justified publication',[25] while Dicey argued that in labouring to reconcile his inherited intellectual beliefs with 'sympathies which . . . were foreign, if not opposed, to the doctrines of his school', Mill had paved the way for the 'transition from the individualism of 1830–65 to the collectivism of 1900.'[26] Even *On Liberty* was hardly ever employed to reinforce the case against State interference: while it has been suggested that the work was 'conscripted into the later nineteenth century debate about the role of the state in social and economic matters',[27] there is in fact little evidence to suggest that this was the case. Although Ritchie criticized *On Liberty* for its

---

[24] A. V. Dicey, 'Mill', 17.   [25] Stephen, *English Utilitarians*, iii. 224 n.
[26] A. V. Dicey, *Law and Public Opinion*, 430.
[27] S. Collini, 'Liberalism and the Legacy of Mill', *Historical Journal*, 20 (1977), 249.

'abstract' conception of the individual and one Individualist recommended it to 'workingmen who are in search of the truth concerning the sphere and duties of government',[28] most Individualists either ignored the work or urged against it the stock criticisms that the distinction between self- and other-regarding conduct could not be maintained, and that there was an irreconcilable conflict between the principle of liberty and utility.[29] Throughout the 1880s and 1890s Mill's reputation suffered something of an eclipse, so that by 1897 the Spencerian *Liberty Review* could remark that he was 'not quite "up-to-date"' and 'must be regarded as an exponent of the most enlightened thought of his day, rather than a teacher whose dicta shall hold good for all time.'[30] The Spencerian Individualist Thomas Mackay summed up their assessment when he wrote:

Mill was by no means a representative of the scientific Liberalism of Cobden and his school . . . I suspect when history comes to be written it will be found that the so-called philosophic Radicalism of Mill was the force which, seemingly from the inside, broke up, for the time being, the authority of the Manchester School of Politics.[31]

Mill's political legatees were Dilke, Morley, and Chamberlain, and thus the Individualists were inclined to regard him not as the liberator of political philosophy from the shackles of an outmoded Benthamism, but as the corruptor of the one true faith.

Nevertheless, it would be wrong to conclude that the Individualists were simply Benthamites trapped at the end of the nineteenth century like flies trapped in amber, and there were a number of issues on which their relationship to the Benthamite philosophy was more complex than these instances might suggest. In the first place, as we stressed at the outset, the Benthamism to which the Individualists laid claim was but one particular (albeit widely accepted) interpretation of Bentham's

---

[28] J. M. Sloan, *For Freedom: Three Addresses on the Fallacies of State Socialism* (London, n.d. [1894]), 10.

[29] A typical example of these criticisms is Lord Pembroke, 'Liberty and Socialism', in id., *Political Letters and Speeches* (London, 1896), 220 f. A propos Pembroke's recognition that 'hardly any actions are purely self-regarding', David Ritchie commented 'We ought to be very grateful to Lord Pembroke for his clear exposure of the principles on which his "League" rests.' (*Principles of State Interference*, 97 n.). This was mischievous; as I have suggested, *On Liberty* was not part of the Liberty and Property Defence League's ideological baggage.

[30] Anon., 'J. S. Mill's Early Writings', *Liberty Review*, 7 (1897), 135. Significantly no mention of Mill's *On Liberty* occurs either in Spencer's *The Man versus the State* or in *The Principles of Ethics*.

[31] T. D. Mackay, 'Empiricism in Politics', *National Review*, 25 (1895), 794.

philosophy; Bentham himself appears to have looked with more favour on the activity of the State than did many of his followers, while his ideas could issue in the interventionist policies of a sanitary reformer like Edwin Chadwick. Furthermore, several examples can be cited of the Individualists having introduced direct modifications into the earlier Benthamite philosophy, even while professing to be merely its defenders. In the remainder of this chapter, I will argue that tensions existed within the Benthamite heritage itself, and it was these tensions which enabled both the New Radicals and the Individualists to lay claim to the same body of doctrine. The tensions in question were specifically those between freedom and necessity in the choice of social institutions; between the principle of utility and the policy of *laissez-faire*; and between the belief in democracy and the belief in the sanctity of the rights of property. Since the first two tensions are extensively discussed in the following chapters, the greatest emphasis will be placed on the Individualists' attitude towards democracy.

II. Social Science and Political Agency

The essence of the Benthamite political creed was faith in the power of conscious reflection, the unceasing criticism of the fabric of human institutions, and the continuous adaptation of all laws and customs to new times and new needs by subjecting them to the test of utility. In contrast to conservative theorists, who contended that governments 'are not made but grow', the old utilitarians maintained that constitutions could be a matter of deliberate, conscious choice. From his initial concern with the abuses of the law Bentham was led, step by step, to a radical reconstitution of society and became, as Mill remarked of him, 'the father of English innovation, both in doctrines and in institutions' who had been 'the great questioner of things established':

If the superstition about ancestorial wisdom has fallen into decay; if the public are grown familiar with the idea that their laws and institutions are in great part not the product of intellect and virtue but of modern corruption grafted on to ancient barbarism; if the hardiest innovation is no longer scouted because it is an innovation—establishments no longer considered sacred because they are establishments—it will be found that those who have accustomed the public mind to these ideas have learnt them from Bentham's school, and that the assault on ancient institutions has been, and is, carried on for the most part with his weapons.[32]

It was the critical spirit of the Benthamites which the New Radical D. G. Ritchie invoked when he argued that 'history has shown perpetually that it is impossible to stand still, and that to do nothing is often to do the greatest wrong.' The achievements of earlier generations of reformers were not honoured by the 'foolish maintenance of effete forms' but by 'endeavouring to do for others what they did for us; that is to say, by endeavouring to hand on to those that shall come after, the privileges we do not enjoy.'[33]

While Benthamism in the political sense was a creed of the rational reform of institutions in accordance with the principle of utility, in its economic beliefs it preached a passive acceptance of social evils as the beneficent consequence of natural laws. Human beings might enjoy freedom to choose the political institutions under which they lived, but in their economic life they were in the grip of an iron necessity described by the laws of Ricardian political economy. In their economic thought the Benthamites argued that individuals were subject to law-like regularities analogous to those of the physical sciences, a doctrine which seemed to imply that humanity could no more alter the economic institutions under which it lived than it could repeal the laws of gravity. If, for example, the wages of workers were paid from the wage-fund then nothing could be done to improve the conditions of their life, except by exhorting them to diminish the supply of labour by having fewer children. The Benthamites themselves did not perceive the tension with their political beliefs since they made the assumption that legislative activism was necessary to reform institutions (like the old Poor Law) which were artificial accretions on the natural order of society. However, given that their distinction between politics and economics was always somewhat arbitrary—especially as they were critical of aspects of existing property law like entail or encumbered estates—it was only a matter of time before the doctrine of rational reform was extended from the sphere of politics and the law into the sphere of economics. This was accomplished by J. S. Mill's famous distinction between the economic laws of production and the laws of distribution; of the former he wrote that they 'partake of the character of physical truths. There is nothing optional, or arbitrary in them', whereas 'It is not so with

---

[32] J. S. Mill, 'Bentham', in id., *Utilitarianism and Other Writings*, ed. M. Warnock (London, 1979), 80.   [33] Ritchie, *State Interference*, 80.

the Distribution of Wealth. That is a matter of human institution solely.'[34] Although Mill was later to qualify this statement, his basic position remained that although the laws of production were 'scientific', the laws of distribution were more complex because they also involved the civil and legal institutions existing in a community. This was a conclusion he was to reaffirm in the review of Thornton's *Labour and its Claims*: once the wage-fund theory had been abandoned, the 'terms of the bargain' between employers and labourers was 'not a matter of necessity, but, within certain limits, of choice' and hence had to be regulated by moral principles. In effect, Mill had reached the conclusion that the distribution of income and wealth in society could be modified by the legislator and he adopted a radical attitude towards the re-distribution of property, especially regarding the laws of inheritance.

This distinction between the laws of production and the laws of distribution enabled the New Radicals to contend that the relief of poverty or human misery could be in part 'effected by reforms in the laws regulating the division of property':

It is manifestly true that, as human society is comprehended in what we call Nature, it must obey her laws; but the laws and institutions, in all their different forms, which decree the acquisition and transmission of property or possession, and hereditary succession, in a word all civil and penal laws, emanate from men's will, and from the decisions of legislators; and if experience, or a higher conception of justice, shows us that these laws are bad, or in any way lacking, we are free to change them.[35]

The New Radical desire to modify the distribution of property by legislation can be regarded as a descendant, via the writings of Mill, of the Benthamite belief that progress consisted in legislative action for the reform of institutions.

By contrast, the Individualists wished to maintain that there was nothing the legislator could do to alter the distribution of property or the underlying conditions of human life, and consequently that social reform was an impossibility. In order to make this argument, they all but abandoned the notion that social and political institutions were a matter for rational, conscious design and instead drew on the aspect of Benthamite creed which had emphasized the beneficent consequences of natural laws. As we have already observed, the Individualists had no doubt about the validity of orthodox economics, and they insisted on the

[34] Quoted in A. Ryan, *J. S. Mill* (London, 1974), 164.
[35] de Laveleye, 'State versus the Man', 502, 503.

'scientific' character of both the laws of production and of distribution; Mill's distinction was attacked on the grounds that

the concrete facts of production, like those of distribution, are partly the results of the customs and legal institutions existing in a community; and the scientific laws of distribution, like those of production, are utterly beyond the disposition of man's desires or volitions.

It followed that the distribution of wealth was beyond the capacity of the legislator to control: 'no legislative changes, no changes whatever which you make in your conduct, can possibly affect the laws of the distribution of wealth.'[36] Nevertheless, the Individualists' argument against State interference did not simply rely on a repetition of the Ricardian orthodoxy in economics. In their view the truths of political economy were comprehended as part of a wider science of society, Spencerian evolutionary sociology, which established that all miseries could be attributed to 'the inevitable and beneficent consequences of natural laws; that these laws, being necessary conditions of progress, any endeavour to do away with them would be to disturb the order of nature and delay the dawn of better things.'[37] The Individualists had not lost their faith in progress, but reconciled it with their defence of the status quo by arguing that, rather than being achieved by the conscious design of human agents, it was to be attained by the working out of the inexorable laws of nature, in particular the laws of biological evolution. This aspect of Individualism, usually crudely caricatured as 'Social Darwinism', was used to establish that progress could not be achieved by the reform of institutions. Whereas the New Radicals wanted to set about relieving poverty and distress by utilizing the mechanism of the State, Individualists contended that the 'Social Problem' could not be resolved by collective action, and that it behoved each individual to improve the conditions of his life through his own actions.

An additional claim of Spencer's evolutionary sociology was that proposals for social reform proceeded in ignorance of the fundamental laws of the development of society. The Individualists' employment of this argument is typified by Thomas Mackay's rejection of 'revolutionary reconstructions' of society, in particular those which aimed to level up 'the condition of the poorer classes by devices designed to confer on the "have nots" the right to live on the taxation of the "haves"', because they were contrary to the fundamental principles of social science:

[36] J. H. Levy, 'Individualism', in E. B. Bax and J. H. Levy, *Socialism and Individualism* (London, n.d. (1904)), 81–2. [37] de Laveleye, 'State versus the Man', 502.

Whether we like it or not, the fabric of society has grown up around the support of certain fundamental principles. These principles are not, of course, absolutely rigid and immutable . . . but viewing the history of their development as a whole, we find that their main tendency is definite and unmistakable . . . We could not attain, and even if we could attain, we could not permanently retain, the advantages resulting from the working of these social tendencies, if we discarded the principles which have given them birth.[38]

Much the same criticism of schemes for social reform was contained in the assertion by another Individualist that 'the poor shallow Socialist-Radical seems quite unconscious that there are such things as laws of nature.' Since these laws could never be 'banished', the trust placed in legislative action was bound to be misplaced.[39]

The 'fundamental laws of nature' on which the New Radicalism was predicted to flounder were contained in the Spencerian analogy between the process of evolutionary growth experienced by a society and that experienced by a biological organism. The Individualists believed that social science had proved the impossibility of reforming society by means of conscious reflection and that social evolution was simply a matter of the working out of the blind, unconscious laws which governed all of the universe, whether organic or inorganic. The conception of society as an organism, usually associated with collectivism and State intervention, was used by Spencer and his followers to support an individualistic social order which their theory suggested was a natural rather than an artificial structure. This observation applied not merely to the economic institutions of a society, but to all of its social institutions, including the form of government. When combined with Spencer's oft-repeated statement that 'political institutions cannot be effectually modified faster than the characters of citizens are modified', the implication of evolutionary sociology was to reaffirm the old conservative saw about constitutions having grown rather than being made. The Individualists were therefore led to deny the aspect of the Benthamite heritage which emphasized the possibility of subjecting existing institutions to critical examination and radical reconstruction, and which had provided the proponents of social reform with their inspiration.

This aspect of Individualism may be regarded as the extreme development of the element of nineteenth-century evolutionary sociology which had stressed the underlying laws of social change at the expense

---

[38] T. D. Mackay, *Public Relief of the Poor: Six Lectures* (London, 1901), 10–11.

[39] H. S. Constable, *The Fallacies and Follies of Socialist Radicalism Exposed* (London, 1895), 19.

of deliberate human intervention and political agency. Mill's *Logic* had represented the first tentative steps in this direction by an English thinker: under the influence of Comte, Mill had attacked all 'philosophic speculators on forms of government, from Plato to Bentham' for having 'attempted to study the pathology and therapeutics of the social body before they had laid the necessary foundations of its physiology.' These thinkers had failed to comprehend 'that there were limits to the power of the human will over the phenomena of society, or that any arrangements which would be desirable, could be impracticable from incompatibility with the properties of the subject matter.'[40] The putative science of society which would replace the older Benthamite political science was to rest on the foundation of ethology, the science of the formation of character both individual and national, and was to be Comtian in its methodology. It would enable the social reformer to determine 'what artificial means may be used, and to what extent, to accelerate natural progress as far as it is beneficial', and thus involved a considerable restriction of political agency in the shaping of social institutions; as one commentator has put it, the suggestion is that 'the effective capacity of the political agent is . . . reduced to that of a pianola-player', who is able to adjust the speed of the music but not the tune which is played.[41]

The Individualists' conception of social science carried them beyond Mill's recognition of the limited scope of political agency: the upshot of the evolutionary sociology was that even the speed of the music was outside political control. Whereas Mill had never lost sight of Comte's slogan 'Savoir pour prévoir, prévoir pour pouvoir', the Individualists' outlook was more accurately expressed as 'prévoir pour faire rien'. Despite Spencer's repeated insistence that his sociological theories had not demonstrated that 'effort in the furtherance of progress is superfluous', few were convinced by his arguments, and he never satisfactorily accommodated political agency within his science of society.[42]

The methodological innovations created by Mill in his break from the Benthamites were also extended by the Individualists' conception of the nature of social Science. At the root of the Benthamite approach to politics and economics was the claim to have established a 'science of man' on the model of Newtonian mechanics. Their methodology, which

[40] Mill, *A System of Logic*, in id., *Collected Works*, ed. J. M. Robson *et al.*, viii (Toronto, 1973), 876.
[41] Collini *et al.*, *That Noble Science of Politics* (Cambridge, 1983), 129.
[42] See the postscript to the Library edn. of *The Study of Sociology* (London, 1880), 405.

Mill was to christen the 'geometrical method', was a priori and deductive, commencing with a few axiomatic propositions about human nature—for example that each person is the best guardian of his or her own interests or that each person aims to maximize their own utility. But even in the 1820s, this a priori, deductive approach to political science had been challenged by 'philosophical Whigs' like Macaulay, who had stressed the need to base political prescriptions on inductions from the evidence of concrete historical examples. Mill, who had written the sixth book of the *Logic* as an attempt to discover the truth in the debate between his father and Macaulay, recognized the need to take greater cognizance of the facts of history than had the Benthamites, although he ultimately concluded that the social sciences must be founded on the 'inverse-deductive' method he discovered in Comte's sociology.

By the 1870s, however, the deductive conception of social science was again challenged by the 'historical method', which Dicey defined as 'the habit or practice of examining the growth or history of laws, institutions, customs, and opinions', and which accordingly gave rise to an inductive rather than a deductive social science.[43] This approach to the study of social phenomena derived its authority from evolutionary biology and especially from Sir Henry Maine's pioneering work in historical jurisprudence which one commentator described as being simply an application of Darwin's method to society. Although Maine's own political views shared much in common with those of the Individualists, his methodology appeared to challenge the Benthamite conception of social science by pointing to the immense historical and geographical diversity of human social arrangements. Furthermore, in contrast to the older utilitarianism which had assumed societies to be simply agglomerations of isolated self-maximizing individuals, the historical method stressed the interdependence of institutions, beliefs, and habits and the role of a society's inherited value-system as a force for social cohesion; its immediate effect 'was to rehabilitate the customary and collective at the expense of the contractual and the individual.'[44] In the writings of economists like Cliffe Leslie and Toynbee, the historical method served to reinforce the development of New Radical ideas about State intervention and interference with the rights of property.

[43] A. V. Dicey, *Law and Opinion*, 454n. See also H. Sidgwick, 'The Historical Method', *Mind*, 9 (1886).

[44] Clive Dewey, 'Celtic Agrarian Legislation and the Celtic Revival: Historicist Implications of Gladstone's Irish and Scottish Land Acts 1870–1886', *Past and Present*, 64 (1974), 40–1. Dewey argued that the influence of the historical method was a significant factor the adoption of the Irish Land Acts of 1870 and 1881.

In response to the historicist challenge to the deductivist methodology, the Individualists carried the accommodation with the historical method even further than had J. S. Mill. It has been suggested of Sidgwick, for example, that his work

conceded the legitimacy of much of the critique of the axioms and methods of classical utilitarianism which had been made in the name of historical and cultural diversity, and he abandoned the attempt to deduce historically valid precepts from the 'laws of human nature' on the overworked model of Newtonian mechanics.[45]

Sidgwick adopted propositions like 'each person is the only safe guardian of his own rights and interests' not as universally true but as empirical generalizations 'sufficiently near the truth for practical purposes.'[46] Conclusions which had been deductively arrived at from these premises then had to be checked against the facts of history to establish their validity. He also allowed for differences of national character—a conception Bentham was more likely to have regarded as a case for treatment by the Theory of Fictions—and his recognition of the historical and cultural diversity of human beings developed 'a Burkean respect for the historically formed shape of existing institutions.'[47] Although Sidgwick believed that the study of politics was distinct from the study of history and ought not to be based on it, his own political writings displayed a much greater respect for history and tradition than the Benthamites had ever shown, and in this sense he was much closer to the utilitarianism of Hume than to that of Bentham.

Although Spencer insisted on the validity of a deductive science of society, he also sought an accommodation with the historical method. It was a characteristic feature of Spencer's approach to intellectual questions to hold that there was 'some conceptual truth on both sides of a contradiction', and his attempt to deal with the conflict of methods in the social sciences was no exception to this rule. Behind the diversity of the facts of history and 'that narrative of a nation's actions and fortunes its historian gives us', it was possible to discover general truths about 'the morphology and physiology of society', the relative constants of organization, structure, and function. These general truths were to be arrived at a priori by deduction from the fundamental principle of evolution, but this did not preclude them from being confirmed a posteriori by the

---

[45] S. Collini *et al.*, *That Noble Science of Politics*, 281.
[46] H. Sidgwick, *Elements of Politics*, 10.
[47] Collini, *et al.*, *That Noble Science of Politics*, 292.

immense quantities of historical and anthropological facts which Spencer referred to as 'the data of sociology'.

One final point about the Individualists' accommodation with the historical method remains to be made. Although they were criticized by Idealist and New Liberal philosophers for their adherence to an outmoded, atomistic conception of man and society, the accusation needs to be handled with great care, since 'atomism' was an ambiguous term. In one sense it referred to a conceptual claim about the possibility of conceiving the individual as existing independently of all social relations, a theory that the Individualists certainly endorsed. But atomism could also refer to a factual rather than a conceptual claim to the effect that society is simply an agglomeration of ahistorical individuals 'with given interests, wants, purposes, needs etc.'[48] In this sense the Individualists, unlike the Benthamites, were not atomists. As will be shown in the course of this work, Spencer's use of the social organism analogy meant that the Individualists were able to recognize that the individual was a social product who both moulded, and was moulded by, the society to which he or she belonged.

III. Utilitarianism and Laissez-Faire

The second tension within the Benthamite heritage was between the principle of utility and *laissez-faire*. This tension had been apparent in the utilitarian movement from the beginning, since in Bentham's hands the principle of utility was used to justify a much wider range of State action than the Philosophic Radicals ever countenanced. In the *Constitutional Code* he had envisaged various forms of government interference for the good of the people, including ministries of health and education, and 'indigence relief minister', and an 'interior-communications minister' (i.e. a minister of transport).[49] The Philosophic Radicals, under the leadership of James Mill, minimized the statist implications of utilitarianism by regarding the laws of Ricardian economics as the statement of the conditions productive of the greatest human happiness.[50]

[48] Lukes, *Individualism*, 72.   [49] R. Harrison, *Bentham* (London, 1983), 258.
[50] It is worth noting, however, that even James Mill approved of a State Established Church (of a secular sort) for inculcating proper standards of citizenship; Presbyterianism minus Christianity, so to speak.

Since utilitarianism was a consequentialist moral theory it was necessary to have some means of estimating the likely consequences of the available course of action for it to be applied to actual situations, and it was argued that the knowledge of the consequences of a particular policy had been supplied by the truths of orthodox political economy. According to this view, there was a natural harmony between the self-interested activities of individuals pursuing their own happiness, and thus, as Dicey argued, the Benthamites of the second quarter of the century had failed to grasp that there was no logical connection between *laissez-faire* and the greatest-happiness principle, because 'they could hardly imagine the possibility of a conflict between the true interest of the community and the universal as well as the equal liberty of individual citizens.'[51]

With the waning of confidence in the validity of orthodox political economy, however, the pursuit of the greatest happiness of the greatest number seemed once more to lend support to the kind of State intervention Bentham had advocated. Toynbee stressed that the belief in the 'spontaneous' identity of the individual and common interest was

a perfect instance of the reckless abstractness of the old Political Economy . . . The pressure of competition does undoubtedly tend to the satisfaction of the greatest number of wants at the lowest cost, but not without innumerable evils in the process—evils which, as we now see, the wise regulation of the competitive impulse may . . . avert.[52]

In addition, as T. H. S. Escott argued in the *Radical Programme*,

capital has acquired so predominant a power that it is not safe to leave labour to look after itself; that the economical laws of supply and demand, which are merely generalizations from experience, are not infallible in their operation; and that freedom of contract may be employed as an instrument of oppression as well as of liberty.[53]

When combined with these new social and economic assumptions utilitarianism, which had been converted into a doctrine of *laissez-faire* only by orthodox political economy, appeared to sanction the kind of 'socialistic' interference proposed by the New Radicals and to which the Individualists were so intensely opposed.

Although, as already noted, the Individualists adopted the utilitarian moral theory, the significant role played by the principle of utility in the

[51] A. V. Dicey, *Law and Public Opinion*, 304.
[52] A. Toynbee, 'Ricardo and the Old Political Economy', in id., *Lectures on the Industrial Revolution of the Eighteenth Century in England* (London, 1884), 21–2.
[53] *The Radical Programme* (London, 1885), 53.

development of the New Radicalism should not be neglected, despite the criticisms levelled at it by the Idealists. If the test of legislation was the greatest happiness of the greatest number, and since the majority of the nation were the poor and needy, it was but a short step to the conclusion 'that the whole aim of legislation should be to promote the happiness, not of the nobility or the gentry, or even shop-keepers, but of artisans and other wage earners.'[54] Chamberlain declared that the extensions of the franchise meant that 'the problem of the future' was 'how to promote the happiness of the masses of the people, how to increase their enjoyment of life'[55] and hence 'the greatest happiness of the greatest number, which was formerly only the benevolent aspiration of a philosopher, has become a matter of urgent practical politics.'[56] Lest it be thought that this was mere platform oratory, the Oxford philosopher D. G. Ritchie, although drawing on the Idealist tradition, also claimed a utilitarian justification for the New Radicalism. Bentham's error had consisted in his

abstract and mechanical view of feelings as if 'lots of pleasures' could actually be distributed among the members of a community, like the dividends of a joint-stock company; and his abstract and mechanical view of society, as if it were simply an aggregate of absolutely uniform individuals.[57]

A more adequate version of utilitarianism as involving 'the conception of right conduct which tends to the welfare of the social organism' avoided the 'defects' of the older doctrine, particularly its individualistic and atomistic theory of politics.[58] Given different social conditions and assumptions the principle of utility seemed to demand a degree of State intervention in the economy and regulation of the competitive process; or, as Dicey preferred to describe it, 'the despotic authority of a democratic state.'[59]

Because in the past the link between *laissez-faire* and utilitarianism had been forged by an economic science which the late Victorians were increasingly inclined to question, the Individualists were forced to construct a form of the utilitarian doctrine which reaffirmed the connection between the principle of utility and a limited State by discovering a

[54] A. V. Dicey, *Law and Public Opinion*, 304.

[55] J. Chamberlain, 'The Doctrine of Ransom', Speech at Birmingham, 5 Jan. 1885 in id., *Collected Speeches*, (London, 1914), i. 137.

[56] Id., 'Favorable Aspects of State Socialism', *North American Review*, 152 (1891), 534.

[57] Ritchie, *State Interference*, 168.

[58] Ibid. 169. For an elaboration of this point see M. S. Freeden, *The New Liberalism: An Ideology of Social Reform* (Oxford, 1978), 12 ff.

[59] A. V. Dicey, *Law and Public Opinion*, 307.

substitute for the predictive powers of Ricardian political economy. Given that it was necessary to establish the consequences of a particular course of action a new social science was required, and Spencer argued this was provided by his evolutionary sociology. Bentham had claimed to be engaged in constructing a 'science' of legislation and morality; Spencer took him at his word, and argued that the older form of utilitarianism appeared to support an activist State only because its founder had failed to be sufficiently scientific. 'In Bentham's day the knowledge of physical science was confined to a small number; and, as a result, thoughts about causation were, in nearly all men, vague and undeveloped.'[60] The objective of a 'moral science' was to 'determine how and why certain modes of conduct are detrimental, and certain other modes beneficial'; this the 'Expediency philosophy' had not done since it 'supplied for the guidance of conduct nothing more than . . . empirical generalizations.'[61] The theory of evolution could be employed to reveal the 'scientific' conditions productive of the greatest happiness and these were identified with the Spencerian Law of Equal Freedom. A further consequence of this theory was to rehabilitate the doctrine of natural rights, which Bentham had dismissed as 'simple nonsense' (he reserved the more famous epithet 'nonsense upon stilts' for rights which were 'natural and imprescriptible'). Spencer may be regarded as attempting to mediate between the two very different traditions of English radicalism, the theory of Bentham and the older natural-rights-based doctrines of Paine and Godwin. He argued that respect for the natural rights contained within the equal liberties principle would be productive of the greatest happiness of the greatest number, and the only function for the legislator was to secure the claims of justice. In this way the connection between the principle of utility and a limited State was reaffirmed.

Sidgwick arrived at similar conclusions by a rather different route. Unlike Spencer he was too orthodox a utilitarian to embrace the concept of natural rights, and he accused Bentham not of being insufficiently scientific, but of entertaining an excessively precise conception of the utilitarian calculus. Rather than seeking a substitute for Ricardian political economy, Sidgwick maintained that consequentialist reasoning was so complex that it could be directly employed only infrequently. He argued, like Mill before him, that because of the immense practical difficulties in the way of attaining accurate measurements of the utility

[60] Spencer, *Autobiography* (London, 1904), ii. 89   [61] Ibid. 88.

generated by particular courses of action the utilitarian was forced to
rely on 'axiomata media' for arriving at decisions. The most important of
these for the political theorist was the equal liberties formula, understood as a practical maxim rather than a scientific law. Sidgwick not only
argued for *laissez-faire* as the general rule of public policy, but he
excluded on methodological grounds the possibility of constructing
an ideal code of utilitarian ethics with which to criticize existing
institutions.

Spencer's version of utilitarianism was also conservative in import,
since he made a distinction between 'absolute' and 'relative' ethics
which enabled him to deny the logical implications of his own principles
where they threatened to challenge the existing Victorian social order.
In his hands utilitarianism lost the radical cutting edge it had possessed
in the heyday of Philosophic Radicalism. In this case the Individualists
were forced to modify significantly the doctrines of the Philosophic
Radicals in order to suit them to their conservative purpose.

IV. Individualism and Democracy

A third tension within the old Benthamite creed which was resolved in
different ways by the Individualists and the New Radicals was that
between *laissez-faire* and democracy. Although it has been observed that
'inside and outside England, from Macaulay to Mises, from Spencer to
Sumner, there was not a militant liberal who did not express his
conviction that popular democracy was a danger to capitalism',[62] both
democracy and capitalism were part of the programme of the
Benthamites. The Individualists expressed doubts about the compatibility of the Philosophic Radicals' social and economic reforms and in
so doing they drew on a tendency within utilitarianism which had only
gathered pace after the death of Bentham; here too Mill is something of
a transitional figure, for although he never abandoned his faith in
democracy, he nevertheless came to recognize that pure majority rule
could not be treated as an unmixed good. However, the criticisms of
democracy advanced by the Individualists more closely resembled the
anti-democratic utilitarian case against reform which had been framed
by John Austin in the late 1850s, and was repeated with more vigour a
few years later by Robert Lowe. It was one of the great ironies of political

history that many of those who in 1867 had championed democracy against the arguments of Lowe became convinced in the space of twenty years that they had been mistaken, and subsequently criticized democracy in terms not unlike those Lowe himself had used. A belief in the connection between democracy and socialism led them to question the very principle of 'trust in the people' which the earlier generation of Radicals had espoused. By contrast the New Radicals, while accepting that *laissez-faire* and democracy were not compatible, attempted to present their 'socialistic' policies as the natural consequence of the earlier Radicals' democratic convictions.

Both the New Radicals and the Individualists believed that there was a fundamental conflict between the democratic rights of the people and an economic system founded on *laissez-faire* and a respect for the rights of property. For Bentham the possibility of such a conflict had not arisen since he regarded the propensity to take the property of other people as being stronger among the rich than among the poor.[63] He had argued for universal suffrage subject only to literacy and 'householdership' qualifications, although the first was not really a qualification at all since Bentham believed that anyone could attain literacy in a matter of weeks. The householdership qualification referred to the ability to pay rent and taxes as well as a minimal residency requirement; it was certainly not intended to exclude the poor from the franchise as their interest in good government was as great as that of the rich.[64] J. S. Mill was closer to recognizing a conflict between democracy and the rights of property, and among the shortcomings of democracy he noted was the tendency to enact 'class legislation', i.e. legislation made 'under the influence of interests not identical with the general welfare of the community', even if that 'sectional interest' was the majority. Nevertheless, he shared with Bentham a considerable faith in 'human contrivance'—that is, in institutional mechanisms—as a means of resolving constitutional problems, and he accordingly recommended the adoption of Hare's system of proportional representation, plural voting for the most highly educated, and an expert legislative commission charged with drafting the laws. As Mill noted in his *Autobiography*, although he was 'aware of the weak points in democratic opinions' he had nevertheless 'unhesitatingly decided in its favour, while recommending that it should be accompanied by such institutions as were consistent with its principle and calculated to ward off its inconveniences.'

[63] F. Rosen, *Jeremy Bentham and Representative Democracy* (Oxford, 1983), 178.
[64] Ibid. 132.

The New Radicals endeavoured to present their 'socialistic' policies as the logical culmination of the democratic convictions of the earlier Radicals. One of the cardinal tenets of the old Radical creed, Toynbee observed, was the belief that 'to obtain justice and liberty . . . all classes should be admitted to the suffrage . . . Others might fear, they trusted the people; and nothing shook this faith—not the wild cries of starving multitudes, not ignorant tumults, not violence.'[65] Once having been granted access to political power, the people's demands could not be ignored. Chamberlain explicitly linked his programme for social reform with the extension of democracy, and as he announced in the preface to the *Radical Programme,*

The Reform Acts of 1885 have set the seal on the great change which the Reform Act of 1832 inaugurated . . . At last the majority of the nation will be represented by a majority of the House of Commons, and ideas and wants and claims which have been hitherto ignored in legislation will find a voice in Parliament, and will compel the attention of statesmen.[66]

Laissez-faire and the rights of property were not compatible with democracy, and since the latter had triumphed it belonged to 'the authority and duty of the State—that is to say, of the whole people acting through their chosen representatives' to utilize its power to 'protect the weak, and to provide for the poor, to redress the inequalities of our social system, to alleviate the harsh conditions of the struggle for existence, and to raise the average enjoyment of the majority of the population.'[67] This view was echoed by T. H. S. Escott who remarked that the 1885 Reform Act had served to reinforce the change 'in the direction in which the legislation of the last quarter of a century has been tending—the intervention . . . of the state on behalf of the weak against the strong, in the interests of labour against capital, of want and suffering against luxury and ease.'[68]The State having become fully democratized, it was henceforth to legislate in the interests of the majority of the people, and this required that (when necessary) it would undertake 'socialistic' interference.[69]

[65] Toynbee, 'Are Radicals Socialists?', in id., *Lectures on the Industrial Revolution,* 204–5.   [66] *Radical Programme,* pref.

[67] J. Chamberlain, 'State Socialism and the Moderate Liberals', Speech to the 'Eighty Club', 28 Apr. 1885, in id., *Collected Speeches,* i. 165–6.

[68] *Radical Programme,* 7.

[69] The same argument can be found in *Spectator*'s review of *The Man versus the State*: 'Now that the Government tends to become simply a committee of the people, why should the people object to invest the State to functions superior to those of the policeman, any more than a body of shareholders fears to invest its directors with powers superior to those

The Individualists shared the New Radicals' belief that there was a direct connection between democracy and socialism. Like Goschen, they saw a connection between the emergence of the New Radicalism and the fact that 'it was the year 1880 which saw the commencement of the first Parliament in which the great constitutional change of 1867 made itself fully felt.'[70] But unlike the New Radicals they decided the issue between the democratic rights of the majority and the rights of the propertied minority in favour of the latter. Dicey dated the emergence of the legislative tendency of 'Collectivism' from the introduction of household suffrage; before the 1867 Reform Act the Commons had represented the middle class who were imbued with 'the Benthamism of common sense', whereas after the Act the working class gained the political ascendency and had sought laws 'which might promote the attainment of the ideals of socialism or collectivism.'[71] In contrast to the legislation implemented after the Great Reform Act of 1832, which had the aim of 'purifying the administration and reducing its cost', wrote Godwin Smith, the objective of 'the masses and their leaders' was to seek political power 'in the hope that it may be used to effect a great social change.'[72] The evidence of the legislative tendencies of the Parliaments elected after the 1867 Reform Act seemed to indicate that, as Sir Henry Maine remarked, 'the Radical doctrine of the expediency of an extended suffrage is in fact rapidly mining the Radical doctrines of free ships and free trade, of free transfer and free contract.'[73]

The Individualists came to share the analysis of John Austin and Robert Lowe (whom James Bryce once described as 'a far more stringent and consistent exponent of the harder kind of Benthamism' than was Mill[74]) that democracy was fundamentally incompatible with the sanctity of private property and the freedom of private enterprise. The case against democracy formulated by political thinkers like Austin and Lowe had been based on the alleged utilitarian consequences of popular government, and thus purported to deal not with such terms as 'right, equality, justice', but with the 'working of institutions, with their

---

of auditors?' (Anon., *The Man versus the State* by Herbert Spencer, *Spectator*, 58 (1885), 422). Since *Spectator* was hardly a New Radical journal, it indicates the extent of mainstream liberal consensus on this issue.

[70] G. J. Goschen, 'Since 1880', *Nineteenth Century*, 17 (1885), 723.

[71] A. V. Dicey, *Law and Public Opinion*, 253.

[72] G. Smith, 'The Organization of Democracy', *Contemporary Review*, 47 (1885), 318.

[73] [Sir Henry Maine], 'Radical Patriarchialism', *St. James's Gazette*, 1 (1880), 259–60.

[74] James Bryce, 'Robert Lowe', in id., *Essays in Contemporary Biography* (London, 1903), 304.

faults, with their remedies, with the probable influence which such changes will exert.'[75] They contended that to confer political power on the numerous class of 'men of no property' would be mistaken because of 'their misapprehensions of the purposes and province of government, and their ignorance of the causes which determine their economical condition.'[76] No one could doubt, it was argued, that 'the great majority of the working class are imbued with principles essentially socialist' and a House of Commons representing their 'prejudices' could be expected to 'ruin our finances and destroy our economical prosperity, by insensate interferences with the natural arrangements of society.'[77] These utilitarians went much further than Mill's qualified endorsement of democracy and were prepared to argue for the utility of the British constitution as it existed in the Palmerstonian era.

As a young Fellow of Trinity, Dicey had criticized Lowe for believing that majority rule would enable the working class to act with 'systematic tyranny' against wealth and property; he later came to acknowledge the force of this criticism and explicitly endorsed the utilitarian case against democracy:

Austin, Bowring, W. R. Greg, Robert Lowe and other rigid utilitarians adopted, without any fundamental change of principles, a peculiar type of conservatism. They felt that a Parliament constituted under the Reform Act of 1832 was more likely to legislate in accordance with utilitarian principles than would any more democratic assembly. Their forecast of the future has been justified by subsequent events.[78]

Like the earlier generation of utilitarian critics of democracy, the Individualists believed that the clear consequence of the extension of the franchise was the tendency of the unpropertied majority to seek legislation which conferred 'some advantage upon themselves as a class' and Bruce Smith claimed to be able to discern 'tolerably clear symptoms' of an emerging 'class struggle through the medium of the legislature, which must end injuriously to our best civil interests.'[79]

The Individualists contended that the working class, even though in the majority, were simply one sectional interest among many. Not only was legislation designed to favour them at the expense of the capitalists

---

[75] R. Lowe, *Speeches and Letters on Reform* (2n edn., London, 1867), 4. See also Lowe's anonymous review of 'Reform Essays' in *Quarterly Review*, 123 (1867), 246f.

[76] J. Austin, *A Plea for the Constitution* (2nd edn., London, 1859), 18.

[77] Ibid. 19. See also Lowe, 'Reform Essays', 253.

[78] A. V. Dicey, *Law and Public Opinion*, 164. For Dicey's criticisms of Lowe see id., 'The Balance of Classes', *Essays in Reform* (London, 1867), 74.

[79] [A.] B. Smith, *Liberty and Liberalism*, 10.

misconceived, but it was inevitably also an instance of the 'class legislation' once favoured by the Tory party. Spencer remarked:

A generation ago, while agitations for the wider diffusion of political power were active, orators and journalists daily denounced the 'class legislation' of the aristocracy. But there was no recognition of the truth that if, instead of the class at that time paramount, another class were made paramount, there would result a new class legislation in place of the old.[80]

The language of class legislation had been employed against institutions like the Corn Laws which had favoured the aristocracy at the expense of manufacturers and their workers, and thus had been a feature of the social system the earlier Radicals had striven to overthrow. The Individualists were inclined to regard the New Radicalism as a reversion to the kind of Toryism which had once defended the interests of a class against the interests of the public weal. Spencer, for example, castigated the politics of social reform as 'The New Toryism', while another Individualist, M. D. O'Brien, branded socialism 'the old Tory privilege system applied to Demos.'[81] This theme was also propounded by Bruce Smith who alleged that 'either from want of a clear recognition of the limits to which state interference should go, or from having placed a strained and unscientific interpretation upon the word "liberty"' the new generation of Radicals were 'actually favouring a reaction, in the direction of Toryism—of a democratic type.'[82]

In reply to these criticisms the New Radicals argued that their allegedly Tory policies were simply an attempt to remain true to the doctrine of the earlier generation of Radicals in the changed conditions of late Victorian Britain. Toynbee's response was to contend that the legislation favoured by the New Radicals was not the 'class legislation which Radicals have always opposed.' On the contrary, it did not favour a sectional interest but was 'in the interest of the whole community. We cannot call ourselves safe until all citizens have the chance of living decent lives; the poorest class needs to be raised in the interest of all classes.'[83] Even the moderate, Liberal *Spectator* criticized Spencer for identifying Liberalism with Toryism:

The difference between Toryism and Liberalism consists in this—that the latter seeks freedom for everyone by subjecting everyone to government in the

[80] H. Spencer, *The Principles of Ethics*, ii (London, 1893), 191–2.
[81] M. D. O'Brien, *The Natural Right to Freedom* (London, 1893) 35.
[82] [A.] B. Smith, *Liberty and Liberalism*, 57.
[83] Toynbee, 'Are Radicals Socialists?', 219.

interests of the nation as a whole; while Toryism seeks order by subjecting whole classes to the dominion of other classes, in the interests of the dominant classes.'[84]

The Individualists believed that the reason for the upsurge in 'social-ism' and 'class legislation' was the same as that which Austin had identified, namely that the newly enfranchised voters were ignorant of the 'causes which determine their economical condition.' Pleydell-Bouverie spoke for many of the Individualists when he remarked to a meeting of the Liberty and Property Defence League:

The truth is, as far as I can discern it, that this vast extension of political privileges and franchises . . . has practically turned up a new substratum of political soil . . . which is readily prepared to grow exactly the same weeds of prejudice and ill-understood opinions, which sprang up and prevailed among the more cultivated class two or three hundred years ago, and which has been eradicated from their minds by the experiences of those times.[85]

Some of the older generation of Radicals, like Henry Fawcett, had retained their democratic faith because they believed that the masses could be brought to see the erroneous nature of socialism by being educated in the truths of political economy.[86] This was not generally the position of the Individualists who, like Bruce Smith, argued that the opinion of the majority was almost invariably erroneous since a correct opinion in political or economic matters demanded 'a special knowledge which it takes years to acquire.' In the absence of this special knowledge there was a clear tendency on the part of the newly enfranchised elaborate to regard 'parliament as a sort of scramble for benefits.'[87] Democracy, in passing political power to the uneducated majority, was likely to generate the same myths of protectionism and class legislation which it had been the historical mission of true liberalism to eradicate.

Nevertheless, if Lowe's speeches represented what Bryce was to call the 'swan-song of the old Constitutionalism', the Individualists could not merely express nostalgia for the vanished age. Just as Lowe had transformed utilitarianism into an apology for the Palmerstonian con-stitution, so the Individualists articulated a theoretical defence of the Salisburian political order. Throughout his life Spencer maintained the view that democratic government 'is good, especially good, good above all others, for doing the thing which a government should do. It is bad,

---

[84] Anon., '*The Man versus the State*', *Spectator*, 421.
[85] E. Pleydell-Bouverie, *The Province of Government* (London, 1884), 5.
[86] Stephen, *Life of Henry Fawcett*, 170.
[87] [A.] B., Smith, *Liberty and Liberalism*, 301, 295.

especially bad, bad above all others, for doing the things which a government should not do.'[88] The only legitimate function of government was to protect the liberties of the individual, and hence for democracy and liberty to be reconciled it followed that 'as fast as representation is extended the sphere of government must be contracted.'[89] The evidence from both Britain and America convinced the mature Spencer that there was no guarantee that this process would occur, and indeed the 'diffusion of political power unaccompanied by the limitation of political functions, issues in communism.'[90] Hence he was led to deny one of the fundamental contentions of the *Social Statics*, that the right to vote was a natural right, and he argued that further extensions of the franchise would have to wait upon the evolution of a higher type of character among the citizen body. Political institutions could only be democratized to the extent that individuals acquired a more adequate sense of justice and were thus prepared to respect the liberty (and property) of others. In the interim, Spencer was inclined to look with more favour on the late Victorian constitution; while continuing to profess his detestation of all forms of personal rule, including constitutional monarchy, he was impressed by the 'adaptation to the existing type of man' of 'established governmental forms'.[91] Many of the Spencerians followed their mentor in this direction, Wordsworth Donisthorpe arguing that democracy was impulsive and therefore needed a Court of Appeal which he identified with a reformed House of Lords.[92] Auberon Herbert was virtually alone in remaining true to the undiluted democratic republicanism of his speech on the Civil List.[93]

The task of modifying their democratic commitments was somewhat easier for the empirical Individualists, since they were able to contend that experience had indicated that democracy was only a relative and qualified good. Dicey explained that once it was granted that

the progress of democracy does not always favour the freedom of individuals . . . it becomes impossible to argue that a change is for the good simply because it is

---

[88] H. Spencer, 'Representative Government: What is it Good for?', in id., *Essays: Scientific, Political and Speculative*, iii. 207.   [89] Id., *Autobiography*, ii. 55.

[90] Id., *The Principles of Sociology*, ii. (London, 1882), 751.

[91] Id., *Autobiography*, ii. 465.

[92] W. Donisthorpe, *Individualism: A System of Politics* (London, 1889), 384–5. For another instance of a Spencerian Individualist defending the House of Lords 'as a check on hasty legislation' see Constable, *Fallacies and Follies of Socialist Radicalism*, p. 41.

[93] A. Herbert, *The Right and Wrong of Compulsion by the State* (London, 1885), 33. J. H. Levy was the only other Individualist to continue to espouse the republican and democratic cause into the 1890s.

democratic, for it is quite possible that changes which in one sense favour popular power are inexpedient because they are hostile to liberty or, what is pretty nearly the same thing, to justice.[94]

The most consistently worked out constitutional scheme propounded by an empirical Individualist was contained in the second part of Henry Sidgwick's *Elements of Politics*, which is best understood against the background of the impact of Sir Henry Maine's *Popular Government*, considered by Sidgwick 'the best anti-democratic writing we have had.'[95] By the mid-1880s Maine's proposal to restrict the popular will by borrowing devices from the American constitution had begun 'to excite something like hopeless admiration on the part of thoughtful conservatives', and although Sidgwick was never one to be carried away by a passing fad, his own constitutional innovations reflected the influence of Maine's ideas.[96] As he noted in his diary after a conversation with Dicey

Our idea is to borrow from America the stability for a definite period of the executive, but to keep the original appointment in the hands of the Legislature (as practically in England now).[97]

The advantage of conferring a fixed period in office upon the executive was that it enabled Sidgwick to argue that both chambers of the legislature should possess co-ordinate powers, secure in the knowledge that any dispute between them could not result in the fall of the government. (In the last resort these disputes were to be settled by a referendum.)[98] Although he mentioned the possibility of basing the composition of the Upper Chamber either on some method of appointment or on indirect election, and despite remaining enough of a Radical to believe that no one would advocate the hereditary principle *de novo*, it

---

[94] A. V. Dicey, 'Democratic Assumptions V: Conclusions', *Nation* (NY), 53 (1891), 84.

[95] Quoted in A. S[idgwick] and E. M. S[idgwick], *Henry Sidgwick: A Memoir* (London, 1906), 392.

[96] The debate sparked by Maine's *Popular Government* primarily concerned the extent to which Britain should borrow from the institutions of the US in order to entrench property rights after the passing of the 1884 Franchise Act. It is examined by H. A. Tulloch, 'Changing British Attitudes to the United States in the 1880s', *Historical Journal*, 20 (1977), 825–40.

[97] Record of a conversation with A. V. Dicey at Oxford on 20 May 1888, quoted in A. S[idgwick] and E. M. S[idgwick], *Henry Sidgwick*, 488.

[98] A. V. Dicey, 'Democracy in Switzerland', *Nation* (NY), 42 (1886), 494–6. For the advocacy of the referendum by Dicey and other Individualists see J. Meadowcroft and M. W. Taylor, 'Liberalism and the Referendum in British Political Thought 1890–1914', *Twentieth Century British History*, 1 (1990), 35–56.

was clear from his respect for the established traditions of political societies that the Upper Chamber of his ideal constitution would be not dissimilar to the House of Lords.[99] The Lower House, elected on a household suffrage, would consist of unpaid representatives, a principle marked for abolition by the Chamberlainites and which Goldwin Smith described as 'the only Conservative institution which is really effective,'[100] To complete the institutional machinery, the actual administration of government would be in the hands of a bureaucracy of enlightened utilitarians.[101] As one reviewer noted, the *Elements of Politics* had arrived at the conclusion that 'the ideal form of government must be something not very much unlike that of England or France or the United States, with a few of their most obvious defects and anomalies corrected', and although Sidgwick shared with Mill a belief in the 'relative and qualified desirability of democracy', it is clear that he had moved much closer to an accommodation with the existing British constitution than had Mill in the *Considerations*. Whereas Mill regarded second chambers, however constituted, as redundant, Sidgwick had justified the constitutional position of the House of Lords; he had abandoned universal suffrage (even with weighted voting) in favour of household suffrage; and he rejected the Hare scheme as unworkable.[102]

V. Conclusion

In view of the foregoing discussion it would seem that the unreflective identification of Individualism with the principles of mid-century radicalism would be misconceived. The rival claims to the Benthamite inheritance are far more complex than might prima facie appear to be the case since, as we have seen, Individualists and New Liberals alike claimed to be the true liberals. In addition, while it would be tempting to construe the rivalry to be between the literal followers of the Philosophic

[99] See also A. V. Dicey, 'Unionists and the House of Lords', *National Review*, 24 (1895), 698 f., a plea for a 'reformed and strengthened' House of Lords, which nevertheless retained a substantial hereditary element.

[100] G. Smith, 'The Organization of Democracy', 317.

[101] See Sidgwick, *Elements of Politics*, pt. 2, and W. C. Havard, *Henry Sidgwick and Later Utilitarian Political Philosophy* (Gainesville, Fla., 1959), ch. 7.

[102] It is worthy of note that female suffrage was one of the casualties of the Individualists' change of heart. Sidgwick continued to believe that women of independent means should be able to vote, but the interests of married women could be protected by their husbands; Goldwin Smith reneged on the support he had once given to Mill on the issue; while A. V. Dicey became a vehement opponent of the Suffragists.

Radicals and those who had adopted their spirit of reform, the tensions within the Benthamite heritage were exploited by both sides to the debate; the evident willingness of the Individualists to compromise their principles on the issue of the franchise hardly suggests that they took literalness to extremes. The severe ideological cleavage which developed in the liberal tradition during the closing decades of the century did not occur between a group of traditionalists and a group of innovators, but was between two tendencies both of which represented significant adaptations of the doctrine to which they laid claim. Although the New Liberal revisions of the liberal ideology were more self-conscious than those of the Individualists, the latter also profoundly transformed the mid-century liberal ideology. Thus the Individualists' repeated insistence that they alone represented the historically pure principles of liberalism must be open to question.

It is my contention that, in order to argue in defence of the late Victorian social order, the Individualists were forced to make substantial revisions of the arguments employed by the earlier generation of Radicals, and hence their political conservatism undermined their professions of doctrinal purity. While continuing to share the Philosophic Radicals' enthusiasm for the free market and minimal State, the Individualists had abandoned their faith in human reason being able to construct a more just or more humane social order. In addition, the Individualists went to great lengths to reinterpret the principle of utility and the conception of justice derived from the old radicalism to suit their conservative purpose. In both cases, I shall argue, Individualists introduced substantial modifications into the theoretical conceptions of the tradition to which they laid claim.

In order to establish this point, the remaining chapters of this work will examine a number of the arguments against State interference most commonly advanced by the Individualists. The next chapter will deal with their use of biological theories of evolution (their alleged Social Darwinism), while Chapter 3 examines their argument that an extensive sphere of State action would undermine the virtues of 'character'. Chapter 4 will be devoted to the Individualists' use of the 'social organism' analogy, an intellectual device usually thought to favour the kinds of policies to which they were opposed. The fifth chapter deals with the Individualists' claim that socialism was a retrogressive rather than a progressive development, which will be shown to rest on their perception that it was a reversion to the form of social organization which Spencer called militant.

The remaining two chapters witness a slight shift of emphasis, since they are concerned with ethical, rather than with sociological or bio-logical, arguments: the sixth chapter examines the nature of the Individualists' utilitarianism, while the seventh looks at their various attempts to justify the right to private property. These chapters will be presented as a debate between Spencerian and empirical Individualism, the latter represented by Henry Sidgwick. Because he was sceptical about attempts to find solutions to political and ethical problems in biology or sociology, Sidgwick hardly features in the first four chapters.[103] However, once the issue becomes that of providing a foundation for Individualism in terms of the principle of utility or the doctrine of natural rights, his philosophical thought assumes increased prominence.

It will be shown that each of these six arguments combined the duality of liberalism and conservatism which was characteristic of late Victorian Individualism. On the one hand, each argument endorsed the mid-century liberal view that the best type of society was that based on the limited State, the free market, and freedom of contract. On the other hand, consistent with the Individualists' belief that the social structure of late Victorian Britain conformed to this model, they also lent weighty support to the belief that further progress could not be achieved by the reform of institutions.[104]

---

[103] Sidgwick's scepticism about this intellectual tendency is best expressed by his paper 'The Relation of Ethics to Sociology', in id., *Miscellaneous Essays and Addresses* (London, 1904).

[104] It has been argued by Collini that Individualist argument can be subsumed under four categories, which he refers to as 'the political', 'the economic', 'the scientific', and 'the moral'. (S. Collini, *Liberalism and Sociology: L. T. Hobhouse and Political Argument in England 1880–1914* (Cambridge, 1978), 22 ff., which closely follows the article on 'Individualism' in W. P. D. Bliss (ed.), *Encyclopedia of Social Reform* (2nd edn., London, 1907, 717–24.) He argues that of the four, the political argument, essentially a protest against corruption, privilege, and State inefficiency, 'seemed to call less insistently for refutation' since it had enjoyed its heyday in the anti-aristocratic crusades of the Philosophic Radicals. This conclusion would seem correct, as does his down-grading of the importance of the economic argument on the grounds that, with the exception of Sidgwick, none of the Individualists were sophisticated political economists and the kinds of economic arguments which they invoked were usually a generation or more out of date. The moral argument, which consisted in affirming 'the independent and overriding value assigned to the fostering of "character" as a primary aim of politics' (*Liberalism and Sociology*, 28) is dealt with as part of Ch. 3. However, Collini's category of the scientific argument which 'consisted in presenting an account of Progress such that Individualism figured as both the mechanism of advance and a constitutive part of the goal' would appear to conflate a number of separate issues which are dealt with in Ch. 2, 4, and 5. This categorization also fails to capture a number of other arguments, especially those deriving their force from considerations of justice or utility.

My approach in each of the chapters will be primarily expository rather than critical. Given the absence of Individualism from the standard accounts of the political thought of this period, the most pressing task has appeared to be the identification of the chief arguments and positions of the Individualists. Furthermore, much recent political thought has proceeded on assumptions directly inimical to those made by the Individualists: hence they are either guilty of (by modern lights) the most egregious intellectual blunders, or their defence would require mounting a profound challenge to vast areas of contemporary social and political philosophy. To defend the Individualists on their own terms, for example, would require overthrowing the assumption that genetic questions—for instance concerning the origin of the moral sentiments—are irrelevant to philosophical questions concerning the rightness of a course of conduct. The fact/value distinction, which has effectively undermined attempts to find in scientific doctrines of evolution the true guide to human conduct, would also need to be abandoned. Nevertheless, although I have not engaged in direct criticism of Individualist theories, reference will be made to criticisms of Individualist ideas made in particular by the New Liberals, since these serve to locate Individualism in the context of late Victorian political argument.

The order of the chapters follows the development of ideas in Spencer's Synthetic Philosophy. In making Spencer the focus of this work, it may be argued that a refracted image of Individualism is presented since he represents the most extreme development of the doctrine. However, as was suggested in the Introduction, not only did his *magnum opus* provide many Individualists with a quarry for their arguments against 'socialism', but his standing as England's greatest philosopher demanded that the empirical Individualists define their own position in relation to his, as is indicated by the painstaking nature of Sidgwick's criticisms. In addition, it is also true that Spencer is a major political theorist and sociologist whose work has been neglected and frequently misinterpreted. It is hoped that in locating Spencer's thought in the context of Individualism, the host of lesser figures who drew on the Synthetic Philosophy may cast some light on their source and inspiration, just as a planet may be illuminated by the reflected light of its satellites.

2

PROGRESS AND THE STRUGGLE
FOR EXISTENCE

I. Introduction

Evolutionary theories appealed to the Individualists because they appeared to make possible the reconciliation of two conflicting theoretical commitments. On the one hand, as former Radicals, the Individualists were reluctant to renounce the old liberal belief in progress, and the dream of a human millenium founded on the emancipation of the individual.[1] On the other hand, however, the Individualists were also the defenders of the late Victorian status quo. They were able to square the political circle by insisting that the millenium would arrive, but that it would be brought about only over many generations, by the slow processes of natural evolution, and there was little or nothing political action could do to speed its arrival, although it could do much to hinder it. The present chapter will be concerned accordingly with the Individualists' use of evolutionary theory, and in particular with their appropriation of the Darwinian notion of the struggle for existence as the motive force behind evolutionary processes.

The few references to the Individualists which can be found in studies of late nineteenth-century political thought usually identify the opposition to the socialists and New Liberals with 'Social Darwinism', a theory which has so far eluded precise definition despite the considerable scholarly debate which it has spawned.[2] Probably the most common way of characterizing this theory is that it transposed the Darwinian 'struggle for survival' from the animal kingdom into the social sphere, and held that the evolution of society depended upon the operation of the law of natural selection of favourable heritable varients, a process

---

[1] See e.g. A. Trollope, *An Autobiography* (Oxford, 1980), 293–4.

[2] For references to Individualism in terms of Social Darwinism see I. Bradley, *The Optimists* (London, 1980), 225; A. Arblaster, *The Rise and Decline of Western Liberalism* (Oxford, 1984), 289 f.; and esp. the opaque reference to 'the plethora of defences of vulgar self-interest in the 1880s' in G. Jones, *Social Darwinism and English Thought: The Interaction between Biological and Social Theory* (Brighton, 1980), 57.

best secured by allowing unfettered *laissez-faire*.[3] However, as the present chapter will demonstrate, it is a mistake to regard Spencer's evolutionary theory as being a generalization of Darwinian biology or as simply an application of it to society, and although some Individualists (including Spencer himself) made occasional use of crudely Social Darwinist language, they were reluctant to carry this type of argument to its logical conclusion.

A number of the more sophisticated recent treatments of Spencer have already challenged the Social Darwinist interpretation of his thought, but the argument of the present chapter differs from them in maintaining that his evolutionary perspective was independent of any specific biological theory. While it has been variously claimed that Spencer simply transposed the process which Darwin saw at work in nature to associated human beings, or that he was a generalizer of a Lamarckian biological theory of use-inheritance, it will be argued that both interpretations are mistaken since they share in common the assumption that the inspiration for Spencer's theory was derived from biology. Rather than generalizing biological theories, Spencer regarded them as special cases of a more fundamental principle of evolution which owed more to classical mechanics than it did to biology. In fact, the Lamarckian and Darwinian theories of evolution had to be re-interpreted in order that both might be accommodated within the architecture of his Synthetic Philosophy.

In addition, although Spencer was not simply a generalizer of Darwinian evolution, it will also be demonstrated that he was at pains to show that it could be accorded a place within his system, and was prepared to make tactical use of the support of Darwinian theories when discussing politically charged issues like the Poor Law. This aspect of Spencer's thought was often taken over and exaggerated by some of his followers who consequently expounded a much more crudely Social Darwinist theory than their mentor. Nevertheless, there was no consensus among the Individualists as to the utility of Darwinian biology in support of their political stance, and many of the Individualists found that the use of

[3] This definition is based on R. Hofstadter, *Social Darwinism in American Thought* (New York, 1944), p. vii. Hofstadter's definition of Social Darwinism corresponds to what B. Semmel calls 'internal social darwinism' in contrast to 'external social darwinism' which involves competition between nations or empires (B. Semmel, *Imperialism and Social Reform* (London, 1960)). See also the discussion of the inadequacy of Hofstadter's definition in R. C. Bannister, *Social Darwinism: Science and Myth in Anglo-American Social Thought* (Philadelphia, 1979), 5. Another useful discussion of the definitional difficulties is R. J. Halliday, 'Social Darwinism: A Definition', *Victorian Studies*, 14 (1971), 389–405.

Darwinian language often created tensions with other aspects of their theory. In particular, the occasional use which Spencer made of the Social Darwinist idea of an unfettered struggle for survival in society sat uncomfortably with his oft-repeated insistence that the individual had a considerable personal responsibility to alleviate some of the harsher aspects of social life. Spencer repeatedly insisted that he did not wish to imply that might was right and that the strong had no obligations at all to the weak: competition between individuals in society was not entirely analogous to the struggle for existence in nature since it had to be restricted by the recognition of the rules of justice or even of charity.

The failure of the Individualists to follow Darwinian arguments to a logical conclusion may be regarded as an instance of their social and political conservatism of which we have already had cause to remark. However, some of the Spencer's critics contended, on the contrary, that Social Darwinism was incompatible with fundamental social institutions like property rights and the sanctity of marriage. The Individualists themselves hesitated to draw any conclusions which might offend the moral sensibilities of the average late Victorian, and they were also inclined to overlook the potentially radical implications of the theory with which they aimed to defend the established social order. For it could be argued the only way in which industrial competition would enable the fittest to emerge was to establish initial conditions in which all started equal, and none possessed advantages conferred by the privileges and inequalities inherent in the existing social system.

It should be emphasized that the 'Individualists' referred to throughout this chapter will be the Spencerian Individualists: biologically inspired arguments played little role in the empirical Individualists' defence of the late Victorian social order. Unlike the Spencerian Individualists, political thinkers like Sidgwick, Dicey, and Goldwin Smith were largely uninfluenced by the intellectual fashions of the closing decades of the nineteenth century. Because their outlook remained rooted in the 1860s, they tended to observe later developments, like the application of the theory of evolution to fields far beyond biology, with detachment and occasional scepticism. Consequently in this chapter, and those which it immediately precedes, the empirical Individualists will make only fleeting appearances as critics of the Spencerians' 'scientific' pretensions.

II. The Spencerian Theory of Evolution

Many commentators on Spencer's thought have emphasized its 'Darwinian' aspects and from this has followed his reputation as a callous defender of acquisitiveness and self-interest, a proponent of the doctrine that the weak must go to the wall. The secondary literature abounds with instances of this interpretation. It has been suggested, for example, that the reason why Spencer believed that State intervention would destroy social progress was that he

attributed to economic competition the same role which Darwinism had given natural selection. Economic competition weeded out the 'fit' from the 'unfit', the economic failure from the success. This implied that *laissez faire* was the best condition under which economic competition, and hence social evolution, could take place. It implied also that there was some form of natural acquisitiveness in man.[4]

It has also been suggested by another influential writer that Spencer 'employed the Darwinian theory to supplement the Malthusian argument of the classical economists, to prove that the individualist competitive society of Victorian England had been ordained by nature and was the sole guarantor of progress.'[5]

Although this interpretation appears to have gained currency in proportion to the extent to which Spencer's writings have been neglected, it is not particularly modern. In replying to Spencer's polemic *The Man versus the State*, the Belgian sociologist Émile de Laveleye charged that Spencer was 'anxious to see the law of the survival of the fittest and natural selection adopted in human society.'[6] The New Liberal David Ritchie also alleged that

In the name of Evolution and on behalf of the survival of the fittest Mr. Herbert Spencer cries out against the 'Sins of Legislators' in interfering with the beneficent operation of the pitiless discipline which kills off unsuccessful members of society, and against 'The Coming Slavery' of Socialistic attempts to diminish the misery of the world.[7]

Nor was this interpretation of Spencer's theory confined to his Liberal and socialist critics. The Conservative theorist W. H. Mallock accused Spencer of according excessive emphasis to the Darwinian theory of evolution and criticized him for concentrating exclusively on the dis-

---

[4] Jones, *Social Darwinism*, 56.   [5] Semmel, *Imperialism*, 29.
[6] É. de Laveleye, 'The State versus the Man: A Criticism of Mr Herbert Spencer', *Contemporary Review*, 47 (1885), 492.
[7] D. G. Ritchie, *Darwinism and Politics* (London, 1889), 11.

covery of laws of development for social aggregates. According to Mallock's caricature view of Spencerian evolution, it ascribed the motive force of progress to the fact that

in any community the means of subsistence are being constantly appropriated by the members who are a little stronger than the rest, whilst those who are weaker have an insufficient portion left them. . . . In other words, the Darwinian struggle for existence produces progress by raising the general average of efficiency.[8]

In contrast to this account another has been developed, most notably by J. D. Y. Peel, which has stressed that Spencer saw the mechanism of evolution in terms of Lamarckian use-inheritance rather than in terms of a Darwinian struggle for survival.[9] Although Spencer himself invented the phrase 'the survival of the fittest' it is claimed that he saw the mechanism of human evolution (at least in its civilized stages) as being not Darwinian but Lamarckian, and that this tended to reduce the role played by competition and struggle in his political thought. It is a profound mistake, Peel argues, to view Spencer as a simple translator of the struggle for survival into sociological language. The objectives and achievements of Spencer's theory of evolution were very different from Darwin's and consequently it is 'misguided to see Spencer as a generalizer of the Darwinian theory and so necessarily a corruptor of a proper theory of *social* evolution.'[10] Whereas 'Darwin's theory accounted for the secular transformation of each species by the mechanism of natural selection . . . Spencer's attempted to explain the total configuration of nature, physical, organic and social, as well as its necessary process.'[11] Lamarckian evolution is thus the connecting link between these different elements of the evolutionary process, since only use-inheritance can be used to explain the processes of both biological and cultural evolution.[12]

In this section it will be demonstrated that both parties to this dispute rest their case on the false assumption that Spencer was engaged in generalizing an essentially biological theory into a theory of cosmic evolution. It will be argued that the source of Spencerian evolution was

[8] W. H. Mallock, *Aristocracy and Evolution* (London, 1898), 91–2. While Spencer attempted to discover laws of the development of social aggregates, Mallock believed that progress was primarily due to a struggle for domination between 'exceptionally gifted and efficient' individuals.

[9] Cf. J. D. Y. Peel, *Herbert Spencer: The Evolution of a Sociologist* (London, 1971), 136 ff. Peel was not the first to make this point. Ernest Barker in his *Political Thought from 1848 to the Present Day* (London, 1915), 92, stated bluntly that Spencer 'never became a Darwinian'.

[10] Peel, *Herbert Spencer*, 141.   [11] Ibid. 142.   [12] Ibid. 143.

classical mechanics rather than biology, and that in consequence it owed far more to Grove's proof of the correlation of the physical forces than to Darwin's account of the origin of the species. Spencer's doctrine of evolution was neither Darwinian nor Lamarckian, although both Lamarckian and Darwinian factors can be seen to have been incorporated in the theory of evolution which he propounded. The view of Spencer as advocating competition on the model of a Darwinian struggle for survival may have gained currency in proportion to the neglect which his writings have endured, but the exclusive concentration on Lamarckianism as the mechanism by means of which mankind became more perfectly adapted to its environment has produced a view of Spencer which is as distorted as were the earlier 'Social Darwinist' caricatures. The survival of the fittest clearly did have a role to play, not merely in his biology, but also in his political theory.

Spencer's general theory of evolution is to be found in his volume on *First Principles*, the first of his works to have established his Victorian reputation as a philosopher of note, but which today is viewed simply as the source of his arcane metaphysics: most commentators have displayed a marked tendency to avoid having to deal with Spencer's most philosophically abstract work. For instance, one writer has declared that 'a complete analysis of Spencer's system would be an intolerable infliction upon the reader. We shall confine ourselves to the essentials of his political thought, and leave the Unknowable and other first principles in the vague background where they belong.'[13] Even Peel, the most sophisticated of recent writers on Spencer, has acknowledged that his treatment 'of much of [Spencer's] writing in philosophy in the narrow sense, psychology, ethics, and biology, is cursory and patchy.'[14] However, since the *First Principles* was written to propound the principles of which the remaining nine volumes of the Synthetic Philosphy are merely *illustrations*, it cannot be conveniently ignored as the 'vague background' to the rest of Spencer's thought, and some acquaintance with it must be a prerequisite to understanding the totality of his system. The *First Principles* provides us with the key with which to unlock the whole Synthetic Philosophy.[15]

[13] C. Brinton, *English Political Thought in the Nineteenth Century* (London, 1993), 228.
[14] Peel, *Herbert Spencer*, p. vii.
[15] Refs. to Spencer's *First Principles* are throughout to the 3rd edn. (London, 1875). I have preferred this edn. to later revisions of the work since Spencer subsequently excised much of the illustrative material on the grounds that it was repeated in the vols. of the completed Synthetic Philosophy. However, for the purposes at hand Spencer's illustrations of his principles by sociological material are particularly useful.

According to Spencer the task of philosophy was not to analyse but to systematize and synthesize all human knowledge. He resembled Hegel to the extent that he could not discover a contradiction without attempting to resolve it in a higher synthesis. As he remarked in the *Principles of Ethics*,

After . . . observing how means and ends in conduct stand to one another, and how there emerge certain conclusions respecting their relative claims, we may see a way to reconcile sundry conflicting ethical theories. These severally embody portions of the truth; and simply require combining in proper order to embody the whole truth.[16]

Not only was this true of the conflict between utilitarianism and intuitionism in ethics, but it was also true of that between the deductive and the inductive or historical methods in social science; between idealism and materialism in metaphysics; between associationism and intuitionism in psychology; and between Lamarckianism and Darwinism in biology.

In accordance with this synthetic conception of philosophy, it was defined as 'knowledge of the highest degree of generality', and just 'as each widest generalization of Science comprehends and consolidates the narrower generalizations of its own division; so the generalizations of philosophy comprehend and consolidate the widest generalizations of science.'[17] Spencer, it may be said, aimed at nothing less than a mechanical interpretation of the universe in which every event could be explained in terms of the relations of cause and effect between incident forces. The universe was nothing but a field of forces which acted and reacted upon each other, and life itself was merely a process of adjustment of these forces. The most accurate characterization of Spencerian evolution is in terms of

an assertion of the all-sufficiency of natural law, a denial of intervention from outside at any stage of the process by which the universe has become what it is. Moreover, natural law means here strictly physical law; everything is to be explained in terms of 'matter and motion.'[18]

The one exception to the all-sufficiency of natural law was the necessity of explaining the origin of the observed processes of nature. Spencer considered, and rejected, the various religious attempts to account for

[16] H. Spencer, *The Principles of Ethics*, i (London, 1892), 171.
[17] Id., *First Principles*, 133.
[18] R. Mackintosh, *From Comte to Benjamin Kidd: The Appeal to Biology or Evolution for Human Guidance* (London, 1899), 72.

the creation of the universe: the postulate of God as creator or as the 'first cause' was, he believed, literally inconceivable. On the other hand, atheism had to assume that the universe was 'self-existent', an hypothesis which seemed equally implausible. Hence he concluded that 'the existence of the world with all it contains and all that surrounds it, is a mystery ever pressing for interpretation' but which none of our hypotheses were capable of explaining.[19] This was the greatest of all mysteries, which he referred to as 'the Unknowable'.

The initial data of philosophy comprised three primary truths which Spencer called 'the Indestructibility of Matter', the 'Continuity of Motion', and the 'Persistence of Force'. From the first two of these primary truths it followed that the quantities of matter and motion in the universe were unchanging, while the latter stated 'there can only be changes of state of a constant amount of energy'.[20] Furthermore, Spencer argued, all our experiences of matter and motion could be resolved into experiences of force; given Grove's proof of the correlation of physical forces and Joule's discovery of the mechanical equivalent of heat, it was but a short step to the conclusion that all motions in the universe were mutually convertible.[21] Hence all the diverse phenomena of the universe could be resolved into instances of force, and from the Law of the Persistence of Force it followed that force itself was unchangeable in quantity.

These laws were evidently factors in a more general process, the concomitant redistribution of matter and motion, and it was the law governing this process which would represent the ultimate synthesis of human knowledge which Spencer sought. This synthesis, he believed, must be a statement of the truth that the concentration of matter entailed the dissipation of motion, and conversely that the absorption of motion entailed the diffusion of matter; the cycle of changes passed through by every existence, whether inorganic, organic, or 'super-organic' (i.e. social), entailed 'loss of motion and consequent integration, followed by gain of motion and consequent disintegration.'[22] The first such transformation was called evolution, the second dissolution. As Sir Peter Medawar observed, the *First Principles* was an attempt 'to show that the laws of evolution followed "inevitably" from laws of the indestructibility of matter and the conservation of energy.'[23]

[19] Spencer, *First Principles*, 44.   [20] Ibid. 192c.

[21] Ibid. 197; see also Mackintosh, *From Comte to Benjamin Kidd*, 71.

[22] Spencer, *First Principles*, 285.

[23] P. B. Medawar, 'Herbert Spencer and the Law of General Evolution' in id., *The Art of the Soluble* (London, 1967), 42.

In the simplest possible terms, Spencerian evolution was an affirmation of the growing complexity of the universe, whether inorganic,
organic, or superorganic. 'Evolution means growing complexity; more
complex is more evolved.'[24] The complexity develops according to both
a primary and a secondary redistribution. The primary redistribution is
in evidence in the instance of a concentrating aggregate which loses its
motion rapidly or integrates quickly. For example, a society displays this
aggregative process by the increasing mass of its population and their
concentration in special parts of its area (i.e. towns and cities), as well as
the indirect integrations, like the division of labour, by means of which
the parts are made more mutually dependent. The secondary redistribution, or 'compound evolution', referred to the tendency of the
parts of the aggregate to become more and more unlike each other; 'the
increase of a society in numbers and consolidation has for its concomitant an increased heterogeneity both of its political and industrial
organization.'[25] That is to say, its component elements exhibited a
transformation from homogeneity to heterogeneity. Along with this
increasing heterogeneity the elements of the aggregate also became
more sharply demarcated from each other; there was a movement from
indefinite to definite parts. Finally, with every increase in structural
complexity there was a parallel increase in functional complexity. The
redistribution of matter and retained motion was from a diffused,
uniform, and indeterminate arrangement, to a concentrated, multiform,
and determinate arrangement, and in a statement which Spencer
variously referred to as a 'law', 'formula', or 'definition', evolution was
defined as 'an integration of matter and concomitant dissipation of
motion; during which the matter passes from an indefinite, incoherent
homogeneity to a definite, coherent heterogeneity; and during which
the retained motion undergoes a parallel transformation.'[26] He was at
pains to stress that this process of evolution went on everywhere and
in the same manner, and that there were not different processes
operating in each separate science, but one, single, unitary process
which each science studied from a partial point of view. 'There are
not many metamorphoses similarly carried on; but there is one
single metamorphosis universally progressing, wherever the reverse
metamorphosis has not set in.'[27]

The next stage in Spencer's argument was to show that evolution was
a necessary concomitant of his basic principle of the persistence of

[24] Mackintosh, *From Comte to Benjamin Kidd*, 77.
[25] Spencer, *First Principles*, 544.   [26] Ibid. 396.   [27] Ibid. 546.

force, and the first law to which he appealed was the law of the Instability of the Homogeneous. The universe may be considered as a field of forces, but the forces acting at any two points in that field are not equal. It follows that two different parts of a homogeneous aggregate are subject to different incident forces, and therefore will develop correspondingly different structures. Moreover, any finite homogeneous aggregate must necessarily lose its homogeneity and develop towards greater and greater heterogeneity.

Secondly, the Law of the Multiplicity of Effects decreed that 'every differentiated part is not simply a seat of further differentiations, but also a parent of further differentiations.'[28] By this law, Spencer seems to have had in mind something not unlike a chain reaction in which a particular force is responsible for provoking a whole series of alterations in the field of force, each of which in turn provoke a further series of such perturbations. Since all these processes must have a limit, this 'chain reaction' cannot take place *ad infinitum*: the continual division and subdivision of forces will continue only as long as there remain forces unbalanced by opposing forces, and must ultimately end in rest. The whole process of the redistribution of forces in the universe will finally reach an equilibrium, a state of quiescence in which all force has been dissipated. On the way to this final equilibrium, the dispersion of the smaller and more resisted movements make possible transitional stages which Spencer called 'moving equilibria', among which may be counted all biological and social structures.

It should also be noted that it would be mistaken to assume that the universal tendency to growing complexity was a continuous and uninterrupted process. As one of Spencer's expositors noted:

It is a common error to suppose that evolution is continuous and uninterrupted—that its course may be symbolized by a straight line. A wavy line would, roughly speaking, be a more correct expression . . . [T]hroughout the whole universe motion is rhythmical or undulatory. This is true of all phenomena, from the minutest changes cognizable by science to the latest transformation of societies studied by the economist and the historian.[29]

This corollary of the three fundamental principles Spencer himself referred to as the 'Rhythm of Motion', and it implied that within the overarching cosmic trend towards higher and higher stages of evolution

---

[28] Ibid. 548.
[29] W. H. Hudson, *An Introduction to the Philosophy of Herbert Spencer* (London, 1897), 91.

there would be countless submovements in which both evolution and dissolution were combined. For example, in the animal kingdom, along with the tendency of a species as a whole to progress, individual creatures would be born and die (and therefore suffer dissolution). This law was to receive added significance as part of Spencer's explanation of the 'regression' to socialism in late Victorian Britain.[30]

Rather than the development of a biological theory, whether Darwinian or Lamarckian, into a general theory of evolution, Spencer's *The Principles of Biology* can be seen to represent an application of his general evolutionary principles to the specific case of biological organisms. These were subject to the same laws of evolution as any other aggregate, in so far as they were involved in a process of continual adjustment of their own forces to the forces impinging on them from their environment. For example, the skeleton of an animal passively resists forces like gravity or momentum which tend 'to derange the requisite relations between an organism and its environment' by counteracting them with an equal and opposite force, thus maintaining the 'moving equilibrium'.[31] The moving equilibrium of the organism was being repeatedly disturbed, because the forces operating on it did not always remain constant. In order to regain equilibrium the organism would need to adjust its own inner forces so as to balance the new outer forces; for Spencer, this adjustment was the very essence of the life process: 'Each change is of necessity towards a balance of forces; and of necessity can never cease until a balance of forces is reached.'[32] Moreover, each successive moving equilibrium which the organism attained was a further stage in the evolutionary process, since it produced an increased integration and differentiation of parts and a correspondingly more complex structure. Spencer concluded:

In subordination to the different amounts and kinds of forces to which its different parts are exposed, every individual organic aggregate . . . tends to pass from its original indistinct simplicity towards a more distinct complexity. Unless we deny the persistence of force, we must admit that the gravitation of an organism's structure from an indefinitely homogeneous to a definitely heterogeneous state, must be cumulative in successive generations, if forces causing it continue to act.[33]

Not only would it be mistaken to regard this interpretation of the evolutionary process as simply Darwinism generalized on a cosmic

---

[30] See below, Ch. 5.
[31] H. Spencer, *The Principles of Biology*, i (London, 1864), 154.
[32] Ibid. 432.   [33] Ibid. 430.

scale, but this account is also incompatible with the view that Spencer was a generalizer of Lamarck. On a Lamarckian view, the explanation of the process of evolution was the inherently progressive tendency of nature.[34] But it should be clear from the foregoing account that the inherently progressive tendency of nature played no part in Spencer's explanation of evolution. He explicitly repudiated this aspect of Lamarck's theory, since the

> ascription of organic evolution to some aptitude naturally possessed by organisms, or miraculously imposed on them, is unphilosophical. It is one of those explanations which explains nothing—a shaping of ignorance into the semblence of knowledge.[35]

Instead, Spencer wrote,

> while we are not called on to suppose that there exists in organisms any primordial impulse which makes them continually unfold into the more heterogeneous forms; we see that a liability to be unfolded arises from the actions and reactions of the organisms and their fluctuating environments.[36]

In other words, evolution was a matter of natural law, not of some metaphysical tendency inherent in the organism.

The process of adjustment of the organism to its environment could take one of two forms, which Spencer termed 'direct' and 'indirect' equilibration, and which corresponded respectively to Lamarckian and Darwinian accounts of the evolutionary mechanism. Although Spencer rejected the inherent tendency of organisms to progress as an explanation of evolution, he did attach considerable importance to other aspects of Lamarck's theory. A Lamarckian explanation, in the relevant sense, is one which accounts for the evolution of the species in terms of evolution within the life history of its specimens, which acquire more adaptive characteristics and transmit them to their offspring. An organ not fully suited to the creature's environment becomes more suited as a result of the creature's attempts to use it in that environment; for instance, fins develop into limbs and gills into lungs owing to the attempts of some species of fish to move about on land.[37] This was the aspect of Lamarck's account of evolution which Spencer incorporated into the

---

[34] R. M. Young, 'Malthus and the Evolutionists: The Common Context of Biological and Social Theory', *Past and Present*, 43 (1969), 135. This point is also emphasized by Peel, *Herbert Spencer*, esp. 148.

[35] Spencer, *Principles of Biology*, i. 404.   [36] Ibid. 430.

[37] For this statement of Lamarckian explanation I am indebted to G. A. Cohen, *Karl Marx's Theory of History: A Defence* (Oxford, 1978), 288.

Synthetic Philosophy since, as he remarked, 'direct equilibration is that process currently known as adaptation.'[38] This form of equilibration was to be found wherever a force acted continuously or frequently on the individual members of the species and to which they were therefore required to adjust themselves.

It should be pointed out that Lamarckian explanation in this sense is not teleological since it is 'not the intention of the organism to so alter its equipment: it is altered as a result of a use which is not intended to alter it, but which reflects the environment's demands.'[39] Had an element of teleology been introduced into the Synthetic Philosophy it would have represented a serious flaw since, as John Burrow has noted, 'to imagine Spencer as a teleological evolutionist one would have to rewrite the whole order of his ideas; for him the belief in natural causation was primary, the theory of evolution derivative.'[40]

Furthermore, there is no necessary connection between the Lamarckian mechanism of evolution and competitive pressure on the organism, expressing itself in terms of differential survival rates between well- and ill-adapted organisms. Spencer himself did make use of competitive pressures, but these were supplied by indirect rather than direct equilibration. By 'indirect equilibration' Spencer meant a Darwinian account of the evolutionary mechanism which had as its salient features chance variations (in the sense that they were not caused by requirements of the environment), and selection by competitive pressure. The chance (i.e. non-environmental) variations were caused, Spencer believed, by the action of many 'secondary and tertiary perturbations and deviations, some of which are the still-reverberating effects of disturbing forces previously experienced by the individual, and others which are the still-reverberating effects of disturbing forces experienced by ancestral individuals.'[41] These chance variations meant that the moving equilibria of different specimens of the same species would be differently affected by changes in the environment, and hence would not be absolutely identical. As a result

it cannot but happen that those individuals whose functions are most out of equilibrium with the modified aggregate of external forces, will be those to die; and that those will survive whose functions happen to be most nearly in equilibrium with the modified aggregate of external forces.[42]

[38] Spencer, *Principles of Biology*, i. 435.
[39] Cohen, *Karl Marx's Theory of History*, 288.
[40] J. W. Burrow, *Evolution and Society* (Cambridge, 1966), 205–6.
[41] Spencer, *Principles of Biology*, i. 443.   [42] Ibid. 444.

Whereas direct equilibration was brought into operation by the continuous or frequent action of a force on individual organisms, indirect equilibration resulted from a force which, while not acting frequently on individuals,

acts frequently on the species as whole—either destroying such of the members who are least capable of resisting it, or fostering such of the members who are capable of taking advantage of it. And by the abstraction, generation after generation, of those least in equilibrium with the new factor . . . the species as a whole is eventually brought into complete equilibrium with the new factor—there is indirect equilibration.[43]

In other words, indirect equilibration was simply the Darwinian principle of the survival of the fittest translated into the dialect of the Synthetic Philosophy.

Spencer's account of biological evolution attempted to demonstrate the ultimate compatibility of the factors of adaptation and competitive selection. He argued that indirect equilibration was the form most in evidence at the lower stages of evolution, but that 'along with the gradual evolution of organisms having some activity, there grows up a kind of equilibrium that is relatively direct.'[44] In the *Principles of Biology* he argued that the growing complexity of organisms and their increased mutual dependence meant that indirect equilibration through natural selection became less and less capable of producing specific adaptations and remained fully capable only of maintaining the fitness of constitution to conditions. As a consequence

the production of adaptations by direct equilibration, takes the first place—indirect equilibration serving to facilitate it. Until, at length, among civilized human races, the equilibration becomes mainly direct: the action of natural selection being restricted to the destruction of those who are constitutionally too feeble to live, even with external aid.[45]

As will be shown, Spencer's later political writings did not always conform to this principle.

The theory of evolution propounded by Spencer was not a generalization of a biological theory, but an independent account of the process which resulted in the growing complexity of the cosmos. The theories of biological evolution put forward by both Lamarck and Darwin did not inspire this overarching vision but were incorporated as parts of it, since the purpose of the Synthetic Philosophy was to demonstrate the mutu-

[43] Ibid. 463.   [44] Ibid. 468.   [45] Ibid. 469.

ally reinforcing nature of these apparently incompatible theories. These *biological* theories were simply special cases of the cosmic process Spencer set out to describe, and hence his doctrine of evolution was neither Lamarckian nor Darwinian.

III. The Political Uses of Darwinism

Having established the general principles of Spencerian evolution, there remains to be examined the political uses to which the doctrines of direct and indirect equilibration, of Lamarckianism and Darwinism, were put. Spencer used Lamarckianism to explain the evolution of the moral consciousness: in his view the desired qualities of self-reliance, independence, thrift, a respect of the rights of others, and so on, were to be acquired by the human race by means of direct equilibration, i.e. use-inheritance. A discussion of the political use which he made of Lamarckianism will be deferred until the following chapter, which deals with his account of the formation of 'character', and the remainder of the present chapter will concentrate exclusively on the use which Spencer and his followers made of Darwinian or indirect equilibration.

As J. M. Keynes long ago pointed out, there was a natural affinity between Darwinism and the economics of *laissez-faire*: 'The principle of the survival of the fittest could be regarded as a vast generalisation of the Ricardian economics.'[46] The terminology of Darwinian evolution was too good a weapon for the Individualists to ignore, and it was employed by a number of Spencer's followers in a much cruder form than is to be found in the writings of their mentor. Nevertheless, the Individualists were not unanimous on the applicability of the Darwinian theory to the defence of the late Victorian social order, and even those political theorists who were inclined to employ it recognized that a strict interpretation of Social Darwinism challenged many of the institutions they were most concerned to defend. These thinkers were inclined to opt for social and institutional conservatism rather than to challenge the distribution of property and power in Victorian society for the sake of consistently applying the Darwinian theory.

In defence of his interpretation of Spencer as the generalizer of Lamarckian evolution, J. D. Y. Peel has suggested that Spencer did not

[46] J. M. Keynes, 'The End of Laissez-Faire', in id., *Essays in Persuasion* (Cambridge, 1972), 276.

believe that 'the weakest *must* be made to go to the wall in order for the improvement of the race to occur by natural selection.'[47] Certainly, as will be shown in the next chapter, it is true that an important reason for Spencer's opposition to 'socialistic' legislation was that it would interfere with the process of individual adaptation on which further moral (and therefore social) evolution would have to depend. However, Peel's additional claim that the Darwinist mechanism has no place in Spencer's argument is misleading. It is difficult to square Peel's interpretation with Spencer's blunt remark that

having, by unwise institutions [i.e. the Poor Law], brought into existence large numbers who are unadapted to the requirements of social life, and are consequently sources of misery to themselves and others, we cannot repress and gradually diminish this body of relatively worthless people without inflicting much pain.[48]

As this chapter has already demonstrated, Spencer did not attack Darwinism in the name of Lamarckianism, but was concerned to establish that both factors operated at the level of biological evolution; it would be surprising, therefore, if he abandoned Darwinism in his discussions of politics. Whatever Spencer may have written in the early editions of the *Principles of Biology* about the substitution of direct for indirect equilibration in the social state, in his subsequent political works he did not exclusively stress the Lamarckian mechanism of evolution. As Peel has observed, 'there was a streak in Spencer which was "Darwinian" in the crude sense', although this is something which Peel himself consistently underestimates since he is concerned to establish that Spencer was, above all, a Lamarckian.[49] Nevertheless, as a contemporary commentator remarked, while Spencer was 'hardly to be regarded as a Darwinian in his thinking', he was 'too good a tactician' to refuse help 'from the doctrine, when he finds help offered incidentally, in the biological or historical region.'[50]

One of the most crudely Social Darwinist passages in Spencer's *œuvre* occurs in the *The Man versus The State*. Having quoted a passage from the *Social Statics* in which he had praised the 'beneficent, though severe

---

[47] Peel, *Herbert Spencer*, 148.

[48] H. Spencer, *Principles of Ethics*, ii (London, 1893), 288.

[49] Peel, *Herbert Spencer*, 149.

[50] Mackintosh, *From Comte to Benjamin Kidd*, 76. Bannister argues that between the publication of the 2nd vol. of *The Principles of Biology* in 1867 and the appearance of *The Study of Sociology* in 1873, Spencer had become more pessimistic and the Darwinian mechanism began to receive greater stress at the level of human evolution. (Bannister, *Social Darwinism*, 47.)

discipline' which expressed itself in 'the poverty of the incapable, the distresses that come upon the imprudent, the starvation of the idle, and those shoulderings aside of the weak by the strong, which leave so many in "shallows and miseries"', Spencer continued:

The process of 'natural selection', as Mr. Darwin called it . . . he has shown to be a chief cause (though, not I believe, the sole cause) of that evolution through which all living things . . . have reached their present degrees of organization and adaptation to their modes of life. So familiar has this truth become that some apology seems needed for naming it. And yet, strange to say, now that this truth is recognised by most cultivated people—now that the beneficent working of the survival of the fittest has been so impressed on them that, much more than people in past times, they might be expected to hesitate before neutralizing its action—now more than ever before in the history of the world, are they doing all they can to further the survival of the unfittest![51]

In other words, State interference, 'socialistic' legislation like the Poor Laws, and maudlin private benevolence to the 'undeserving' poor, eliminate present misery at the cost of greater misery hereafter:

Men who are so sympathetic that they cannot let the struggle for existence bring on the unworthy the suffering consequent on their incapacity or misconduct are so unsympathetic that they can, deliberately, make the struggle for existence harder for the worthy, and inflict on them and on their children artificial evils in addition to the natural evils they have to bear.[52]

Yet, Spencer maintained, legislators frequently have been ignorant of this truth, as they have of many other findings of social science. It was this ignorance which was responsible for more human suffering than all the legislation derived from selfish or class interests combined.

Many other examples of Spencer's use of crudely Darwinian terminology in his political writings may be discovered. For example, in a section of *The Study of Sociology* which significantly was entitled 'Preparation in Biology', Spencer wrote that:

Besides an habitual neglect of the fact that the quality of a society is physically lowered by the artificial preservation of its feeblest members, there is an habitual neglect of the fact that the quality of a society is lowered, morally and intellectually, by the artificial preservation of those who are least able to take care of themselves . . .

Fostering the good-for-nothing at the expense of the good, is an extreme cruelty. It is a deliberate storing up of miseries for further generations. There is no greater curse to posterity than that of bequeathing them an increasing

---

[51] H. Spencer, *The Man versus the State*, ed. D. G. Macrae (1884; Harmondsworth, 1969), 141.   [52] Ibid. 144.

population of imbeciles and idlers and criminals. To aid the bad in multiplying is, in effect, the same as maliciously providing for our descendants a multitude of enemies. It may be doubted whether the maudlin philanthropy which, looking only at direct mitigations, persistently ignores indirect mischiefs, does not inflict a greater total of misery than the extremest selfishness inflicts.[53]

Almost twenty years later Spencer was to return to the same theme, using almost exactly the same language. In the *Principles of Ethics*, published in 1893, he considered the positive obligations of the individual towards the relief of the poor. While stressing that such obligations were real, he also insisted that 'the impolicy, indeed the cruelty, of bequeathing to posterity an increasing population of criminals and incapables' issued in the requirement that 'true beneficence will be so restrained as to avoid fostering the inferior at the expense of the superior' and he also noted that

If left to operate in all its sternness, the principle of the survival of the fittest, which, ethically considered, we have seen to imply that each individual shall be left to experience the effects of his own nature and consequent conduct, would quickly clear away the degraded.[54]

Given the occurrence of such crudely Darwinian language in Spencer's own writings, it is not surprising to find that these ideas were accorded a significant role in the publications of a number of his professed followers. For instance, Spencer's identification of the social 'struggle for existence' with the 'industrial battle' of economic competition was echoed by a number of other Individualists.[55] As H. S. Constable remarked in his pamphlet *The Fallacies and Follies of Socialist Radicalism Exposed*,

---

[53] Id., *Study of Sociology* (1873; 15th edn., London, 1889), 343–5. The passage is also quoted by Peel, *Herbert Spencer*, 149 in recognition of the 'crudely Darwinian' streak in Spencer's thought.

[54] Spencer, *Principles of Ethics*, ii. 408. For the principle of the survival of the fittest 'ethically considered' see Ch. 7, below, where it is referred to as 'the Law of Conduct and Consequence'.

[55] It is also worthy of note that, despite his emphasis on the 'Great Man' as a motive force of progress, W. H. Mallock also believed that a secondary factor in evolution was the competition for subsistence between labourers. Thus if the Darwinian evolutionary mechanism did have a social counterpart, this was to be found 'in the contemporary competition of labourers to find remunerative employment, and in the fact that those who are least successful in finding it would, if left to themselves, be continually dying off.' Since Mallock assumed that in a progressive society there would always be more labourers available for work than tasks for them to perform, it followed that a struggle 'was involved in obtaining work of any kind; and for the higher kinds of work the struggle is very keen.' (Mallock, *Aristocracy*, 147.)

If the laws of nature demand, as they undoubtedly do, in the struggle of life on the earth, extinction of the indolent and the vicious, a country must suffer if Socialists succeed in counteracting these laws.[56]

Similarly, M. D. O'Brien, having invoked a well-worn Individualist comparison between socialism and the system established in Peru by the Jesuits, argued that the latter was 'unquestionably the greatest attempt ever made to dodge the natural law expressed in that well-known Darwinian phrase "the weakest must go to the wall".'[57] By implication, socialism, in attempting to subvert this natural law, would suffer the same fate as its predecessor.

Writing in his second book, *The Natural Right to Freedom*, O'Brien more explicitly identified economic competition with a Darwinian struggle for survival:

Industrial struggle is at once both the condition and the opportunity of the really efficient man, and the more there is of it the more will efficiency flourish and inefficiency come to grief; as, indeed, what can be more just than that the latter should 'get the worst of it'? since, in this great battle of life, somebody must lose; somebody must go to the wall in this universal and irrevocable struggle for existence.[58]

It followed from this identification of industrial competition with the biological struggle for survival that wealth in general was simply 'the wealth of the fittest survivors of the commercial struggle for existence.' This identification was also echoed by Sir Henry Maine, a writer who shared much ideological ground in common with the Individualists, and who quoted Spencer with approval. In his polemic *Popular Government*, Maine drew an admiring picture of the United States on the grounds that there 'has hardly ever before been a community in which the weak have been pushed so pitilessly to the wall, in which those who have succeeded have so uniformly been the strong, and in which in so short a time there has arisen so great an inequality of private fortune and domestic luxury.'[59] In Maine's view, the prosperity of mankind depended on motives called into activity by the strenuous and never-ending struggle for existence, the beneficent private war which makes one man strive to climb on the shoulders of another and remain there through the law of the survival of the fittest.[60]

[56] H. S. Constable, *The Fallacies and Follies of Socialist Radicalism Exposed* (London, 1895), 7.   [57] M. D. O'Brien, *Socialism Tested by the Facts* (London, 1892), 91.
[58] Id., *The Natural Right to Freedom* (London, 1893), 323–4.
[59] Sir H. S. Maine, *Popular Government: Four Essays* (London, 1885), 51.
[60] Ibid. 50.

The Spencerian who perhaps carried the Darwinian argument to its most extreme development was Thomas Mackay, for whom the English poor were 'an incipient species'.[61] According to Mackay, those members of society who 'have not inherited, or cannot acquire, or who acquiring cannot keep enough to maintain themselves', were analogous to the 'unfittest' of Darwinian biological theory.[62] In the 'natural course of things' there was a 'tendency' for these 'lower types' to 'disappear', and even in primitive human societies the poor died 'like flies in winter'.[63] With the advance of civilization, and mankind's growing success in its struggle with nature, the wealthy members of society were moved by religious doctrines to help those who could least help themselves. This had the result that the existence of the 'lower types' had been 'unnaturally prolonged':

It is not too much to say that man has made all other species his ministers; but the conflict still rages between the members of his own species; and . . . philanthropy obliges him to provide for the unfittest that fall in battle. This operation we may call the domestication of the unfittest by the fit.[64]

Mackay's attitude to this process of domestication was ambivalent, to say the least, and he went to great lengths to praise the 'cruel, but in the end beneficent rules, under which the battle of life is fought in the world of nature.' In an argument which clearly owed much to Malthusian fears about population growth, Mackay insisted that if unskilled workers multiplied out of proportion to the availability of remunerative employment 'congestion of population and enforced idleness are occasioned.'[65] He attacked the 'narcotics of poor law and charitable relief' and claimed that

the tendency downwards towards uneconomic conditions of existence must be carefully restrained. If poor law guardians and enthusiastic philanthropists insist on making eligible provision for all who cannot support themselves in economic independence, it is difficult to see how the rottenness of the foundation on which society then rests can be repaired.[66]

In the writings of Mackay, therefore, the Individualists' Social Darwinist imagery of a struggle for existence in society was combined

[61] T. D. Mackay, *The English Poor* (London, 1889), 21.

[62] Ibid. 4.   [63] Ibid. 5.   [64] Ibid. 6.

[65] Ibid. 178. The Malthusian fears which underpinned Mackay's vision of the 'lower types' expanding to a point at which they destroyed the 'healthy stock' also found echoes in the work of Sir Henry Maine. See his articles 'Mr. Godkin on Popular Government', *Nineteenth Century*, 19 (1886), 366–79, and 'Malthusianism and Modern Politics', *St. James's Gazette*, 1 (1880), 524–5.   [66] Mackay, *English Poor*, 184–5.

with the older Malthusian fear of the consequences of excessive population growth; only by encouraging self-help and a sense of personal responsibility could the 'laws' of population be held in check.

IV. Social Darwinism and its Difficulties

Despite the evident relish with which Individualists like Mackay, O'Brien, and Constable were prepared to contemplate an industrial struggle for existence in which they presumably regarded themselves as victors, Social Darwinist arguments were not without their difficulties from the standpoint of Individualism. In the first place, a number of New Liberal critics pointed out that to ensure the survival of the fittest in society many, if not all, of the fundamental elements of civilization would have to be abolished. As David Ritchie argued:

> To get the real benefits of natural selection, we should . . . abolish all such institutions as inheritance of property, marriage for life, probably all law and order—everything that separates us from the animals. Simply to abolish all factory Acts and land Acts and sanitary Acts . . . would leave us still very far away from the region of unimpeded natural selection.[67]

Spencer himself appeared aware of the strength of this criticism, and in a reply to the critique of *The Man versus the State* by de Laveleye he endeavoured to answer it. In the first place, he maintained that the survival of the fittest in its social applications did not mean the survival of the physically strongest or most cunning, but rather 'the survival of the industrially superior and those who are fittest for the requirements of social life.'[68] Although Spencer did not deny that the struggle for existence took place in the higher forms of social organization, he emphasized that it was to be distinguished from its 'brutal form' in which physical aggression triumphed.

In the light of the passages quoted above, it is clear that this part of Spencer's reply was disengenuous to say the least: if the kind of struggle for existence he invoked differed so fundamentally from that described by Darwin, there would appear to be no warrant for claiming the biologist's authority for an attack upon the Poor Law. An uncharitable interpretation would be that Spencer was prepared to cite Darwin in his

[67] D. G. Ritchie, *Studies in Political and Social Ethics* (London, 1902), 27.
[68] H. Spencer, 'M. de Laveleye's Error' repr. from *Contemporary Review* (Apr. 1885) in id., *Various Fragments* (enlarged edn., London, 1900), 107.

support whenever there was some tactical advantage to being associated with a scientist of such stature, but was prepared to withdraw whenever the implications of this association threatened to bring down the rest of his system.

More satisfactory was the second part of Spencer's defence. In this context, the part of his reply to de Laveleye which has the greatest significance was his contention that 'the struggle for existence as carried on in society, and the greater multiplication of those best fitted for the struggle, must be subject to rigorous limitations.'[69] In other words, rather than claiming that the survival of the fittest should go on unhindered, Spencer argued in very un-Darwinian terms that the process of evolution demanded that the human mind had to be 'disciplined into that form which itself puts a check upon that part of the cosmic process which consists of the unqualified struggle for existence.'[70] Spencer insisted that he was not reworking the jaded doctrine that might makes right, but was arguing on the contrary that the principles of right imposed a check on the competitive process. His early work on moral philosophy, the *Social Statics*, could be regarded 'as an elaborate statement of the conditions under which, and limits within which, the natural process of elimination of the unfit should be allowed to operate.'[71] Even in O'Brien's case the Darwinian struggle was not directly transposed into the social sphere since, like Spencer, he insisted that industrial competition must be regulated by ethical considerations, in particular 'exemption from aggression and from fraud, the equivalent of aggression.'[72] The function of ethics was to impose a check on the untrammelled struggle for existence which otherwise would operate with the same ferocity in the human world as it did in the animal kingdom.

Therefore, contrary to Ritchie's argument, the struggle for existence in society did not require the abolition of all the achievements of civilization, but could only take place within the framework created by justice, in Spencer's sense of the Law of Equal Freedom. Given Spencer's insistence that he did not want 'to establish a reign of injustice under its most brutal form', the struggle for existence in society was subject to the mutual limitation of spheres of action, which in turn implied respect for the rights of life, liberty, and property. It was the function of the State to ensure that these rights were respected and that the competitive struggle was conducted according to the dictates of

[69] Ibid.

[70] D. Duncan, *The Life and Letters of Herbert Spencer* (London, 1908), 336.

[71] Spencer, 'M. de Laveleye's Error', 106.　　　[72] O'Brien, *Natural Right*, 337–8.

justice. In other words, Ritchie was mistaken to think that the survival of the fittest in society would mean the disappropriation of the weak by the strong, as it did in the animal kingdom.

Nevertheless, ethical considerations created an additional problem for the Individualists, since their Social Darwinist arguments appeared to run counter to one of the most cherished elements of the Victorian moral sensibility. They seemed to amount to an attack, not merely on State assistance to the poor, but also on charity and private philanthropy. It was possible to interpret the Individualists as maintaining that nothing should be done to interfere with the processes of natural selection as they operated in society, and this seemed to deny that charity really was a virtue. Spencer himself argued that this was a misrepresentation of his views: while the 'stern' reign of justice would 'quickly clear away the degraded', he recognized that this outcome would hardly correspond to our most deeply felt moral sentiments. Justice had to be tempered by benevolence, especially by private charity to the poor, without which 'a social life may be carried on, though not the highest social life.'[73] Spencer's ethical theory not only permitted, but positively demanded, a degree of individual benevolence: he regarded the development of the altruistic moral sentiments as being an essential factor in the moral evolution of humanity, and believed that, like all faculties, they would grow stronger with exercise. Despite his comments quoted earlier, Mackay adopted a similar approach, arguing that 'it was inevitable and right that humanity should mitigate the rigour of this struggle for existence.'[74] One of the chief forms of the mitigation of the struggle for existence was the Poor Law, although Mackay argued for its 'strict application' in order to ensure that the 'incipient species' did not multiply to an extent where it would threaten the 'healthy existence' of the parent stock. Like Spencer, he also praised private benevolence, particularly of the kind exercised by the Charity Organisation Society, of which Mackay himself was a member and a leading apologist.

This attempt to defuse some of the more unpalatable aspects of the Darwinian theory when it was applied to society generated a powerful tension within the Individualists' theory which they could never successfully resolve. In the first place, the struggle for existence served to retard the development of altruistic sentiments like generosity, pity, and mercy since, as Spencer wrote, not only did it involve 'the necessity that personal ends must be pursued with little regard to the evils entailed on

---

[73] Spencer, 'M. de Laveleye's Error', 109.
[74] Mackay, *English Poor*, 18–19.

unsuccessful competitors; but it also involves the necessity that there shall not be too keen a sympathy with that diffused suffering inevitably accompanying this industrial battle.'[75] Secondly, the development of the altruistic sentiments could also run counter to indirect equilibration by promoting ill-directed voluntary benevolence to help the undeserving poor, rather than allowing them to be subject to the processes of natural selection. The same kind of sentimentality and misplaced sympathy which resulted in the increasingly interventionist tendencies of the Liberal party was also responsible for the abuse of private charity and of institutions like the Poor Law. Charity had to recognize certain limits, Spencer argued, since 'a reign of generosity without justice—a system under which those who work are not paid, so that those who have been idle and drunken may be saved from misery—is fatal; and any approach to it is injurious.' In the *Principles of Ethics*, he was at pains to emphasize that voluntary charitable effort should only be directed to the deserving poor, those who were destitute through no fault of their own. Mackay additionally argued that Christian 'charity' might sometimes require that one acted in a conventionally uncharitable way. For example, it was not to display charity to a starving man to give him food if this would dissuade him from making efforts on his own behalf.[76] Ethics could produce, it seemed, only the most limited mitigation of the sufferings of mankind.

The altruistic sentiments which Spencer invoked to mitigate the harsher aspects of the struggle for existence and on which, as we shall see, he pinned his faith in the improvement of humanity, implied that mutuality and co-operative endeavour were part of the highest form of social life. Spencer's ideal, it is often forgotten, was not a society of self-interested individuals, but one in which people voluntarily formed organizations for mutual assistance, for only thus could the 'higher' faculties, like benevolence and sympathy, be fostered. In making this argument, the Individualists revealed the extent to which they had remained wedded to the voluntary principle of the older radicalism, and to the emphasis on mutuality and co-operative endeavour which that entailed. According to the latter, society would be

organized largely through voluntary associations . . . These associations would be of various sorts: the religious, social and educational life of the various denominations, the self-sustaining friendly societies and charities, the trade

[75] H. Spencer, *The Principles of Psychology*, ii (1855; London, 1872), 611.
[76] See T. D. Mackay's discussion of the nature of 'charity' in id., *The State and Charity* (London, 1898), ch. 1.

unions and professional organizations, and the vast plethora of other Victorian associational bodies, self-regulating, but with the discrete legal support of the state.[77]

The problem was that this model of society did not sit comfortably with the idea of a struggle for existence in which the 'weak go to the wall'; the Darwinian model of society was one based entirely on self-interest and the desire for self-preservation, whereas the voluntary principle was based on the assumption that individuals were sufficiently capable of setting aside the persuit of their selfish ends to make social co-operation possible. Moreover, the voluntary principle seemed to imply that the activities of associations like the Charity Organisation Society were legitimate, while the Darwinian streak to Individualism condemned these same activities as a dangerous interference with the natural processes of evolution. This conflict was at its most acute in the writings of Mackay, where the crudely Darwinian streak which we have already explored was balanced by advocacy of mutual associations, which extended even to a particular form of co-operative bank.[78]

A third difficulty in the use of biologically inspired arguments by the Individualists related less to their attempts to make such arguments consistent with conventional moral notions, than with the need to defuse the potentially radical political implications which could be drawn from them. The Individualists tended to assume, not merely a simple identification between success in economic competition and the biological fitness to survive, but also that success in economic competition as defined by the conditions prevailing in late Victorian Britain, could be identified with success in the Darwinian struggle for survival. It will be recalled, for instance, that Mackay defined the socially unfit in terms of those members of society who 'have not inherited, or cannot acquire, or who acquiring cannot keep enough to maintain themselves'; but it is by no means obvious that the inheritance of a substantial fortune should be regarded as evidence of an individual's superiority in the struggle for existence.

The assumption that the late Victorian social system permitted the fit to rise and the unfit to perish was explicitly challenged by one of Spencer's own followers, Wordsworth Donisthorpe:

[77] H. C. G. Matthew, introd. to *The Gladstone Diaries*, vols. x and xi (Oxford, 1990), p. xxxv.
[78] T. D. Mackay, 'People's Banks', *National Review*, 22 (1894), 636–47. In this article Mackay championed agricultural co-operative banks on the model of those established in Germany, Austria, and the Netherlands by F. W. Reiffisen.

Doubtless the unfit will be eliminated, and the fit will survive. But is it quite certain that under existing arrangements it is the absolutely unfit who will go to the wall? At any rate, it is an open question. That they are the unfit under the present system of industrial organisation is proved by the fact that they are short of the means of subsistence . . . But . . . is it not possible that under a better system of industrial organisation many of those whom the callous political economist stigmatises as the unfit might turn out to be the cream of the race?[79]

Donisthorpe's musings were untypical of the Individualists. They were also largely inspired by the desire to make propaganda on behalf of his own scheme for profit-sharing which he called 'Labour Capitalisation', and were in no sense intended as a challenge to the existing social order. Nevertheless, the point was one with potentially far-reaching implications, since it suggested that, at least on one interpretation, Social Darwinism would require the fundamental transformation of existing competitive conditions.

This challenge was taken up by Alfred Russel Wallace, Darwin's 'co-discoverer' of natural selection, and a strong advocate of the nationalization of the land. Wallace remarked that 'it is strange that Mr. Spencer did not perceive that if this law of the connection between individual actions and their results is to be allowed free play, some social arrangement must be made by which all may start in life with an approach to equality of opportunities.'[80] Even if justice did require that the fittest should experience the benefits of their superiority and the weaker the burdens of their inferiority, it was only possible to identify the superior and inferior as a result of 'absolute fair play between man and man in the struggle for existence.'[81] But, given the actual conditions of late Victorian society, in which many individuals were 'brought up from childhood in low and degrading surroundings . . . and have to struggle amid fierce competition for the bare necessities of life' it was manifestly absurd to maintain 'that they receive the legitimate results of their own nature and actions only.'[82] Therefore, Wallace argued, Spencer's principle required that every person should be provided with 'the best education they are capable of receiving; that their faculties shall be well trained, and their whole nature obtain the fullest moral, intellectual, and physical development.' Furthermore, 'equality of opportunity requires that all shall have an endowment to support them during the transition

[79] W. Donisthorpe, *Law in a Free State* (London, 1895), 38–9.

[80] A. R. Wallace, 'Herbert Spencer on the Land Question: A Criticism", in id. *Studies Scientific and Social* (London, 1900), ii. 342.

[81] See Id., 'True Individualism—The Essential Preliminary of a Real Social Advance', in id., *Studies*, ii. 516.   [82] Id., 'Spencer on the Land Question', 342.

period between education and profitable employment.'[83] Only thus could the struggle for existence take place on anything approaching equal terms.

Spencer would doubtless have argued that the degree of State intervention proposed by Wallace would prove inconsistent with the principle it was supposed to help realize. Nevertheless, the fact remains that it was possible for the Individualists' invocation of the struggle for existence to bear a much more radical interpretation than they were prepared to countenance. Not only does this point provide evidence of the Individualists' social and political conservatism, but it also illustrates a related point which will recur throughout the following chapters: their theoretical principles often threatened to carry them far beyond their desired resting-place, and they were frequently engaged in a struggle to defuse the potentially radical implications of their own ideas.

V. Conclusion

When applied to social development, Spencer's theory of evolution attempted to make possible the reconciliation of two apparently irreconcilable political commitments. In the first place, the Individualists in general identified themselves with the tradition of mid-century liberalism, one of the most characteristic features of which was the 'passion for improvement':

Zeal for improving mankind was a characteristic feature of the Victorian Liberal Mind. It manifested itself in an obsession with the efficiency and reform of institutions, in a desire to clear away anomalies and obstacles to social progress and advancement, and in the passionate involvement of so many liberals in crusades to right some wrong and make the world a better place.[84]

The Individualists laid claim to the tradition of which this reforming zeal was part, and Spencer insisted that his 'opposition to socialism results from the fact that it would stop the progress to . . . a higher state and bring back a lower state.'[85] Yet despite their protestations that they had not abandoned their belief in progress, the Individualists' own writings were often marked by quietism and by a complacent acceptance of the status quo. Rather than expressing the 'passion for improvement' of the older radicalism, they exhibited a preference for established institutions

---

[83] Id., 'True Individualism', 516.   [84] Bradley, *Optimists*, 200.
[85] Spencer, 'From Freedom to Bondage', in T. D. Mackay (ed.), *A Plea For Liberty* (London, 1891), 24.

over those which were untried, and argued that the existence of an institution created a presumption in favour of its utility.

The theory of evolution enabled the Individualists to contend that the defence of existing institutions was itself a means to the end of progress. The Individualists had not abandoned the belief in progress characteristic of earlier liberals, but contrary to the views of the latter, they believed that it was to be achieved by a 'natural' process rather than by means of conscious human intervention. In general, the institutions of late Victorian Britain provided the framework of rights and liberties within which this natural process could take place; hence the primary objective of the liberal legislator was to ensure their preservation, and secondarily to endeavour to eliminate or emasculate those remaining institutions (like the Poor Law) which interfered with the natural processes. The problem of poverty was best dealt with by allowing these natural processes free play, subject to the conditions imposed by the equal liberties conception of justice. Therefore, as Mackay argued,

[t]he object of statesmanship should be, not to plunge forward into the unlimited slough of social legislation but, cautiously, and with due regard to existing circumstances, to withdraw these uneconomic conditions of life, and to allow them to be replaced by the healthy vigorous expanding framework of individual right and liberty.[86]

This argument for Individualism gave support to the combination of liberalism and conservatism which was characteristic of Individualist political thought. On the one hand, the idea that progress was best promoted by the competition of individuals implied that the function of the State was the minimal one of ensuring that the competition took place within the framework of just rules, primarily the protection of rights to life, liberty, and property. On the other hand, the reliance on evolutionary theories was conservative in so far as it suggested that present miseries were not the result of unjust political or social institutions, but were the social consequences of fundamental natural laws, and 'there is no purpose to be achieved by the reform of institutions.'[87]

The conservative aspect of the Spencerian theory of evolution was well recognized by its New Liberal critics. Although Hobhouse's assumption that these evolutionary arguments had their source in Darwinian biology can now be seen to have been mistaken, he gave an admirably clear exposition of the practical consequence of the evolutionary argument:

[86] Mackay, *English Poor*, 194–5.
[87] L. T. Hobhouse, *Democracy and Reaction* (2nd edn., London, 1909), 90.

No doubt there remained even in human society many features which are at first sight objectionable. But here again the evolutionist was in the happy position of being able to verify the existence of a soul of goodness in things evil. Was there acute industrial competition? It was the process by which the fittest came to the top. Were the losers in the struggle left to welter in dire poverty? They would the sooner die out. Were housing conditions a disgrace to civilization? They were the natural environment of an unfit class, and the means whereby such a class prepared the way for its own extinction. Was infant mortality excessive? It weeded out the sickly and the weaklings.[88]

Nevertheless, Spencer's belief that the struggle for existence was in need of ethical limitation, while creating a unresolved tension within his own thought, offered the New Liberals a means of overcoming the conservatism of this evolutionary theory. They argued that in a civilized society reason, as embodied in the State, could suspend the necessity of struggle. As L. T. Hobhouse again remarked, Spencer's theory 'meant that the human mind must be regarded as an organ like the lungs or liver evolved in the struggle for existence with the function of adjusting the behaviour of the organism to its environment', and was to be thought of 'as a sort of glorified reflex action'.[89] In contrast, Hobhouse argued, mind, rather than being a mere reflex action which assisted human beings in the struggle for existence, enabled them to exercise control over the blind forces of evolution. This in turn implied that mankind could take control over the underlying conditions of life:

Now it seemed to me that it is precisely on this line that modern civilisation has made its chief advance, that through science it is beginning to control the physical conditions of life, and that on the side of ethics and religion it is forming those ideas of the unity of the race, and of the subordination of law, morals, and social constitutions generally to the needs of human development which are the conditions of the control that is required.[90]

In other words, a point was reached in the evolutionary process which produced an organism no longer subject to the evolutionary struggle for existence. Instead of being forced to adapt itself to its environment, this organism was able to gain control over its environment with the aim of moulding it in accordance with ethical norms. Whereas the Individualists assumed that the environment was a constant to which the individual must adapt, the New Liberals challenged this view by arguing that the environment could be shaped by conscious human design.

---

[88] Id., *Social Evolution and Political Theory* (New York, 1911), 20–1.
[89] Id. *Development and Purpose* (London, 1913), p. xv.   [90] Ibid., pp. xxii–xxiii.

3

THE FORMATION OF CHARACTER

I. Introduction

In the previous chapter it was shown that Spencer's theory of evolution incorporated both Darwinian and Lamarckian elements. Having examined the role which the Darwinian notion of the struggle for existence played in Individualist political thought, the focus of the present chapter will be on the political implications of the Lamarckian theory of use-inheritance, and in particular its role in developing an account of character formation which underpinned the Individualists' fears that a substantial sphere of State activity would be antithetical to the virtues of self-reliance, independence, and respect for the rights of others. It will be argued that Spencer used Lamarckianism to support his view that the virtues of character were not to be promoted by the conscious design of the legislator, but only by the individual being prepared to develop inherited 'natural' faculties of the mind. As part of his attempt to confer scientific credibility on this theory of the formation of individual character, Spencer also transformed the classical associationist psychology in a direction which provides additional confirmation for our central contention that Individualism represented a conservative adaptation of the liberal tradition.

Among the reasons cited by the Individualists as a justification for resisting any substantial sphere of State interference, one of the most frequently employed was the need to foster the normative virtues of character. As Spencer remarked in the *Principles of Ethics*,

the end which the statesman should keep in view as higher than all other ends, is the formation of character. And if there is entertained a right conception of the character which should be formed, and of the means by which it may be formed, the exclusion of multiplied state-agencies is necessarily implied.[1]

---

[1] H. Spencer, *The Principles of Ethics*, ii (London, 1893), 251.

This passage merely reinforced his earlier statement in *The Study of Sociology*, that 'of all the ends to be kept in view by the legislator, all are unimportant compared with the end of character-making; and yet character-making is an end wholly unrecognised.'[2]

The Victorian concept of character contained both a descriptive and a normative element.[3] The descriptive content referred to an individual's settled dispositions, as for example in Alexander Bain's *On the Study of Character* which dealt with the ancient problem of constructing a typology of individual personalities. In the normative sense, 'character' referred not simply to strongly developed dispositions, but to habits of action of certain desirable kinds; in other words, 'character' meant 'moral qualities highly developed or strikingly displayed.'[4] This evaluative sense of character was constituted by a basic core of qualities which included self-restraint, perseverance, strenuous effort, courage, self-reliance, thrift, and a sense of personal responsibility and duty. It was a conception which enjoyed such an extraordinary status and centrality in Victorian thought that it transcended all the conventional political categories. Indeed, as Collini has remarked, by the end of the nineteenth century there was a 'swelling chorus of politicians of all parties who professed to stand in the same relation to any scheme which might be said to weaken character as the preacher did to sin.'[5] It would be mistaken to suppose that fundamentally different interpretations were attached to the term by the contending parties; as Freeden has pointed out, 'nowhere in liberal thought was there a reversal of faith in the individual virtues of self-reliance, personal exertion and the like.'[6]

The Individualist argument that an extensive sphere of State action was a threat to these virtues was one which their opponents treated with great respect. As the New Liberal Walter Lyon Blease noted in his *A Short History of English Liberalism*,

The philosophical argument against Social Reform which has most weight . . . is the argument . . . that by helping individuals the State deprives them, in whole or in part, of the disposition to help themselves, and that they tend to rely more and more upon the social organization and less upon their own strength.

[2] Id., *The Study of Sociology* (1873; 15th edn., London, 1889), 372.

[3] S. Collini, 'The Idea of "Character" in Victorian Political Thought', *Transactions of the Royal Historical Societies*, 35 (1985), 31–50.

[4] *OED*, definition 2, quoted in id., *Liberalism and Sociology: L. T. Hobhouse and Political Argument in England 1880–1914* (Cambridge, 1978), 16.

[5] Id., '"Character"', 46.

[6] M. S. Freeden, *The New Liberalism: An Ideology of Social Reform* (Oxford, 1978), 174. This point is echoed by Collini, *Liberalism and Sociology*, 31.

Everything in the way of public assistance is thus regarded with suspicion. To feed school children is to weaken parental responsibility. To raise wages by legislation is as demoralizing as to distribute doles. To offer a pension of five shillings a week in old age is to discourage thrift in youth.[7]

However, at the same time that the Individualists could oppose State interference on the grounds that it undermined character, the New Liberals could insist that an important reason for advocating State interference in such spheres as housing, education, and health-care was the promotion of these same virtues.[8] The crucial premiss of their argument was the individual's 'dependence on his environment in the widest sense of the term—human and non-human. Moral improvement became thus a question of reforming the framework in which the individual functioned.'[9]

It has been argued that the opponents of the New Liberal emphasis on the role of the social environment in the formation of character embraced the view that the positive virtues of character could be achieved only as a consequence of exercising 'individual and autonomous will power'.[10] Character was 'not geared to the claims of the environment' but was 'based on an independent entity', i.e. the actions of an autonomous moral agent.[11] This philosophical theory had its roots in the Idealist tradition, and the most obvious example of the doctrine is the ideology of the Charity Organisation Society, of which Bernard Bosanquet was the chief theorist. Bosanquet's argument for treating character as the creation of the will of an autonomous moral agent 'was a qualified and developed form of the Kantian argument that morality is a self-imposed maxim.'[12] From the Kantian requirement that truly moral actions must be self-imposed it was but a short step to the inference 'which Kant and T. H. Green made only with hesitation, but Bosanquet boldly, . . . that self-maintenance by the individual in nearly all aspects of his life was the key to morality and the real will.'[13] Rather than character being the creation of an individual's social conditions and circumstances, Bosanquet argued, the circumstances of an individual's life were the product of his character.[14]

---

[7] W. L. Blease, *A Short History of English Liberalism* (London, 1913), 337.

[8] On the New Liberal adoption of the objective of the promotion of character as an end of legislation, see Freeden, *New Liberalism*, 170 ff., and Collini, *Liberalism and Sociology*, 31.   [9] Freeden, *New Liberalism*, 170–1.

[10] Ibid. 170.   [11] Ibid. 172.

[12] A. W. Vincent and R. Plant, *Philosophy, Politics and Citizenship: The Life and Thought of the British Idealists* (Oxford, 1984), 108.

[13] Ibid. 107–8.   [14] Ibid. 109.

Yet the Idealist theory of character formation drew on philosophical assumptions which were deeply antithetical to the empiricist epistemology and sensationalist psychology which the Individualists had inherited from the Philosophic Radicals. A key assumption of the radicalism of the second quarter of the nineteenth century, which the Individualists shared in common with the New Liberals, was a belief in the formation of character by environmental influences. Given this philosophical inheritance the Individualists were clearly precluded from making use of the Idealist dichotomy of 'character' and 'environment'. One of the objectives of this chapter is to explain how it was possible for them to insist on the determination of character by the environment while at the same time being able to regard social reform as at best irrelevant, and at worst antithetical, to the development of character.

The explanation of this apparent paradox is to be found in Herbert Spencer's *The Principles of Psychology*, which purported to be a work in the mould of the associationist psychology, one of the pillars of Benthamite utilitarianism. But although Mill commended the work for its 'searching analyses of complex mental phenomena' and 'mastery over the obscurer applications of the associative principle', he also suggested that Spencer's principle of evolution was 'quite inconsistent with the philosophy of the work it is prefixed to.'[15] Mill might have been less perplexed had he realized the extent to which Spencer was prepared to use Lamarckianism to depart from classical associationism. Before Spencer's innovations can be appreciated, however, it is first necessary to examine the classical theory of associationism and its place in the politics of the Philosophic Radicals.

II. Associationism and Radicalism

Associationism in its primary signification referred to a 'principle of explanation put forward by an important school of thinkers to account generally for the facts of mental life.'[16] This was the doctrine that the human mind was composed of atomic sensations, which were held together by certain combinatory laws. It had its origin in Locke's 'new

---

[15] Quoted in *The Letters of J. S. Mill*, ed. H. S. R. Elliot (London, 1910), i. 197, ii. 7.
[16] G. Croom Robertson, 'Associationism', in *Encyclopaedia Britannica* (9th edn., London, 1875), ii. 730. A much more extensive discussion of associationism is to be found in H. C. Warren, *A History of the Association Psychology* (London, 1921).

way of ideas' and especially in the Humean observation that the mind consisted of impressions and ideas, the former being the data of sense, the latter being simply less vivid copies of the former. David Hartley soon transformed Hume's philosophical theory into an empirical psychology which held that

any sensations A, B, C and co., by being associated with one another a sufficient number of times, get such a power over the corresponding ideas a, b, c, and co., that any one of the sensations A, when impressed alone, shall be able to excite in the mind b, c, and co., the ideas of the rest.[17]

For example, the sensations of the taste, colour, shape, and smell of an apple having been repeatedly associated in my experience, and having produced the corresponding ideas in my mind, it follows that whenever I experience the scent of an apple, the ideas of its taste, colour, shape, etc. are immediately recalled. From this example it is clear why the classical associationist doctrine made the principle of the combination of ideas one of contiguity, 'or the repetition of impressions synchronous or immediately successive.'[18]

Although Hartley is usually credited with being the founder of the association psychology, it was effectively refounded by James Mill's *Analysis of the Phenomena of the Human Mind* which, as Flugel has written, represented 'the climax of associationism in its most rigourous and mechanical form', and which explained 'mind' as simply 'a mosaic of sensations built up by a series of purely mechanical processes.'[19] The case of the elder Mill also illustrates the connection which traditionally existed between the association psychology and Philosophic Radicalism of which it had been one of the pillars; as Passmore has observed, 'from Priestly to J. S. Mill the associationists were all of them radicals, both in politics and religion.'[20]

Writing in his *Autobiography*, J. S. Mill brought out the connection between his father's politics and his psychological views in a very clear way:

In psychology, his fundamental doctrine was the formation of all human character by circumstances, through the universal Principle of Association, and the consequent unlimited possibility of improving the moral and intellectual condition of mankind by education. Of all his doctrines, none was more important than this, or needs to be insisted on: unfortunately there is none which

---

[17] Croom Robertson, 'Associationism', 732.   [18] Ibid.

[19] J. C. Flugel, *One Hundred Years of Psychology* (London, 1933), 32.

[20] J. Passmore, *The Perfectibility of Man* (London, 1970), 190. See also E. Halevy, *The Growth of Philosophic Radicalism* (London, 1972), 7 ff.

is more contradictory to the prevailing tendencies of speculation, both in his time and since.[21]

It is possible to argue that the associationist psychology was as much a Utopian as a radical doctrine. Its political implications derived from the fact that the theory 'declared that a teacher could inculcate whatever moral values he chose, by associating them with the pleasures and pains of the childish psyche.' The only difference between James Mill and a Utopian like Robert Owen was that 'Owen tended to stress the natural sympathy which children possessed, where James Mill was inclined to emphasize the way in which discipline worked upon the child's selfish feelings.'[22] In either form, the classical doctrine of associationism placed immense power in the hands of the educator and legislator to transform individual character for good or ill.

John Stuart Mill remained true to his father's faith in the capacity of the principles of associationism to explain the phenomena of the human mind, as well in the correlative belief in the power of education to transform individual character. According to Leslie Stephen, Mill treated the principle of association as 'omnipotent': 'As it can make the so-called necessary truths, it can transform the very essence of character.'[23] The 'science of human character', which Mill termed 'Ethology', was parasitic on the laws of association, and would, if constructed, be a 'deductive science', consisting of corollaries from psychology, the 'experimental science':

If . . . we employ the name Psychology for the science of the elementary laws of mind, Ethology will serve for the ulterior science which determines the kind of character produced in conformity to those general laws, by any set of circumstances, physical or moral. According to this definition, Ethology is the science which corresponds to the art of education; in the widest sense of the term including the formulation of national or collective character as well as individual.[24]

The utility of the science of ethology from the point of view of Mill's ultimate project of elevating the character of the race was obvious. 'It would be a statement of the way in which society was actually to be built up out of the clusters of associated ideas, held together by the unit Man.'[25]

---

[21] J. S. Mill, *Autobiography*, in id., *Collected Works* ed. J. M. Robson *et al.*, i (Toronto, 1963), 109–11. [22] A. Ryan, *J. S. Mill* (London, 1974), 18.

[23] L. Stephen, *The English Utilitarians* (London, 1900), iii. 150.

[24] J. S. Mill, *A System of Logic* (London, 1919), 869.

[25] Stephen, *English Utilitarians*, iii. 151.

Furthermore, Mill insisted on the radical implications of associationism in one additional respect. He regarded it as posing a fundamental
challenge to one of the bulwarks of conservatism, namely, the view that
there were innate differences between human characters, not only
between individuals, but also between the sexes. This view, Mill argued,
was 'one of the chief hindrances to the rational treatment of great
social questions and one of the greatest stumbling blocks to human
improvement.'[26]

III. Spencer's Lamarckian Associationism

As we have seen, the classical theory of associationism enabled both
James and John Stuart Mill to draw radical political conclusions from a
psychological doctrine which stressed the possibility of 'improving the
moral and intellectual condition of mankind' by education and legislation. It will now be argued that Spencer introduced a biological and
evolutionary element into associationism which had the effect of trans-
ferring the influence of the environment from the individual to the race
as a whole. This effectively removed the possibility of radical reform by
means of moral and intellectual education and also resulted in a defence
of the allegedly innate differences between individuals and sexes which
Mill had regarded as constituting an obstacle to human improvement. In
short, Spencer transformed the association psychology into a form
which lent support, not to political radicalism, but to the conservative
adaptation of mid-century liberalism which, we have argued, was
characteristic of Individualism.

Spencer insisted that rational legislation had to be founded on 'a
true theory of conduct, which is derivable only from a true theory of
mind'.[27] But this was a requirement which legislators were inclined to
overlook, and in so far as they based legislation on a theory of human
nature, it was derived from unsystematic 'empirical notions' rather than
from 'generalizations expressing the ultimate laws of Mind.'[28] He
regarded an adequate psychological theory as an essential part of his
social and political thought, and in the *Social Statics* he had drawn
heavily on phrenology in contending that the mind consisted of a

---

[26] Mill, *Autobiography*, 111.
[27] Spencer, *Study of Sociology*, 358.   [28] Ibid. 356.

number of pre-given faculties.[29] After the completion of this work, however, he became a convert to associationism under the influence of Mill's *Logic*, and commentators have declared unanimously that *The Principles of Psychology* is a work in this tradition.[30]

Spencer took as the basic unit of consciousness a 'nervous shock' like that felt when we experience a sudden noise or flash of lightning. This is the 'primordial element of consciousness' out of which the 'countless kinds of consciousness may be produced by the compounding of this element with itself and the recompounding of its compounds with one another in higher and higher degrees: so producing increased multiplicity, variety, and complexity.'[31] Spencer's primary concern was not with these 'ultimate' constituents of mind, but was with its 'proximate' components which he divided into two main groups—'feelings' and the 'relations between feelings'. Spencer employed the term 'feeling' much as it had been used by James Mill, to denote

any portion of consciousness which occupies a place sufficiently large to give it a perceivable identity; which has its individuality marked off from adjacent portions of consciousness by qualitative contrasts and which, when introspectively contemplated, appears to be homogeneous.[32]

Spencer assumed that such a feeling would be compounded from a number of nervous shocks: the analogy being with a series of taps which, exceeding a rate of more than sixteen per second, would appear to form a single musical note. A particular feeling, for example the experience of coloured patch, would be formed from a rapid succession of such nervous shocks. The 'relations between feelings' (or 'cognitions' as they were more commonly called) were characterized by contrast as 'occupying no appreciable part of consciousness. Take away the terms it unites, and it disappears along with them; having no independent place, no individuality of its own.'[33] Relations between feelings can be analysed into the detection of differences between two successive feelings: they last no appreciable amount of time and consist purely in the recognition of the amount of (un)likeness between a feeling and that which immediately succeeds it in the mind.

[29] The transformation of Spencer's psychological doctrines and the relationship between the *Social Statics* and phrenology is admirably dealt with by R. M. Young, *Mind, Brain, and Adaptation in the Nineteenth Century* (Oxford, 1970), 151 ff.

[30] For this point see Warren, *Association Psychology*, 119 ff.; Flugel, *A Hundred Years of Psychology*, 115 ff.; J. M. Baldwin, *History of Psychology* (London, 1913), ii. 82 ff.; H. Elliot, *Herbert Spencer* (London, 1917), 277.

[31] H. Spencer, *The Principles of Psychology*, i. (1855; 2nd edn., London, 1870), 120.

[32] Ibid. 164.   [33] Ibid.

Feelings may in turn be divided into 'emotions' and 'sensations', the difference between them consisting of the larger or smaller proportions of the relational elements present. Emotions are vaguely demarcated from each other and have indefinite relations, whereas sensations by contrast are characterized by an abundance of sharp and definite relations. In addition, whereas sensations readily enter into associations, emotions do not, and whereas sensations can be easily recalled, emotions cannot.

Having identified the proximate components of mind, Spencer attempted to explain the manner in which the variety and complexity of consciousness could be created out of these elements. The 'method of composition remains the same throughout the entire fabric of Mind', Spencer wrote, for the same process which creates a feeling out of a succession of nervous shocks can also account for the formation of the higher emotions like the love of liberty, property, or justice. The differences between feelings result from the different rates of occurrence of nervous shocks, and each sensation is generated by the 'perpetual assimilation of a new pulse of feeling to pulses of feeling immediately preceding it: the sensation is constituted by the linking of each vital pulse as it occurs, with the series of past pulses that were severally vivid but have severally become feint.'[34] The process of the composition of mind is 'no other than this same process carried out on higher and higher platforms, with increasing extent and complication.' In other words,

Mind is constituted only when each sensation is assimilated to the faint forms of antecedent like sensations. The consolidation of successive units of feeling to form a sensation, is paralleled in a larger way by the consolidation of successive sensations to form what we call a knowledge of the sensation as such or such—to form the smallest separable portion of what we call thought, as distinguished from mere confused sentiency. So too it is with the relations among those feelings that occur together and limit one another in space or time.[35]

It should be noted that Spencer had abandoned the classical associationist principle of association by contiguity in favour of a principle which links sensations according to their degrees of likeness or unlikeness. As Croom Robertson wrote, Spencer maintained

that the fundamental law of all mental association is that presentations aggregate or cohere with their like in past experience, and that, besides this law, there is in strictness no other, all further phenomena of association being incidental. Thus,

[34] Ibid. 184.   [35] Ibid. 185.

in particular, he would explain association by Contiguity as due to the circumstances of imperfect assimilation of the present to the past in consciousness.[36]

Spencer also argued that the development of mind, in the form of the compounding and recompounding of primitive sensations into higher states of consciousness, obeyed the laws of general evolution in the sense that it exhibited the same features of integration, differentiation, and increased definiteness as did the rest of creation. In the first place, mind displayed an increasing integration; in the initial phases of its evolution a sensation is created from 'an integrated series of nervous shocks or units of feeling' while in the more advanced stages 'by an integration of successive like sensations, there arises the knowledge of a sensation as such or such.'[37] Accompanying this process of integration is a process of differentiation or increased heterogeneity. Sensations which are composed of units all of one kind are rendered heterogeneous by the combination and recombination of these units in a multitude of ways. Finally, feelings also take on an increasingly definite character. As mind develops, so feelings become increasingly clearly demarcated from each other, culminating in the visual sensations, by far the most important part of our intellectual operations, which are more definitely circumscribed than any others. Thus mind manifests the same traits followed by evolution in both biology and sociology.

The evolutionary process of the compounding and recompounding of sensations was paralleled by a process of the growing complexity, definiteness, and heterogeneity of the central nervous system. The claim that each mental event has a physiological counterpart was to be found in Hartley's version of associationism, but had dropped from view in the purely mentalistic account contained in James Mill's *Analysis*. Spencer returned to the earlier conception of associationism, and insisted that for each occurrence of a sensation there was a corresponding disturbance of the nervous system, and that these were to be regarded as the mental and physical instantiations of the same event. This was not a materialist theory of mind, a charge Spencer repeatedly denied, but was a species of what modern philosophers would describe as 'psychophysical parallelism', the theory that for every mental phenomenon there must be a neural counterpart.[38] Spencer argued that what was subjectively a mental event was objectively a molecular motion,

---

[36] Croom Robertson, 'Associationism', 733.

[37] Spencer, *Principles of Psychology*, i. 187.

[38] For a critical account of psychophysical parallelism see N. Malcolm, *Wittgenstein: Nothing is Hidden* (Oxford, 1986), 193 ff.

and that in both human and inferior beings feelings were the accompaniments of changes in the nervous system. For every feeling there was a corresponding nervous discharge. This parallelism of feeling with nervous action was confirmed by a number of considerations: that the circumstances which hinder or facilitate nervous actions are also circumstances which similarly facilitate or hinder feelings; that both feeling and nervous action last an appreciable time; that, *ceteris paribus*, the intensity of a feeling is proportionate to the intensity of a nervous action; and so on. Although it was impossible to obtain 'immediate proof' that 'feeling and nervous action are the inner and outer faces of the same change, yet the hypothesis that they are so harmonizes with all the observed facts' and, Spencer concluded, no other verification was either necessary or possible.[39]

It followed that the 'primordial element of consciousness', a nervous shock, corresponded to an objective event, a wave of molecular motion. Just as what we call feelings are compounded from a rapid succession of nervous shocks, so the 'nerve current' is

intermittent—consists of waves which follow one another from the place where the disturbance arises to the place where its effect is felt. The external stimulus in no case acts continuously on the sentient centre, but sends to it a series of pulses of molecular motion. Hence, in concluding that the subjective effect, or feeling, is composed of rapidly recurring mental shocks, we simply conclude that it corresponds to the objective cause—the rapidly recurring shocks of molecular change.[40]

Furthermore, if mental composition is compared with nervous structure, feelings can be seen to correspond to the molecular changes of which nerve-corpuscles are the seats, and relations between feelings to the molecular changes transmitted through the fibres which connect the nerve-corpuscles. 'Speaking generally,' Spencer wrote, 'feelings and the relations between feelings, correspond to nerve-corpuscles and the fibres which connect nerve-corpuscles; or rather, to the molecular changes of which nerve-corpuscles are the seats, and the molecular changes transmitted through fibres.'[41]

The development of mind on its subjective side, as we have seen, is determined by the laws of evolution. Therefore, just as it is (subjectively) an increasing integration of feelings on successively higher stages, along with which there occurs increasing heterogeneity and definiteness, these traits correspond to (objective) developments in the evolution of

---

[39] Spencer, *Principles of Psychology*, i. 128.   [40] Ibid. 152.   [41] Ibid. 190.

the nervous system in which 'along with growing distinctness and multiformity of structure, there is throughout an advancing integration of structure as well as of mass.'[42] Spencer offered an account of the evolution of the nervous structure which explained this process of increased integration, heterogeneity, and definiteness in terms of the adaptation of the organism to its environment. Initially, organisms are undifferentiated specks of protoplasm which have direct experience of environmental stimuli, but given the Law of the Instability of the Homogeneous, these stimuli will not act equally or continuously on all parts of the organism, and a stage will be reached when a stimulus will habitually be experienced by particular parts of the organism. From these points of contact waves of molecular change will spread throughout the entire organism. Furthermore, given the law that forces follow the path of least resistance, and as a result of differences in the composition of the various parts of the organism, the molecular waves will pass more readily through some parts rather than others. Over the course of evolution, the repeated passage of waves of molecular motion along the same path will facilitate further such passages, just as water running over sand does not spread evenly over the whole but cuts out a number of channels leaving the intermediate areas dry. Over time, strands of specially adapted protoplasm will extend throughout the organism which will constitute channels of easy communication between its various parts.

The connection between the evolution of the objective structures of the nervous system and the subjective association of ideas was brought out very clearly by one of Spencer's expositors, John Fiske. He pointed out that

The continual redistribution of nervous energy among the cells is the objective side of the process of which the subjective side is the recompounding of impressions . . . [F]or every revived association of ideas, there is a nervous discharge between two or more cells, along formerly used sets of transit fibres; and for every fresh grouping of impressions, for every new connection of ideas, there is a discharge along new transit lines.[43]

The formation of a new association involves 'the establishment of a new transit line or set of transit lines, while the revival of an old association involves merely the recurrence of motion along old transit lines.'[44] The

---

[42] Ibid. 192.
[43] J. Fiske, *An Outline of the Cosmic Philosophy, based on the Doctrine of Evolution* (London, 1874), ii. 139.   [44] Ibid. 141.

association of ideas is accompanied by the formation of a fibrous transit line between two nerve-cells and the more often this path is traversed the stronger will be the association.

It followed from Spencer's identification of subjective associations of ideas with transit lines in the physical nervous structure that, if the latter could be transmitted from generation to generation by the mechanism of Lamarckian evolution, then the corresponding associations of ideas could also be inherited. As we saw in the previous chapter, the mechanism of the evolutionary process referred to by Spencer's term 'direct equilibration' was one in which progress occurred because of the efforts of individual organisms to become better adapted to their environment. Where the environment is simple, the organism is simple, but progress to higher stages of life implies the ability of the organism to respond to special and complex changes in the environment. The frequent experience of an environmental stimulus by an organism will establish new associations of ideas, and consequently will give rise to new fibrous transit lines within its central nervous system, and this new part of the structure of the nervous system will be transmitted to its progeny according to the mechanism of Lamarckian use-inheritance. As generation succeeds unto generation the association of ideas, and its counterpart in the nervous system, will become more strongly established. An organisms's response to the environmental stimulus, which initially required the exercise of will and deliberation, in time may become instinctive and eventually automatic. Through the transmission of inherited variations, particular associations of ideas will become organic in the race.

This point may be illustrated by an example, used by Spencer himself, drawn from the animal kingdom. He remarked that it was well known that 'on newly-discovered lands not inhabited by man, birds are so devoid of fear as to allow themselves to be knocked over with sticks; but that in the course of generations, they acquire such a dread of man as to fly on his approach; and that this dread is manifested by young as well as by old.'[45] The only way in which this phenomenon could be explained, he thought, was if we suppose that 'in each bird that escapes the injuries inflicted by man . . . there is established an association of ideas between the human aspect and the pains, direct and indirect, suffered from human agency.'[46] At first the bird is motivated to take flight by a state of consciousness which is 'nothing more than an ideal reproduction of

[45] H. Spencer, 'Bain on the Emotions and the Will', in id., *Essays: Scientific, Political and Speculative*, i (London, 1868), 315.   [46] Ibid.

those painful impressions which before followed man's approach'; that is, the bird's flight is an exercise of will.[47] Over the course of many generations, the tendency to flight becomes instinctive, in the young as well as in the old. Spencer concluded:

> it is an unavoidable inference that the nervous system of the race has been organically modified by these experiences: we have no choice but to conclude that when a young bird is thus led to fly, it is because the impression produced on its senses by the approaching man entails, through an incipiently-reflex action, a partial excitement of those nerves which in its ancestors had been excited under like conditions[48]

This law holds equally in the case of human beings, and it implies that 'the nature which we inherit from an uncivilized past, and which is still very imperfectly fitted to the partially-civilized present, will, if allowed to do so, slowly adjust itself to the requirements of a fully-civilized future.'[49] Indeed, Spencer believed that the future development of mankind would take the form of its greater adaptation to the requirements of the social state as the appropriate associations of ideas were strengthened over time, and were transmitted to each successive generation.

The upshot of Spencer's identification of the subjective principles of association with the formation of the objective structure of the nervous system, and the corresponding use which he made of Lamarckianism, was fundamentally to alter the nature of associationism. Whereas James Mill's version of the doctrine had supported the view that individual character was infinitely malleable since the educator could, given sufficient skill, establish whatever associations were desired, Spencer held that associations were simply the subjective counterparts of objective structures and could change only to the extent that the objective structures were themselves changed. The trains of ideas of classical associationism were now deemed to run on physiological tracks worn by the associations of many previous generations, and hence they were substantially predetermined for any given individual. Such biological tracks, i.e. the strands of nervous fibre, changed only slowly, over the course of many generations, while particular configurations of nervous structure were transmitted from parent to children according to the Lamarckian inheritance of acquired characteristics.

---

[47] Ibid. 316. Spencer defined a voluntary act as 'nothing beyond a mental representation of the act, followed by a performance of it.' (*Principles of Psychology* (1st edn., 1855), 613.)   [48] Id., 'Bain', 316.   [49] Id., *Principles of Ethics*, ii. 258.

Spencer argued, therefore, that the individual human mind was not a *tabula rasa*, but that the individual was the inheritor of a whole series of characteristics and capacities which had been acquired as the result of ancestral experience. R. M. Young has pointed out in one of the few recent studies of Spencerian psychology, 'evolutionary associationism was incompatible with a simple *tabula rasa* view of the mind', and Spencer can be found making the same criticisms of the classical doctrine of associationism as did anti-sensationalist psychologists like Jean Francis Gall: 'it could not explain individual and species differences, and it ignored the fundamental importance of the biological endowment of varying brain structures.'[50] Even in his later writings, after his 'conversion' to associationism, Spencer continued to employ the conception of the human mind as consisting of certain faculties, like those of justice or benevolence, which he had derived from phrenology; however, rather than these faculties being part of an eternally fixed order of nature, they were now seen to be the product of the interaction of many generations of individuals with their environment, both natural and social. The phrenological faculties had evolved out of racial experience and were transmitted according to the mechanism of use-inheritance. In the words of one historian of psychology, J. M. Baldwin, the 'native, *a priori*, forms of the mind are looked upon as solidified social experience—acquired, stiffened and transmitted by heredity . . . Innate ideas are the petrified deposits of race experience.'[51]

The associations of ideas and characteristics which were innate in the individual were the result of the accumulated experience of the race, inherited by each new generation by means of the Lamarckian mechanism of transmission. As Young has again observed,

By replacing the *tabula rasa* of the individual with that of the race, Spencer was able to maintain the basic position of sensationalism while recognizing inherited biological endowments of the nervous system and avoiding the risk of the rationalist belief in innate ideas. The term 'innate' thereby lost its Cartesian terrors for the empiricist.[52]

This point was regarded by many of Spencer's commentators as constituting his most important contribution to psychology, since it appeared to offer a reconciliation of the profound issues raised by the debate between the empiricism of J. S. Mill and the intuitionism of Sir

---

[50] Young, *Mind, Brain, and Adaptation*, 173.
[51] Baldwin, *History of Psychology*, ii. 82.
[52] Young, *Mind, Brain, and Adaptation*, 178.

William Hamilton. In the case of mathematics, for instance, Mill had believed that individual exprience would be sufficient to confirm the 'inductive truth' that 'two plus two always equals four'; this had been denied by Hamilton, who had argued for the existence of a special faculty of mathematical intuition. Although Spencer disagreed with Mill's view that the experience available to any particular individual would be sufficient to establish inductively the truths of mathematics, he did not therefore support Hamilton's contention of the existence of a special faculty of mathematical intuition which was prior to all experience. The truths of mathematics were confirmed inductively, by experience, but the necessary weight of evidence was derived from the experience of all the generations of mankind, and thus the mathematical faculty could be seen to have evolved from the experiences of the race as a whole.

Spencer's unique combination of associationism with the theory of evolution explained the formation of character by circumstances and condition, and was fundamentally at odds with the Idealist theory of character formation. It also differed from the older associationism in that the circumstances which went to make up character were primarily those of ancestral experience rather than those experienced by the individual. The environment continued to shape character, but rather than acting through the experience available to an individual during a single lifetime it acted on the accumulated experience of the race as a whole. As Spencer wrote in the first edition of *The Principles of Psychology*, the 'greater part' of the psychological cohesions in the mind of the individual 'constituting what we call his natural character' have been determined 'by the experience of antecedent organisms; and the rest by his own experiences.'[53] The character of the individual is simply the product of that 'general antecendent life whose accumulated results are organized in his constitution', i.e. the experiences of the many generations of individuals out of which his nervous system has evolved.

IV. From Psychology to Politics

While Spencer's contemporaries tended to concentrate on the philosophical implications of his attempt to reconcile empiricism and intuitionism, the political implications of his evolutionary associationism went largely unremarked. Nevertheless, the claim that environment

[53] Spencer, *Principles of Psychology* (1st edn., 1855), 616.

influences character only over the course of many generations, and the associated belief that the human mind comprised certain faculties which were (from an individual point of view) innate, were doctrines which were also loaded with important political consequences.[54] Spencer derived both a negative and a positive political conclusion from his psychological theory. The negative conclusion concerned the impossibility of altering individual character by changes in the immediate environment, such as those proposed by the social reformers. The positive conclusion related to the importance of individual liberty and a limited State as the pre-condition for the development of each individuals' innate facilities. In this section the negative conclusion will be examined, while the following section will explore the positive conclusion.

In the first place, Spencer's argument suggested that there were innate differences between individuals as the result of the differences in the constitution of their respective nervous systems, a point which was brought out especially sharply in terms of the different 'natural characters' of the sexes. True to the classical doctrine of associationism, J. S. Mill had insisted that there were no innate differences in the mental characteristics of men and women:

A long list of mental and moral differences are observed, or supposed to exist, between men and women; but at some future, and, it may be hoped, not distant period, equal freedom and an equally independent social position come to be possessed by both, and their differences of character are either removed or totally altered.[55]

By contrast, Spencer argued that to claim that men and women are mentally alike 'is as untrue as that they are alike bodily.'[56] Adaptation to maternal rather than paternal functions determines the difference which exist, not merely between the physical structures of men and women, but also between their 'psychical structures'. Because of the necessity of conserving female energy for the task of reproduction, women come to maturity earlier than men and this results in 'a rather smaller growth of the nervo-muscular system'. Two fundamental consequences for the female mind followed from this fact: first, that 'mental manifestations have somewhat less of general power or massiveness'; and secondly, that

[54] It is also worthy of note that Spencer regarded the theory of evolutionary associationism as a way of supporting the doctrine of a moral sense which had been presupposed by the *Social Statics*.

[55] Mill, *Logic*, 566. See also id., *The Subjection of Women* (London, 1867).

[56] Spencer, *Study of Sociology*, 373.

there is a perceptible falling short in those two faculties, intellectual and emotional, which are the latest products of human evolution—the power of abstract reasoning and that most abstract of the emotions, the sentiment of justice—the sentiment which regulates conduct irrespective of personal attachments and the likes or dislikes felt for individuals.[57]

In addition to these differences resulting from the respective parental functions of the sexes, Spencer also noted a number of secondary differences which resulted from their relations with each other: women are characterized by 'the ability to please, and the concomitant love of approbation', and are particularly inclined to admire both powerful men and power in general.[58]

Although Spencer recognized that the course of evolution was eventually likely to lead to 'a diminution of the mental differences between men and women', for the present the 'traits of intellect and feeling which distinguish women' had to be considered for their impact on social policy.[59] In particular, the less developed sense of justice and the 'love of the helpless, which in her maternal capacity woman displays in a more special form than man', predisposes women to support the kinds of social policies which yield benefits apart from deserts. Women also possess a 'vivid imagination' for 'simple direct consequences' at the expense of the ability to grasp 'consequences that are complex and indirect', while they also exhibit 'awe of power and authority'. In combination, these factors mean that women respect freedom less than men, and their influence 'goes towards the maintenance of controlling agencies, and does not resist the extension of such agencies.'[60] This argument provided Spencer with intellectual justification for his opposition to female suffrage, one of the chief consequences of which, he believed, would be to assist in the extension of State interference.

Another important political implication of evolutionary associationism stemmed directly from Spencer's doctrine that the character of the individual was shaped by the environment only by indirect means, as mediated through the accumulated experiences of his ancestors.[61] This doctrine supported the conclusion that the attempt to mould character 'artificially' either by education or social reform was destined to fail. Given that character is contained within the inherited physiological constitution of the individual, and that any lasting biological changes will

---

[57] Ibid. 374.   [58] Ibid. 377.   [59] Ibid. 379.   [60] Ibid. 380.
[61] This argument was intended to supplement Spencer's contention that the evolution of human association from militancy to industrialism removed the ethical warrant for the discipline of the individual by society in its corporate capacity. (*Principles of Ethics*, ii. 254.)

take many centuries to realize, it was obviously absurd to suppose that 'society in its corporate capacity' had the means to attempt to inculcate particular dispositions in its members by systems of education, discipline, or culture.[62]

Spencer's belief that it was impossible artificially to mould individual character was a constant theme in his writings. The malleability of character was rejected as early as his volume on *Education: Intellectual, Moral and Physical* in which he argued that the view that individuals might be moulded by the deliberate inculcation of moral precepts was based on an unsound pyschology. The notion that 'an ideal humanity might be forthwith produced by a perfect system of education', he wrote, was one which was not acceptable 'to such as have dispassionately studied human affairs.'[63] Similarly, in the *Study of Sociology* he suggested that although human nature is infinitely modifiable, it can be modified only with glacial slowness by the processes of evolution, and hence 'all laws and institutions and appliances which count on getting from it within a short time, much better results than present ones, will inevitably fail.'[64] Spencer challenged what he alleged was the prevalent opinion that 'there needs but this kind of instruction or that kind of discipline, this mode of repression or that system of culture, to bring society into a very much better state.'[65] There was ample evidence— illustrated by the experience of the Christian Church—to support the view that deliberate attempts to reform character by education do not work: 'Throughout a Christendom full of churches and priests, full of pious books, full of observances directed to fostering the religion of love, encouraging mercy and insisting on forgiveness, we have an aggressiveness and a revengefulness such as savages have everywhere shown.'[66] A conclusion which could be seen to follow a priori from Spencer's psychological principles, could be seen to be confirmed a posteriori by the evidence of history.

The necessary slowness of any change in the natural character of individuals meant that evolutionary associationism could also be used against those social reformers who believed that a higher type of character might be produced by changes in social conditions or institutions. For example, it was argued that the objective of State intervention in order to provide free libraries, a system of education, and better

---

[62] Ibid. 257.
[63] Id., *Education: Intellectual, Moral, and Physical* (1861; Thinker's Library edn., London, 1929), 100–1.   [64] Id., *Study of Sociology*, 120.
[65] Ibid.   [66] Id., *Principles of Ethics*, ii. 257.

sanitary and housing conditions in the cities, was the improvement of the character of the people, but such views rested on a misapprehension of the 'appropriateness of the appliances' by means of which this objective was to be realized: 'Here we read that "it is necessary completely to re-fashion the people whom one wishes to make free": the implications being that a re-fashioning is practicable.'[67] Yet it was this very implication which evolutionary associationism denied, since, as Mackay remarked, 'human character is the growth of centuries' and could be refashioned, if at all, only over the course of many generations.[68]

This point was elaborated by another Spencerian Individualist, H. S. Constable, in the context of an explicit attack on J. S. Mill's use of associationism to support Radical politics. Constable accused Mill, 'like many a foolish living Radical', of having based his teachings on the belief 'that every man comes into the world a blank sheet of paper, and that his subsequent character, talents, and actions depend entirely on his education and surroundings; so that any black Australian savage or white British savage in our slums would be an Isaac Newton if he had the same education.'[69] Against this *tabula rasa* view of the mind Constable invoked 'science' in the shape of Herbert Spencer as proof that 'the effect of education and surroundings is almost nothing compared with the inborn, ages-long, inherited nature.'[70] Although it could not be denied that education had its effect, the fact remained that 'inborn nature is the chief thing', and consequently the Radicals' ambition of fostering the virtues of character by improving social conditions was bound to be thwarted.[71] The same point was made by Spencer himself when he wrote:

A further endowment of those feelings which civilization is developing in us—sentiments responding to the requirements of the social state—emotive faculties that find their gratification in the duties devolving on us—must be acquired before the crimes, excesses, diseases, improvidences, dishonesties and cruelties that now so greatly diminish the duration of life, can cease.[72]

A lasting improvement in society could be brought about only by a fundamental change in human nature which itself could not be transformed by an improvement in social conditions. Social reform might alter the environment in which the individual lived, but, according to

---

[67] Id., *Study of Sociology*, 120.
[68] T. D. Mackay, 'The Joining of Issues', *Economic Review*, 1 (1891), 200.
[69] H. S. Constable, *Radicalism and its Stupidities* (London, 1896), 56.
[70] Ibid. 56–7.
[71] Id., *The Fallacies and Follies of Socialist Radicalism Exposed* (London, 1895), 87.
[72] H. Spencer, *The Principles of Biology*, ii. (London, 1867), 497.

Spencer's pyschological theory, an individual's natural character was substantially predetermined and could be modified, if at all, only by experiencing the natural consequences of his conduct, and Spencer criticized Comte for believing that 'society is to be re-organised by philosophy' when it could be reorganized only by 'the accumulated effects of habit on character.'[73]

Evolutionary associationism also served to distance Spencer from other theorists, like Bosanquet and the leading members of the Charity Organisation Society, who argued that the improvement of society was to be brought about by the deliberate inculcation of moral ideals. This point of view lent itself to an approach to social reform by means of the transformation of individual souls rather than by means of the 'mechanical' theories of socialists, and it regarded itself as a higher form of individualism than the individualism of private selfishness allegedly preached by Mill and Spencer.[74] The higher individualism, wrote one of its proponents, 'respects every person as having something of infinite worth in him, and would begin to improve the world by elevating the single spirit, counting no advance permanent that is not based on reformed and cultivated individuals. This method fully deserves the epithet "Christian"'.[75] Although the Individualists shared with these theorists the fundamental assumption that it was only by means of an alteration of individual character that permanent social change was to be achieved, they believed that this improvement could be produced by the natural processes of evolution and not by moral exhortation. The deliberate inculcation of moral ideals in the individual was bound to fail, and the pain resulting from indolent or feckless living was a far better moral guide than the preaching of sermons.

V. The 'Natural' Formation of Character

As we remarked earlier, Spencer believed that human nature was becoming more perfectly adapted to the requirements of living in

[73] Id., 'Reasons for Dissenting from the Philosophy of M. Comte', in id., *Essays*, iii (London, 1874), 77.

[74] This theory was attacked by Hobson as a 'convenient' doctrine which released the individual 'from fighting in those coarser and more brutal frays which engage the ungovernable passions and disturb the foundations of the existing social order.' The endeavour to 'solve economic problems by direct appeal to the moral conduct of individual members', he argued, was 'fordoomed to failure.' J. A. Hobson, *The Social Problem* (London, 1901), 132–4.

[75] N. P. Gilman, *Socialism and the American Spirit* (London, 1893), 325.

society, and that (like all other evolutionary processes) the progress of mankind was tending towards an equilibrium. 'The ideal social being', he wrote, is one who is 'so constituted that his spontaneous activities are congruous with the conditions imposed by the social environment formed by other such beings.' Moreover, it was 'only by the process of adaptation itself' that the type of character could be produced 'which makes social equilibrium spontaneous.'[76] In contrast to the Darwinian aspects of his theory, which had stressed the inevitable and ruthless struggle for survival, his Lamarckianism gave rise to the claim that progress ensured that human beings were becoming more interdependent and more suited for a life of social co-operation. The equilibrium towards which human evolution was tending was the perfect adaptation of the individual to the social state in which there is a correspondence between 'the promptings of nature' and 'the requirements of life in society':

The adaptation of man's nature to the conditions of his existence, cannot cease until the internal forces we know as feelings are in equilibrium with the forces they encounter. And the establishment of this equilibrium, is the arrival at a state of human nature and social organization, such that the individual has no desires but those which may be satisfied without exceeding his proper sphere of action, while society maintains no restraints but those which the individual voluntarily respects. The progressive extension of the liberty of citizens, and the reciprocal removal of political restrictions, are the steps towards which we advance towards this state. And the ultimate abolition of all limits to that freedom of each, save those imposed by the like freedom of all, must result from the complete equilibration of man's desires and conduct necessitated by surrounding conditions.[77]

If the negative political conclusion drawn from Spencer's evolutionary associationism was that it was impossible to improve individual character by a change in social conditions, its positive conclusion was that the desirable qualities of character, and the associated social

[76] H. Spencer, *Social Statics* (1851; 2nd edn., London, 1868), 310.

[77] Id., *First Principles* (3rd edn., London, 1875), 512–13. It is worth pointing out that there was an important difference between Spencer's earlier and later work in this regard. In the *Social Statics*, Spencer wrote as if he believed that completely spontaneous social equilibrium was actually realizable, and that the goal of human evolution was destined to be an anarchistic utopia. In the later philosophy, however, while continuing to believe that human evolution still *tended* in this direction, he had become convinced that perfect adaptation would take an infinite time, and hence the future goal he had once predicted for mankind was 'a goal ever to be recognized, though it cannot actually be reached.' (Id., 'Absolute Political Ethics', in id., *Essays* (1874; enlarged edn., London, 1891), iii. 228.) This point is discussed more extensively in Ch. 5, below.

equilibrium, could only be fostered by encouraging the exercise of those faculties which were innate in each individual. An individual's capacity for self-help, as well as the altruistic sentiments, were conceived on the analogy of the thews and sinews of the body; should the State assume the burdens which the faculties rightfully ought to bear then they would atrophy in exactly the same way as an unused muscle.[78] As one of Spencer's followers remarked, 'according to all laws of evolutionary science, instincts grow stronger as they are exercised', and to transfer the responsibility for the relief of suffering from the individual to the state would be to promote the withering of these sentiments by their disuse.[79] Spencer himself wrote in the *Social Statics* that 'no one can need reminding' that

demand and supply is the law of life as well as the law of trade. Would you draw out and increase some feeble sentiment? Then you must set it to do, as well as it can, the work required of it. It must be kept ever active, ever strained, ever inconvenienced by its incompetence. Under this treatment it will, in the slow course of generations, attain to efficiency; and what was once an impossible task will become the source of a healthy, pleasurable and desired excitement. But let a state-instrumentality be thrust between such a faculty and its work, and the process of adaptation is at once suspended. The embryo agency now superseded by some commission—some board and staff of officers, straightaway dwindles; for power is inevitably lost by inactivity as it is gained by activity.[80]

The development of the individual faculties was influenced by every change in social conditions, among which must be included every law which compels, restrains, or aids a man over the course of time, and Spencer accused legislators of having given inadequate consideration to the point that every law is capable of either encouraging or stunting the growth of the faculties of the individual.

Spencer further argued that human beings could begin to approach the state of 'spontaneous' social equilibrium only on the condition that the widest possible sphere of individual liberty was preserved. Given the condition that the individual be allowed the greatest possible sphere of free action, compatible with a like freedom for other individuals, each person would experience the 'natural' consequences of his conduct. If human beings were allowed the freedom to experience the con-

---

[78] Compare J. S. Mill, *On Liberty* (1859): 'The mental and moral, like the muscular powers, are improved only by being used.' (*Utilitarianism, Liberty and Representative Government*, ed. H. B. Acton (Everyman edn., London, 1972), 116–17.)

[79] T. D. Mackay, *The English Poor* (London, 1889), 12.

[80] Spencer, *Social Statics*, 309–10.

sequences of their conduct then, over a period of time, the adaptive mechanisms would operate to bring about an adjustment of the natural character of the human organism to match the requirements of social life. The natural consequence of improvidence, for example, is (as Mr Micawber might have said) misery. Hence an association of ideas would be established between improvidence and specific types of pain. These unpleasant experiences would provide the individual with the stimulus to modify his character by an exercise of will; he would choose to be careful with money, to save for contingencies, and so on. After repeated attempts, the associations of ideas would strengthen and the physiological lines of communication constituted by nervous fibres would begin to form. This physiological constitution would be inherited by each subsequent generation, who would further develop and strengthen the channels of communication by their own conscious efforts to avoid improvidence. Thus, over the course of many generations, the nervous system appropriate to a more fully adapted life would become organic in the race, prudence would become instinctive, and improvidence would disappear. A similar process would also occur with regard to the other moral dispositions, for example self-help, responsibility, and the love of justice, of property, and of liberty. In physiological terms, the strands of the nervous system, which are the objective counterparts of these higher emotions necessary to the creation of the most perfect human communities, will be formed only by many generations of individuals receiving the natural consequences of their conduct. Once formed, these strands of nervous fibre will be transmitted from one generation to the next according to the mechanisms of Lamarckian evolution.

By contrast, Spencer argued, the attempt to mould character deliberately meant that it would become 'deformed to fit the artificial arrangements instead of the natural arrangements. More than this: it has to be depleted and dwarfed for the support of the substituted agencies.'[81] These sentiments were echoed by Mackay who argued that 'attempts to improve the delicate mechanism of the harmonious progression inherent in a free society, by the forceful action of the State, must result in reaction and hinder the growth of the true social instincts.'[82] It was 'impossible for artificial moulding to do that which natural moulding does', since the essence of the spontaneous formation of character was that 'each faculty acquires fitness for its function by performing its

---

[81] Id., *Principles of Ethics*, ii. 259.
[82] T. D. Mackay, 'Empiricism in Politics', *National Review*, 25 (1895), 791.

funtion.'[83] The only way in which the faculties of the mind could be further developed was to allow the individual the liberty for their exercise, and the problem with the artificial moulding of character was that the social reformers proposed 'to divorce conduct from consequence', and to go against the primary condition for the occurrence of this process of adaptation.[84] O'Brien contended that the root of the evils besetting society was 'the depraved nature of man' which could never be improved 'by a vast and elaborate system of laws. Instead of working for the better, collective slavery but makes bad worse.' The only remedy was to allow individuals their freedom since by the use of their liberty alone 'can men ever learn their folly; and therefore to destroy liberty is to cut off the very conditions of improvement.'[85] Nothing could be a more fundamental absurdity than to propose to improve social life by breaking the fundamental law which punished dissolute conduct and rewarded self-discipline, and yet this was precisely the consequence of State interference.

Therefore not only did evolutionary associationism provide a justification for the Individualist contention that no lasting social change could come about without a change in individual character, but it also lent 'scientific' credibility to one of the most widely employed of all the arguments against State intervention, the claim that the dispositions of character could not flourish in the shadow of the State. A typical example was Lord Bramwell's criticism of legislation like the Ground Game Act, the Employers' Liability Act, and the Irish Land Act on the grounds that 'legislation which treats people as helpless . . . instead of teaching them to struggle for themselves, adds to their feebleness by a mischievous taking care of them.'[86] George Brooks also objected to 'State-meddling' because he believed it would

dwarf, and ultimately destroy, mental self-hood, by eliminating from human nature . . . that vital and essential element of true manhood and womanhood— the power of judgement, of discrimination, of choice, of decision, by which power human beings are able to take their own way, choose their own lot, develop their own faculties, and make the best of themselves generally.[87]

In addition, the incompatibility of character with an interventionist State was affirmed by Mackay:

[83] Spencer, *Study of Sociology*, 368.   [84] Id., *Principles of Ethics*, ii. 260.
[85] M. D. O'Brien, *Socialism Tested by the Facts* (London, 1892), p. xxiv.
[86] Lord Bramwell, *Laissez Faire* (London, 1884), 21.
[87] G. Brooks, *Industry and Property* (London, 1895), 148–9.

Endless Acts of Parliament have been passed, now to protect, now to coerce the poor, and as a consequence atrophy has settled down on some of the instincts which might otherwise have protected them. The first lessons in thrift, the first motives to refrain from consuming wages on the day they are earned, arise from the desire of men to provide against the uncertainties of an unknown morrow, and for the inevitable period of sickness and old age.[88]

Another Individualist of a Spencerian hue, J. McGavin Sloan, argued in his *Three Addresses on the Fallacies of State Socialism* that 'faculty' was 'the child in the main, of individual responsibility and self-reliance. Let the state make the citizen secure of all things needful from youth to old age, and faculty would soon be smitten with senility and decreptiude.'[89] The effect of 'State-meddling', it was alleged, would be to destroy liberty, individuality, and independence, and to transform the nation 'into helpless children and slaves'.[90] And O'Brien argued that 'nothing is more demoralizing than government; nothing tends more to destroy character than the regulation of minorities by majorities; hence nothing needs more keeping within the narrowest possible limits than that corporate action of individual despots called the State.'[91]

The Individualists concentrated their criticisms of the demoralizing effects of government interference on a number of specific institutions, chief among which was the Poor Law. Whereas the empirical Individualists were content to assist the 'deserving' poor within the framework of the 1834 Act, the attitude of the Spencerians towards this institution ranged from outright hostility (in the case of Spencer himself) to grudging acceptance (in the case of most of his followers).[92] Spencer regarded the Poor Law as 'a kind of social opium eating' and as the cause of immense misery which had, over many centuries, destroyed the dispositions to thrift and self-help. He insisted that the habitual improvidence of the English was due to their having been 'for ages disciplined in improvidence' by State relief of the poor: 'Extravagance has been made habitual by shielding them from the sharp penalties extravagance brings. Carefulness has been discouraged by continually showing to the careful that those who were careless did as well, or better than, themselves.'[93] Furthermore, it had discouraged the development

---

[88] Mackay, *English Poor*, 12–13.

[89] J. M. Sloan, *For Freedom: Three Addresses on the Fallacies of State Socialism* (London, n.d. (1894)), 20.   [90] Constable, *Fallacies and Follies of Socialist Radicalism*, 18.

[91] M. D. O'Brien, *The Natural Right to Freedom* (London, 1893), 7.

[92] For the empirical Individualists' attitude towards the Poor Law see Ch. 6.

[93] Spencer, *Study of Sociology*, 368.

of the faculty of beneficence, which 'has the best effects when individually exercised. If, like mercy it "blesses him that gives and him that takes", it can do this in full measure only when the benefactor and beneficiary stand in direct relation.'[94] Despite his recognition that the abolition of the Poor Law would be the cause of much suffering among the 'large numbers who are unadapted to the requirements of social life', Spencer insisted that it should be replaced by voluntary action, thus encouraging the development of both self-help and the altruistic sentiments.

Many of Spencer's followers shared his belief that the Poor Law had a demoralizing effect and that the institution had contributed to the spread of 'drunkenness and idleness' by filling the country 'with the offspring of wretched people, who become every generation more drunken, idle, and vicious according to the law of heredity.'[95] On the other hand, they also recognized that the alternative to some minimal provision for the destitute would be to have people dying in the streets, and hence the Poor Law could be regarded as 'a necessary evil, to prevent completely intolerable ones'.[96] Their view was that the Poor Law should be maintained, subject to the proviso that outdoor relief was to be minimized. This was the position adopted by Mackay, an experienced Poor Law administrator, who believed that the best cure for pauperism was to 'reduce the encouragement to pauperism held out by our present system of out-door relief.'[97] He contended that human nature had a 'natural capacity for independence' and that 'dispauperization means the restoration of independence, not the abolition of poverty', which could be achieved only by the wider diffusion of property according to the natural laws of society and not by 'socialistic' institutions like the Poor Law.[98]

The proposals for the State provision of old age pensions which gathered momentum throughout the 1890s were also combated by the Individualists because of their allegedly demoralizing effects. Spencer believed that proposals of this kind would serve to intensify rather than cure the habitual improvidence of the English:

Men who have been made improvident by being shielded from many of the evil results of improvidence, are now to be made more provident by further shielding them from the evil results of improvidence. Having had their self-control

---

[94] Id., *Principles of Ethics*, ii. 403.
[95] Constable, *Fallacies and Follies of Socialist Radicalism*, 35.   [96] Ibid.
[97] T. D. Mackay, 'Politicans and the Poor Law', *Fortnightly Review*, 57 (1895), 408.
[98] Id., 'Empiricism in Politics', 802.

decreased by social arrangements which have lessened the need for self-control, other social arrangements are devised which will make self-control still less needful; and it is hoped to make self-control greater.[99]

For Mackay legislation represented no solution to 'the question of old age' since it was not 'in this or any other matter a constructive social force.' But whereas the statutory provision of old age pensions would prove destructive of the virtues of character, employing the

ties of family; the natural sympathy which obtains between man and man; the persistency by which human wants, whether they relate to manhood or old age, discipline us to effort and self-control; . . . liberty of enterprise, and security of tenure in their property assured for rich and poor alike
would foster these same virtues.[100]

W. E. H. Lecky also objected to State pensions on the grounds that they proposed

to teach the working population to look to the state, and not to themselves, for the provision of their old age . . . Can it be seriously believed that the addition of many millions a year to the state funds directly employed in the relief of poverty will, in the long run, tend to diminish pauperism or to encourage self-reliance and thrift?[101]

Lecky's ideal was that of the 'classic type of English liberalism' who was 'a robust, healthy, self-reliant type, extremely jealous of all extensions of government interference, extremely tenacious of individual liberty, and habitually preferring spontaneous action . . . to the disciplined action of a controlling power.'[102]

The tone of these arguments was predominantly moralistic; although it was sometimes argued that fostering the dispositions of character was merely a means to an end, and that without them productive industry would cease, it was more usual for the development of character to be treated as an end in itself, and for freedom and responsibility to be regarded as the indispensable conditions for attaining this goal.[103] Spencer's achievement was to have transformed this moralistic argument about the necessity of freedom for the development of character

---

[99] Spencer, *Study of Sociology*, 371.
[100] T. D. Mackay, 'Old Age Pensions', *Quarterly Review*, 182 (1895), 279.
[101] W. E. H. Lecky, 'Old Age Pensions', in id., *Historical and Political Essays* (London, 1903), 309.
[102] Id., *A History of England in the Eighteenth Century* (4th edn., London, 1890), vi. 241.
[103] For examples of Individualists who saw the virtues of character as the 'mainspring of production', see id., *Democracy and Liberty* (2nd edn., London, 1898), ii. 367; [A.] B. Smith, *Liberty and Liberalism*, 550.

into a 'scientific' demonstration of the conditions under which the desirable type of character could be formed. The incompatibility of character with an interventionist State was no longer an article of faith capable only of constant reaffirmation, but was the logical outcome of his psychological theory. Evolutionary associationism clearly indicated that the human mind comprised a number of faculties, for example of benevolence, justice, or self-help and that these could be developed only on the condition that the freedom and opportunity for their exercise was available to the individual.

VI. Conclusion

In conclusion it would appear that Spencer's theory of the formation of character could offer 'scientific' justification for two standard Individualist arguments: first, that extensive State action would undermine the virtues of character; and second, that lasting social improvement was only possible as the result of the accumulated effects of habit on individual character. Moreover, the theory of evolutionary associationism represented a considerable modification of the classical associationist doctrine, and the innovations which Spencer introduced had profound political implications for this formerly radical psychological theory.

In the first place, although evolutionary associationism was not blind to the significance of environmental influence on the formation of character, this factor entered into the theory in a different way to that of the classical form of the theory. In the short term, the Individualists held, character was relatively constant, since it possessed a physiological basis in the individual's nervous system. Deliberate attempts to mould the environment, or deliberate attempts at moral or intellectual education, would prove to be futile. In the longer term, however, the environment did assume importance since character was modified by the accumulated efforts of many generations of individuals consciously to adapt themselves to it. The environment provided the stimulus to which the organism would respond by exercising its will. Despite Spencer's repeated insistence that 'ultimately' the process of evolution would achieve the objective of moulding character to a form appropriate to the social state, his conclusion was altogether contrary to that of the Philosophic Radicals who contended that it was within the power of the legislator or the educator to create in the mind of the individual whatever associations of ideas were desired. Nevertheless, while the emphasis on the malleability of individual character, which had suffused the thought of both James and John Stuart Mill, was explicitly denied by the Individualists, it continued to perform a vital function in the New Liberalism. As Freeden has remarked,

on the basis of the new political and scientific theories, a collective effort to control environment was no longer contrary to the essence of human nature. And by collective effort the rational control of mind over matter, of the human spirit over it material environment, could yet be attained.[104]

Although the New Liberal emphasis on collective effort was a distinctively new aspect of the theory, the belief that changes in character could be brought about by changes in the environment was a theme which forged a link between the new liberalism and the old, and which differentiated both from Individualism. The seeds of the New Liberal project of improving individual character by means of social reform were contained in the associationist doctrine of the orthodox utilitarians which had stressed the possibility of the legislative and educational improvement of mankind.

The second consequence of evolutionary associationism was to affirm that the individual human mind comprised certain faculties which had evolved out of the experience of the race as a whole. Although there were no innate ideas, in the sense of ideas prior to all experience, certain ideas were 'innate' in each individual. For example, every individual possessed a mathematical faculty, itself the product of the experiences of many generations of individuals, which enabled him or her to recognize the 'intuitive' truth of mathematical propositions. Similarly, the 'moral sense' enabled individuals to recognize the intuitive rightness of certain courses of conduct, a capacity which was also based on generations of ancestral experience.[105] By providing the doctrines of intuitionism with apparent intellectual respectability, Spencer had not merely brought about a fundamental change in the nature of associationism but he had also transformed it in a conservative direction since, as we have seen, the younger Mill explicitly connected intuitionism with conservatism. The doctrines that each individual could recognize the intuitive rightness of certain courses of conduct, or that different sexes and races possessed different inherent characteristics, were regarded by

---

[104] Freeden, *New Liberalism*, 175.   [105] See below, Ch. 6.

Mill as dangerous obscurantism, intellectual mists dissolved by the light of the association psychology. Spencer's achievement was to return credibility to these doctrines by employing the same instrument Mill had used to destroy them.

With reference both to the malleability of human character and the doctrine that there were innate ideas accessible to special faculties of the human mind, Spencer's evolutionary associationism represented a conservative adaptation of the classical doctrine, and was another instance of the conservatism which pervaded Individualism as a whole. Even in the 1850s Spencer had resisted the radical implications of classical associationism, but the conservative nature of his doctrine did not become fully apparent until the project of reform became transformed into the New Liberalism. While the task of liberalism remained destructive (i.e. removing obstacles to the formation of characters), Spencer's disagreement with both James and John Stuart Mill did not fully emerge; but once, towards the end of the century, the radicalism of the liberal creed took a more constructive turn, the conservative implications of Spencer's version of associationism rapidly became apparent. His evolutionary associationism still held out the hope of a future state of human perfection, but it could be achieved only over the course of many generations and as a consequence of the misery of the idle, the improvident, and the destitute.

4

INDIVIDUALISM AND THE ORGANIC
CONCEPTION OF SOCIETY

I. Introduction

The politically conservative nature of Individualism is illustrated, not only by its transformation of the association psychology or of the liberal conception of progress, but also by the attempts of some Individualists to secure support for their principles from a biologically inspired science of society. In the first volume of *The Principles of Sociology* Spencer had drawn an extensive analogy between a biological organism and the social aggregate, and this conception of the 'social organism' did much to determine the principal concerns of social science in the closing decades of the nineteenth century. The present chapter will be concerned with the attempts of Spencer and other Individualists to use the conception of society as an organism as part of the defence of an individualistic social order.

The ambition of the first generation of sociologists had been to construct a social science which could be used as an instrument to facilitate the project of social reform. As was noted in an earlier chapter, this objective was in evidence in Mill's *A System of Logic* as much as in the writings of Comte. Mill remarked that the 'object of the Social Science' was to 'understand by what causes' any given condition of social affairs had been 'made what it was; whether it was tending to any, and to what, changes; what effects each feature of its existing state was likely to produce in the future; and by what means any of those effects might be prevented, modified, or accelerated, or a different class of effects superinduced.'[1] However, the ambition of Spencer and those Individualists who borrowed from his sociological work was quite different. As Richard Hofstadter has perceptively noted, Spencer was

animated by the desire to foster a science of society which would puncture the illusions of legislative reformers who, he believed, generally operated on the assumption that social causes and effects are simple and easily calculable, and

---

[1] J. S. Mill, *A System of Logic* (1843; London, 1919), 573.

that projects to relieve distress and remedy ills will always have the anticipated effect. A science of sociology, by teaching men to think of social causation scientifically, would awaken them to the enormous complexity of the social organism, and put an end to hasty legislative panaceas.[2]

The objective of Spencerian sociology, unlike that of Comte or Mill, was not to serve as a basis for social engineering, but rather to show that all such engineering was an impossibility.

From the Individualists' point of view, the virtue of a justification for their creed based on the organic conception of society was that it combined a defence of an individualistic social order with the view that society was not an object of conscious human design. The Individualists could argue that the nature of society was such that any attempt by the centralized authority to overstep the limits imposed on it by the protection of rights and the administration of justice would result in disruption to the whole social organism, and hence it was not possible to employ the State as an instrument of social reform. Once again, the characteristic of a key Individualist argument was the bipolarity of liberalism and conservatism on which we have already had cause to remark. The upshot of the social organism analogy as it was used by Spencer and his disciples was that the State was structurally determined to perform only those functions which were assigned to it by individualistic liberalism.

Many of Spencer's critics have regarded the attempt to marry organicism with Individualism as fundamentally misconceived, and he has been accused of having failed to recognize that his sociology made use of two irreconcilable ways of conceptualizing society. It will be argued that this alleged incompatibility between Individualism and the organic conception of society rests on a confusion of the several distinct senses in which society might be compared to a biological organism. Perhaps it is because most commentators have persisted in regarding Spencer as merely the generalizer of Darwinian biology that they have interpreted his social organism analogy in the strictest possible sense, as implying that society resembled an organism in all its particulars. In fact, however, Spencer's own use of the analogy had nothing to do with the idea that the State or society possessed a will or purposes of its own, distinct from those of its members, but related primarily to a fundamental parallelism of structure, especially to the fact that both societies and biological organisms possessed systems for production, distribution, and regulation. The points of similarity were quite limited and specific,

[2] R. Hofstadter, *Social Darwinism in American Thought* (New York, 1944), 29.

and Spencer believed that any attempt to impute a closer resemblance than this between society and an organism was destined to fail.[3]

Nevertheless, it is also true that a more literal organic conception of society was adopted by one of Spencer's self-professed disciples, Wordsworth Donisthorpe, who believed that the social organism possessed a group purpose and a group will distinct from that of its members. Since this particular version of organicism is more usually associated with an active, interventionist State, the present chapter will also consider Donisthorpe's attempt to reconcile an individualistic social order with the notion that society had a will of its own which was directed to the group welfare.

The views of Spencer's New Liberal opponents will also be examined. They accused him of having illegitimately restricted the organic analogy to the basic structural similarities resulting from the systems of production, distribution, and regulation; had it not been for the distorting influence of Spencer's outmoded political views, they argued, he would have realized that the analogy between social and biological organisms was much more profound than this limited parallelism of structure and that it implied the existence of a centralized, directive intelligence which could be identified with an interventionist State. The 'scientific' analysis of society seemed to support political conclusions which were the very opposite of those which Spencer himself wished to draw.

II. The Social Organism and Individualism

Despite Spencer's ambition to put Individualism on a secure social scientific foundation, many of his critics have alleged that he had failed

---

[3] The argument of this ch. broadly agrees with that set forth by T. S. Gray, 'Herbert Spencer: Individualist or Organicist?', *Political Studies*, 33 (1985), 236–53. Gray claims that 'the accusations of conflict between individualism and organicism in Spencer's writings are essentially the result of rigid or emotive conceptualizations of the two terms on the part of critics. Most commentators have arbitrarily confined their attention to a restricted range of the possible meanings of the two concepts, and have read into them more than, or less than, Spencer himself intended, thereby tilting at a straw man.' (p. 246.) Unfortunately, Gray's otherwise excellent article is marred by a number of misconceptions about the nature of Spencer's organicism which arise from reading his work out of its context in mid-Victorian radicalism. Contra Gray (p. 240), Spencer's defence of free belief and worship was not in conflict with his recognition of the valuable social role played by religion: they could be reconciled on condition that Churches were regarded as *voluntary* associations. Moreover, the suggestion that Spencer supported the 'state provision of certain public goods' like sanitation (p. 239) is quite simply wrong.

to recognize that Individualism is incompatible with the centrepiece of his sociology, the organic conception of society.[4] As early as 1871 T. H. Huxley argued in his essay on 'Administrative Nihilism' that, taken seriously, Spencer's theory of the social organism led to the conclusion that there was much the State would be justified in doing, beyond the limited functions Spencer had ascribed to it. The real force of the analogy, Huxley suggested, was 'totally opposed to the negative view of State function':

Suppose that, in accordance with this view, each muscle were to maintain that the nervous system had no right to interfere with its contraction, except to prevent it from hindering the contraction of another muscle; or each gland, that it had a right to secrete, so long as its secretion interfered with no other; suppose every separate cell left free to follow its own 'interest' and *laissez faire* Lord of all, what would become of the body physiological?[5]

In the present century Sir Ernest Barker argued that there was a tension between Spencer's theory of natural rights, in which society is made up of atomistic individuals who form the State only for the limited purpose of the protection of their liberty and property, and his view of society as forming an organic unity. Since these were incompatible ways of conceptualizing society, Spencer's political theory began and ended in 'an incongruous mixture of Natural Rights and physiological metaphor.'[6] More recent commentators have continued to make this claim. L. A. Coser, for instance, has pointed out that 'in spite of the individualistic underpinnings of his philosophy, Spencer developed an overall system in which the organicist analogy is pursued with even more rigour than Comte's work.'[7] Stanislav Andreski, a contemporary sociologist who otherwise displays considerable sympathy for Spencer, has also argued that his theory of society

should have led him to expouse some form of authoritarian collectivism because the organisms regarded as higher display a greater centralization of the nervous system, and a greater subordination of the parts to the whole. Indeed, his system provides a much more logical justification for socialism (as practised rather than preached) than Marx's theory of class struggles.[8]

---

[4] See ibid. 236–7 for an impressive list of these critics.

[5] T. H. Huxley, 'Administrative Nihilism', quoted by H. Spencer, 'Specialized Administration', in Spencer, *Essays: Scientific, Political and Speculative*, iii (London, 1874), 144.

[6] E. Baker, *Political Thought in England 1848 to the Present Day* (London, 1915), 71.

[7] L. A. Coser, *The Masters of Sociological Thought* (2nd edn., New York, 1977), 98. For an additional statement of this argument see W. M. Simon, 'Herbert Spencer and the "Social Organism"', *Journal of the History of Ideas*, 21 (1960), 294–9.

[8] S. Andreski, *Herbert Spencer: Structure, Function, and Evolution* (London, 1972), 28.

And David Wiltshire concluded a notably unsympathetic reading of Spencer's use of the organism analogy with the remark that 'no one after Spencer attempted to reconcile the incompatibles of organicism and individualism.'[9]

While the majority of recent commentators are agreed that Spencer tried, but failed, to reconcile his sociology with his political views, another recent interpretation has suggested that his sociological theories have no connection whatsoever with his Individualism. In his 'Renewed Appreciation' of Spencer, Jonathan H. Turner has attempted to rehabilitate Spencer's reputation as one of the founders of sociology by claiming that as 'the first general systems theorist', there was no connection at all between his sociology and his political views. Spencer's '*laissez-faire* ideology' is 'easy to ignore', Turner writes, because it

hardly appears in Spencer's sociology. And yet, so many just assume that Spencerian sociology is riddled with references to 'survival of the fittest' and ideological tracks (*sic*) on the virtues of *laissez-faire*. This is just not the case.[10]

Given this weight of argument, Spencer's belief that the conception of society as an organism could not only be reconciled with his Individualism, but could even render an intellectual justification for it, appears to be utterly incomprehensible. The solution to the paradox is to be found in the varied meanings which could be (and were) invoked by a late Victorian political thinker when making use of the social organism analogy. For the sake of simplicity, these different meanings of the term 'organic' can be reduced to three broad categories. In the first place, 'organicism' might be used to refer to the Burkean notion that society was not an artificial construct but was a natural growth. This sense of the analogy did not favour any particular conception of the role or functions of the State, but merely indicated that social changes ought to take place slowly and with due respect for the historically evolved traditions and customs of the society. Secondly, the 'organic conception of society' might refer only to certain basic structural similarities between society and a biological organism; for example, that they both possessed systems for nutrition and regulation. Any conclusions concerning the legitimate functions of the State would have to await a more detailed explication of the nature of the parallel which was being drawn.

---

[9] D. Wiltshire, *The Social and Political Thought of Herbert Spencer* (Oxford, 1978), 242.

[10] J. H. Turner, *Herbert Spencer: A Renewed Appreciation* (Beverly Hills, Calif., 1985), 83. As I shall argue, there are ways in which Spencer's sociology supports his Individualism without his having to resort to such crude propagandizing.

Thirdly, the 'social organism' analogy might be used in order to indicate that, just as a biological organism possessed consciousness and intentions which were not those of its component parts, the State or society possessed a will, purpose, or interest of its own which was distinct from that of the will, ends, or interests of any of its members, considered either collectively or individually. In this sense, the organic analogy (which I shall refer to as the conception of society as a 'collectivity') seemed to support collectivism and State intervention in order to realize this notion of the common good. This sense of organicism was most commonly associated with philosophical Idealism, which denied that society could be conceptualized in terms of discrete individual atoms, and which regarded the dichotomy between State and individual as merely the product of a false empiricism; on this view a system of social relations might also be described as organic in the sense that they were harmoniously interconnected. Because it is essentially a statement about ontology, this last sense of organicism belonged to a higher plane of abstraction than did the others, and hence it can be eliminated from the present investigation which is concerned primarily with the political and sociological applications of the organic analogy.[11] By concentrating on the three different senses of the social organism conception identified above—the Burkean, the structural, and the collective—it will be demonstrated that the error into which commentators on Spencer have fallen is in failing to distinguish between these various senses, and as a consequence they have convicted him of having failed to draw the implications of a version of the analogy which it was no part of his intention to expound. Although the three categories are not, prima facie, mutually exclusive, neither does one logically entail any of the others. The application of the analogy which Spencer himself utilized was primarily concerned with the similarities of structure between the social organism and a biological organism, and he stopped short of developing the analogy in a direction which would have conferred the social organism with a will or interests of its own.

There was another aspect of Spencerian organicism which echoed the Burkean notion that society was a natural growth not an artificial structure. In her study of British Social Darwinism, Greta Jones has suggested that in the late nineteenth century, organicism, which had

---

[11] It should be noted that the Idealist version of the organic analogy might not necessarily manifest itself in any profound differences with the political doctrine of Individualism, as the case of Bosanquet indicates, although it also lent support to the more interventionist stance of Ritchie or Haldane.

been formerly a conservative notion, was appropriated by Liberals like Spencer and Stephen. Their organicism required that account be taken 'of the "social tissue" binding society together. This excluded violent disruption. But it was nonetheless possible to envisage major social change paralleling natural change.'[12] On the contrary, it will be demonstrated that rather than the Individualists having made use of a formerly conservative instrument for their own purposes, Spencer's use of the social organism analogy was itself profoundly conservative in its implications. Not only did Spencer use the analogy to demonstrate that the limitation of the functions of the State was a natural corollary of the processes of evolution, but he also used it to establish that society was a complex, natural growth which it was beyond the capacity of social reformers to transform.

With regard to the first aspect of his use of the social organism analogy, Spencer argued that evolution produced specialization of both the structure and function of particular organs, and since this was true of society as much as of a biological organism, the functions of the State could be no exception to this law. In accordance with his attempt to systematize and synthesize all human knowledge, which was discussed in the first chapter, Spencer attempted to demonstrate that the process of the emergence of an individualistic social order could be subsumed under general laws of evolution. Evolution is the progressive integration of matter accompanied by the dissipation of motion, and embodies a continuous change from incoherent homogeneity, illustrated by the lowly protozoa, to coherent heterogeneity, manifested in man and the higher animals. Everywhere one finds evidence of a general direction of change from those things which are 'small, loose, uniform, and vague in structure' to those which are 'large, compact, multiform and distinct'.[13] Since the homogeneous is inherently unstable it will inevitably develop into the heterogeneous and this process of evolution from simplicity to complexity is the principle common to everything in the known universe.

The principles of evolution which were in evidence in the natural world were also to be found in the 'superorganic' evolution of human societies. Social phenomena conformed to laws of their progress and development in identical fashion to biological organisms, and thus sociological laws were discoverable in the same way as were those of biology. The truths of sociology bore the same relation to history as

[12] G. Jones, *Social Darwinism in English Thought: The Interaction between Biological and Social Theory* (Brighton, 1980), 41.
[13] H. Spencer, *The Principles of Sociology*, ii (London, 1882), 646.

those of biology did to the biography of an individual human being, a point which Spencer developed in *The Study of Sociology*, a work intended as a popular introduction to the subject. It might be thought that the 'incalculableness of a child's future'—whether he will survive infancy, whether he will enjoy success in a career, whether he will marry, whether he will eventually father children—means that the child presents 'no subject-matter for science'. But this would be to ignore the fact that behind the 'inconstant' phenomena of human life, that is to say the biography of the individual, there stand the 'constant' phenomena of the anatomy and physiology of Man. Despite the inexactness of some of the generalizations of the study of human biology, and despite the fact that the general truths which this study propounds admit important exceptions, nevertheless 'no one doubts that the biological phenomena presented by the human body, may be organized into a knowledge having the definiteness which constitutes it scientific, in the understood sense of that word.'[14] Thus although in societies 'causes and effects are related in ways so involved that prevision is often impossible',[15] Spencer argued that the relationship between history and sociology paralleled that between an individual's biography and his physiology:

The kind of relation which the sayings and doings that make up the ordinary account of a man's life, bear to an account of his bodily and mental evolution, structural and functional, is like the kind of relation borne by that narrative of a nation's actions and fortunes its historian gives us, to a description of its institutions, regulative and operative, and the ways in which their structures and functions have gradually established themselves.[16]

Not only were sociological laws of the same epistemic status as those of biology, but society also exhibited a process of evolution from simplicity to complexity, from the undifferentiated to the differentiated, and from the independence of its parts to their integration, analogous to that to be found in the animal kingdom. And as each of its parts became more fully integrated they gradually assumed more and more specialized functions, just as the organs of an animal become more specialized with its greater complexity. Moreover, it should be noted that for Spencer this comparison between society and an organism dealt 'not with a figurative resemblance but a fundamental parallelism.'[17]

Spencer argued that there were five points of analogy between a society and an organism. In the first place, they both 'conspicuously

---

[14] Id., *The Study of Sociology* (1873; 15th edn., London, 1889), 57.
[15] Ibid. 53.   [16] Ibid. 58.   [17] Ibid. 328.

exhibit augmentation in mass', in other words they both undergo a process of growth.[18] Secondly, this increase in size is accompanied by the development of structure in terms of the multiplication and differentiation of parts: 'while at first so simple in structure as to be considered structureless, they assume, in the course of their growth, a continually increasing complexity of structure.'[19] Thirdly, 'the progressive differentiation of structures is accompanied by the progressive differentiation of functions.'[20] The differentiation of parts follows from the diversity of functions they perform, so that they 'grow into unlike organs having unlike duties.' Fourthly, in both societies and organisms, evolution establishes 'not differences simply, but definitely connected differences—differences such that each makes the other possible.' The mutual dependence of parts to which this gives rise is expressed in the division of labour,

that which in the society, as in the animal, makes it a living whole. Scarcely can I emphasize sufficiently the truth that in respect of this fundamental trait, a social organism and an individual organism are entirely alike.[21]

Finally, the life of the aggregate can immensely exceed that of its components; the

life and development of a society is independent of, and far more prolonged than the development of any of its component units; who are severally born, grow, work, reproduce, and die, while the body politic composed of them survives generation after generation, increasing in mass, completeness of structure, and functional activity.[22]

From the standpoint of Spencer's Individualism, the most important of these parallels was that between the differentiation of social structure and the tendency of the organs of the body to become increasingly specialized. Peel has argued that 'differentiation, specialization, the division of labour come about because they are more adaptive', but this is to confuse process with cause.[23] In adapting itself to the environment the organism does take on an increasingly complex structure, but the reason why this structure develops is not that it is more adaptive but because homogeneous structures are inherently unstable. It was demonstrated in the second chapter that Spencer believed that all aggregates are subject to the Law of the Instability of the Homogeneous,

[18] Id., *The Principles of Sociology*, i. (London, 1876), 467.
[19] Id., 'The Social Organism', in id., *Essays*, i (London, 1868), 391.
[20] Id., *Principles of Sociology*, i. 468.   [21] Ibid. 470.
[22] Id., 'Social Organism', 392.   [23] Peel, *Herbert Spencer*, 139.

and social aggregates are no exception to this law: 'the social mass, homogeneous when minute, habitually gains in heterogeneity along with each increment of growth; and to reach great size must acquire great heterogeneity.'[24] This differentiation of structure 'cannot occur without changes of function',[25] for in both biological and social organisms,

vitality increases as the functions become specialized. In either case, before there exist variously adapted structures for performing unlike actions, these are ill-performed . . . But along with advance of organization, every part, more limited in its office, performs its office better . . . each aids all and all aid each with increasing efficiency; and the total activity we call life, individual or national, augments.[26]

In other words, the efficient co-operation of the parts of the social organism demands that they obey the law of increased specialization of function. As will now be demonstrated, this aspect of the conception of the social organism placed a limitation on the sphere of State action by stressing the progressive specialization of functions of the various parts of the organism.

According to Spencer the most important differentiation between the parts of any organism is that between its inner and outer organs. The external parts of the organism are 'those which deal with environing existences—prey, enemies, etc.', while the internal parts are those which 'utilize for the benefit of the entire body the nutritious substances which the external parts have secured.'[27] As a theory of social structure and function this conception was given its clearest and most concise statement in the course of Spencer's essay on 'Specialized Administration', in which he asserted that 'the primary differentiation in organic structures . . . is the differentiation between outer and inner parts—the parts which hold direct converse with the environment and those which do not hold direct converse with the environment.'[28] What Spencer appears to have had in mind by this distinction was a division between those organs which enabled the individual organism to defend itself or to acquire food and those internal organs which provided its various parts with nutrient. In any organism, whether biological or social, there had to be both a system regulation or control and a system which provided the diverse organs with the means of 'sustenation'. In addition, once these inner and outer systems had been marked off a third system developed, 'lying between the two and facilitating their co-operation.

---

[24] Spencer, *Principles of Sociology*, i. 489.
[25] Ibid. 504.   [26] Ibid. 508–9.   [27] Ibid. 511.
[28] Id., 'Specialized Administration', 131.

Mutual dependence of the primarily contrasted parts, implies intermediation; and in proportion as they respectively develop, the apparatus for the exchange of products and of influences must develop too.' In other words, some means was also required of distributing the nutrient produced by the organs of sustenation.

Spencer distinguished, in sociological terms, between the regulating system of society, of which the State was part, and between systems of production and distribution. The sustaining (or producing) system consisted of those parts 'carrying on alimentation in a living body and the parts carrying on productive industries in the body politic.' These parts of the social organism were internally differentiated according to certain laws. For example, differences in the organic or inorganic environment initiated differences of occupation; a coal-mining industry could only develop where there were deposits of coal, or a shipbuilding industry where there was access to the sea as well as to supplies of iron. The industrial system, like the digestive system of an individual organism.

takes on activities and correlative structures determined by the animals, minerals and vegetals, with which its working population are in contact; and . . . industrial specialisations in parts of its population are determined by differences, organic and inorganic, in the local products those parts have to deal with.[29]

These industrial structures of society were able to 'extend themselves without reference to political divisions, great or little', and hence could overrun parish, county, or even national boundaries.

In any but the simplest social organisms, the diversity of the process of production creates the need for a system of distribution. The 'distributing system' means, in the first instance, the physical infrastructure like roads, railways, and canals which carry people and commodities, but it can also mean the physical movements along these channels of communication as well as the 'circulating currents themselves'.[30] The commodities which circulate throughout the social system correspond to the nutritive fluid of animal organisms, and just as the organs of body take from the blood certain elements for their sustenation and return to it the particular elements which they produce, so the physical processes of the industrial structure operate on the same principles. Each industry 'allowing various materials to pass through its streets untouched, takes out of the mixed current those it is fitted to act upon; and throws into the

[29] Id., *Principles of Sociology*, i. 523.   [30] Ibid. 533.   [31] Ibid. 535.

circulating stock of things . . . the articles it has prepared for general consumption.'[31] Furthermore, competition occurs between the various organs, both social and biological, so that although indirectly they are all mutually dependent 'yet, directly, each is antagonistic to the rest.' They are in an antagonistic relationship since they 'both depend for their existence on a common stock of produce.'[32] Moreover, the ability of an industry to remove items from the circulating stock of commodities will depend on its state of activity since the competition between the organs causes 'high nutrition and growth of parts called into greatest activity by the requirements of the rest.'[33]

The third differentiation with respect to function is the regulating system. Whereas the alimentary systems of animals and societies are 'developed into fitness for dealing with substances, organic or inorganic, used for sustenation', the regulating and expending systems (nervo-motor in animals and governmental–military in societies) 'are developed into fitness for dealing with surrounding organisms, individual or social—other animals to be caught or escaped from, hostile societies to be conquered or resisted.'[34] In consequence, society 'has a set of structures fitting it to act upon its environment—appliances for attack and defence, armies, navies, fortified and garrisoned places' which correspond to the external parts of the organism, and governmental structures owe their origin and efficiency to wars between societies.[35]

Whereas in the earliest stages of society the governmental or military structure is not clearly distinguished from the rest of society, since 'the army is simply the mobilized society and the society is the quiescent army',[36] social evolution divides the regulating system from the industrial process and at the same time differentiates it into two separate and distinct systems. This follows from the general law of organization that 'distinct duties entail distinct structures.' In the case of the external organs of the social organism, 'success in conflicts with other societies implies quickness, combination and special adjustment to ever-varying circumstances' which in turn requires a 'centralized agency which is instantly obeyed.'[37] The outer parts, like those of the individual, are under rigorous central control since they 'must be capable of prompt combination; and that their actions may be quickly combined to meet each exigency as it arises, they must be completely subordinated to a

---

[32] Id., 'Specialized Administration', 139.   [33] Id., *Principles of Sociology*, i. 536.
[34] Ibid. 539.   [35] Id., 'Specialized Administration', 138.
[36] Id., *The Man versus The State*, ed. D. G. Macrae (1884; Harmondsworth, 1969), 114.
[37] Id., *Principles of Sociology*, i. 562.

supreme executive power—armies and navies must be despotically controlled.'[38]

On the other hand, the industrial organization of society requires no 'quick, special and exact adaptations . . . but only a general proportion and tolerable order among actions which are not precise in their beginnings, amounts or endings.'[39] The 'comparatively uniform' activity of the industrial system produces a regulating system which is very different to the centralized and hierarchical organization of the State. Like the digestive or visceral system of an individual, the industrial system functions according to its own controlling mechanism which provides manufacturers and the manufacturing centres with spurs or checks to production. 'Partly by direct orders from distributors and partly by indirect indications furnished by the market reports throughout the kingdom, they are prompted to secrete actively or to diminish their rates of secretion.' It might seem as if at this point Spencer had pre-empted the Hayekian idea that the price mechanism is essentially a system for conveying information, but it is apparent that the system of control he has in mind is rather the messages which 'from hour to hour . . . pass between all the chief provincial towns, as well as between each of them and London; from hour to hour prices are adjusted, supplies are ordered hither or thither, and capital is drafted from place to place, according as there is greater or less need for it.'[40] As this passage makes evident, Spencer thought adjustments in prices were the consequences of the transfer of information, not themselves the means of its transfer.

As a result of the process of functional and structural differentiation, the industrial system has become divorced from the governmental organization, and whereas in the primitive societies 'industrial organization is ruled by the chief', in the more advanced stages of civilization industry 'has evolved for itself a substantially independent control.'[41] The upshot of this process of development is a specialization of the State's functions:

There is now no fixing of prices by the State, no prescribing of methods. Subject to but slight hindrance from a few licenses, citizens adopt what occupations they please. The amounts grown and manufactured, imported and exported, are unregulated by laws; improvements are not enforced nor bad processes legislatively interdicted; but men, carrying on their business as they think best, are

---

[38] Id., 'Specialized Administration', 140.
[40] Id., 'Specialized Administration', 140–1.
[39] Id., *Principles of Sociology*, i. 560.
[41] Id., *Principles of Sociology*, i. 565.

simply subject to the legal restraints that they should fulfil their contracts and not aggress upon their neighbours.[42]   ·

It follows that industrial production can be conducted without inter-ference from the executive centre which controls the external organs, with the single exception of the 'one all-essential influence which these higher centres exercise over the industrial activities—a restraining influence which prevents aggression direct and indirect.'[43] In order for the industrial process to function correctly it is necessary that the materials exhausted in work and waste shall be replaced, and 'securing this is nothing less than securing fulfilment of contract.' An organ which adequately performs its function but which is not repaid in blood will dwindle causing great damage to the organism itself; similarly, 'an industrial centre which has made and sent out its special commodities, must decay.' Since this is the only aspect of the industrial system which is not self-regulating, the executive centre must also concern itself with the protection of individual rights and especially with ensuring the fulfilment of contracts in addition to the function of defending the social organism against external aggressors. Spencer claimed that 'far from contending for a *laissez-faire* policy in the sense which the phrase commonly suggests, I have contended for a more active control of the kind distinguishable as negatively regulative.'[44] In particular the legal system was in need of radical overhaul to improve its efficiency.

Thus, as a result of the process of evolution, the State's functions become more specialized and more narrowly focused. Despite the State having attempted in earlier periods of history to regulate the systems of production and distribution, with the increased differentiation and structuration of the social organism it came to specialize in those functions which it was uniquely placed to perform. In other words, the State was limited to securing the conditions under which each citizen was enabled to receive the full benefit of his character and activities, subject only to the limitations necessarily imposed by the presence of fellow-citizens having like claims. Spencer called this function 'negative regulation', which aimed to protect 'each individual against others', and which comprised the administration of justice, the enforcement of contracts, and defence against aggression by other States. In the higher social organisms the function of the State was merely to ensure that there was no interference with the fundamental laws of life. For it to have performed any other function would be an encroachment on the

---

[42] Ibid.   [43] Id., 'Specialized Administration', 141.   [44] Ibid. 167.

'office' of some other social structure, and would lead to inefficiency in the co-operation and co-ordination of the diverse organs of society. This was merely a specific instance of the general law, 'universally illustrated by organizations of every kind' that 'in proportion as there is to be efficiency, there must be specialization, both of structure and function—specialization which, of necessity, implies accompanying limitation.'[45]

Spencer argued that in claiming that the social organism analogy supported positive regulation by the State, Huxley had failed to grasp the point that the specialization of function of an organ entailed a corresponding limitation of its sphere of activity, so that in advanced social organisms the State performed negatively regulative functions only. Morever, contrary to Coser's claim, Spencer's use of the organic analogy was not a 'more rigorous' application of it than is to be found in Comte's writings. In explicit repudiation of Comte's conception of society constituting a collectivity, Spencer insisted that 'there exists no analogies between the body politic and a living body save those necessitated by that mutual dependence of parts which they display in common.'[46] This argument against the Comtean conception of the social organism was reinforced by the most significant disanalogy between a biological organism and a social organism which Spencer acknowledged. He made the assumption that although the social organism could display a mutual dependence of parts and a subdivision of functions, this did not extend to the kind of differentiation 'by which one part becomes an organ of feeling and thought, while other parts became insensitive.'[47] While in a biological organism consciousness is concentrated in a small part of the aggregate, in the social organism it is diffused throughout the aggregate and 'all units possess the capacity for happiness and misery, if not in equal degrees, still at least in degrees that approximate.' This 'cardinal difference' between biological and social organisms was such that it 'entirely changes the ends to be pursued.'[48] Since Spencer took a utilitarian view of ethics, the capacity of all members of the organism to experience pleasure and pain was a fact of great moral significance.[49] Since the social organism itself lacked a 'sensorium', and was therefore incapable of states of consciousness, whether pleasant or unpleasant, it followed that

---

[45] Ibid. 168. [46] Id., *Principles of Sociology*, i. 613. [47] Ibid. 478.
[48] Id. 'Specialized Administration', 138.
[49] Spencer's utilitarianism is discussed in greater detail in Ch. 6.

the welfare of the aggregate, considered apart from that of the units, is not an end to be sought. The society exists for the benefit of its members; not its members for the benefit of society.

Despite the great efforts made for the prosperity of the body politic,

the claims of the body politic are nothing in themselves, and become something only in so far as they embody the claims of component individuals.

Spencer's belief that the social organism was incapable of experiencing pleasure or pain, and that therefore it possessed moral significance only as a means to the happiness of its members, indicates the misconception in Wiltshire's remark that 'Spencer, who numbered himself among progressive thinkers, adopted an analogy the subsequent applications of which led directly to Fascism, in Benito Mussolini's literally "corporate" state.'[50] Nothing could be further from Spencer's own understanding of the analogy he drew than the claim that society is everything and the individual nothing.[51]

In addition to the argument from the differentiation of social structure, Spencer also attempted to give a social scientific foundation for his Individualism by insisting on the almost incomprehensible complexity of the social system. This line of argument displayed the same bipolarity of the liberalism and conservatism which was characteristic of many Individualist theories. On the one hand, it suggested that market mechanisms were capable of spontaneously producing social organization and hence that the State's role need only be the strictly limited one of administering justice and ensuring that contracts were respected. One the other hand, the emphasis on the complexity of the relations among the parts of the social aggregate had the effect of placing the Individualists in the company of those thinkers, predominantly conservative, who have argued that society is an organism of incomprehensible complexity and that it is beyond the power of governments or of any other human agency to produce any fundamental alteration in its constitution.

In Spencer's view the basis of the industrial order was spontaneous voluntary co-operation, not the hierarchical system of command which is characteristic of the external organs, and he gave expression to a sense

---

[50] Wiltshire, *Herbert Spencer*, 229.

[51] As C. W. Saleeby pointed out in a slim volume on *Sociology* (London, n.d. [1906]), 44–5: 'the State has no consciousness of its own and therefore the welfare of the State never means more or other than the welfare of the citizens . . . This assertion . . . is of the very first importance because it is essentially a democratic assertion.'

of wonder that social order should emerge unplanned from the self-interested actions of a multitude of individuals:

The world-wide transactions conducted in merchant's offices, the rush of traffic filling our streets, the retail distributing system which brings everything in easy reach and delivers the necessaries of daily life to our doors, are not of government origin. All these are the results of the spontaneous activities of citizens, separate or grouped. Nay, to these spontaneous activities Governments owe the very means of performing their duties. Divest the political machinery of all the aids which Science and Art have yielded it—leave it those only which State-officials have invented; and its functions would cease. The very language in which its laws are registered and the orders of its agents daily given, is an instrument not in the remotest degree due to the legislator; but is one which had unawares grown up during men's intercourse while pursuing their personal satisfactions.[52]

It has been the spontaneous co-operation of individuals which has done much more than governmental agencies to promote the cause of social development, whether the progress concerned has been from wigwams to houses or the formation of complex trading networks.

Furthermore, Spencer argued, 'this spontaneously formed social organisation is so bound together that you cannot act on one part without acting more or less on all parts.'[53] It also follows from this claim that society is so constituted that an attempt to interfere with the spontaneous order at a particular point will have repercussions throughout the social system, and because of the complexity of the system these will be impossible to predict. Spencer gave expression to this idea in a passage in the *Study of Sociology* of inspired comedy in which he likened the action of the legislator to the attempts of someone to flatten a buckled metal plate:

You see that this wrought-iron plate is not quite flat: it sticks up a little here towards the left—'cockles' as we say. How shall we flatten it? Obviously, you reply, by hitting down on the part that is prominent. Well, here is a hammer, and I give the plate a blow as you advise. Harder you say. Still no effect. Another stroke? Well, there is one, and another, and another. The prominence remains,

---

[52] Spencer, *The Man versus The State*, 134–5. It should be noted that the notion of spontaneous order has recently been revived in defence of Individualism by F. A. Hayek. In discussing his use of the notion, Hayek has remarked that 'very complex orders, comprising more particular facts than any brain could ascertain or manipulate, can be brought about only through forces inducing the formation of spontaneous orders.' (Hayek, *Law, Legislation, and Liberty* (London, 1973), i. 38.) Society is just such a spontaneous order. This is exactly the same idea as Spencer expresses in the passage just quoted, although Hayek does not acknowledge Spencer's influence, at least in the work referred to.   [53] Spencer, *The Man versus The State*, 135.

you see: the evil is as great as ever—greater indeed. But this is not all. Look at the warp which the plate has got near the opposite edge. Where it was flat before it is now curved. A pretty bungle we have made of it . . . Is humanity more readily straightened than an iron plate?[54]

The difficulty from the legislator's point of view is that 'in proportion as an aggregate is complex, the effects wrought by an incident force become more multitudinous, confused and incalculable, and that a society is of all kinds of aggregates the kind most difficult to affect in an intended way and not in unintended ways.'[55] It should be clear, therefore, that the point concerning the impossibility of a piece of legislation producing the intended outcome is simply an application of the Law of Multiplicity of Effects which was examined in the second chapter. Since any incident force, in this case the legislative measure, is likely to be the cause of perturbations throughout the entire social organism it is impossible to predict the total effect it will produce. We can be sure, however, that it is likely to be the seat of many unintended adjustments throughout the structure of society and that these are likely to defeat its initial purpose.

While Spencer's philosophical justification for this view was not widely invoked, the notion that misguided 'socialistic' legislation stemmed from a failure to study its ultimate rather than the immediate effects become part of the stock of Individualist argument. Bruce Smith, for example, alleged that while the tendency towards socialism was in part due to the cupidity of the lower classes,

the over-legislation of the present day is equally the outcome of misconception as to results—miscalculations, as it were, of political arithmetic arising from the . . . habit of regarding the immediate effects of a statute, while ignoring, or at least neglecting to give due consideration to, those which are less easily discerned.[56]

Mackay singled out the Poor Law as proof of the theory that 'even if benefit is derived from a socialistic law in one direction, it is counter-balanced by unexpected evils which arise in another direction' since 'in ministering to the wants of the body' it had done much 'to injure the character of the poor.'[57] Government action would always produce

---

[54] Id., *Study of Sociology*, 270–1.   [55] Ibid. 270.

[56] [A.] B. Smith, *Liberty and Liberalism*, (London, 1887), 320.

[57] T. D. Mackay, 'The Joining of Issues', *Economic Review*, 1 (1891), 195. Spencer's work was also cited in support of the contention that 'State-meddling' would have unpredictable effects by H. S. Constable, *The Fallacies and Follies of Socialist Radicalism Exposed* (London, 1895), 28.

unintended effects which would disturb the delicate social mechanism which was the growth of ages; although why it should be that the unintended effects would always produce undesirable consequences was never clearly demonstrated.

The Individualists argued that because the relations of cause and effect in society could not be determined with any precision, the best that organized knowledge could do was to teach willing submission to the blind forces of evolution. Even if legislators were educated in genuinely scientific ways of thinking about society (and Spencer was critical of classical education for failing to provide such knowledge) the complexity of society was such that they could not be certain of the outcome of a proposed measure. The legislator should be prepared to acknowledge his ignorance and be prepared to forgo his meddling legislation on the grounds that what he does not understand is best left alone. This Burkean sense of organicism was employed by Wordsworth Donisthorpe who remarked that since

the science of society has met with general acceptance of late years . . . (thanks chiefly to Mr Spencer) even the most impatient reformers recognize the fact that the State is an organism and not an artificial structure to be pulled to pieces and put together on a new model whenever it pleases the effective majority to do so.[58]

The idea that society was a complex, natural growth which the reformer should let alone was also present in a passage from one of Leslie Stephen's works which demonstrates the degree to which the Individualists had departed from the Benthamism they professed to defend:

Society is not a mere aggregate of independent atoms, but a complex living organism. However faulty may be its operations, it represents a system worked out by the experience of generations. Its structure has been developed by the wants of mankind; the principles on which it rests have been felt out, not reasoned out; and though it is undoubtedly in need of constant improvement . . . genuine reform is only possible by a careful examination of the functions discharged by its various constituent parts and a provision for wants by which their constitution has been actually, if unconsciously, determined. The rash reformers, who undertake to cut and carve and remould in obedience to some *a priori* guesses, or in wrath provoked by real grievances, are managing it at the risk of vital injury.[59]

---

[58] W. Donisthorpe, 'The Limits of Liberty', in T. D. Mackay (ed.), *A Plea for Liberty* (London, 1891), 67.

[59] L. Stephen, *The Life of Henry Fawcett* (1885; 3rd edn., London, 1886), 150–1. See also id., *The Science of Ethics* (London, 1882), 112 f. which describes social organization in terms reminiscent of Spencer: 'The society, like the individual, has its organs of self-defence and nutrition, its apparatus corresponding to the brain, the stomach, and so forth, though it would be absurd to press the analogy too far.'

Stephen's distinction between rash reformers and those who have conducted a careful examination of the social organism might appear to support Jones's contention, quoted above, that Stephen had adapted organicism to a liberal purpose. However, it is significant in the light of this passage that in another work Stephen singled out Malthus as a leading example of the kind of thinker which 'argued that society formed a complex organism, whose diseases should be considered physiologically, their causes explained, and the appropriate remedies considered in all their bearings.'[60] It would seem, therefore, that the kind of social reform Stephen had in mind was not that promoted by New Radicals.

Stephen was unusual among the empirical Individualists in making extensive use of the social organism conception, since their ranks included some of the most incisive critics, most notably Henry Sidgwick and the Earl of Pembroke, of the attempt to ground Individualism on this conception. Nevertheless, it is significant in this regard that neither of these critics suggested that Spencer had undermined Individualism by his use of the organic conception of society. Pembroke, for example, believed the organic analogy to have demonstrated that the industrial and trading (i.e. nutritive) functions of society were best promoted by the self-interested activities of individuals, but the 'functions about which there is most dispute are precisely those in which the analogy helps us little, if at all.' Just as there were physiological functions which 'lie between those that are purely self-working, and those that are always directed by the brain and nerves' and with which 'the brain and nerves may be said to interfere, or not according to the circumstances of the particular case', so there were social functions which were similarly hybrid. National education was just such an example, in part self-working but also in need of external regulation.[61] Sidgwick accepted that Spencer had identified important structural parallels between societies and organisms, but he also believed that there were disanalogies of equal significance.[62] Since he subjected most of the Spencerian philosophy to sustained and detailed criticism, he might have been expected to have highlighted any potential inconsistencies between Spencer's political views and his concept of the social organ-

---

[60] Id., 'The Sphere of Political Economy' in id., *Social Rights and Duties* (London, 1896), i. 119.

[61] G. R. C. Herbert, 13th Earl of Pembroke, 'Liberty and Socialism', in id., *Political Letters and Speeches* (London, 1896), 211 ff.

[62] H. Sidgwick, 'The Relation of Ethics to Sociology', in id., *Miscellaneous Essays and Addresses* (London, 1904), 253 ff.

ism. But the fact that neither he nor Pembroke criticized Spencer's organic conception of society on these grounds lends prima facie support to the contention of this chapter that, correctly understood, the social organism conception and Individualism did not necessarily come into conflict.

III. Individualism and Group Welfare

Spencer's use of the social organism analogy drew on the Burkean and structural categories identified earlier, and at no point carried the implication that society might possess a will, interests, or consciousness distinct from that of its individual members. Nevertheless, this latter conception of society as a collectivity was employed in defence of Individualism by Wordsworth Donisthorpe. Although he lauded Spencer for having 'contributed more to the scientific study of society than any other thinker', it is obvious that Donisthorpe had completely misunderstood the nature of the analogy which Spencer drew since his writings make no reference to the structural and functional aspects of Spencerian sociology.[63] Instead, Donisthorpe's own organic conception owed far more to the third sense of organicism, in the sense of imputing a group will and a group purpose to society, than it did to Spencer's limited analogy.

Donisthorpe's political theory also suffered from a lack of rigour and frequent ambiguities in terminology; for example, he referred variously to the organic nature of the 'State', of 'society', and of the 'group'. These terms may be treated as rough synonyms, but to confuse matters Donisthorpe also used the term 'State' in a narrower sense to mean the machinery of government. He also made considerable use of an ambiguity in the term 'law', as meaning both statute and physical regularity, again without keeping these senses clearly distinct. Yet despite Donisthorpe's obvious shortcomings as a political thinker, his work deserves consideration since he was described by no less an authority than T. H. Huxley as an 'acute thinker and vigorous writer . . . whose work on Individualism is at once piquant, learned, and thorough-going.'[64]

---

[63] W. Donisthorpe, *Individualism: A System of Politics* (London, 1889), p. v.

[64] T. H. Huxley, 'Government: Anarchy or Regulation?', *Nineteenth Century*, 27 (1890), 860.

Donisthorpe's use of the organic conception of society involved both the Burkean and collectivist senses of organicism which we have identified. The emphasis which Donisthorpe placed on the necessary slowness of social change has already been noted in this chapter, but he also believed in the existence of a group will or purpose. To describe society as an organism, Donisthorpe believed, meant that it was 'a whole not to be expressed in terms of its component parts, any more than a man can be expressed in terms of the cells of which he is composed.'[65] Furthermore, just as an individual man has a consciousness which cannot be reduced to those of the cells of his body, it followed from this conception that there was a group consciousness and a group will. Unlike Spencer, Donisthorpe believed that it was possible to conceive of the State possessing a consciousness which was not that of its members, and it was

absolutely essential to conceive of the group or state as acting in accordance with the motives of sympathy or antipathy; such acts taking the form of charity, compensation or reward in the one case, and of spoilation, compulsory restitution, or punishment in the other.[66]

Donisthorpe identified the group will with the will of the sovereign as expressed by the classical theory of sovereignty. In *The Man versus the State*, Spencer had criticized Hobbes and Austin for affirming the 'unlimited authority' of the sovereign, a doctrine which had laid the foundation for a theory of majoritarian democracy lacking the limitations on political power imposed by natural rights. Donisthorpe argued, on the contrary,

all that Hobbes and Austin contend is, that what the group wills, it does, and that those members who happen to be in line with the group act may be called the effective majority. No-one pretends that any determinate person, or number of persons, ever did have or could have the making of the group will.[67]

The 'effective majority' is the section of society which wills in accordance with the group will and this is to be distinguished from the mere numerical majority. Although the effective majority may be outnumbered, it nevertheless possesses a superiority of force. 'Force in the form of wealth, intellectual force, moral force, and many other and derivative and combined forces, pour into the common stream . . . and the resultant of these and other forces is the group-will.'[68] The State is

---

[65] Donisthorpe, *Individualism*, 276.
[66] Ibid. 292.   [67] Ibid. 275–6.   [68] Ibid. 275.

the embodiment of the effective majority—the *force majeure*—of the country and this is the reason why Hobbes described its power as absolute.

Spencer had also challenged the classical theory of sovereignty because he could find no 'assignable warrant' for the unlimited power of the sovereign, but Donisthorpe contended that it was fruitless to search for the justification of the authority of the State. No one would think to ask

by what particular virtue or authority or warrant or justification, the greater overcomes the less. And yet when the subject of the inquiry is not the organism a human being, but the organism a society, [Spencer] searches everywhere for an 'assignable warrant' and bitterly complains that Austin while admitting that a government is actuated by group-morality furnishes none.[69]

Donisthorpe also thought that it was a further implication of his theory that it would be folly to attempt to set any limit on the State's powers *ab extra*, by institutional means:

To contend that the state, when it had once made up its mind, rightly or wrongly, to act in such or such a way, is subject to restraints is to say that which has no meaning. The group will, once made up, necessarily manifests itself in action, and it is no more subject to restraints from without than is the will of a single human being.[70]

The question which Spencer ought to have addressed concerned the criterion according to which the group acts were to be considered good or bad, right or wrong. On Donisthorpe's account, there could only be one answer to this question: 'the welfare of the group. This is the warrant, this the justification.'[71] The welfare of the group was to be distinguished from that of its members in the same way that the group will was to be distinguished from the majority will:

We are not even bound to show that all the units of the group are benefited by the operation of the law; nor that the majority of the individuals are benefited; nor that *any* of the individuals are benefited. It is true there are powerful forces tending to bring about coincidence between the will of states and the wills of their component units, but this may be regarded for the present purposes as accidental.[72]

Donisthorpe's version of the social organism analogy had arrived at a conception of society or the social group as a collectivity, having a consciousness, will, and purpose independent of that of its members.

[69] Ibid.   [70] Ibid. 261.   [71] Ibid. 276.   [72] Ibid. 277.

Such a conception was obviously a far cry from that expounded by Spencer, who had attempted to avoid the pitfalls of collectivism by arguing that the analogy broke down on these very points. Thus Donisthorpe was confronted with the problem of establishing a defence of an individualist social order from a basis which apparently undermined his own case.

The reconciliation between organicism and individualism was achieved by Donisthorpe's conception of the kinds of laws which were conducive to the group welfare and which were therefore willed by the group will. It is important to recognize in this context that Donisthorpe used the word 'law' in two very different senses. In the first place, 'out of deference for popular usage' he employed the term to refer to 'so-called State laws, statutes, decrees, edicts etc.' By contrast, law in the 'nomological sense' meant the statement of 'an invariable sequence of which the antecedent is an act of an individual citizen or individual citizens and the consequent is the act of the group or state.'[73] The notion of law in the nomological sense referred to a number of 'middle principles or maxims' which were based on experience and confirmed by induction. In the realm of individual morality, for example, we are guided by moral principles, not because they are deductions from a higher law, but because 'we have found them trustworthy a thousand times, and our parents and friends have trusted them too. Do not lie. Do not steal. Do not hurt your neighbour's feelings without cause. And why not? Because, as a general rule, it will not pay.'[74] The principles of morality were like the prudential Hobbesian 'laws of nature'. The same applied to 'group morals or state laws' as to individual morality. We must abandon all hope of deducing good laws from 'high general principles' and instead must rest content with 'these middle principles which originate in experience and are verified by experience. And we must search for these middle principles by observing the tendency of civilization.'[75] These middle principles are discovered by the science Donisthorpe called nomology which dealt with the 'true statical laws which operate in societies, of their tendency, and of the dynamical laws of their change and development.'[76] Nomological laws, which are 'true laws in the scientific sense', were to be discovered by 'making inductions from the minor social rules which have stood the test of time' and not by deduction from first principles.[77]

---

[73] Ibid. 283.   [74] Id., 'The Limits of Liberty', 75.
[75] Ibid.   [76] Id., Individualism, 304.   [77] Ibid. 284.

Donisthorpe expressed the relationship between law in the nomological sense and law in the sense of statute in the following terms:

The invariable sequences which actually tend to hold good at any given time in any country, may be called the statical laws or internal group-morals of that particular State at that stage of its development. The laws as expressed are necessarily but imperfect and often distorted reflections of these true laws, the distortion being due not only to imperfect expression and the inadequacy of language but more especially to the false generalisation of law-makers of one sort or another.[78]

Nomology did not only study the statical laws of the social organism but also the dynamical laws of their development:

It must not be supposed that the empire of the individual was defined once and for all by some social compact, or that it has come to maturity at some past time, and is now definite and unalterable. On the contrary, it is still in a state of growth, like all other products of evolution.[79]

Donisthorpe observed that some laws were repealed or ceased to be operative, and the reason for this was to be found in the fact that 'tribes whose laws conduce to the well-being of the race necessarily outlive and thrust out of existence those tribes whose laws, however apparently reasonable or just, do not conduce to the group-welfare.'[80] While the welfare of the group was not the cause of the origin of laws 'it is the cause of their survival—of their present existence.' For example,

the strong man who first deferred to the wish of a weak man was not actuated by solicitude for the well-being of his race. But it was the compatibility of such acts with the well-being of his race which preserved and rendered organic the habit of such acts. Tribes practising such acts predominated by elbowing other tribes out of existence, and by perpetuating a race of men actuated by like promptings.[81]

If the members of a tribe were prepared to compromise over their self-seeking claims they would experience fewer internal conflicts, and as a result force would be greatly economized. Tribes who could channel their energies outwards into external defence or aggression, rather than being expended in internecine warfare, would tend to predominate and the 'State whose members practised the rule would tend to survive.'[82]

Donisthorpe appears to have believed that the process of natural selection operated with regard to groups or societies rather than to

---

[78] Ibid. 270.   [79] Id., *Law in a Free State* (London, 1895), 18–19.
[80] Id., *Individualism*, 286.   [81] Ibid. 278.   [82] Ibid. 280.

individuals. In the struggle for existence it was 'the superior social organisation which tends to survive, and not necessarily that of the individual type of man.'[83] The superior social organisms were those which had adopted the laws most conducive to the group welfare and a pattern or tendency could be observed in the development of civilization, in which one conception of justice came to prevail over its rival. Donisthorpe argued that justice consisted of two distinct and antagonistic principles: the first had its origin in self-interest and involved a 'spirit of compromise', expressed both by the willingness of individuals to make contracts with each other, and in the preparedness of the strong to defer to the wishes of the weak. The other principle had its origin in parental love and denoted 'those group interferences between individual citizens which aim at more or less equalising the conditions of the competition.'[84] The former principle was the principle of individualism, while the latter was the principle of socialism. The tendency of history was for justice as 'selfish compromise' to finally 'absorb the whole field of law. Altruism tends to become wholly voluntary and law to become wholly based on average individual advantage and implied voluntary contract. Thus scientific anarchy is shown to be the end towards which society is moving.'[85] In the anarchic state which is the goal of history, 'voluntary association would practically effect what the state does now in all that is necessary, and therefore good' but for the time being some degree of State interference was indispensable and therefore had to be tolerated. The final result 'to which we shall ever approximate, but never attain, will be perfect civil liberty, or the greatest liberty which is compatible with the utmost well-being of society as a whole.'[86]

Nevertheless, although the history of civilization was a transition from a socialistic to an anarchic state, the process by which this was brought about was one of slow, evolutionary growth, and to impose a 'more advanced form on an organism not yet ripe for it is not to hasten but to

---

[83] Ibid. 20.

[84] Ibid. 281. Donisthorpe's distinction between the two principles of justice had much in common with Spencer's belief that the 'continuance of every higher species of creature depends on conformity, now to one, now to the other, of two radically opposed principles.' Within the family group the principle of altruism and benevolence is the ruling one; in society in general, however, each adult 'gets benefit in proportion to merit—reward in proportion to desert: merit and desert in each case being understood as the ability to fulfil all the requirements of life.' A mother can show pity on her weak and unsuccessful offspring, but society encourages its failures at its peril. Woe-betide the well-meaning but misguided legislator who seeks to inject the ethics of the family into the social organism. (Spencer, *The Man versus The State*, 137.)

[85] Donisthorpe, *Individualism*, 282.   [86] Ibid. 303.

retard its development.'[87] In regarding the social organism as a natural growth and in emphasizing the consequent slowness of any change affecting it, Donisthorpe had adopted the Burkean aspects of Spencer's organicism, even while ignoring the 'fundamental parallelism' of structure in favour of a conception of society with a will and interests of its own.

While admiring Spencer's contributions to sociology, Donisthorpe also believed that he had vitiated his own 'scientific' insights into the nature of society by attempting to provide Individualism with an alternative justification in terms of natural rights. Due to Spencer's deluded belief 'in abstract justice, as something anterior to society or even to man—something immutable and absolute', the attempt to formulate a natural-rights defence of Individualism resulted in an 'absolutist' demand for the immediate abolition of many of the State's functions.[88] In opposition to this view he argued that it was impossible to settle the functions of the State according to some a priori formula of justice, like the Law of Equal Freedom, since whether or not a particular measure or state function was conducive to the group welfare at any particular stage of its development was something which could be determined only by induction. Although the aim of the legislator was to obtain 'the greatest possible freedom of the individual from state interference, compatible with the well-being of the social organism', the degree of freedom which was possible would vary according to the stage of development which the social organism had reached.[89]

This was not to deny that the science of nomology was incapable of providing any guidance to the legislator in deciding the practical questions of the day. Donisthorpe argued that '[b]y the use of the comparative method, we shall possibly be enabled to detect permanent tendencies which will guide us in predicting the probable limitation of State action among civilised communities in the future.'[90] In the first place, nomology had established that 'as civilisation advances the State tends to throw off one claim after another to interfere with the free action of its members, while at the same time it becomes stronger, more regular, speedier and more certain in performing the functions that remain to it.'[91] Since personal liberty was the outcome of the process of evolution and not its cause, 'as each class and each individual fights for

---

[87] Ibid. 282.
[88] Ibid. 271. Spencer's natural-rights defence of Individualism is examined in Ch. 7.
[89] Ibid. 295.
[90] Id., *Law in a Free State*, 5.   [91] Id., *Individualism*, 300.

his own hand, he will find that the lowest price at which he can obtain his own greatest freedom is in the granting of equal liberty to others in certain departments of activity which experience, and experience alone, can demarcate.'[92] Because the tendency of the times was towards throwing off various forms of State control it followed that 'when we see an agitation for the purpose of adding to the duties of the state, we may reasonably conclude *prima facie* that it is an agitation in the wrong direction.'[93] Moreover, it also followed that 'when we see the State interfering in matters having little in common with what is more and more clearly marked out as its normal province . . . we are again logically justified in presuming that such matters ought to be removed from the domain of state control. Upon those who maintain a contrary opinion must rest the *onus probandi*.'[94] The 'scientific' legislator, as distinguished from the 'rule of thumb' politician, attempted to apply the general principles which had been discovered by nomological social science. As Donisthorpe remarked,

the art of politics is the application of the science of nomology to the concrete . . . Yesterday we were all Free Traders and 'Let Be', to-day we are on the high road to socialism; tomorrow the Fates only know where we shall be. The only cure for the policy of drift is a patient and intelligent study of nomology, whereby middle principles of practical application will be brought to light and the absurd fallacies of the social doctrinaires put to flight for ever.[95]

The social doctrinaires who were to be thus routed included not only socialists and New Radicals but also 'absolute' Individualists like Auberon Herbert and J. H. Levy. However, as the latter pointed out in his response to Donisthorpe's attacks, nomology could provide no criterion for distinguishing between good laws and bad. It simply stated that whatever is, is right, and even appeared to make right identical with might. Although it was undoubtedly true that 'those who wield the *force majeure* can make what laws they like, and can thus confer on themselves any legal rights they choose' it was useless for the purpose of judging law to refer to the law itself.[96] The reason was that

the question at issue is a moral, not a legal one. The frequent sneers at 'right' by which the nineteenth century essayed to show its superiority to the eighteenth, are but a covert attempt to remove morality, or at least justice, from politics, and

---

[92] Ibid. 302.   [93] Ibid. 300.   [94] Ibid.   [95] Ibid. 305.
[96] J. H. Levy, 'Individualism', in E. B. Bax and J. H. Levy, *Socialism and Individualism* (London, n.d. [1904]), 142.

to make the government of man by man, at best, a thing of the expediency of the hour.[97]

Nevertheless, as proof of the general proposition that political disputes are at their most acrimonious between those who are in substantial agreement, Donisthorpe was much closer to Herbert and Levy than he was to the empirical Individualists, and he joined the former in condemning the Poor Law, State education, monopolies, and the Church establishment, and agreed with them on the need to reduce the number of the departments of the State.

Although Donisthorpe claimed he owed his greatest debt to Spencer the sociologist, it is clear that he employed the organic analogy in a manner completely at odds with that to be found in the *Principles of Sociology*. In arguing that there was a group will or group purpose, Donisthorpe had apparently conceded to collectivism the view that society possessed a corporate consciousness and corporate interests. He was able to extricate himself from this compromising position by arguing that since Individualism promoted the group welfare the corporate consciousness of society, which always desires the group welfare, therefore desired an individualistic social order. In other words, rather than relying on an aggregative notion of the common good, which was characteristic of Individualist thinkers as diverse as Spencer and Sidgwick, Donisthorpe defended a policy of non-interference from the standpoint of a corporate conception of the group welfare. This had the neat implication that although Individualism may not have been desired by the majority of Donisthorpe's fellow countrymen, especially the working classes whom he held in such disdain, it was nevertheless uniquely in accordance with the well-being of society and was the object of the group will. Donisthorpe consistently held a low estimation of the capacity of the working class, describing one of his audiences at a Liberty and Property Defence League meeting as 'worms' and regarding the poor as too weak and divided to challenge the propertied effective majority: 'The man who cannot overcome the temptation of a glass of grog when his wife and children have to pay for it with their dinner, is not the man to refuse the gold of the rich to stab his fellow-worker in the

---

[97] Ibid. 142–3. Compare the criticism *Economic Review*, 5 (1895), 275: made by R. R. Marett in 'Review of *Law in a Free State* by Wordsworth Donisthorpe', 'We are not to try to find out *why* State supervision has been relaxed in any given set of cases, in order that we may proceed to consider whether the reason is a good one, and one according to which our own policy may be directed. We are simply to notice *that* it has been relaxed, and forthwith to abandon ourselves to the stream of tendency.'

back.'⁹⁸ Although outnumbered, the Individualist élite willed in accordance with the group will, and were therefore justified in regarding themselves as the effective majority.

IV. Individualist Critics of New Liberal Organicism

The conception of the social organism which Donisthorpe employed in defence of Individualism was far more frequently used by the New Liberal theorists who attempted to demonstrate that the organic conception of society 'seems to admit of more easy applications to the defence of just those very views about the state which Mr. Spencer most dislikes.'⁹⁹ The chief point of the New Liberal criticisms of Spencer was to contend that, had he not been blinded by his Individualism, he would have recognized that the analogy between society and a biological organism went much deeper than the limited structural parallel he had drawn in his sociological writings, and an extensive sphere of State action could be seen to be a necessary corollary of the organic conception of society once it was grasped in its full complexity. The New Liberals did not suggest that the social organism conception and Individualism were incompatible given Spencer's own understanding of the analogy, but instead argued that the organic conception of society could be extended in ways which Spencer himself was reluctant to admit because of his 'out-moded' political views.

In the *Principles of Sociology*, for example, Spencer had argued that one of the most significant disanalogies between social and biological organisms was that the social organism did not possess a corporate consciousness, but Ritchie suggested that it was merely 'his political creed of individualism which leads Mr. Spencer to deny the existence of a social sensorium, and to deny to the social organism the important characteristic of all organisms—the dependence of the parts on the whole.'¹⁰⁰ As J. A. Hobson put the same point, having found society 'a low grade organism without a sensorium' Spencer had made the mistaken assumption that it must always remain so because 'in politics he fell back on the Atomism of the so-called Liberty of a wrongly

---

⁹⁸ Donisthorpe, *Individualism*, 238.

⁹⁹ D. G. Ritchie, *Principles of State Interference* (London, 1891), 22. For a discussion of Ritchie's employment of the organic analogy and its place in New Liberal thought see M. S. Freeden, *The New Liberalism: An Ideology of Social Reform* (Oxford, 1978), 97 ff.

¹⁰⁰ Ritchie, *State Interference*, 17.

conceived individual and of a society composed of a mechanical balance of individual rights.'[101]

This argument amounted to a profound challenge to Spencer's attempt to provide his Individualism with a foundation in social science, since it suggested that there was a greater analogy between society and an organism than he had been prepared to admit; his reluctance to press the organic conception of society to its logical conclusion stemmed only from dubious political motives. Hobson expanded this criticism in *The Crisis of Liberalism* by arguing that Spencer's belief that the organic analogy broke down at certain key points could be questioned in the light of developments in biological thought. The denial that society possessed a corporate consciousness could be answered in two ways. First of all,

the whole evolution of organic life is from forms in which there is no discernible sensorium towards forms which are more distinctly specialised in this regard. If, then, we could find no sensorium in society, we are not therefore entitled to deny its organic nature, but only to conclude that it is as yet a low order of organism.[102]

Secondly, Spencer had mistakenly concentrated only on the physical life of society, but

whatever view we hold about Society on the physical plane as a collection of individual bodies living in some sort of union, it can, I think, be made quite clear that Society is rightly regarded as a moral rational organism in the sense that it has a common psychic life, character, and purpose, which are not to be resolved into the life, character, and purpose of its individual members.[103]

It was a fact, Hobson believed, that the habits of thinking, feeling, and acting together transform the minds of the individual members of a community into a single mind and this was what was meant by the doctrine of the general will.[104]

Further developments in biology also suggested that the individual cell of an organism is closer to an individual member of society than previously had been thought and that it was

a more distinct, a more individual vital unit than was supposed, that it is itself of an organic structure, that it is not physically continuous with other cells, that it performs what may be termed free acts, giving out effort and even exercising choice in movement and in the selection of its food from its environment.[105]

[101] J. A. Hobson, 'Herbert Spencer', *South Place Magazine*, 9 (1904), 52, repr. in *J. A. Hobson: A Reader*, (ed. M. S. Freeden (London, 1988), 63–4.
[102] Id., *The Crisis of Liberalism: New Issues of Democracy* (London, 1909), 72.
[103] Ibid. 73.   [104] Ibid. 76.   [105] Ibid. 71–2.

The findings of modern psychophysics also suggested to Hobson that the specialization of consciousness in the brain is not complete, but that 'some degree of cellular consciousness pervades the body.'[106] Whereas Spencer had argued that the discreteness of individual members of society, and the multiplicity of centres of consciousness, had no sociological counterpart, Hobson argued on the contrary that a biological organism was itself a social mechanism.

Another point of view was expressed by Ritchie, who argued that while Spencer had failed to follow through the true implications of the organic conception of society, in another sense he was guilty of taking it too seriously. He treated the conception as the 'key to all mysteries' rather than as something of merely heuristic value which could help political theory out of the confusions of Individualism. Ritchie also challenged Spencer's view that society was a natural spontaneous order which governments should let alone. The theory, he argued, was impaled on the horns of a dilemma: either government is part of the organic structure of society, in which case it should be left to fight it out with the individual on the principles of natural selection, or it is not part of the organic order and there is some flaw in Spencer's sociology. Yet this dilemma was itself the product of a false dichotomy, Ritchie alleged, for the choice was not simply between society's having been made or its having grown, since 'social organisms differ from other organisms in having the remarkable property of making themselves; and the more developed they are the more consciously do they make themselves.'[107] This aspect of Ritchie's criticism amounted to a radical rejection of the idea that the social structure was itself part of the natural order of things and was therefore beyond human control. It was an affirmation of the ability of human beings to take collective control over their own destiny and to reconstruct society according to some more rational or humane ideal. This was the very opposite of what the social organism analogy meant to Spencer and to the other Individualists, since for them it supported the kind of conservatism which regarded a society of free competition and the minimal State as the inevitable form which civilized societies must take.

Nevertheless, this use of the social organism analogy by the New Liberals was not without its Individualist critics. The most decisive rejections of the organic analogy by Individualist political theorists are to be found in Auberon Herbert's article 'Lost in the Region of Phrases',

---

[106] Ibid. 72.   [107] Ritchie, *State Interference*, 49.

which was part of an exchange with Hobson, and in M. D. O'Brien's book, *The Natural Right to Freedom*.[108] As a good Spencerian, Herbert was careful to distinguish between two different senses of the social organism, and he admitted that there was a 'resemblance . . . between an individual and certain social wholes, in which he is included, and . . . between an organism and its component parts.'[109] The nature of this resemblance was identical to that which Spencer himself had noted, namely

All parts included in wholes have a generic likeness to each other of a certain kind. A brick in a house, a muscle in a body, have each of them relations to their own whole (the house and the body) which may be compared to the relations existing between an individual and the various social bodies in which he is included.[110]

Herbert also followed Spencer in insisting that the disanalogies between an organism and society were almost as important as the analogies. In particular, while in the case of the body the whole is greater than the part since a muscle does not exist 'for its own sake', this is not true of the relationship between the individual and society, since the former is always 'an end in himself'.[111] He was critical of the conception of the society employed by Hobson because it represented 'an attempt to reduce the individual to nothingness, and on the ruins of the individual to exalt and glorify "the social organism".'[112]

Whereas Hobson had argued that the social organism conception established that society possessed something resembling a 'common psychic life', Herbert was equally convinced that society was nothing more or less than the individuals comprising it: 'If a crowd, a town, a nation, is not in each case a collection of individuals—more or less acted upon, it is true, by certain common feelings, more or less possessing certain common interests—what can it be?' Thus, he argued, to contend that

John Smith and Richard Parker are under the influence of the same class of feelings or are engaged in seeking the same ends, . . . does not in any way get rid of the individuals John Smith and Richard Parker, or put in their place a new sort of being made up half of Smith and half of Parker, or—to state the case of the Social Entity even more exactly—made up of some twenty or thirty millions of Smiths and Parkers.[113]

[108] A. Herbert, 'Lost in the Region of Phrases', *Humanitarian*, 14 (1899), 320–30; M. D. O'Brien, *The Natural Right to Freedom* (London, 1893).

[109] Herbert, 'Lost in the Region of Phrases', 324.

[110] Ibid.   [111] Ibid. 325.   [112] Ibid. 321.   [113] Ibid. 323.

The most extreme rejection of the social organism conception by an Individualist was to be found in O'Brien's diatribe against Ritchie's *Principles of State Interference*. His theory could be described, not inaccurately, as a throwback to the pre-sociological views of earlier generations of liberals since O'Brien gave expression to the kind of crude atomistic view of society which many commentators have alleged is characteristic of classical liberal thought:

The Socialist's pet theory is that we all belong to a vague and indistinct entity called 'Society'. The only intelligible meaning of this term, when used in relation to the individual, is—'other people.' 'Society' is so many duplicates of yourself; you cannot, so argues the Socialist, belong to yourself, but you can belong to a crowd of similar 'yous' who cannot belong to themselves![114]

While he rejected the organic conception of society outright, O'Brien's target was not the Spencerian structural analogy but the third sense of organicism which we identified earlier in this chapter, society as a collectivity. O'Brien recognized that to think of society as an organism possessing interests and a conception of the good which were not those of its individual members gave powerful support to socialism. Taking the term 'State' in its widest sense as being synonymous with 'society', O'Brien declared that

strictly speaking there is no such thing as the State . . . All that really exists is the individual surrounded by a number of beings similar to himself . . . The individual is the basis of society; for the social aggregate is simply the unit multiplied.[115]

There was no such thing as a conception of the common good in the organicist sense, and the 'freest possible individual development' was 'the only good *common* to all'.[116]

O'Brien also argued that although it was often claimed that the State was an organism, it was impossible to conceive of society apart from its component units, that terms like 'State', 'Society', and 'Social Organism' were nothing more than useful classificatory metaphors, and he emphasized the same disanalogies identified by Spencer. In the first place, a biological organism possessed physically continuous parts, yet this was precisely what the individual parts of a society were not.[117] Only 'under a system of absolute command and slavish obedience', in which the units of society 'move together like one body' might the organic analogy have any purchase, but the evolution of society was away from

[114] M. D. O'Brien, *Socialism Tested by the Facts* (London, 1892), 202.
[115] Id., *Natural Right to Freedom*, 10.   [116] Ibid. 13.   [117] Ibid. 14.

systems of command and obedience and was towards a regime of individual liberty. Furthermore, the application of the social organism conception was itself vague since it left unanswered a number of vital questions; for example, did all the inhabitants of the earth form a single social organism? Was the British Empire a social organism? And could a voluntary association be described as a social organism? In the absence of any answers to these questions, O'Brien believed that the organic conception of society was fundamentally flawed. Yet in arguing that society was nothing but an aggregation of individuals, O'Brien had failed to distinguish between the conception of the social organism as a collectivity and Spencer's notion that the social organism was an aggregate possessing definite relations which remained comparatively constant while the individuals occupying them changed.

Thus in the criticisms of Spencer made by the New Liberals, and in the Individualists' criticisms of the latter's conception of the organic nature of society, it was never suggested that there was a basic incompatibility between organicism and Individualism. It was generally agreed that on Spencer's understanding of the analogy it certainly did give support to his Individualism. The disputes arose over the New Liberals' attempts to formulate a much closer analogy between society and a biological organism than was possible within the framework of Spencerian organicism. While one side contended that this closer parallel could not be drawn, the other argued that there was no warrant for thinking of society as organic in only the limited sense implied by the structural parallel unless one had already adopted Individualism as a political creed.

V. Conclusion

The conclusion of this chapter is that Spencer was not guilty of having committed the kind of fundamental error of which he has been accused by many commentators. Rather than being unaware of the implications of his own analogy between society and a biological organism, Spencer avoided the collectivist implications of the organic analogy by employing it in a quite limited and specific sense. He may have possessed no more justification for this limited employment of the analogy than a desire to make it consonant with his Individualist political views, but this is a very different point to the accusation that he had failed to realize that his organicism was incompatible with his individualistic politics. As W. H.

Hudson argued, Spencer's Individualism 'so far from being artificially foisted on to the rest of his system . . . grows naturally out of and therefore properly belongs to it—is an organic part of his doctrine of universal evolution.'[118]

Even if we succeed in holding distinct the different senses of organicism, it is also clear that Donisthorpe believed that even the collectivist version of organicism could be made compatible with Individualism. The fact that society possessed a group will and a group purpose seemed to him to present no obstacle to the defence of an individualistic social order, once it was recognized that the common good was best served by a regime of the greatest possible individual liberty compatible with the existence of the social organism. Thus even this sense of organicism could be made to serve Individualist ends.

Furthermore, both Spencer and Donisthorpe shared the Burkean notion of organicism in the sense that they believed that all changes in the direction of Individualism had to take place slowly and over the course of many generations. In this respect, both versions of the organic conception of society were deeply conservative. Spencer's account was conservative in an even more fundamental sense since it affirmed that society *necessarily* possessed a given structure for each stage of social development, and that the limitation of State function was a 'natural' concomitant of the processes of evolution. The upshot of the organic analogy was to insist that the individualistic social structure and the liberal minimal State were the expression of the natural order of things, and were the only possible form of social organization appropriate to advanced societies. The conservatism of this theory was given its clearest expression by Goldwin Smith, who observed that the one consequence of the waning of religious faith had been to undermine the patience of the masses with the 'inequalities of the social system' since they no longer believed the system to be 'a providential ordinance'. He anticipated that, in future, 'scientific conviction, derived from the study of the social organism, may supply the place of religious impressions as a motive for acquiescence in things as they are.'[119] In other words, if it is the essence of conservatism to declare that social and political institutions cannot be radically reformed, then Spencer's deterministic thesis also lent itself to a conservative defence of the existing order of society.

[118] W. H. Hudson, *An Introduction to the Philosophy of Herbert Spencer* (London, 1897), 141.
[119] G. Smith, 'The Organization of Democracy', *Contemporary Review*, 47 (1885), 318, 319.

5

THE INDIVIDUALIST THEORY OF HISTORY

I. Introduction

The Individualist philosophy of history provides further evidence in support of the contention that the Individualists endeavoured to combine liberal principles with a conservative defence of the late Victorian social order. It will be argued in the present chapter that the Individualists' interpretation of history enabled them to present themselves, in accordance with their claim to be the genuine heirs of the Benthamites, as the true progressives and correspondingly to portray the New Radicalism as a retrogressive creed. In their view, social reformers were engaged in a retrogressive rather than a progressive enterprise, since they were undermining the very conditions of progress and re-creating the repressive type of society from which mankind had only recently emerged. On the other hand, this same theory of history provided the Individualists with a justification for their conservatism, since they could argue that further progress required the maintenance of the free market and limited State of late Victorian Britain. Their interpretation of history enabled them to present institutional conservatism as the truly progressive creed and to claim that the New Radicalism served the cause rather of reaction than of progress.

Individualist political thinkers can be seen to have given expression to a particular theory of history in which the freedom of the individual and an individualistic social order were presented as the ultimate goal of social evolution. The theory of history which they propounded involved a sequential development from a custom-bound, hierarchical society based on relations of status and subordination to the open, free, progressive society of classical liberalism with its voluntarily assumed social relations. Furthermore, they all agreed that socialism was not an innovation but was a reversion to the type of social organization which already had been superseded by the advent of a social order based on the principles of Individualism. The Individualists believed that socialism, far from being a progressive force, would re-create the same relations of command and obedience, of hierarchy and subordination, which had characterized more primitive forms of social organization. The Individualist theory of history did not only purport to establish that the greatest possible individual liberty, compatible with the like liberty of others, was the end towards which society was tending but it also demonstrated that socialism and social reform were ultimately 'reactionary' creeds.

This chapter will begin with an examination of Sir Henry Maine's generalization that 'the movement of progressive societies has hitherto been a movement *from Status to Contract*', which is generally recognized to be the earliest statement of the theory.[1] It will be argued that Maine's generalization can be seen to be part of a sophisticated theory of history in which the emergence of individual rights to property, an individualistic social order, and civilization itself were all of a piece. This account will be contrasted with that of Spencer who incorporated Maine's generalization (although without accepting the underlying social theory) as part of his own theory that the processes of evolution were transforming society from a 'militant' into an 'industrial' type. Contrary to many commentators on Spencer's political thought, who have concentrated on tracing the historical antecedents of this distinction, this chapter will be concerned with demonstrating the role which the ideal types of militancy and industrialism played in the political argument of late Victorian Britain.[2]

In order to locate Spencer's ideal types of society in their polemical context, their employment as part of his critique of socialism in the essay on 'The Coming Slavery' will be examined. It will be argued that many other Individualists besides Spencer expressed the view that history was the story of the emancipation of mankind from the tyranny of the socialistic institutions of the past, and that the final decades of the nineteenth century had witnessed a regression towards a more militant social order.

Finally, it will also be shown that the Individualist interpretation of

---

[1] Cf. S. Collini, *Liberalism and Sociology: L. T. Hobhouse and Political Argument in England 1880–1914* (Cambridge, 1978), 27.

[2] Although I have employed the Weberian terminology of 'ideal types' with regard to militancy and industrialism, it should be noted that Spencer's approach to the methodology of the social sciences was far removed from that of the German sociologist. Given Spencer's scientific background, it might be more accurate to say that he regarded the two social types as pure substances which were compounded to varying degrees in all actually existing societies.

history was itself open to two possible interpretations. The first of these shared with A. V. Dicey the view that the goal of history had been reached with the high-tide of Individualism in mid-century and that the only function remaining to liberalism was to preserve its achievements.[3] The empirical Individualists believed all that was necessary to preserve the Individualist order was to maintain the limits of State action which had been recognized before the *fin de siècle* resurgence of socialism. While the conservative implications of this version of the theory are obvious, there was also another version of it, mainly held by those thinkers who were inspired by Spencer, which regarded anarchy as the goal towards which human history was tending. From this point of view the mid-century limited State was merely a stage in a more far-reaching process which would eventually result in complete disappearance of all forms of coercive authority. Nevertheless, even this version of the theory could be made to serve a conservative purpose because it implied that all changes in the direction of anarchy had to take place slowly and organically, while the shared perception of social reform as retrogressive enabled both strands of Individualists to make common cause against socialism.[4] Hence even the interpretation of history formulated by the Individualists can be seen to have exhibited the dual features of liberalism and conservatism which we have already indicated as the common feature in all their arguments.

II. From Status to Contract

Sir Henry James Sumner Maine was one of the most distinguished legal historians of the Victorian period. His work on *Ancient Law*, published in 1861, was widely regarded as a path-breaking work which was to inspire a whole generation of legal historians, among them Maitland and Pollock, as well as sociologists and anthropologists. The work also contains Maine's most famous generalization, that the 'the movement of progressive societies has hitherto been a movement *from Status to*

---

[3] A. V. Dicey, *Lectures on the Relation of Law and Public Opinion during the Nineteenth Century* (London, 1905), *passim*.

[4] This distinction between the two versions of the Individualist theory of history does much to explain the tensions within a group like the Liberty and Property Defence League, which consisted of both the more conservative Individualists and 'philosophic anarchists' who were followers of Spencer. On this tension see E. Bristow, 'The Liberty and Property Defence League and Individualism', *Historical Journal*, 18 (1975), 761–89.

Contract' which was the prototype of the Individualist theory of history as the transition from 'socialism' to freedom. He was impressed by the way in which individuality was the product of a precarious and rather fortuitous historical development and shared with Spencer a conception of this process as involving a transition from a custom-bound hierarchical society to one based on liberty and freedom of contract. To understand the exact meaning of this generalization, however, it is necessary to examine the theory of human progress and development which was first put forward in *Ancient Law* and subsequently elaborated in Maine's other writings. This theory provided the often unspoken background to many of Maine's writings on society and even to his arguments against democracy in *Popular Government.*

The great social contract theorists, Hobbes and Locke, had argued that the state of nature was a state of perfect liberty, some portion of which had to be surrendered in order to institute civil society and government. By contrast, Maine believed that this notion of a state of nature, and the corresponding belief in the natural liberty of the individual, could be shown to be false when examined under the lens of the historical method.[5] In the preface to *Popular Government*, he remarked that his earlier work on the *Ancient Law* had been obstructed 'by a number of *a priori* theories which, in all minds but a few, satisfied curiosity as to the Past and paralysed speculation as to the Future.' These theories were specifically the hypotheses of a law and a state of nature, and they had not only obscured thinking about the private laws of mankind but they were also responsible for misconceptions about the nature of political institutions. Yet the application of the historical method demonstrated that such assumptions were 'unhistorical and unverifiable' and that as a result of his investigations 'some assumptions commonly made on the subject must be discarded.'[6]

The contrast between Maine's social theory and the political thought of Hobbes is, as K. D. Smellie suggested, especially fruitful. In so far as the state of nature could be said to have existed, Maine believed, it was not a Hobbesian state of unlimited liberty but one in which the individual was subordinated within the patriarchal family-state:

To Hobbes men, finding the state of Nature 'nasty, brutish and short', surrendered their power to a sovereign. Any tampering with that full delegation

---

[5] This contrast was first invoked by K. B. Smellie, 'Sir Henry Maine', *Economica*, 8 (1928), 64–94. I am heavily indebted to Smellie's paper in this section.

[6] Sir H. S. Maine, *Popular Government: Four Essays* (London, 1885), v.

would mean anarchy. To Maine the state of nature was a tyranny of custom from which some men had escaped when a favourable combination of circumstances led to the discovery of institutions which were the conditions of freedom. Any tampering with these might destroy that freedom.[7]

The state of nature, far from being Hobbes's state of absolute liberty, was the subordination of the individual to the crushing tyranny of blind obedience to custom; civilization, on the other hand, was 'a condition of social organisation which made possible a constant succession of new ideas. It was a condition which was secured by a favourable combination of order and liberty.'[8] But what were the conditions of freedom and what were the favourable circumstances which had led to their discovery? In *Ancient Law* Maine had traced the evolution of individual rights and duties out of communal customs, identifying the calculus of social justice elaborated by the Roman jurists as the crucial turning-point in this development. This process demanded two prerequisites: first of all, the existence of patriarchal families, which were literally tiny states whose members were subject to the capricious commands of the father-legislator. Secondly, the existence of an organized force—kingship—capable of enforcing some solution of the conflicts which would inevitably occur between such families. The ancient law was simply the international law which existed between these family-states and

civilisation is born with the transformation of the heavy technical formalities that were in ancient law the only legal transactions possible, and were between group and group, into the comparative simplicity of modern legal concepts. Roman law is important because it gives us an almost complete history of this change.[9]

It is in the light of this account that Maine's generalization that the movement of progressive societies was one from status to contract has to be viewed. Maine believed that the emergence of an open society out of a closed one was marked by the emergence of individual rights out of communal customs and this was the criterion of human progress. This point was made very clearly with reference to individual rights of property:

Property in land as we understand it, that is, several ownership, ownership by individuals or groups not larger than families, is a more modern institution than joint property or co-ownership, that is, ownership in common by large groups of men originally kinsmen and still, wherever they are to be found . . . believing or

---

[7] Smellie, 'Maine', 65.   [8] Ibid. 66.   [9] Ibid. 68.

assuming themselves to be in some sense kin to one another . . . Individual property in land has arisen from the dissolution of co-ownership.[10]

Maine continued:

Civilization is nothing more than a name for the old order of the Aryan world, dissolved but perpetually reconstituting itself under a vast variety of influences, of which infinitely the most powerful have been those which have, slowly, and in some parts of the world less perfectly than others, substituted private property for collective ownership.[11]

The emergence of property and free contract was all of a piece with the emergence of civilization, understood in the sense of a social organization which permitted a constant succession of new ideas. To attack private property would be to undermine the very conditions of civilized life: 'Nobody is at liberty to attack several property and to say at the same time that he values civilization. The history of the two cannot be disentangled.' This overwhelming sense of the precariousness of civilization, and an intense awareness of the rare conjunction of conditions which had produced it, engendered in Maine a Burkean respect and reverence for the existing constitution of society.[12] For Maine history was 'the record of our failures from which we might glean the causes of a success which had become ours by accident.'[13] If he did not think of society as being literally an organism in Spencer's sense, then he was strongly aware of the subtle interdependence of its parts and of its having grown, like an organism, independently of the will or intention of any of its constitutive members. History provided Maine with a sense of the rarity and fragility of civilization and with an awareness of the delicate constitution of the social organism, while the historical method provided the key to studying society as an organic growth.

---

[10] Sir H. S. Maine, *The Effects of the Observation of India in Modern European Thought* (London, 1875), 27.

[11] Ibid. 30.

[12] The comparison between Burke and Maine has been drawn not only by Smellie but also by Ernest Barker in *Political Thought in England from Spencer to the Present* (London, 1915), 162. In addition, *Saturday Review* in its notice of *Popular Government* remarked that Maine might be regarded as 'the Burke of the new secession of the Whig aristocracy from a party now once more tainted with revolutionary doctrines.' (Anon., 'Review of *Popular Government*', *Saturday Review*, 60 (1885), 782.) However, the comparison is not altogether appropriate. Maine's rationalistic, secular, and unsentimental approach to institutions hardly corresponds to that of Burke, while rather than looking nostalgically on the regime of status he celebrates its supersession by contract.

[13] Smellie, 'Maine', 80.

III. From Militancy to Industrialism

Like Maine, Herbert Spencer also propounded a theory of history involving a sequential development from a custom-bound, aggressive, hierarchical type of social organization based on relations of command and subordination to the open, free, progressive society of classical liberalism with its voluntarily assumed contractual social relations.[14] Many commentators have discussed Spencer's theory that human history involved a transition from militancy to industrialism, but the secondary literature which exists on this topic is almost exclusively concerned with establishing the historical antecedents of this distinction. Peel, for example, has identified a similar conception in the writings of (among others) Harriet Martineau, Andrew Ure, and H. T. Buckle. He argues that these different versions of the contrast between militancy and industrialism can be traced to a common root in the society/polity distinction of the eighteenth-century English radicalism of Godwin and Paine, in which society is regarded as the realm of authentic virtue and polity as something to be avoided or minimized.[15] Wiltshire has also remarked that the notion of stages of development was a 'common manifestation of nineteenth century political theory' and that 'Henry Maine (status to contract), Walter Bagehot (the age of discussion) and Auguste Comte (the law of the three stages) shared Spencer's liking for compartmentalized progress.'[16] Nevertheless, neither Peel nor Wiltshire has attempted to relate Spencer's theory of history to that of the other Individualists. In concentrating on what may be termed a 'vertical' investigation into the intellectual origins of this distinction, they have neglected a 'horizontal' examination of its place in the political argument of late Victorian Britain. The following section will attempt to rectify this omission, but first the broad outlines of the ideal types of militancy and industrialism will be sketched.

The first point to be noted is that the militancy/industrialism distinction was integral to the organic conception of society.[17] It was demonstrated in the previous chapter that Spencer believed the process of evolution, as applied to the social organism, implied that society 'considered apart from its living units, presents phenomena of growth,

---

[14] For recent discussions of Spencer's militancy/industrialism distinction see esp. J. D. Y. Peel, *Herbert Spencer: The Evolution of a Sociologist* (London, 1971), 192 ff.; D. Wiltshire, *The Social and Political Thought of Herbert Spencer* (Oxford, 1978), 243 ff.

[15] Peel, *Herbert Spencer*, 192 ff.   [16] Wiltshire, *Herbert Spencer*, 194.

[17] This point deserves stressing since it receives too little emphasis in much of the secondary literature, most notably Wiltshire, *Herbert Spencer*.

structure, and function, like those of growth, structure, and function in an individual body; and these last are needful keys to the first.'[18] The Spencerian conception of the social organism had a double aspect. First of all, society resembled an organism in terms of the *structure* and *function* of its various component parts. Institutions were to be explained in terms of their function as part of the social organism, just as organs of the body were explained by their contribution to the maintenance of the living system. Secondly, society also passed through stages of evolutionary *growth* which exactly paralleled the process of development apparent in organic evolution. Initially, societies were simple, unstructured, small, and uniform; they gradually became complex, structured, large, and individuated. In this sense, therefore, the theory of the social organism was an attempt to explain the dynamic processes of human history. Whereas the organic conception in its first aspect may be regarded as constituting the foundation of Spencer's functionalist sociological theory, in its other aspect it gave expression to his theory of history.

The origins of society, Spencer believed, were to be found in the compounding of families and tribes into what were initially loose, almost homogeneous, aggregations. The parallel between the development of a social organism and an individual organism was again apparent; the foundation of the latter was the 'definite nucleated cells' out of which it was aggregated, while 'well-developed, simple social groups are those out of which, by composition, the higher societies are eventually evolved.'[19] As the aggregate became more complex and closely integrated, the separateness of the cells 'gradually give place to structures in which the cell-form is greatly masked or almost lost', and consequently 'the family groups and compound family groups which were the original components eventually lose their distinguishableness.'[20] In this respect the theory might appear to have much in common with Maine's account of social development, and Spencer believed that there was a degree of truth to the generalization that the individual had replaced the family as the unit of modern societies. Nevertheless, Spencer was also explicitly critical of the patriarchal theory. He argued that Maine incorrectly held that patriarchal family was the social unit of all primitive peoples, whereas it was in fact distinctive to the pastoral mode of existence, and there was no one single primitive group out of which society grew.

---

[18] H. Spencer, *The Study of Sociology* (1873; 15th edn., London, 1889), 330.
[19] Id., *The Principles of Sociology*, i. (London, 1875), 737.   [20] Ibid. 737.

Moreover, Spencer also criticized Maine's belief that all property ownership was originally tribal.

Contrary to Maine's account of the evolution of society from patriarchy to individualism, the basis for Spencer's distinction between militant and industrial types of societies rested on the observation that the co-operation which constituted the foundation of all societies may take two radically different forms. In the first place, there is the kind of spontaneous co-operation which unintentionally arises from the pursuit of private ends, giving rise to the division of labour and to the system of production and distribution which relies on the pursuit of gain by individuals. This spontaneous co-operation, which is achieved without the instrument of coercive power, produces 'a combined action which directly seeks and subserves the welfares of individuals, and indirectly subserves the welfare of society as whole by preserving individuals.'[21] On the other hand, there is also a form of co-operation which is consciously devised and which implies a distinct recognition of public ends which are often at variance with private wishes. Spencer called this latter form of co-operation 'governmental' since it employed coercive agency to achieve its ends and it exhibited a 'combined action which directly seeks and subserves the welfare of society as a whole, and indirectly subserves the welfare of individuals by protecting society.'[22] The spontaneous co-operation of individuals gave rise to the industrial social type, while governmental co-operation created militant social organizations.[23]

The militant form of social organization took historical precedence over industrialism since the earliest co-operation of individuals had been for the purpose of mutual protection in an environment of warlike and unsocialized individuals in whom the altruistic sentiments of justice and generosity were largely undeveloped.[24] The model for militant society, Spencer thought, was the army and this type of society was to be found in its purest form in primitive communities in which the 'army is simply the mobilized society and the society is the quiescent army.'[25]

---

[21] Ibid. ii (London, 1882), 247.   [22] Ibid.

[23] It is important to note that both industrialism and militancy were of the nature of ideal types. Spencer made it plain that actually existing societies exhibited a combination of elements of both, albeit compounded in different degrees. Although industrialism had not been anywhere completely realized it was nevertheless possible to regard British society as having undergone a *transformation towards* industrialism in the first half of the 19th cent.   [24] See above, Ch. 3.

[25] H. Spencer, *The Man versus the State*, ed. D. G. Macrae (1884; Harmondsworth, 1969), 114.

Like an army, the social structure of a militant society is characterized

by a regime of status, since its members stand one towards another in successive grades of subordination. From the despot down to the slave, all are masters of those below and subjects of those above.[26]

Even the ecclesiastical system exhibits an elaborate hierarchy closely resembling the hierarchy of the political system. In addition, the militant social type is founded on the principle of inheritance and hereditary, so that the position of each individual in the society is determined by birth. Since Spencer held that the 'acquirement of function by inheritance conduces to rigidity of structure' and 'succession by descent favours that which exists', this serves to make the social structure rigid and unchanging.[27]

Nevertheless, the militant type of society was characterized by much more than a regime of status. Concerted action, which entails the subordination of the individual to the whole, is necessary to obtain military success. The life of the unit is not his own 'but is at the disposal of his society' and he possesses only 'such liberty as military obligations allow.'[28] Furthermore, even where private ownership is recognized, in the last resort the citizen is 'obliged to surrender whatever is demanded for the community's use.'[29] In a militant type of social organization, not only the citizen's property, but ultimately even the citizen himself, is owned by the State.

A militant society sets the terms of social co-operation compulsorily by force and aggression, and this in turn implies the necessity of 'a coercive instrumentality' since this type of union for corporate action is impossible without 'a powerful controlling agency'.[30] This need for a controlling agency creates a highly centralized social structure, and 'organizations other than those forming parts of the State-organization, are wholly or partially repressed.'[31] The public authority, occupying and regulating all fields of social life, excludes all private or voluntary combination.

Because military efficiency is the overriding concern of the militant type of society its economic system, which is under the direction of the centralized authority, is exclusively geared towards needs engendered by the requirements of offence and defence. Thus not only does the government perform 'negatively regulative' functions, it also exercises

---

[26] Id., *Principles of Sociology*, ii. 663.   [27] Ibid. 257.
[28] Ibid. 661.   [29] Ibid. 662.   [30] Ibid.   [31] Ibid. 666.

those which are 'positively regulative': 'It does not simply restrain; it also enforces. Besides telling the individual what he shall not do, it tells him what he shall do.'[32] Moreover, the economic system of this social type is predominantly autarkic since militant societies exist in an environment composed of similarly warlike societies, with the result that there is little prospect of their being able to engage in mutually beneficial trade.

In the previous chapter it was shown that Spencer believed that social and political institutions were dependent on the existence of a particular type of character among the individuals of a society; for example, there was little point in extending the franchise in a society in which the virtues of justice and self-restraint were so little developed that democracy would lead directly to socialism. He also argued that both militancy and industrialism had a particular type of character appropriate to them. Militancy was naturally associated with the martial virtues; in particular, fearlessness, delight in the forcible exercise of mastery, the pursuit of vengeance, little regard for life or liberty, and unswerving obedience.[33] As reflecting this type of character, as well as the average life of the community, the religion was one of enmity and was marked by the prominence of 'stern and repulsive' doctrines.

Although the military and industrial activities of society are antagonistic, Spencer also believed the former had played the main part in the development of the latter throughout the whole course of social evolution. In the first place, the military struggle for existence between societies had been essential for their internal consolidation, while each new integration brought about by conquest has ultimately replaced the warlike relations formerly existing between the integrated communities with relations of a peaceful character.

Neither the consolidation and re-consolidation of small groups into large ones: nor the organization of such compound and doubly-compound groups; nor the concomitant development of those aids to a higher life which civilization has brought: would have been possible without inter-tribal and inter-national conflicts.[34]

Although the universal antagonism of mankind may have caused inconceivable horrors, without it 'the world would still have been inhabited only by men of feeble types, sheltering in caves and living on wild food.' Yet the warlike phase of human existence was over, Spencer believed, and 'from war has been gained all that it had to give.'[35] Having done its work of creating the initial conditions of social solidarity, and of fostering within itself the social system destined to replace it, the military instinct is destined to disappear.

The developmental process which, in the case of the organic conception of society, was presented as a transition from a simple, undifferentiated, and unstructured social organization to one which was complex, differentiated, and structured, could also be regarded under another aspect as the transformation of militancy into industrialism. Whereas the chief features of militancy are a comparatively undeveloped and undifferentiated social structure, with little mutual dependence of parts, and no clear demarcation between the systems for production and regulation, industrialism represents its complete opposite. Given that the development of spontaneous co-operation and the division of labour has made individuals more mutually dependent, 'a corporate action subordinating individual actions by uniting them in joint effort, is no longer requisite.'[36] It is thus a regime of contract rather than status, and since the market system formed by spontaneous co-operation is also subject to its own regulating mechanism, the State can retreat from interference with the industrial and commercial activities of mankind. In addition, the concomitant ethical evolution of the individual and the corresponding decline in warlike behaviour also implies that corporate action, which is called into existence 'by those aggressive traits of human nature which chronic warfare has fostered', will diminish in function and become more limited in scope.

In the *Social Statics* Spencer had believed that the ethical evolution of humanity would eventually make the State as such redundant. By contrast, the Synthetic Philosophy presented industrialism as a form of social organization in which government was limited to the 'negatively regulative' functions, not one in which there was no government at all. By the time that he came to write *The Principles of Sociology*, the highest type of society which he was prepared to countenance was one in which the governmental agency will concern itself only with keeping private action in due bounds, and he was also prepared to speculate on the political constitution of such a State.[37] In the militant type of society the individuality of the citizen is submerged in the collectivity, but the

[36] Ibid. 728.

[37] Cf. F. W. Maitland, 'Mr. Herbert Spencer's Theory of Society', *Mind*, 8 (1883), 361 f., where this point is well made. The issue is further discussed in Ch. 6, and the reasons for Spencer's abandonment of anarchy as the goal of history are examined in greater detail later in this ch.

primary object of the corporate agency in the industrial social order is the defence of his individuality; this 'becomes society's essential duty . . . internal protection must become the cardinal function of the state.'[38] The State thus becomes negatively regulative only, concerning itself with the maintenance of justice in the sense of the 'preservation of the normal connexions between acts and results—the obtainment by each of as much benefit as his efforts are equivalent to—no more and no less'.[39] In his mature writings, therefore, the chief contrast between militancy and industrialism was not a contrast between unlimited government and anarchy, but between unlimited and limited government.

As society evolves towards industrialism, voluntary or spontaneous co-operation comes to predominate over the coercive governmental co-operation which characterized militancy. The model for industrialism was not the army but the productive association, and instead of being organized for the waging of war, this type of society is 'organized exclusively for carrying on internal activities, so as most efficiently to subserve the lives of citizens.'[40] Although Burrow has described this as the 'liberal, individualistic, rational bourgeois society *par excellence*', in which the only social relations are those which arise from the economic division of labour, this ignores Spencer's considerable emphasis on the scope for voluntary association under industrialism, something which would be further enhanced by the natural sympathy which he assumed would be developed during the process of evolution.[41] It was noted in Chapter 2 that the Individualists' model of society as a collection of atomistic, self-interested individuals who were locked into a Darwinian economic struggle for existence was counterbalanced (and perhaps contradicted) by an alternative model in which individuals were capable of voluntary co-operation for mutually beneficial ends. The State could not legitimately provide poor relief or privilege the position of a particular religious denomination, but there was nothing wrong with individuals voluntarily combining for charitable or religious ends. The narrow range of public organization will create the scope for the formation of a wide range of private, voluntary organizations to perform functions which were once the province of the governmental power. Moreover, Spencer also made it clear that the family would not

---

[38] Spencer, *Principles of Sociology*, ii. 697.
[39] Ibid. 700.   [40] Ibid. 728.
[41] J. W. Burrow, *Evolution and Society* (Cambridge, 1966), 222.

dissappear and indeed claimed that its excessive weakening was responsible for the misguided belief in the paternal duty of the State.[42]

Finally, Spencer also stressed that the type of individual character
appropriate to industrialism differed fundamentally from that associated with militancy. The light regard in which life and liberty had been
held was replaced by the love of freedom; in the place of delight in the
exercise of authority was respect for the claims of others and a respect
for property; in the place of the desire for vengeance was a love of
justice; and the belief in the virtue of obedience was replaced by the
strengthening of the desire for independence.

The growth of industrialism out of militancy was, as we have seen,
simply another instantiation of the general law of evolution which was at
work throughout the whole of creation, and social organisms, like their
biological counterparts, necessarily reflect the demands which the
environment imposes on them. A social organism which exists in a
warlike environment must necessarily assume a structure suited to
military operations; in the lower stages of evolution the survival of
societies depends on their powers of offence and defence, and thus
'*relative to these temporary requirements* those with the most centralized
regulating systems' will survive.[43] On the other hand, the advance of
industrialism will bring about conditions in which the survival of
societies depends mainly on 'those powers which enable them to hold
their own in the struggle of industrial competition' and it will promote
the development of the industrial system at the expense of the structures
of militancy.[44] The struggle for existence between societies does not
disappear with the predominance of the industrial over the militant type,
but merely takes a different form, since principle of selection will
operate to favour those societies which have developed furthest along
the road to industrialism. In other words, the societies in which life,
liberty, and property are secure and all interests justly regarded will be
those to survive since 'they must prosper more than one in which they
are not; and consequently, among competing industrial societies, there
must be a gradual replacing of those in which personal rights are
imperfectly maintained, by those in which they are perfectly main-

---

[42] 'This recognition of the individual, even when a child, as the social unit, rather than
the family, has indeed now gone so far that by many the paternal duty of the state is
assumed as self-evident; and criminals are called "our failures" . . . [However], so far
from expecting disintegration of the family to go further, we have reason to suspect that it
has already gone too far.' Spencer, *Principles of Sociology*, i. 738–9.

[43] Ibid. 618b.   [44] Ibid.

tained.'[45] As so often in Spencer's philosophy, Providence operates to secure the outcome most desirable from the standpoint of Individualism.

Spencer was not alone in interpreting history as a transition from a condition of subordination to one of liberty, and his theory had a particular resonance with the late Victorian Individualists, who regarded the anti-aristocratic crusades of Benthamite radicalism as simply the most recent manifestation of the struggle for freedom. Thomas Mackay, for example, argued that although it often had been assumed that 'Socialism is something new, and that in the past human destiny has been entrusted to the care of the individualistic principle', nothing could be further from the truth. On Mackay's account the principles of individualism and socialism had been locked in perpetual struggle throughout history; the individualistic rule of conduct obliged man 'to adapt his character to his environment' while the 'socialistic instinct' was the tendency to avoid this rule by submitting to the guidance of groups or associations in the search for happiness. Very early in human history the socialistic instinct had triumphed and had 'set on men's necks a central government, which acted in a narrow class spirit, and devoted itself according to the lights of the time to preserving class distinctions and to making each class perform the duties which an ill-informed legislature thought necessary or important.'[46] Progress was a continuous process of human emancipation from the institutions created by this socialistic instinct and of liberation 'from the slavery of custom and superstition towards freedom of action and thought.'[47] He went so far as to claim that 'the dominant principle of human affairs has been socialism. History is the record of the gradual and painful emancipation of the individual from the socialistic tyranny of slavery, feudalism and centralised authority.'[48] Donisthorpe also gave expression to this theory of history, remarking that 'from a condition of tribal Socialism, Englishmen have taken many centuries to attain their present degree of civil liberty.'[49]

---

[45] Ibid. ii. 698.   [46] T. D. Mackay, *The English Poor* (London, 1889), 7.
[47] Ibid. 13.   [48] Ibid., p. v.
[49] W. Donisthorpe, *Law in a Free State* (London, 1895), 5.

IV. The Late Victorian 'Regression' to Socialism

It has been suggested by one recent critic of Spencer that although he recognized and denounced the late Victorian drift to socialism, he was unable to explain it within the framework of the Synthetic Philosophy, and consequently his 'elaborate explanatory system withered under Britain's drift towards socialism in the latter half of the nineteenth century.'[50] However, as was pointed out in an earlier chapter, it would be mistaken to believe that Spencer thought of evolution as a continuous and uninterrupted process, following an undeviating course. The law which Spencer termed 'the Rhythm of Motion' implied that all change alternated between progression and retrogression. This alternation was as true of social changes as of any others: 'social progress' could be interpreted as 'one slow movement towards individual liberty frequently interrupted by retrogression.'[51] As Spencer himself remarked in his *Autobiography*:

On recognizing the universality of rhythm, it becomes clear that it was absurd to suppose that the great relaxation of restraints—political, social, commercial— which culminated in free trade would continue. A reimposition of restraints, if not of the same kind then of other kinds, was inevitable; and it is now manifest that whereas during a long period there had been an advance from involuntary co-operation in social affairs to voluntary co-operation (or, to use Sir Henry Maine's language, from *status* to contract), there has commenced a reversal of the process.[52]

The first such manifestation of this reversal was the imperialism and militarization of late Victorian Britain which Spencer inevitably viewed as leading to a regression towards militancy.[53] On these grounds he opposed such apparently innocuous organizations as the Salvation *Army*, which he believed were expressive of the resurgence of militaristic sentiments abroad in the nation. Hence also his opposition to the Boer War and colonial expansion which, despite his stance on other issues, aligned him with the party of progress.

In addition to this process of 're-barbarization', Spencer also believed that another retrogressive movement was taking place in terms of the

---

[50] E. F. Paul, 'Herbert Spencer: The Historicist as Failed Prophet', *Journal of the History of Ideas*, 64 (1983), 634. Paul has since repeated the charge in 'Liberalism, Unintended Orders and Evolutionism', *Political Studies*, 36 (1988), 251–72. For a critique of Paul see my 'The Errors of an Evolutionist: A Reply to Ellen Frankel Paul', *Political Studies*, 37 (1989), 436–42.

[51] A. E. Hake and O. E. Wesslau, *The Coming Individualism* (London, 1895), 11.

[52] H. Spencer, *Autobiography* (London, 1904), ii. 369.

[53] See e.g. the various essays collected in id., *Facts and Comments* (London, 1902).

internal structure of the social organism. This he associated with the 'socialistic' tendencies of both major parties in late nineteenth-century Britain and with the growing role of the State in industrial and commercial activities. In the article on 'The Coming Slavery' Spencer had invoked the distinction between militancy and industrialism to argue that the tendency of recent legislation was towards a new militancy. The process which had been set in train by the collectivist legislation of the two decades prior to the publication of *The Man versus the State* was the re-creation of the superseded militant form of social organization. Spencer alleged that under socialism the regulative apparatus of the State would everywhere control all kinds of production and distribution, and would everywhere apportion the shares of the product required for each locality, working establishment, and individual:

[T]he changes made, the changes in progress, and the changes urged, will carry us not only towards state-ownership of all land and dwellings and means of communication, all to be worked and administered by state agents, but towards state usurpation of all industries.[54]

As socialism advanced the State would take ever greater control over public and private life, thus unleashing an irresistible tyranny. Consequently, as Mackay insisted, the advocates of a compromise between Individualism and socialism were badly misguided: 'Those who talk of compromise seem not to realize that the knell of the period of compromise has sounded . . . We are falling under a tyranny more absolute and unrelenting than anything the world has ever seen.'[55] The upshot of the general establishment of a socialistic organization, Spencer argued, would be to place untrammelled power in the hands of a class of officials who

using without check whatever coercion seems to them most needful in the interests of the system (which will practically become their own interests) will have no hesitation in imposing their rigorous rule over the entire lives of actual workers; until, eventually, there is developed an official oligarchy, with its various grades, exercising a tyranny more gigantic and more terrible than the world has seen.[56]

---

[54] Id., *The Man versus the State*, 105.
[55] T. D. Mackay, 'Empiricism in Politics', *National Review*, 25 (1895), 792.
[56] H. Spencer, 'From Freedom to Bondage', in T. D. Mackay (ed.), *A Plea For Liberty* (London, 1891), 24. The idea that modern capitalism might actually require bureaucracy for its efficient operation does not seem to be one which Spencer considered. As Hyndman pointed out, he neglected entirely that the private companies had become 'really as much organised bureaucracies, with as little volition left to the individual employees, as they would be if managed by the state.' (H. M. Hyndman, *Socialism and Slavery* (London, 1884), 9.)

Echoing these sentiments, Hake and Wesslau contended in their book *The Coming Individualism* that the officials would enjoy 'absolute control of all the resources of the country, and the power to order individuals about. . . [I]n a State where work is compulsory, the officials would have a powerful means of coercion at their elbow ready to crush out any insubordination.'[57]

The consequence of the growing power of the bureaucracy, Spencer argued, would be the formation of a system of slavery, for if that 'which fundamentally distinguishes the slave is that he labours under coercion to satisfy another's desires' then this would be the fate of those subjected to this tyranny.[58] Socialism would force the individual to labour without option for the society, awarding him from the general stock such a portion as the society thought fit. It would make no difference that his master was a whole society rather than a person; he would be undeniably a slave. O'Brien put the same point more colourfully when he warned that socialism would transform England into 'a gigantic West Indian sugar plantation of the old-fashioned type. There is no starvation, but in its place a swarm of men, who walk in and out everywhere, whip in hand, thrashing without mercy every idler and every lagger.'[59]

Having partially freed himself from the shackles of the earlier militant type of society with its enforced co-operation and philosophy of 'do your work and take your rations', humanity was again building a new regime of bondage for itself. Spencer believed that mankind,

having by long struggles emancipated itself from the hard discipline of the ancient regime and having discovered the new regime into which it has grown, though relatively easy, is not without its stresses and pains, its impatience with these prompts the wish to try another system, which system is, in principle if not in appearance, the same as that which during past generations was escaped from with much rejoicing.[60]

The usual Individualist explanation of the 'regression' to socialism, in terms of the extension of the franchise, was extensively discussed in Chapter 1. But in the essay on 'The Coming Slavery' which was quoted from earlier, Spencer also developed a more sophisticated account of the causes of the 'regression', and he argued that the momentum which was being built up behind corporate action at the expense of individual action had a number of distinct sources. The lower classes supported

---

[57] Hake and Wesslau, *Coming Individualism*, 119.
[58] Spencer, *The Man versus the State*, 100.
[59] M. D. O'Brien, *Socialism Tested by the Facts* (London, 1892), 18.
[60] Spencer, 'From Freedom to Bondage', 10.

regulation because it was in their apparent interests; since it seemed to be to their immediate advantage they did not stop to consider the likely long-term consequences. And their support for these measures increased exponentially: 'every additional tax-supported appliance for their welfare raises hopes of further ones. Indeed the more numerous public instrumentalities become, the more is generated in citizens the notion that everything is to be done for them, and nothing by them.'[61] As generation succeeds unto generation, the belief that governmental agencies are the only ones available will grow, and this fallacy will be fostered by popular education and by popular literature of the kind which deals with 'pleasant illusions rather than . . . hard realities.' But the impetus for socialistic legislation does not derive solely from the desires of the working class; the upper ten thousand were equally culpable. For example, Spencer laid much of the blame at the door of the practical politician, who thinking only of the proximate results of a measure, failed to pay attention to its long-term consequences or to see it as part of a larger pattern of social change.

Dwelling only on the effects of his particular stream of legislation, and not observing how such other streams already existing, and still other streams which will follow his initiative, pursue the same average course, it never occurs to him that they may presently unite into a voluminous flood utterly changing the face of things.

He was 'unconscious that he is helping to form a certain type of social organisation' and that the cumulative effect of his measures will be to make the realization of this type of organization all the more irresistible.[62] Furthermore, the chiefs of the great political parties outbid each other in an irresponsible grab for popularity; rather than exposing the delusions underlying the popular clamour for legislative interference they pander to them and MPs become 'unconscientious enough to vote for Bills which they believe to be wrong in principle, because party needs and the demands of the next election demand it.'[63] Finally, the extension of the regulative agencies of the government also serves the interests of the middle classes, who are able to find their sons respectable careers in the government bureaucracy.

Spencer concluded 'The Coming Slavery' by writing that socialism would revive the regime of status, 'the system of compulsory co-

---

[61] Id., *The Man versus the State*, 95–6.
[62] Ibid. 91.   [63] Ibid. 97.

operation, the decaying tradition of which is represented by the old Toryism, and towards which the New Toryism is carrying us back.'[64] The idea that socialism was nothing new, and that it would inevitably entail the revival of a superseded condition of society, was widely shared among the Individualists. George Brooks summed up their attitude of weary condescension towards schemes of 'socialistic' reform:

There is nothing new under the sun. The nostrums which are now being proposed by Socialistic demagogues as a cure for the ills of labour have all been proposed before, and tried, and this in our own country: and they have ignominiously failed. Hundreds of years ago the State tried the experiment of regulating the hours of labour; having intermeddled with the hours of labour it felt constrained to interfere with the wages of labour; having fixed the hours and wages of labour it proceeded to determine how the labourer was to spend his wages . . . Having been delivered from this Egyptian darkness and oppression by the light of knowledge and the power of truth, it might have been hoped that we had for ever left such folly and tyranny behind us. But lo! the errors of four hundred years ago are now proclaimed to us as heaven sent truths and we are exhorted, with a confidence which could only be born of ignorance, to do the very things which our forefathers tried to do but failed to accomplish.[65]

Many examples could be cited of other Individualists adopting the same attitude towards Socialism, and the criticism of the Irish Land Act broached in the Introduction, that it involved a reversion to a regime of status, was part of this tendency.[66] But perhaps the most extensive discussion of the idea that socialism was a regression to a more primitive type of society occurs in Bruce Smith's book *Liberty and Liberalism* in which late Victorian socialism was compared to the sumptuary laws of the Tudors. In his book Smith had set out to return the Liberal party to its true principles by attempting to demonstrate that it was the inheritor of a tradition going back to the Norman Conquest. This was Whig history with a vengeance, the story of liberalism as the story of the gradual emergence of English freedom from under the Norman Yoke. The Charter of Henry I, the Magna Carta, the Petition of Right, the Habeas Corpus Act, the Declaration of Right, the struggle for American Independence, and Catholic Emancipation were all part of the history and growth of liberalism. Smith believed that these pieces of legislation marked the development of a principle

[64] Ibid. 110.

[65] G. Brooks, *Industry and Property* (London, 1895), 88–9.

[66] See e.g. Donisthorpe, *Law in a Free State*, 56; H. S. Constable, *The Fallacies and Follies of Socialist Radicalism Exposed* (London, 1895), 30, 81; id., *Radicalism and its Stupidities* (London, 1896), 138.

which has, at various periods, been recognized and acted upon, under different and changing titles, and has, at all times, spurred on, to fresh thoughts and fresh actions, all who could see in the future, an improved condition of civil and religious freedom, based on an ever broader principle of the 'equality of man.'[67]

The notion of equality which was at the root of all true liberalism was the principle of equal liberties, the abolition of legal privileges based on birth, creed, or station. Smith's brand of liberalism conferred on individuals equality of opportunity in the exercise of whatever faculties and abilities they might happen to possess and its chief object was the abolition of class privileges, whether the result of prescription or of Act of Parliament. But whereas true liberalism attempted only to grant to an individual the liberty to do whatever his fellow citizens could do, its perverted 'socialistic' form aimed to secure for him not only opportunities for the exercise of his abilities but also the material wherewithal. Yet 'spurious' liberalism had only the effect of 'curtailing the liberty of citizens instead of widening it; involving the State in commercial pursuits instead of leaving the field to private enterprise; or of interfering with the recognized rights of property.'[68] In pursuing the chimera of material equality, which Smith believed was contrary to all sound social science, spurious liberalism would result in the destruction of all real liberties.

Smith had little difficulty in pointing out that there were many historic instances of this spurious liberalism which had demonstrably failed to achieve their desired result. For example, he could point to the abortive attempt to regulate the price of bread in the reign of Henry III; to equally futile historical efforts to regulate the price of wool or to stimulate its production; to failed attempts to prevent the export of wool or iron, to regulate the price of labour, to prevent usury, to fix the locality of manufactures, and to regulate workmen's meals by legislation. These instances of failed 'socialistic' legislative meddling proved 'that the repeated attempts to produce happiness or success for the people, by Act of Parliament, have not only failed to effect their purpose, but, in many cases, produced results entirely opposite to those which were intended and anticipated.'[69]

Nevertheless, the growth of the knowledge of economic laws among the ruling class had meant that they had set aside as futile these abortive efforts to promote human happiness by means of legislation. They had

[67] [A.] B. Smith, *Liberty and Liberalism* (London, 1887), 79.   [68] Ibid. 256.
[69] Ibid. 263–4. Compare Spencer's discussion of this point in Ch. 3.

come to recognize that the only secure foundation for the welfare of the citizen and society was the principle of equal opportunities and they had accordingly enlarged the sphere of individual liberty by abolishing many unnecessary State functions. By the end of the nineteenth century, however, power was being wrested from the hands of the educated and enlightened classes and transferred to the new mass electorate who were as ignorant of the truths of political economy as had been the ruling class of old, and Smith anticipated with some trepidation a return to the kind of 'overlegislation' which had characterized State policy under the Tudors, inflicting 'endless injury, loss, inconvenience, and misery as the result of their incompetence.'[70] Yet although the immediate prospects for the welfare of society were very bleak, ultimately the democracy would, like the aristocracy before it, learn by its experiences. In virtue of 'unalterable and unaccommodating economic laws' the follies of the mass electorate would 'throw back on their authors practical and sorrowful proofs of their unwisdom, and thus instil some wholesome lessons for subsequent guidance.'[71] Having run its course, the tendency to overlegislation which had emerged in the closing decades of the nineteenth century would once again be supplanted by the principles of Individualism.

The idea that socialism belonged to the distant past was not confined to the Spencerian Individualists. A similar view of late Victorian radicalism was expressed by the historian William Lecky, who declared that 'few things are more curious to observe in the extreme Radical speculation of our times than the revival of beliefs which had been supposed to have been long since finally exploded—the aspirations to customs belonging to early and rudimentary stages of society.'[72] Among the allegedly exploded doctrines which were being revived Lecky included land nationalization which was 'avowedly based on the remote ages, when a few hunters or shepherds roved in common over an unappropriated land.'[73] Like Spencer, he discerned a long ancestry for the proposals of modern socialistic legislation:

The system of making different forms of industry monopolies in the hands of different corporations, of restricting each labourer to one kind of labour, of regulating minutely by authority the hours, the wages, and all other conditions of labour has been abundantly tried in the past. It may be seen in the castes of the East, which descend from a period beyond the range of authentic history, and it

---

[70] Ibid. 281.   [71] Ibid. 326.
[72] W. E. G. Lecky, *Democracy and Liberty* (London, 1896), ii. 185.   [73] Ibid. 186.

was equally apparent in the medieval guilds and other corporations that were abolished at the French Revolution, and in the restrictive Tudor legislation which lingered in England till the first decade of the nineteenth century. All these ideas of restriction and control are once more in full activity among us, and many of them are rapidly passing into legislation.[74]

Lecky regarded this reaction as simply the expression of a general desire to escape from the 'many and violent agitations of modern life' and to 'revert to archaic types of thought and custom' which was in evidence in such tendencies of the times as Tractarian theology and Pre-Raphaelite art. Although both these movements had largely lost their force by the last decade of the century, the 'reaction towards Tudor regulation of industry and an almost Oriental exaggeration of the powers of the State' was continuing virtually unabated.[75]

Sir Henry Maine, whose theory of history as the progression from status to contract provided the Individualists with the basis for their interpretation of the historical process, also echoed Spencer's belief that the tendency of late nineteenth-century radicalism was to regress towards a more primitive type of society. Maine wrote that the policies of Radicals who had supported 'socialistic' measures like the Ground Game Act, the Employers' Liability Act, and the 1881 Irish Land Act were a form of 'Radical Patriarchalism', a description of great significance in the light of his social thought. The social theory of the Tories of the previous generation, he argued, was one 'tinged with a rather sentimental benevolence and tending towards a mild Patriarchalism. The Tories wished that society should be preserved and protected all round.' Through the efforts of Bentham and the elder Mill this view had been discredited as theory and destroyed in practice, and the self-regulation of society 'through the utmost liberty of contract and transfer' had been substituted in its place.[76] Nevertheless, the New Radicals had gone so far in reversing the doctrine of *laissez-faire* 'that we have almost a return to Tory patriarchalism' and the intellectual descendants of the Philosophic Radicals were preaching the very 'heresies' which Bentham and Mill had devoted themselves to exposing.[77]

The problem with this critique of socialism was that the proposed social system was not, strictly speaking, a *regression* to militancy since the object for which the corporate authority would be exercised was quite different to that of the militant type of society. Spencer himself

[74] Ibid. 186–7.   [75] Ibid. 189.
[76] [Sir Henry Maine], 'Radical Patriarchalism', *St. James's Gazette*, 1 (1880), 259–60.
[77] Id., 'Patriarchal Radicalism', *St. James's Gazette*, 2 (1881), 1467–8.

recognized this point in his reply to de Laveleye's criticisms of *The Man versus the State*, when he remarked that 'my assertion was that the coercive system employed [by socialism] was like that employed in militant society: the *ends* to which the systems are directed being quite different.'[78] If Spencer had followed the logic of this reply it would have necessitated the development of a third ideal type to stand alongside militancy and industrialism, and the fact that he did not do so probably indicates that the insight was lost in the heat of polemical controversy. But the point was elaborated by Ritchie who criticized Maine and Spencer for reducing history to 'only one great formula', namely that 'society advances from status to contract—and sticks there or else goes backwards.'[79] Drawing on the conceptual apparatus of Idealism, he alleged that beyond these 'one-sided extremes' there was a higher type of society which synthesized the best elements of both, and thus involved an advance 'to a stage in which all that is most precious in individualism must be retained along with the stability of social condition which individualism has destroyed.'[80] Another Fabian to have been influenced by Idealism, Sidney Ball, elaborated on this criticism of the Individualists' theory of history:

There is a higher form of society than that of mere status, or of mere contract, and that is regulated contract, i.e., contract under conditions of freedom and morality, secured by the public power. Freedom of contract, where it is really freedom of coercion, the State very properly regulates: it regulates it in the interest of free competition, and it regulates it further in the interests of that morality which society as a whole is concerned in maintaining.[81]

This higher form of society was best described as socialism.

V. The Goal of History is Anarchy

At the beginning of this chapter it was noted that the Individualists' theory of history was open to two divergent interpretations. If the end of history was held to be the liberation of the individual from all those restraints which were unnecessary other than to secure the like liberty of other individuals, then it could be contended either that this goal had

---

[78] Spencer, 'M. de Laveleye's Error', repr. from the *Contemporary Review* (Apr. 1885), in id., *Various Fragments* (enlarged edn., London, 1900), 104.
[79] D. G. Ritchie, *Darwinism and Politics* (London, 1889), 69.   [80] Ibid. 71.
[81] S. Ball, 'A Plea For Liberty: A Criticism', *Economic Review*, 1 (1891), 342–3.

been achieved by the mid-Victorian limited State or that it remained an objective for the future. Bruce Smith spoke for many Individualists who adopted the former interpretation when he remarked that the advanced stage of liberalism had been attained already, and that consequently the policy of Liberals ought to be 'to *preserve* that state of things; to watch . . . for any attempt to encroachment upon that domain of freedom or "equal opportunities".' Smith readily acknowledged that this was a conservative outlook. If the essence of conservatism was 'merely a maintenance, or a preservation of institutions as they are, then society, having reached the desired social condition at which liberalism aims, we should have two political schools, Conservatives and Liberals, embracing the same policy.'[82] Nevertheless, Smith was untypical of the Spencerians and this interpretation of history was stronger among the empirical Individualists, the former University Radicals, who, although clothing their Toryism in 'sackcloth and ashes', shared Henry Sidgwick's conviction of the necessity 'of conserving our glorious constitution pro tem.'[83]

While an interpretation of history in which the mid-Victorian State was represented as the pinnacle of human liberation had clearly conservative implications, they are less immediately obvious in the account of the historical process propounded by Spencer and many of his followers. Most of the Spencerians took the view that late Victorian society could not be described as purely Individualist, since it exhibited a number of features which were obviously incompatible with the ideal type of industrialism, and several Individualists even shared the youthful Spencer's belief that mankind was evolving towards a future state of perfect individual liberty. According to Spencer himself, all hitherto existing societies had been either militant or a compound of militancy and industrialism. While numerous examples of the militant type of society could be identified, the chief traits of the industrial type had to be

generalized from inadequate and entangled data. Antagonism more or less constant with other societies, having been almost everywhere and always the condition of each society, a social structure fitted for offence and defence exists in nearly all cases, and disguises the structure which social structure alone otherwise originates.[84]

It followed, as Hake and Wesslau argued, that 'the economic systems of all civilised States are hybrid systems, being partly Collectivist, partly

[82] [A.] B. Smith, *Liberty and Liberalism*, 253.
[83] A. S[idgwick] and E. M. S[idgwick], *Henry Sidgwick: A Memoir* (London, 1906), 398–9.   [84] Spencer, *Principles of Sociology*, i. 584.

Individualist.'[85] This was also true of Victorian society, and until it had rid itself of militant structures like military garrisons and naval fleets, and until the State had ceased its positively regulative 'meddling' in such areas as the Factory Acts and the Poor Law, the ideal of industrialism would not be realized. The suggestion that late Victorian society as yet imperfectly embodied their ideals enabled the Individualists to contend that the evils of society identified by social reformers were due to remnants of the old militancy:

Unfortunately they regard our present system, with its many Socialistic features, its monopolies, its government meddling, its defective defence of individual liberty, as a fair pattern of a free system, and do not understand that we now live in a half-way house towards Socialism, and suffer accordingly.[86]

The problem with Individualism, as George Bernard Shaw remarked of Christianity, was that it had never been tried.[87]

If it was true that late Victorian society was industrialism with the fragments of the shell of the old militancy on its head, then this 'hybrid' society was clearly incompatible with the ideals of the 'more advanced individualists and philosophic anarchists', like Wordsworth Donisthorpe, who believed that 'absolute freedom from state-interference is the goal towards which society is making.'[88] In the anarchic state which they believed to be the goal of history, 'voluntary association would practically effect what the state does now in all that is necessary, and therefore good.'[89] It remains to be explained, therefore, why the views of the more extreme Spencerians did not issue in demands for immediate political action to abolish the functions of the Victorian State which were incompatible with their vision of complete individual liberty.

The answer is to be found in the doctrine of evolution, which in Spencer's *Social Statics* had subsisted in an uneasy relationship with his instinctive political radicalism; as Burrow has noted, these contrasting features of the work were reconciled only by 'the assumption that civilization was on the verge of opening the last envelope.'[90] But by the time the mature Spencer had 'revised and abridged' the *Social Statics*, his radical instincts had waned and a corresponding acquiescence in the gradual processes of social evolution meant that the opening ceremony

---

[85] Hake and Wesslau, *Coming Individualism*, 11.   [86] Ibid. 113.

[87] This argument is also to be found e.g. in J. H. Levy, 'Individualism', in E. B. Bax and J. H. Levy, *Socialism and Individualism* (London, n.d. (1904)), 133 f.

[88] W. Donisthorpe, 'The Limits of Liberty', in Mackay (ed.), *Plea for Liberty*, 67.

[89] Donisthorpe's political theory was discussed in greater detail in Ch. 4.

[90] Burrow, *Evolution and Society*, 227.

had been somewhat delayed. The waning of Spencer's radical instincts is illustrated by his abandonment of his earlier, neo-anarchist, faith that the ethical evolution of mankind would permit the State to wither away. He had come to recognize that the process of adaptation, upon which so much depended, necessarily became slower the more closely that mankind approximated to perfection: 'The rate of progress towards any adapted form must diminish with the approach to complete adaptation, since the force producing it must diminish; so that, other causes apart, perfect adaptation can be reached only in infinite time.'[91] But since dissolution would have set in long before mankind could have enjoyed the infinite time necessary to achieve perfect adaptation to the social state, it followed that the ideal of a stateless society could never be attained. Furthermore, the slowing of the process of adaptation meant that reaching even an approximation of the never-to-be-attained ideal was likely to take a considerable length of time, so that although Spencer continued to believe 'in the words of the song, "there's a good time coming", it now seems to me that the good time is very far distant.'[92] Once the 'temporary wave of reaction' had spent its force, the evolution of mankind towards industrialism would resume, but progress was to be achieved only by individual adaptation over the course of many generations, and not by political action.

Spencer's view that only the slow processes of evolution could prepare the ground for the attainment of a truly Individualist society was echoed by a number of other political theorists, many of whom had not followed him in abandoning anarchism as the goal of history. M. D. O'Brien, for instance, wrote that the State was destined to be outgrown, since 'outer compulsion is the sign of inner weakness, and dies in proportion as the knowledge of the law grows.' At the present time, however, man was so far below 'his true, his rational nature' that the institution of government was required as 'the clumsy scaffolding within which the spirit of man is slowly and painfully building a nobler temple.' Only 'when men are free of their personal infirmities' would they 'be free of the tyranny of one another. Then shall there be for them a new heaven and a new earth.'[93] Donisthorpe also regarded the State as a necessary evil for certain stages of social development, and one which could not be dispensed with more rapidly than evolution allowed. Mankind was not yet ready for unconditioned liberty, which was a type

[91] H. Spencer, *The Social Statics* (1851; abridged and rev. edn., London, 1892), 31 n.
[92] Id., *Autobiography*, ii. 369.
[93] M. D. O'Brien, *The Natural Right to Freedom* (London, 1893), 16.

of society suited for the distant future, and hence '*for the present*, we must recognize some form of state interference as necessary and beneficent.'[94] Because 'we are not yet ripe for absolute individualism' the process of liberating mankind from the 'considerable remnants of the old patriarchal socialism' which still remained was likely to require 'many years, decades, and perhaps centuries'.[95] In the interim, Individualists were best advised to defend the 'empire of the individual' so far established by the gradual processes of evolution, since 'the experience of ages has, at least, stamped the status quo with the hall-mark of genuineness.'[96] By locating the goal of 'absolute individualism' in the distant future, Donisthorpe was able to draw out the relativistic implications of his political theory on which we remarked in the previous chapter.

Thus the conservatism of even the Spencerian version of the theory should be apparent since, like the organic conception of society, it placed great emphasis on the gradualness of any changes which might take place in the direction of the Individualist goal of history. Spencer clearly regarded the process as one which would require many generations to reach completion, since social institutions could only be modified as rapidly as the characters of individual citizens. In practical terms it resulted in a political position which was virtually indistinguishable from that promoted by empirical Individualists who took the view that the objective of political action should be to prevent the activities of the mid-Victorian State from being extended by socialists. It mattered little that 'philosophic anarchists' like Donisthorpe regarded this as a relative and qualified objective, since the hope of a future stateless society had receded so far into the distance as to possess hardly any operational value at all.

VI. Conclusion

Despite the differences between the empiricists and the Spencerians over the issue of whether or not the goal of history had been attained, this should not detract from the considerable ground they shared in common. Both sides expounded a vision of history in which Individualism had emerged only with difficulty from the barbarism of the past. The liberal social order based on individual liberty, private property,

---

[94] Donisthorpe, 'The Limits of Liberty', 68.   [95] Id., *Law in a Free State*, 5.
[96] Ibid. 19.

freedom of contract, and economic competition was the product of slow evolutionary development which enjoyed at best uncertain prospects of survival. The superseded condition of society, whether described as militancy or as status, was identified with the characteristics of hierarchy, subordination, and the command economy, and it was all too easy to identify proposals for social reform or extensive social reconstruction via the medium of the State with a return to this primitive social order.

From the point of view of this theory of history, therefore, socialism could not be interpreted as a progressive force, but was inherently retrogressive. This account of the historical process could be used to give 'scientific' credibility to the notion that Individualism represented the summit of human development. If the history of mankind was the history of progressive emancipation from the compulsory co-operation enforced by the State, then 'socialistic' attempts to extend the province of the public authority could only be portrayed as a regression to an earlier mode of social organization and as a threat to the order which had produced and sustained individuality.

Furthermore, having demonstrated that Individualism was the goal of progress, the Individualists also drew conclusions from this interpretation of history which were, in the context of late Victorian politics, profoundly conservative. On the one hand, the empiricists could contend that resistance to the New Radicalism and the preservation of the existing social order was the only certain way of securing the benefits of progress. On the other, Spencer could argue that although the social order of late Victorian Britain fell some way short of the ideal of industrialism, since it continued to contain many fragments of the old militancy, nevertheless the only alternative to its preservation was a regression towards subordination and tyranny. He recognized that hope of further progress in the direction of industrialism was in advance of the 'temporary needs' of the time, and the most that could be achieved was to prevent the 'broad, vague form of sympathy with the masses' which 'spends itself in efforts for their welfare by multiplication of political agencies' from the further elaboration of 'a social organization at variance with that required for a higher form of social life.'[97] Both 'conservative' Liberals and 'philosophic anarchists' could make common cause in the defence of the existing constitution of society, and once more Individualism displays the duality of conservatism and liberalism which was its hallmark.

[97] Spencer, *Principles of Sociology*, ii. 754–5.

6

THE REWORKING OF UTILITARIANISM

I. Introduction

In the preceding chapters it has been observed that the Individualists frequently employed the arguments of the Philosophic Radicals, but reinterpreted them to serve a conservative purpose. This was true, for example, of Spencer's transformation of the associationist psychology or of the conception of sociological laws which lay at the heart of his analogy between society and a biological organism. The contention that the Individualists gave a conservative twist to previously radical arguments is also supported by the subject of the present chapter and the foundation stone of Philosophic Radicalism, the principle of utility.

True to the Individualists' self-image as the inheritors of the mantle of the Philosophic Radicals, many of them continued to espouse the ethical theory of utilitarianism. At the same time, however, the versions of the utilitarian doctrine defended by the most philosophically sophisticated Individualists, Spencer and Sidgwick, represented considerable departures from the classical theory. In the present chapter I shall argue that the modifications which they introduced into classical utilitarianism represent two different strategies designed to accomplish the same objective of purging the doctrine of its potentially statist implications. From its very inception, utilitarian thought had been ambiguous in its relation to the State, being pulled between enlightened State intervention and *laissez-faire*.[1] By the closing decades of the nineteenth century, the potential for justifying an extensive sphere of State activity was

[1] This thesis was, of course, first advanced by E. Halévy, *The Growth of Philosophic Radicalism* (London, 1972), esp. 118 ff. His contention that there was a contradiction between Bentham's jural and economic assumptions has been challenged by recent scholarship, esp. R. Harrison, *Bentham* (London, 1983), 122, and J. Steintrager, *Bentham* (London, 1977), 64 f. Nevertheless, the central fact remains that the connection between utilitarianism and *laissez-faire* was contingent on a variety of economic assumptions which were being increasingly challenged in the late 19th cent. On this point see Arnold Toynbee, 'Ricardo and the Old Political Economy', in id., *Lectures on the Industrial Revolution of the Eighteenth Century in England* (London, 1884), 21 f.

beginning to be exploited by Radical politicians like Chamberlain and by the political theorists of the New Liberalism. Spencer and Sidgwick aimed to construct a version of the doctrine which could lend justification to the actual distribution of wealth and property, to an industrial system based on free contract, and which would re-establish the connection between the principle of utility and a limited State.

The problem which confronted the Individualists, therefore, was that of adapting the utilitarian doctrine, which in the late Victorian era apparently lent support to an activist State, to the conservative purpose of resisting any substantial sphere of State interference. Spencer regarded his 'rational' or 'deductive' utilitarianism as transcending the orthodox, Benthamite version of the doctrine. He argued that utility was to be regarded as the ultimate rather than the immediate end of action, and that the greatest happiness could be promoted only by conforming to the scientifically discoverable conditions for happiness. This strategy was also adopted by Bruce Smith, although he stopped short of embracing the full evolutionary trappings of Spencer's version of the theory. The aim of maximizing utility was not to be achieved directly but indirectly, by promoting the conditions for the production of happiness. This had the effect of severely restricting the legislator's capacity to pursue the greatest happiness of the greatest number as a matter of deliberate policy. Although it might appear possible to take legislative short cuts to maximizing utility, for example by introducing extensive State relief for the poor, such policies violated the necessary conditions for the attainment of the ultimate objective, and hence in the long run would prove to be self-defeating.

Spencer's theory also seemed to entail a number of consequences which, at least in his mature years, he was reluctant to acknowledge, in particular the nationalization of the land. In an attempt to make his ethical theory conform more closely to the late Victorian social order, Spencer introduced the distinction between 'relative' and 'absolute' ethics, arguing that what was ethically correct for a perfectly evolved humanity was not necessarily correct when the distorting factors of a 'partially civilized' human nature were taken into account. By this method the radical elements in the theory were defused and Spencer was enabled to engage in an Individualist defence of the existing social order, including the private ownership of land.

The conservatism engendered by Spencer's distinction between absolute and relative ethics was also present in the form of the utilitarian doctrine expounded by Henry Sidgwick. Like Spencer, he was concerned to confine State action within certain narrow limits, and to resist any substantial interference with the free market. He also shared Spencer's view that the principle of utility was not to be applied directly to political decisions but was in need of mediation through legislative principles like the Law of Equal Freedom. However, Sidgwick disagreed with Spencer on questions of methodology and substance. Rather than basing his case on scientific 'laws' for the production of happiness, Sidgwick remained committed to the empirical method of orthodox utilitarianism. Yet he also claimed that this method was so difficult to employ that most utilitarian decisions could only be reached by the application of 'middle axioms'—among which were to be counted the rules of common-sense morality and the principles of nineteenth-century legislation. A further corollary was that it was impossible to construct an ideal code of utilitarian ethics which could be used to criticize existing social arrangements, including established moral beliefs. Consequently, the most that the utilitarian philosopher could hope to achieve were specific and piecemeal reforms. Sidgwick's ethical theory did not transcend Benthamism, but was a transformation of it which remained rooted in the classical doctrine.

Secondly, whereas Spencer insisted that the rules of morality were always to be adhered to irrespective of a direct estimate of the utility produced by particular acts falling under them, Sidgwick argued that a consistent utilitarian could not accord moral rules anything more than dependent validity since in some circumstances they might fail to be maximally felicific. Because this point also applied to the legislative principle of equal liberties, he drew the limits of legitimate State action more broadly than did Spencer. This has led many commentators to argue that Sidgwick's political theory was intended to support a substantial extension of the sphere of State action, but a comparison of his views with those of other Individualists like Lord Pembroke, Goldwin Smith, and Dicey reveals that he remained firmly within the Individualist fold. Sidgwick drew conclusions about the legitimate functions of the State which were generally conservative, but the philosophical route by which he arrived at them was quite different to that followed by Spencer.

II. Benthamism Transcended: Spencer

Spencer regarded himself as a utilitarian moral philosopher, and by his own account he was distressed to find himself categorized among the anti-utilitarians by J. S. Mill in the latter's essay on *Utilitarianism*.[2] The basis for this self-description was his repeated insistence that pleasure was the ultimate standard of value: it was undeniable, Spencer thought, that 'taking into account immediate and remote effects on all persons, the good is universally the pleasurable.'[3] He believed that conventional moral judgements, as well as all the competing schools of moral philosophy, were necessarily forced to rely on the assumption that conduct was good or bad 'according as its aggregate results, to self or others or both, are pleasurable or painful' and that our ideas of the goodness or badness of actions originate 'from our consciousness of the certainty or probability that they will produce pleasures or pains somewhere.'

Nevertheless, Mill's characterization of Spencer as an anti-utilitarian was not entirely groundless. As the previous chapters have shown, Spencer's ambition was to resolve the key intellectual disputes of his day by combining the competing schools of thought in a higher synthesis: Darwinism and Lamarckianism, associationism and the faculty psychology, deductivism and the historical method, could all be shown to be partial statements of the true view which was available only from the perspective of evolution. The same was true of the conflict between Utilitarian and Intuitionist ethical theories which, Spencer wrote, 'severally embody portions of the truth; and simply require combining in the right order to embody the whole truth.'[4] Hence, despite his utilitarian conception of value, he was also prepared to admit an element of truth to the theories of the critics of utilitarianism, and he attempted to combine elements of both schools of thought in a philosophical doctrine which would resolve the outstanding debates of Victorian moral philosophy.

The key issue in British moral philosophy in the nineteenth century concerned 'the attempt to determine whether or not there is a rational basis for setting moral limits to the principle of utility.'[5] The chief rival to utilitarianism, Intuitionism, insisted that wrongness of actions consisted in some kind of non-empirical property perceived by a special

---

[2] H. Spencer, *Autobiography* (London, 1904), ii. 88 f.

[3] Spencer attempted to demonstrate on a number of occasions that the theory of evolution could prove that 'pleasure is the ultimate good'. For a pains-taking critique of these attempts at a proof see H. Sidgwick, *Lectures on the Ethics of T. H. Green, H. Spencer, and J. Martineau* (London, 1902), 135 f. One of Spencer's attempts to establish the connection between evolution and ethical hedonism was exhibited by Sidgwick as 'a good specimen of Mr. Spencer's hasty inferences.' (p. 151.)

[4] H. Spencer, *The Principles of Ethics*, i (London, 1892), 171.

[5] J. B. Schneewind, *Sidgwick's Ethics and Victorian Moral Philosophy* (Oxford, 1977), 9.

faculty or moral sense; moral truths were just what people of a normal moral development saw when they looked at a situation in the appropriate moral light. This theory had the effect of conferring a privileged status upon the dictates of the ordinary moral conscience, and the Intuitionists claimed that the pursuit of pleasure, happiness, or welfare should be limited by conventional virtues and by widely acknowledged rights and obligations. Since utilitarianism led to paradoxical or shocking moral conclusions, it was to be rejected as an ethical theory. To the Benthamites, such a suggestion was merely the product of superstition, or bad education, or an outmoded philosophy, and they denied that the ordinary moral conscience was the product of a special faculty for perceiving a transcendental realm of moral values. As Mill put this point in his criticism of the Intuitionist Adam Sedgwick, the utilitarians contended

that the morality of actions is perceived by the same faculties by which we perceive any other of the qualities of actions, namely our intellects and our senses.[6]

Following the associationist psychological theory, Mill explained the origins of the conscience in terms of the repeated connection between particular courses of action and an individual's experience of pleasurable or painful sensations. As his critics pointed out, however, the lifetime of an individual appeared too short to provide the wealth of experience and frequency of sensation required to generate something as powerful and as complex as a moral conscience.

Spencer's resolution of this dispute bore striking similarities to his resolution of the debate between associationism and the faculty psychology, of which it was the direct outgrowth. In Spencer's view, the Intuitionists had been correct to the extent that the conscience was innate to each individual, and Mill was mistaken in believing that the experience of a single individual would be sufficient to generate the dictates of morality. On the other hand, utilitarians like Mill had been correct to argue that the moral conscience was not a special transcendental capacity, independent of all experience. The conscience was innate to each individual because, like the other faculties of the human mind, it had been formed by generations of ancestral experience. As Spencer explained in a letter to Mill subsequently published in *The Principles of Ethics*, his solution to this dispute, like his solution to the

6 J. S. Mill, 'Whewell on Moral Philosophy', quoted by A. Ryan, *J. S. Mill* (London, 1974), 100.

debate between associationism and the faculty psychology, was to transfer the influence of the environment from the individual to the race as a whole:

[C]orresponding to the fundamental propositions of a developed moral science there have been and still are developing in the race certain fundamental moral intuitions; and . . . though these moral intuitions are the results of accumulated experiences of utility, gradually organised and inherited, they have come to be quite independent of conscious moral experience . . . I believe that the experiences of utility organised and consolidated through all past generations of the human race have been producing corresponding nervous modifications which, by continued transmission and accumulation, have become in us certain faculties of moral intuition—certain emotions responding to right and wrong conduct, which have no apparent basis on the individual experiences of utility.[7]

Because our moral intuitions are the results of the 'accumulated experience of utility', it followed that their authority could outweigh any direct estimates of pleasure and pain made by a particular individual. After all, the individual possessed only his own limited experience of the utility or disutility of a given course of action, whereas his moral intuitions were based on the experience of countless generations of ancestral individuals. This directly challenged the Benthamite notion of a felicific calculus, by means of which each individual could establish for himself the rightness of a course of conduct. One of Bentham's key mistakes, Spencer wrote, was to make the 'unwarranted assumption that it is possible for the self-guided human judgement to determine, with something like precision, by what methods it [the greatest happiness] may be achieved.'[8] In addition, Bentham's theory relied on the assumption that mankind were 'unanimous in their definition of "greatest happiness"', whereas on the contrary 'no fact is more palpable than that the standard of happiness is infinitely variable.' Because the conception of happiness varied so much from one person to another, it was impossible to appeal to it directly as a guide for conduct.

Nevertheless, Spencer was far from abandoning the notion of a moral science in favour of an irrational and unreflective dependence on the deliverances of each individual's conscience, as had the Intuitionists. He argued that although

the moral sentiments generated in civilized men by daily conduct with social conditions and gradual adaptation to them, are indispensable as incentives and

[7] Spencer, *Autobiography*, ii. 89.
[8] Id. *Social Statics*, (1850; 2nd edn., London, 1868), 19.

deterrents; and though the intuitions corresponding to these sentiments, have, in virtue of their origin, a general authority to be recently recognised; yet the sympathies hence originating, together with the intellectual expressions of them, are, in their primitive forms, necessarily vague. To make guidance by them adequate to all requirements, their dictates have to be interpreted and made definite by science.[9]

To clarify the point of this passage, Spencer drew a parallel between moral intuitions and the intuition of space: just as the latter 'responds to the exact demonstrations of geometry, and has its rough conclusions interpreted and verified by them, so will moral intuitions respond to the demonstrations of moral science, and will have their rough conclusions interpreted and verified by them.' Spencer's fundamental objection to Benthamism was not that it had entertained the ambition of constructing a science of ethics, but that in pursuing this object it had failed to be sufficiently scientific; as Burrow has written, Spencer thought that the Benthamite version of the greatest happiness principle 'is no more than a statement of good intentions. We do not know what means to adopt to achieve the desired ends.'[10]

Spencer distinguished between orthodox or empirical utilitarianism on the one hand, and his own brand of deductive or rational utilitarianism on the other. The cardinal error made by the Benthamites was to assume that 'utility is to be directly determined by simple inspection of the immediate facts and estimation of the probable results'; elaborating on this point in the *Principles of Ethics*, Spencer accused orthodox, empirical, utilitarianism of attempting to distinguish good conduct from bad by mere induction and observation:

Conduct, according to its theory, is to be estimated by observation of results. When in sufficiently numerous cases, it has been found that behaviour of this kind works evil while behaviour of this kind works good, these kinds of behaviour are to be judged as wrong and right respectively.[11]

The problem with this approach, Spencer believed, was that it made the connection between an act and its good or bad results appear 'accidental'. It affirmed the existence of only '*some* relation between cause and effect' whereas 'a completely-scientific form of knowledge' would be able to discover a *necessary* relation between them.[12] This was the essence of deductive utilitarianism, namely the rational or 'scientific'

---

[9] Id., *Principles of Ethics*, i. 172.
[10] J. Burrow, *Evolution and Society* (Cambridge, 1966), 216.
[11] Spencer, *Principles of Ethics*, i. 56.   [12] Ibid. 57.

determination of 'the conditions by conforming to which this greatest happiness may be obtained.'[13] It was the business of a moral science, Spencer asserted, 'to deduce from the law of life and the conditions of existence, what kinds of action necessarily tend to produce happiness, and what kinds to produce unhappiness.'[14] The objective of the Synthetic Philosophy was thus to prove a priori 'that expedience must be a misleading guide, that it must be in the nature of things essentially bad to swerve a hair's breadth from the lines laid down by the strictest Individualism.'[15]

The origin of this distinction between empirical and deductive utilitarianism is to be found in Mill's *A System of Logic* where a contrast was drawn between the deductive and experimental sciences.[16] A science was experimental, wrote Mill, 'in proportion as every new case, which presents any peculiar features, stands in need of a new set of observations and experiments—a fresh induction.'[17] It dealt only with 'Empirical Laws', 'those uniformities which observation or experiment has shown to exist', on which one ought not to rely 'in cases varying much from those which have been actually observed, for want of seeing any reason *why* a law should exist.'[18] By contrast, a science was deductive to the extent that 'it can draw conclusions, respecting cases of a new kind, by processes which bring those cases under old inductions.' It was able to do this because its laws were laws of nature rather than empirical, in the sense that they 'state the explanation, the *why*, of empirical law . . . the ultimate causes on which it is contingent.'[19] As Ryan has pointed out, these laws of nature may be identified with the few ultimate causal laws (like those of Newtonian mechanics) which explain the multiplicity of empirical laws, the observed uniformities in nature.[20]

Mill insisted that the progress of a science consisted of its developing an increasingly deductive character, subsuming empirical regularities under explanatory causal laws.[21] Similarly, Spencer thought, the problem with empirical utilitarianism was that its adherents failed to recognize that they had 'reached but the initial stage of Moral Science', since

---

[13] Id., *Social Statics*, 82.   [14] Id., *Principles of Ethics*, i. 57.

[15] F. B. Jevons, 'A Review of Spencer's *Justice*', *Economic Review*, 2 (1892), 134.

[16] It is noteworthy that although Spencer's criticisms of Benthamite utilitarianism remained remarkably constant, the terminology of 'deductive' and 'empirical' utilitarianism did not appear in the *Social Statics*, which was written before Spencer had encountered Mill's *A System of Logic*. See Spencer, *Autobiography*, ii. 487, app. B.

[17] J. S. Mill, *A System of Logic* (London, 1919), 144.   [18] Ibid. 338.

[19] Ibid.   [20] A. Ryan, *The Philosophy of John Stuart Mill* (London, 1970), 68 ff.

[21] Cf. Mill, *System of Logic*, 145.

although observing regular connections between certain acts and good or bad results, they did not attempt to account for these connections in terms of causality.[22] Deductive utilitarianism was alleged to transcend its Benthamite predecessor in the same way that Newtonian physics transcended the astronomical observations of Tycho Brahe.

Spencer believed that the true account of the causal connections between means and ends in ethics was to be obtained from the theory of evolution. Moral phenomena had to be considered as phenomena of evolution, he argued, because 'they form a part of the aggregate of phenomena which evolution has wrought out':

> If the entire visible universe has been evolved—if the solar system as a whole, the earth as part of it, the life in general which the earth bears, as well as each individual organism—if the mental phenomena displayed by all creatures, up to the highest, in common with the phenomena presented by the aggregates of these highest—if one and all conform to the laws of evolution; then the necessary implication is that these phenomena of conduct in these highest creatures with which morality is concerned, also conform.[23]

Since 'conduct at large, including the conduct which Ethics deals with, is to be fully understood only as an aspect of evolving life', Spencer argued that the rules of morality could be identified by investigating 'the most highly evolved conduct as displayed by the most highly evolved being, man' and thus required a 'specification of those traits which his conduct assumes on reaching the limit of evolution.'[24]

It followed from the identification of morality with completely evolved conduct that the principles of ethics were to be discovered by consideration of the 'behaviour of the completely adapted man in the completely evolved society.'[25] This conception was in turn based on extrapolation from the 'fundamental truths' common to each of the special sciences of physics, biology, psychology, and sociology.[26] For example, psychology had demonstrated that human beings were becoming increasingly adapted to the social state through the development of the 'higher' faculties. Whereas it was inevitable that the actions of imperfectly adapted beings would produce pain as well as pleasure in their performance, Spencer argued that the further development of the moral faculty

---

[22] Spencer, *Principles of Ethics*, i. 58.

[23] Ibid. 63.   [24] Ibid. 281.

[25] Ibid. 275. However, contrary to G. E. Moore's argument in *Principia Ethica* (Cambridge, 1959), 45 ff., Spencer did not define 'good' as 'more evolved'. Like Mill and other utilitarians he defined the concept in terms of pleasure, and assumed that more highly evolved beings would be capable of experiencing greater pleasure.

[26] Spencer, *Principles of Ethics*, i. 63.

meant that fully evolved humanity would be capable of acting so as to produce pleasure unsullied anywhere by pain. From a utilitarian point of view a society composed of such ideally perfect human beings would be the best conceivable. The nature of this society was further delineated by the findings of sociology:

The fundamental requirement is that the life-sustaining actions of each shall severally bring him the amounts and kinds of advantage naturally achieved by them; and this implies firstly that he shall suffer no direct aggressions on his person or property, and secondly that he shall suffer no indirect aggressions by breach of contract.[27]

The completely evolved society of Spencerian moral philosophy was one governed by the Law of Equal Freedom, which asserted that 'Every man is free to do that which he wills, provided he infringes not the equal freedom of any other man.'[28] Moreover, the moral constitution of the fully adapted individuals living in this society was such that each would spontaneously respect this law, and none would aggress on the rights and liberties of others. For Spencer, justice primarily meant a rule of conduct which defined the equitable relations among perfect individuals.

The Law of Equal Freedom was not exhaustive of the rules governing Spencer's ideal society: he recognized the existence of duties of positive and negative beneficence as well as a sphere of conduct which he idiosyncratically styled 'the ethics of individual life', involving certain duties to the self like 'rest', 'activity', and 'nutrition'. Nevertheless, while Spencer insisted that the highest type of social life could not be attained without beneficence, 'the exchange of services beyond agreement', it was clear that the Law of Equal Freedom was the fundamental part of his moral code.

Spencer considered that the Law of Equal Freedom had a double aspect, since it was both a statement of the scientifically determined conditions for the attainment of the greatest happiness, and a rule of conduct which demanded an individual's allegiance 'irrespective of a direct estimation of happiness or misery'.[29] Considered in the latter sense this law should be made the direct object of conduct:

For if there are any conditions without fulfillment of which happiness cannot be compassed, then the first step must be to ascertain these conditions with a view to fulfilling them; and to admit this is to admit that not happiness itself must be

[27] Ibid. 149.
[28] Ibid. ii. (London, 1893), 46. A more extensive discussion of this principle will be deferred until the next ch.   [29] Ibid. i. 57.

the immediate end, but fulfillment of the conditions to its attainment must be the immediate end.[30]

Nevertheless, Spencer also insisted that 'rational utilitarianism . . . takes for its immediate object of pursuit conformity to certain principles which, in the nature of things, *causally determine* welfare.'[31] This notion constituted the essence of Spencer's criticisms of orthodox utilitarianism in terms of its failure to transcend empirical inductions with causal laws. But if the Law of Equal Freedom is literally a statement of causality, then we can have no choice in obeying it, any more than we have a choice in obeying the law of gravity, and yet the conception of a moral rule would seem to entail an element of choice in deciding whether or not to obey it.[32] Consequently it is difficult to see how the Law of Equal Freedom can be regarded as a moral imperative, and Spencer appears to equivocate between two very different senses of natural law: that of the scientist, and that of the moralist.

Spencer did not succeed in resolving the tension inherent in his dual conception of the Law of Equal Freedom, but its existence should give pause for thought before he is consigned to the twentieth-century category of 'rule utilitarianism', which holds that 'an act is right if, and only if, it conforms to a set of rules general acceptance of which would maximize utility.'[33] This is not to deny that there are grounds for describing Spencer in this way, since he maintained that the violation of the rule of conduct was not justified even in those cases where it might appear to promote a greater amount of utility than conformity to the rule. Nevertheless, an account of Spencer's ethical theory shorn of its evolutionary and quasi-scientific trappings engenders many fundamental misunderstandings of his moral philosophy, symptomatic of which is the claim that 'both Mill and Spencer adhere to what Spencer calls "rational utilitarianism"' since for both of them 'the tendencies of actions were captured in statable empirical laws.'[34] But this is to overlook Spencer's distinction between empirical and deductive laws. He would have agreed with this statement as a characterization of Mill,

---

[30] Ibid. 167.   [31] Ibid. 162. Italics added.

[32] 'When we say of these fully-evolved men that they will obey the law of equal liberty or any other law, we can only mean that they will obey in the sense that matter is sometimes said to obey the law of gravity. In short, our ideal code is a code "formulating" not regulating "the behaviour of the completely-adapted man in the completely-evolved society."' F. W. Maitland, 'Mr. H. Spencer's Theory of Society', *Mind*, 8 (1883), 359.

[33] D. Lyons, *The Forms and Limits of Utilitarianism* (Oxford, 1965), 140.

[34] J. N. Gray, 'Spencer on the Ethics of Liberty and State Interference', *History of Political Thought*, 3 (1982), 472.

for the latter's defence of liberty was based on induction and observation: experience shows, for example, that on the whole a sane adult was the best judge of his own interests. Yet in Spencer's terms this was simply an empirical law and as such needed to be transcended by a scientific investigation into the conditions which causally determine the greatest happiness. Only a moral theory based on this type of investigation was worthy of the description of 'rational utilitarianism'.[35]

Spencer argued that in failing to be sufficiently scientific in the determination of the conditions productive of the greatest happiness, the empirical utilitarians had opened the way for the evils of 'state superintendence'. Benthamite utilitarianism seemed to embody 'the belief that government ought not only to guarantee men the unmolested pursuit of happiness, but should provide the happiness for them and deliver it at their door.'[36] In consequence the statute book was simply a 'record of unhappy guesses' of 'empirical attempts at the acquisition of happiness.'[37] Although from a Benthamite perspective it might seem that a policy of State intervention would promote the greatest happiness of the greatest number, a scientific examination of the causal laws which were productive of the greatest happiness could demonstrate that such a policy would be ultimately self-defeating. Rational utilitarianism, Spencer argued, gave rise to a conception of the limited State.

Nevertheless, on at least one interpretation, Spencer's ideal society should have permitted no role for government at all. The 'perfectly-adapted man in the perfectly-evolved society' was so constituted that he would instinctively act so as to respect the rights and liberties of others; it followed that there would be no need for coercion of any kind. The individual would not need to 'coerce' himself since there would be no conflict between his emotion and reason, while society would not need to coerce the individual since he would 'spontaneously' act in a socially desirable way. In the *Social Statics* Spencer had held out this anarchic state as the goal towards which humanity was rapidly moving, and government was considered merely a temporary expedient while the conditions for social equilibrium were established.[38] Later statements

---

[35] The differences between Mill and Spencer bear many similarities to those between Spencer and Sidgwick discussed later in this ch.

[36] Spencer, *Social Statics*, 308. It has been argued that the *Social Statics* was, at least in part, intended as an attempt to rescue utilitarianism from its potentially statist implications. See J. D. Y. Peel, *Herbert Spencer: The Evolution of a Sociologist* (London, 1971), 83. For his later criticisms of Benthamism see *The Man versus the State*, ed. D. G. Macrae (1884; Harmondsworth, 1969), 155 ff.   [37] Id., *Social Statics*, 21.

[38] Cf. ibid. 311.

of Spencer's ethical philosophy retained elements of this conception, but they tended far more to emphasize that government was an inescapable part of the human condition. In both the *Principles of Sociology* and the *Principles of Ethics*, Spencer seemed 'to contemplate as the final condition of humanity a condition which neither he nor others would call absolutely perfect' because 'society will still coerce the individual but only for a few purposes.'[39] Having reached the conclusion, discussed in Chapter 5, that perfect adaptation would be unattainable, Spencer was lead to abandon his earlier anarchism, and to assign a role to government even in his 'perfect' society.

The function ascribed to government by the *Principles of Ethics* was that of upholding the Law of Equal Freedom. Conformity to this law, Spencer argued, demanded only that the government guaranteed the 'scientific' conditions for the pursuit of happiness, and did not aim to promote the general welfare by its direct action. In other words, since the Law of Equal Freedom was a statement of the principle of justice, the function of the State may be stated more positively as being to uphold and defend justice:

Each citizen wants to live, and to live as fully as his surroundings permit. This being the desire of all, it results that all, exercising joint control, are interested in seeing that while each does not suffer from breach of the relation between acts and ends in his own person, he shall not break those relations in the persons of others. The incorporated mass of citizens has to maintain the conditions under which each may gain the fullest life compatible with the fullest lives of fellow citizens.[40]

The State, or 'the incorporated mass of citizens', was thus strictly limited to the administration of justice; with the advance of peaceful relations between nations even the function of external defence would eventually cease to be necessary. If the State should seek to do more than uphold justice it would instantly itself become a transgressor: 'If justice asserts the liberty of each limited only by the like liberties of all, then the imposing of any further limit is unjust; no matter whether the power imposing it be one man or a million of men.' The State exists to enforce rights and if 'instead of preserving them, it trenches upon them, it commits wrongs instead of preventing wrongs.'[41] Consequently Spencer regarded as illegitimate State functions which had long been part of the Victorian conception of the role of government, and were not primarily matters of contention between the two wings of liberalism, like

[39] Maitland, 'Spencer's Theory of Society', 363, 361.
[40] Spencer, *Principles of Ethics*, ii. 213–14.   [41] Ibid. 222.

the Poor Law, the State issue of currency, the provision of light-houses, the Factory Acts, and public-health legislation.[42]

A number of Spencer's followers, most notably Auberon Herbert and J. H. Levy, abandoned any pretence of employing this kind of utilitarian justification for a limited State and founded their Individualism on the natural rights of the individual.[43] Nevertheless, Spencer's deductive utilitarianism did find favour with many other Individualists. For example, O'Brien echoed Spencer's criticisms of empirical utilitarianism in a passage which was practically a précis of the relevant chapters of the *Social Statics*:

[S]ecuring liberty is more important than promoting happiness. For if happiness be the goal, liberty is the only way to it . . . Even 'the greatest happiness of the greatest number' cannot be achieved unless men are individually free to move towards it. Add to this, that 'happiness' is relative to each individual character . . . But liberty is the same for all; . . . it is definite and objective, whereas happiness is vague and subjective; and in securing it we are allowing to everyone as much happiness as he can get without taking it at the expense of his fellows. Liberty secures the maximum of the general happiness, while at the same time it prevents the particular tyrant from buying joy with the slavery of his fellow.[44]

A more extensive statement of this argument was to be found in Bruce Smith's book *Liberty and Liberalism*. Government, he argued, had to aim at the greatest good of its citizens which he defined in terms of the greatest happiness. In addition, it had to pursue this goal for the race as a whole rather than of a single generation since 'every government has been entrusted with the charge of a great inheritance, which has to be handed on, again, to its successors.'[45] The government had to strive to attain the *ultimate* as well as the *immediate* happiness of the people, and as Smith remarked,

the more one knows of legislation, the less it will be believed capable of actually producing happiness for the people, that is to say, happiness of a positive nature. It can prevent aggression and abuse by one citizen over another. It can guarantee to every citizen the freedom to do the very best for himself. But parliament possesses no mysterious power.[46]

The most that the government could do was to ensure that the necessary conditions for human happiness were respected. Smith argued that

---

[42] See e.g. Spencer's discussion of the 'limits of state-duties', ibid., pt. IV.
[43] Their theories are considered in Ch. 7.
[44] M. D. O'Brien, *Socialism Tested by the Facts* (London, 1892), 194–5.
[45] [A.] B. Smith, *Liberty and Liberalism* (London, 1887), 241.   [46] Ibid. 420.

social science had revealed these necessary conditions of human happiness to be three in number: security of the person, security of property, and individual liberty. In securing to every man the fruits of his labour or of his ingenuity, Individualism encouraged improved methods of work and production and thereby increased prosperity and the sum total of human happiness. Smith concluded that:

in order to obtain for a community the largest aggregate amount of happiness, each member of it should have secured to him the most absolute freedom or liberty; subject only to such limitations as are necessary in order to secure equal freedom or liberty to all other members.[47]

Furthermore, since the progress, prosperity, and happiness of mankind require only the security of the person, property, and liberty of the individual, it was possible to deduce broad guidelines for the liberal legislator to follow. In the first place, 'the state should not impose taxes or use the public revenue for any purpose other than that of securing equal freedom to all citizens.' Secondly, this objective provides the only justification for the State interfering with the legally acquired property of any section of its citizens 'and in the event of any such justifiable interference amounting to appropriation, then, only conditional upon the lawful owner being fully compensated.' Finally, the State should not restrict the personal liberties of its citizens for any other purpose than that of guaranteeing the equal liberty of all.[48]

III. Absolute and Relative Ethics[49]

The rules of rational utilitarianism prescribed the ideally optimific behaviour for human beings who were perfectly adapted to the social state, but there remained the question of the applicability of this ideal code to the actual decisions of imperfect humanity. Furthermore, although rational utilitarianism excluded the possibility of the State acting to promote the happiness of its citizens directly, there was a divergence between the rights prescribed by the principle of justice and those actually established by law. In particular, the nationalization of the

[47] Ibid. 222.   [48] Ibid. 450.
[49] The issues dealt with in this relatively short section are discussed more extensively in Ch. 7.

land and universal suffrage were both logical corollaries of the theory which the mature Spencer was unwilling to acknowledge.[50]

Spencer's proposed solution to both these problems was the distinction between absolute and relative ethics. By being regarded as analogous to the truths of 'abstract mechanics or absolute mechanics', which were capable of practical application only if due allowance was made for distorting factors like friction and air resistance, the principles of ethics were to be made at once applicable to actual decisions and less radical in their implications.[51] Although 'absolute mechanics' dealt with an ideal world of 'forces and motions considered as free from all interferences resulting from friction, resistances of media, and special properties of matter' it was nevertheless 'indispensable for the guidance of real mechanics.'[52] In like manner, the code of absolute ethics was indispensable for the guidance of less than completely evolved conduct; having deduced from the evolutionary 'laws of life' the code of ethics appropriate to a perfect humanity, this could be applied to practical decisions once due allowance had been made for the 'imperfect adaptation' of human nature to the requirements of living in the social state. This resulted in an analogue of 'real' mechanics, a code of relative ethics, which was intended 'to serve as a standard for our solving, as well as we can, the problems of real conduct', and prescribed conduct which was 'relatively right' or 'least wrong'.[53]

The upshot of this distinction between absolute and relative ethics was that many of the radical implications of Spencer's ethical theory were defused. Although absolute ethics might seem to demand equal

---

[50] My conclusions about Spencer's later 'drift to conservatism' broadly agree with those propounded by D. Wiltshire, *The Social and Political Thought of Herbert Spencer* (Oxford, 1978). This thesis has been challenged by W. L. Miller, 'Herbert Spencer's Drift to Conservatism', *History of Political Thought*, 3 (1982), 483–97, which alleges that the 'drift to conservatism' thesis is based on a misunderstanding of the nature of the *Social Statics*. Miller contends that this was not a 'blueprint for immediate social reform', but was a description of an ideal state which could only be reached by mankind as a result of a long process of evolution (p. 483 f.). It belonged to what Spencer would later call 'absolute' ethics, and hence there is no discrepancy between his earlier and later views. However, this argument would appear to overlook two points. (1) Spencer's views on the time-scale involved in human evolution underwent a considerable re-evaluation between his earlier and later work. (2) In his later work absolute ethics is not presented as a distant goal, but as a never-to-be-realized ideal analogous to the perfectly rigid lever of absolute mechanics. It was thus 'a goal ever to be recognized, though it cannot actually be reached.' ('Absolute Political Ethics', in *Essays: Scientific, Political and Speculative* (1874; enlarged edn., London, 1891), iii. 228.) In the earlier work, by contrast, Spencer seems to have believed that his Utopia could be achieved, and sooner rather than later.

[51] Spencer, 'Absolute Political Ethics', 222.

[52] Ibid. 223.   [53] Id., *Principles of Ethics* i. 275.

political rights for men and women or the abolition of private ownership of the land, the realization of these demands was made contingent on the glacially slow evolutionary processes which would remove the 'mis-adaptations' of human nature to the social state. As Spencer remarked in the *Principles of Ethics*, the principle of justice 'is an idea appropriate to an ultimate state, and can be but partially entertained during transitional states; for the prevailing ideas must, on the average, be congruous with existing institutions and activities.'[54] The ethical conceptions appropriate to each stage of human existence were determined by the proportions of the ideal types of militancy and industrialism present in any given society; the closer a society conformed to the ideal type of industrialism, the more closely its code of ethics would correspond to absolute ethics:

[A]bsolute justice being the standard, relative justice has to be determined by considering how near an approach may, under present circumstances, be made to it. As already implied in various places, it is impossible during stages of transition which necessitate ever changing compromises, to fulfill the dictates of absolute equity; and nothing beyond empirical judgements can be formed of the extent to which they may be, at any given time, fulfilled.[55]

It followed that the ethical code appropriate to an imperfectly evolved society like late Victorian Britain would diverge from the code of absolute ethics in many important respects. Spencer was able to contend that although his principle of justice might appear to demand universal suffrage, justice in late Victorian Britain required a limited franchise since 'in the absence of a duly-adapted character liberty given in one direction is lost in another.'[56] To hand political power to the majority, who were incapable of respecting the principle of justice, would destroy the liberty of the property-owning class to use and dispose of their possessions as they saw fit. The nationalization of the land would also either involve the expropriation of landowners or the payment of such great sums in compensation that the scheme would be practically disastrous.[57]

On the other hand, the relativistic implications of Spencer's distinction between absolute and relative ethics were also open to exploitation by his critics. If it was true that the completely evolved society of industrialism was still some way from being realized, then it seemed to follow that the theory conferred legitimacy, pro tem, on the remaining

[54] Ibid. ii. 43.   [55] Ibid. i. 286.
[56] Id., *Principles of Sociology*, ii. 750.   [57] Cf. Ch. 7, below.

elements of militant social organization, including an extensive sphere of State action. The *Westminster Review*, for one, thought that 'there are reasons why we should not be in too great a hurry to complete the transition from a predominately militant to a predominately industrial type of national life.'[58] These included the continuing necessity of Britain being able to protect itself against aggression by other States, and the recognition that the militant social type had not completed its work in moulding an individual character suited to the social state. The *Westminster Review* concluded that Spencer's principles 'are not adapted to our present state of society and may be considered as ideals far in advance of practicability.'[59]

By making the distinction between absolute and relative ethics, Spencer had arrived at a kind of naturalized Hegelianism in which the gradual emergence of the ethical Idea could be discerned in each stage of human history, and in which the actual could be identified with the rational. Despite the discrepancies between the absolute principle of justice and the prevailing distribution of property and power in late Victorian Britain, Spencer could none the less contend that it was a transitional stage necessary to the attainment of the ultimate goal and hence these departures from the principle could be justified.[60] Not only did deductive utilitarianism set itself against the intervention of the State to reduce inequalities in society, but it was also opposed to all forms of radical social change. But Spencer's relativism was a two-edged weapon: it was only by adopting this approach that his formerly radical ideals could be made consistent with a defence of the late Victorian status quo, but at the same time it threatened to make his dire warnings about the consequences of the drift to socialism appear at best overstated and at worst irrelevant.

IV. Benthamism Tamed: Sidgwick

The empirical utilitarianism which Spencer had set out to supersede with his scientifically determined code of conduct was represented in

---

[58] Anon., 'Contemporary Literature', *Westminster Review*, 66 (1884), 554.

[59] Ibid. 555.

[60] Spencer's notion of a conception of justice apropriate to each stage of human social development has certain parallels with Marx's theory of justice. For Marx see A. Wood, *Karl Marx* (London, 1981), 130 ff.

the closing decades of the nineteenth century by the Knightbridge Professor of Philosophy at Cambridge, Henry Sidgwick. As Sidgwick himself stressed, however, he shared a considerable amount of ground in common with Spencer; both believed that the greatest happiness was the ultimate end of action and that 'in the main' the service which 'any one sane adult should be legally compelled to render to others should be merely the negative service of non-interference.'[61] On the other hand they were separated by two chief differences, one methodological and the other practical.

'The main difference between me and Mr. Spencer', wrote Sidgwick, 'is as to the value of Absolute Ethics.'[62] By contrast to Spencer's methodology in the Synthetic Philosophy, Sidgwick insisted that a completely evolved society was too far removed from present reality to afford any guidance as to what we ought to do now. In the first place, even if it were possible to 'conceive as possible a human community which is from a utilitarian point of view perfect' it would be impossible to 'forecast the natures and relations of the persons composing such a community, with sufficient clearness and certainty to enable us to define even in outline their moral code.' If Spencer might reply to this point that it merely indicated the limitations of Sidgwick's imagination, his second criticism was more telling. Even if such a construction were possible it would not be 'of much avail in solving the practical problems of actual humanity.' A society in which there was no such thing as punishment, for example, 'is necessarily a society with its essential structure so unlike our own, that it would be idle to attempt any close imitation of its rules of behaviour.'[63] Therefore, the construction of an ideally perfect code of utilitarian ethics, which was of dubious utility and was probably impossible to construct, was to be abandoned.[64]

Methodologically Sidgwick remained an empirical utilitarian, for whom right conduct was to be determined, not by elaborate deductions

---

[61] H. Sidgwick, *Lectures on Ethics*, 278.

[62] Ibid. 199. The substance of Sidgwick's criticisms of Spencer in these posthumously published lectures appeared during his lifetime in a number of articles, most notably the 'Critical Notice of *Justice*', in *Mind*, NS 1 (1892), and 'Mr. Spencer's Ethical System', *Mind*, 5 (1880).

[63] Id., *The Methods of Ethics (1874*; 7th edn., London, 1907), 470. See also Maitland's claim that in Spencer's ideal state 'if such words as right, duty, ought survive at all, they will survive as petty archaisms of uncertain meaning.' (Maitland, 'Spencer's Theory of Society', 359.)

[64] The best exposition of Sidgwick's methodology is to be found in S. Collini *et al.*, *That Noble Science of Politics* (Cambridge, 1983), 279–307.

from the 'laws of life', but by what he referred to as the 'empirical–reflective method of Empirical Hedonism.'[65] This was Bentham's 'felicific calculus' under another name, and it involved calculating the potential surplus of pleasure over pain by representing

> beforehand the different series of feelings that our knowledge of physical and psychical causes leads us to expect from the different courses of action which lie open to us; judge which series, as thus represented, appears on the whole preferable, taking all probabilities into account; and adopt the corresponding line of conduct.[66]

Nevertheless, this method embroiled the individual 'in much perplexity and uncertainty'. To form an estimate of the pleasure likely to be derived from a future course of action an individual both had to attempt to compare his own past feelings in respect of their pleasantness, and to forecast his future pleasures from his past experiences, but in either case 'it seems difficult or impossible for him to avoid errors of considerable magnitude.'[67] When one also considered that the individual might have to estimate the character of his own potential experiences from the experiences of others, and that he would have to take into account the effects of his actions on all sentient beings, the difficulties in the way of this empirical–reflective method seemed insuperable.[68] Yet despite Sidgwick's conclusion that the felicific calculus would be almost impossible to use, he also believed that a utilitarian had no alternative but to fall back on the empirical–reflective method.

He was rescued from this paradox by the convenient observation that, in the great majority of cases, the received opinion on moral questions could be shown to be supported by the principle of utility in the sense that many common-sense moral rules have 'some manifest felicific tendency'. According to Sidgwick's conception of the role of philosophy in *The Methods of Ethics*, it aimed to produce a systematization of principles already in evidence in accepted moral rules, and it was part of the argument of the book that utilitarianism provided just such a systematization of the morality of common sense.[69] Although he did not claim that the rules of common sense were themselves the product of

---

[65] H. Sidgwick, *Methods of Ethics*, 460.
[66] Ibid. 131.   [67] Ibid. 460.   [68] Ibid. 147 ff.
[69] See J. B. Schneewind, *Sidgwick's Ethics and Victorian Moral Philosophy* (Oxford, 1977), ch. 6. It should be pointed out that Sidgwick distinguished between egoism (the pursuit of personal happiness) and utilitarianism (in the sense of a doctrine of 'Universal Benevolence' directed to the maximum happiness) which might require the sacrifice of egoistic goals. This distinction had not been clearly made by earlier utilitarians.

utilitarian calculation, it was nevertheless 'but a short and easy step to the conclusion that in the Morality of Common Sense we have ready to hand a body of Utilitarian doctrine', and that the 'apparent first principles of Common Sense may be accepted as the "middle axioms" of utilitarian method.'[70] Instead of the utilitarian philosopher standing aloof from ordinary morality, and using the principle of utility as a tool with which to cut through the irrationalities and confusions of accepted beliefs, Sidgwick was forced to concede that in the vast majority of cases utilitarian decisions could only be reached by employing the rules of common sense. Thus despite their very different methodologies, Sidgwick and Spencer can be seen to have arrived at substantially similar conclusions regarding the relationship between utilitarianism and the dictates of the ordinary moral conscience.

The practical difference between Spencer and Sidgwick was connected to their methodological differences and arose from the fact that Spencer insisted on taking his principle of justice—the Law of Equal Freedom—'as an absolute or ultimate ethical principle, having an authority transcending every other.'[71] It was on this issue, Sidgwick remarked, that Spencer 'conceives the main practical issue to lie between his own view and the more empirical Utilitarianism that I represent.'[72]

Spencer, as we have noted, believed that conformity to the Law of Equal Freedom determined the rightness of an act irrespective of the utilities it produced; the principle of utility being employed only in order to justify this law. Sidgwick also believed that on many occasions a utilitarian would be justified in retaining the rules of common-sense morality even when their own proper consequences were not maximally felicific, since the utility of the possession of a rule would outweigh the utility to be derived from its violation. As Schneewind has written in an excellent exposition of the place of rules in Sidgwick's theory:

We must be able to make reliable predictions about each other's conduct in moral matters, and we could not do so if each of us had to make complete utilitarian calculations of right and wrong prior to each decision . . . Hence some acts are allowed to pass as right even when their own proper consequences are less than maximally felicific. The reason is that the second-order benefits derived from using the decision-procedure which justifies doing them make up for the deficiencies in the consequences of the individual acts.[73]

---

[70] H. Sidgwick, *Methods of Ethics*, 461.
[71] Ibid. 279.   [72] Ibid. 278.   [73] Schneewind, *Sidgwick's Ethics*, 348.

Nevertheless, even counting the utility to be derived from the possession of a rule, it would be irrational for a utilitarian to refuse to break the rule in circumstances in which he was quite certain that to do so would produce a greater utility. Although Sidgwick believed that the accumulated experience of mankind as embodied in moral rules would make these exceptions exceedingly rare, he adopted the conventional utilitarian view that the rightness of an act was determined, not by its conformity to a rule, but by its being productive of greater utility than any of its alternatives. He argued that 'a Utilitarian must hold that it is always wrong for a man knowingly to do anything other than what he believes to be conducive to the greatest happiness',[74] and a consistent utilitarian could not act upon 'any absolute practical maxims: but only general rules of a relative and limited validity.'[75]

As we shall see in the following section, this difference over the status which a utilitarian could accord to his decision-rules was to have important consequences for Sidgwick and Spencer's respective views on the limits of State action. For the present, however, the most important point is that although Sidgwick allowed rules of conduct an important function in his ethical theory, he accorded them a different status to that which they had been assigned by Spencer. Whereas for Spencer the rules of conduct themselves determined the rightness of an act, and were statements of causal laws, for Sidgwick rules were primarily 'axiomata media' or practical aids to utilitarian decision, the rightness of an act being determined by its producing a greater surplus of pleasure over pain than any alternatives.

Both these methodological and substantive differences between Sidgwick and Spencer emerged in the former's justification of a limited State. In making the transition from his reworked version of utilitarianism to Individualism, Sidgwick's methodology in *The Elements of Politics* closely corresponded to that which he employed in *The Methods of Ethics*, but rather than dealing with the principles of common-sense morality, the *Elements of Politics* was founded on an appeal to 'the common sense of mankind, as expressed in actual legislation.'[76] Analogous to Sidgwick's argument in the *Methods of Ethics* that common-sense moral rules possessed 'some manifest felicific tendency' was his contention that the principles which had determined the course of

---

[74] Sidgwick, *Methods of Ethics*, 492, quoted in Schneewind, *Sidgwick's Ethics*, 348.
[75] H. Sidgwick, 'Review of James Fitzjames Stephen's *Liberty, Equality, Fraternity*', *Academy*, 4 (1873), 392.
[76] Id., *The Elements of Politics* (London, 1891), 44.

legislation in Britain throughout much of the nineteenth century possessed a utilitarian justification. The utilitarian legislator could employ these principles as a ready-to-hand code for reaching political decisions in the same way that the utilitarian moralist could employ commonsense morality as a ready-to-hand code for ethical decisions.

Sidgwick argued that the problems which had undermined the utility of the empirical–reflective method as a means of reaching moral decisions also meant that its applicability to political decision-making was limited. Rather than seeking to apply the principle of utility directly to legislation, the utilitarian political theorist had to 'establish or assume some subordinate principle or principles, capable of more precise application, relating to the best means for attaining by legislation the end of Maximum Happiness.'[77]

The first such subordinate principle to be considered was the Law of Equal Freedom which decreed that the sole end of legislation was to secure mutual non-interference between individuals. Sidgwick argued that rather than the Law of Equal Freedom being the absolute moral principle of Spencer's theory, the justification of the 'Individualistic Minimum' of governmental interference required

an individualistic maxim definitely understood as a subordinate principle or 'middle axiom' of utilitarianism: i.e. that individuals are to be protected from deception, breach of engagement, annoyance, coercion, or other conduct tending to impede them in the pursuit of their ends, so far as such protection is conducive to the general happiness.[78]

The reason why the equal liberties principle had to be understood as a middle axiom of utilitarianism, rather than as 'absolutely desirable as the ultimate end of law and of all governmental interference', was that Spencer's version of the principle could not sustain even a limited State.[79] For example, Spencer's conception of harm was cast in terms of an infringement of liberty, but the protection of property rights in their existing form seemed to go well beyond what would be required to secure an individual against infringements of his liberty in the ordinary sense of 'the absence of physical and moral coercion.'[80] Thus, Sidgwick claimed,

all governments and most Individualists practically go beyond this, and aim at the protection of the governed from pain—and loss or diminution of their means

---

[77] Ibid. 39.   [78] Ibid. 55.   [79] Ibid. 44.
[80] For a more extensive discussion of this point see Ch. 7.

of gratifying their desires—caused by the action of human beings. In so doing, they adopt by implication a utilitarian view of the mutual interference that law ought to prevent,—even while expressly disavowing the utilitarian criterion.[81]

The parallel between this point and Sidgwick's other criticisms of Spencer's deductive utilitarianism is evident: a consistent utilitarian could not accord the Law of Equal Freedom the status of an absolute principle, but only the status of a subordinate maxim of utilitarianism. Although the Law of Equal Freedom was not to be accorded the status of an absolute moral principle, it was a useful middle axiom or practical aid for the application of the principle of utility to decisions concerning legislation and public policy. Sidgwick argued further that the Individualistic Minimum provided a satisfactory theoretical foundation for a large part of the legislation which existed in civilized communities. He also was in broad agreement with orthodox political economy that 'wealth tends to be produced most amply and economically in a society where Government tends to leave industry alone.'[82] As a general rule, therefore, 'the state should enforce all contracts made between sane adults, if they have been made without coercion and wilful or careless misrepresentation, and if the effects they were designed to produce involve no violation of law or damage to third parties or the community at large.'[83]

It should be noted that although Sidgwick's formula of Individualism did not possess the absolute status which it had been accorded by Spencer, he did not mean to imply that the equal liberties principle was to be overridden on every occasion on which it failed to maximize utility. The self-limiting nature of Sidgwick's utilitarianism, which was discussed in relation to moral rules, was also apparent in his discussion of *laissez-faire*. Sidgwick did not aim to show that government intervention was always expedient, even where 'laisser faire leads to a manifestly unsatisfactorily result; its expediency has to be decided in any particular case by a careful estimate of advantages and drawbacks requiring data obtained from special experience.'[84] Like the rules of moral common sense, which a utilitarian could be justified in following even though the proper consequences of a particular act falling under them did not produce maximally felicific results, Sidgwick believed that there could

---

[81] H. Sidgwick, *Elements of Politics*, 47.

[82] Id., 'Economic Socialism' in id., *Miscellaneous Essays and Addresses* (London, 1904), 201–2, first published in *Contemporary Review*, 50 (Nov. 1886).

[83] Id., *Elements of Politics*, 85.   [84] Ibid. 168

be utilitarian grounds for abiding by the rule of *laissez-faire* even when it did not produce the greatest happiness in a particular case.

Despite the important methodological and substantive differences between Sidgwick and Spencer their fundamental conclusions were remarkably similar. In the first place, just as Spencer had produced a version of the utilitarian doctrine which was adverse to any substantial alteration of the late Victorian social order, Sidgwick's conclusions were also essentially conservative. Instead of seeking radical social change, the utilitarian philosopher must content himself with piecemeal criticism and reform, commencing 'with the existing social order and the existing morality as part of that order.'[85] As the New Liberal theorist D. G. Ritchie observed, '[i]f this is Benthamism, it is Benthamism grown tame and sleek.'[86] He also noted that Sidgwick revealed an almost Hegelian willingness to discover the rational in the real, a point which was brought out especially clearly by the remark that 'the form of society' to which the utilitarian philosopher's practical conclusions relate 'will be one varying but little from the actual, with its actually established code of moral rules and customary judgements concerning vice and virtue.'[87]

In addition, both Sidgwick and Spencer agreed that in general the direct application of the principle of utility to particular decisions would not produce the greatest total utility. Although they disagreed with each other over the reasons why this would be the case, and although Sidgwick could not accept the absolute status Spencer accorded the Law of Equal Freedom, both were consequently opposed to political strategies which aimed to maximize utility by the frequent and direct intervention of the State.

V. The Limits of *Laissez-Faire*

Despite Sidgwick's endorsement of the general principle of *laissez-faire* he also believed that the Individualistic Minimum was inadequate as a complete account of the limits of State action. He was aware of 'certain difficulties and doubts which arise when we attempt to work out . . . a consistent and exclusive individualist system' and accordingly con-

---

[85] Id., *Methods of Ethics*, 474.

[86] D. G. Ritchie, 'Review of *The Elements of Politics*', *International Journal of Ethics*, 2 (1892), 255.   [87] Sidgwick, *Methods of Ethics*, 474.

sidered 'to what extent, and under what carefully defined limitations, it is expedient to allow the introduction of paternal and socialistic legislation, with a view to remedy these inadequacies.'[88]

Because Sidgwick argued that the legitimate functions of the State went beyond Spencer's Individualistic Minimum of defence against external aggression and the enforcement of contracts, some comment-ators have suggested that his conclusions demanded a range of State functions which are no longer consistent with Individualism. In this regard, it has been claimed, Sidgwick sought a compromise between the principles of Individualism and socialism:

In much the same way that he used the principles of utilitarianism and common sense intuitionism (*sic*) to supplement one another in *The Methods of Ethics*, so he invoked the principles of socialism for those cases in which 'the individualistic basis' of liberalism tended 'to be inadequate to produce the attainable maximum of social happiness'.[89]

It also has been alleged that Sidgwick's *Elements of Politics* 'represents something of a landmark in the transformation of British political thought', for breaking with the hitherto dominant creed of *laissez-faire* liberalism.[90] An alternative formulation of this claim is cast in terms of a comparison between Sidgwick's utilitarianism and the Idealism of T. H. Green:

Oxford Idealists and Cambridge rationalists [i.e. Sidgwick and Marshall] were both preoccupied by contemporary social problems, both formulated essentially social philosophies concerned with the right conduct of individuals in their relations with each other, and both arrived at comparable policy prescriptions at almost exactly the same time.[91]

Finally, in the only full-length study of Sidgwick's political theory, William Havard has suggested that he 'humanised' the doctrine of individualism and thus stood 'on the threshold of the doorway through which L. T. Hobhouse passes in the twentieth century.'[92]

In contrast to this widely accepted interpretation, it will now be demonstrated that Sidgwick was simply part of a more widespread approach to the issue of the legitimate limits of State action, which,

[88] Id., *Elements of Politics*, 43.
[89] J. T. Kloppenberg, *Uncertain Victory: Social Democracy and Progressivism in European and American Thought 1870–1920* (Oxford, 1986), 185. [90] Ibid. 182.
[91] C. J. Dewey, '"Cambridge Idealism": Utilitarian Revisionists in Late Nineteenth Century Cambridge', *Historical Journal*, 17 (1974), 63.
[92] W. C. Havard, *Henry Sidgwick and Later Utilitarian Political Philosophy* (Gainesville, Fla., 1959), 133.

while it recognized exceptions to the rule of *laissez-faire* going beyond anything Spencer might allow, did not depart substantially from the recognized functions of the State in late Victorian Britain.[93] Far from marking a 'transformation' of British liberal thought, Sidgwick's views were close not only to those of the empirical Individualists, but also to those of some of Spencer's self-professed disciples.

Because the Law of Equal Freedom was a middle axiom and not an absolute moral principle, Sidgwick argued that there were circumstances in which utilitarian considerations would require it to be set aside. It was dependent on the validity of two assumptions: the first was psychological, 'individuals are likely to provide for their welfare better than the government', the second sociological, 'the common welfare is likely to be best promoted by individuals promoting their private interests intelligently.'[94] The former, if true, would exclude 'paternalist' legislation, the latter 'socialist' legislation. But, Sidgwick argued, neither was *absolutely* valid. Since each was no more than a 'rough induction from our ordinary experience of human life . . . in no way proved to be even an approximately universal truth' they could be true only as a general rule, and hence the Law of Equal Freedom was subject to important qualifications.[95]

With regard to the psychological assumption, Sidgwick considered a number of cases in which 'indirectly individualist' legislation or governmental intervention might be justified. This would involve the prohibition of 'acts or omissions not directly or necessarily mischievous to others, but attended with a certain risk of mischief.' An example of this would be the legal enforcement of a system of standard weights and measures to prevent deception by sellers with regard to the quantity of good sold. These considerations shaded over into directly paternalist ones. If it is demonstrated that men are liable to ruin themselves by gambling or opium-smoking, or if they knowingly incur easily avoided dangers in industrial processes, then 'it would, I think, be unreasonable to allow these practices to go on without interference merely on account of an established presumption in favour of laissez-faire.'[96] Sidgwick

---

[93] This argument has also been made by S. Collini, in 'Idealism and "Cambridge Idealism"', *Historical Journal*, 18 (1975), 171–7, and *Liberalism and Sociology*, 17 ff. However, Collini has misidentified the target of Sidgwick's criticisms. He regards Sidgwick's book as a polemic against 'Collectivists like Hobhouse' (*Liberalism and Sociology*, 20), whereas I suggest that Spencerian Individualism rather than Collectivism was Sidgwick's primary target.

[94] H. Sidgwick, *Elements of Politics*, 143–6.

[95] Ibid. 136–7.   [96] Ibid. 137.

inferred that the government would be entitled to prosecute the owners of gambling houses or of opium dens, and to set basic standards of safety in industrial processes. Similar considerations also justified the government in taking action to secure 'adequate qualifications in any class of professional men', for example to eliminate quackery in the medical profession.[97]

In the context of the late nineteenth century these arguments were not radical, and it is possible to find other empirical Individualists expressing much the same view of paternalistic legislation like the Factory Acts. For example Goldwin Smith, hardly a socialist himself, argued that

it is difficult to see why the enforcement of hygienic regulations or safeguards for life and limb is more socialistic in the case of a factory than in the case of a city, or why the protection of women and children who cannot protect themselves against industrial cruelty and abuse is more socialistic than the protection of them against wife-beating or infanticide.[98]

In this he was supported by Brodrick, who remarked that 'whatever objection may be raised against any one of these measures, it is clear that, if all be condemned as Socialistic, hardly any sphere will be left for the legitimate action of law and government.' Such measures, he insisted, could not

properly be called Socialistic, inasmuch as they were not dictated by a desire to promote the Socialistic ideal of equality . . . When the public clamours for legislation to preserve the lives of miners or sailors against preventible accidents, it is not with the idea of disturbing the distribution of profits between labour and capital, but only of putting a stop to a scandalous waste of human life.[99]

He argued that it was a fallacy 'countenanced alike by cunning advocates of Socialism and by partisans of the Liberty and Property Defence League, that every legislative restraint of individual liberty is, in its essence, Socialistic.'[100] Sidgwick's ambition in the *Elements of Politics* was to place arguments like these on a sound utilitarian footing.

In dealing with the second, 'sociological', assumption Sidgwick argued that although in general the common interest is best achieved by allowing the pursuit of individual self-interest 'abstract theory shows

[97] Ibid.

[98] G. Smith, 'Social and Industrial Revolution', in id., *Essays on Questions of the Day, Political and Social* (New York, 1893), 12. (This essay is largely a reprint of his pamphlet *False Hopes; Or Fallacies Socialistic and Semi-Socialistic Briefly Answered*, (London, 1886)).

[99] G. C. Brodrick, 'Democracy and Socialism', *Nineteenth Century*, 15 (1884), 627–8.

[100] Id., 'The Socialistic Tendencies of Modern Democracy', in id., *Literary Fragments* (London, 1891), 217.

several cases in which the individual's interest does not tend in the direction most conducive to the common interest—even assuming that utility to society is measured by market value.'[101] If we take the sociological assumption to be simply an assertion of that 'natural harmony of interests' which, according to Halévy, underpinned the political thought of the first generation of Benthamites, then Sidgwick's point amounts to the allegation that individual interests do not always harmonize in the prescribed fashion. As a result, it was necessary that, in some cases at least, the State should intervene in order to bring about an artificial identity of interest.

While Sidgwick referred to such State interference as socialistic, the point does not lend weight to the contention that he 'supplemented' the principles of liberalism with those of socialism. In the first place, the limited nature of the 'socialistic' interference in question is revealed by Sidgwick's definition of socialism in terms of 'the requirement that one sane adult, apart from contract or claim for reparation, shall contribute positively by money or services to the support of others.' This definition was supplemented by another which described as socialistic 'any limitation on the freedom of action of individuals in the interest of the community at large, that is not required to prevent interference with other individuals or for the protection of the community against the aggression of foreigners.'[102] In the broad sense in which it was employed by Sidgwick, the term socialism clearly encompassed a wide range of policies or measures which did nothing to subvert the existing industrial system, and very little to transform it. It meant, in fact, practically any extension of the State's activities beyond Spencer's Individualistic Minimum of the enforcement of contracts, the administration of justice, and military defence.[103]

According to this broad definition of socialism, many of the activities performed by the mid-Victorian limited State were socialistic. Sidgwick cited, for example, the protection of land against floods and the protection of animals against infectious diseases; the former dated back at least to Peel's administration. Such intervention was justified, he argued, because 'where uniformity of action or abstinence on the part of a whole class of producers is required for the most economical produc-

---

[101] Sidgwick, *Elements of Politics*, p. xiv, see also ch. 10, sect. 2

[102] Ibid., pp. 42–3. These two definitions do not appear to be coextensive, although Sidgwick seems to have regarded them in this light.

[103] This 'broad' usage of the term 'socialism' was not unique to Sidgwick, but was typical of late Victorian political thought. See Freeden, *New Liberalism*, 25 f.

tion of a certain utility, the intervention of Government is likely to be the most effective way of obtaining the result.'[104] The State is able to act in those cases where a voluntary association would lack the appropriate sanctions to maintain an agreement which is collectively beneficial, but which is open to exploitation by 'free riders'; the protection of fisheries is a case in point. Sidgwick also believed that the evils of monopolies could become rampant, particularly given the tendency to trusts and cartels exhibited by the economy of his own time, and therefore that it was impossible to dispense with an element of governmental control in these areas.

Furthermore, Sidgwick also recognized that there were public goods which pure Individualism could not be relied upon to produce. It was possible, for example, that 'laissez faire may fail to furnish a supply of some important utility' in cases where 'a particular employment of labour or capital may be most useful to the community, and yet the conditions of its employment are such that the labourer or capitalist cannot remunerate himself in the ordinary way'.[105] A case in point would be a lighthouse which cannot adequately secure the remuneration for the service it renders. Moreover, there were 'certain kinds of utility . . . which Government, in a well-organised modern community, is peculiarly adapted to provide.'[106] The government, being financially more stable than private individuals and companies, is better placed than they to give security to creditors, and thus Sidgwick did not endorse the free banking theories of the Spencerians.

Sidgwick also defended the Poor Law system which had been established by the Act of 1834. In the *Elements of Politics* he was characteristically circumspect, as befitted the author of a textbook, but explicit endorsement of the existing Poor Law system is to be found in a work hitherto neglected in the scholarly disputes over Sidgwick's attitude to the legitimate functions of the State, the preface to P. F. Aschrott's *The English Poor Law System*.[107] In both the *Elements of Politics* and the preface to Aschrott, which was written while Sidgwick was working on his book on political theory, he made plain his disapproval for an exclusively voluntary system of poor relief, as operated in France, which was inefficient and resulted in the paradoxical situation that the State provided for the physical needs of criminals but not of non-

[104] H. Sidgwick, 'Economic Socialism', 207.
[105] Ibid. 209. [106] Ibid. 206.
[107] Id., pref. to P. F. Aschrott, *The English Poor Law System* (London, 1888).

criminal paupers.[108] This distanced Sidgwick from some of Spencer's more extreme supporters, but he also criticized the German model of compulsory State insurance on the grounds that it was 'anti-individualistic', basing his objection not on opposition to the principle of compulsion as such, but rather on a preference for a scheme in which 'the burden of the provision is thrown on the persons who receive the benefit of it.'[109] A middle way between these two alternatives was the English system of poor relief in which responsibility for the welfare of the poor was divided jointly between the State, which provided for their most basic needs, and private charity to which was assigned the task of distinguishing differences of desert.[110] The English system, he wrote, recognized the State's responsibility to provide for the most basic needs of members of society, and accordingly 'secures adequate sustenance from public funds to all persons who are in destitution, while it aims at minimizing the encouragement thus offered to idleness and unthrift by attaching unattractive . . . conditions to public relief given to ordinary adult paupers.'[111] This State provision was, however, to be supplemented by 'the amount of philanthropic effort and sacrifice habitually devoted by private persons to the supply of social needs'.[112] Yet Sidgwick also recognized the 'increasing difficulty of performing well the discriminative operation . . . so long as private almsgiving is un-systematized, and is left to individuals acting without concert', and he praised the work of the Charity Organisation Society in promoting 'rational almsgiving'.[113] Those commentators who have interpreted Sidgwick's political theory as a precursor of the New Liberalism would do well to consider that the chief criticism of the existing system which he made in the preface to Aschrott was that the workhouses failed to provide work 'which the labourer can take an interest in, and which may stimulate in him, if he is still able-bodied, both the desire and the hope of making his way back to self-supporting independence.'[114] Sidgwick was well aware of the possibility that manual labourers were likely to use their new-won political power 'in the direction of diminishing the

---

[108] Id., *Elements of Politics*, 157; id., pref. to Aschrott, *Poor Law System*, p. viii.

[109] Id., *Elements of Politics*, 158; id., pref. to Aschrott, *Poor Law System*, p. viii. The German model of compulsory State insurance was advocated for Britain by W. H. Dawson in his book *Bismarck and State Socialism* (London, 1891), and by Canon Blackley in numerous articles.

[110] H. Sidgwick, pref. to Aschrott, *Poor Law System*, p. vi. Sidgwick derived this distinction from J. S. Mill, *The Principles of Political Economy*, v, Ch. 11.

[111] H. Sidgwick, *Elements of Politics*, 158.   [112] Ibid. 159.

[113] Id., pref. to Aschrott, *Poor Law System*, p. vii.   [114] Ibid. x.

deterrent character of our poor law administration', and although he recognized that these demands might have to be met by 'partial concessions', it was clear that this was a development he was far from welcoming.[115]

In addition to the Poor Law, Sidgwick believed that a further instance of legitimate 'socialistic' interference was the expenditure of public funds on the education of labourers, even when it was not in the interest of the labourers themselves or of their parents, so far as this outlay 'tends to increase the productive efficiency of the persons who profit by it to an extent that more than repays the outlay.'[116] The provision of public education was consistent with individualistic principles since it could be regarded as compensation for the fact that in appropriating natural resources 'beyond what the individualistic theory justifies', the propertied classes had restricted the 'equality of opportunity' of labourers. A similar justification could be given of State-aided emigration.[117]

Sidgwick's views on 'socialistic' interference, like those on paternalist legislation, were shared by the other empirical Individualists. G. J. Goschen, for example, insisted that '"Laissez Faire" has suffered in reputation, because its advocates have pushed its claims to public favour to extremes.' Like Sidgwick, he declared himself not to be 'a blind and unreasonable champion of "Laissez Faire" under all circumstances.'[118] Similarly, A. V. Dicey insisted that the *laissez-faire* principle was to be used as 'a good working rule of political practice . . . tempered by the common sense of prudent statesmanship', and it was a quality which he found in evidence in Lord Pembroke's *Speeches and Letters*.[119] Pembroke, he noted, did not rigidly adhere to a policy of *laissez-faire* and he exhibited 'a width of mind not always to be found among the strictest economists. He perceives . . . that the maxim *laissez faire*, though in many cases a sound practical rule, cannot be treated as an absolute principle in the strict following whereof consists the whole of statesmanship.'[120]

Pembroke had argued in his essay on 'Liberty and Socialism' that, like egoism and altruism, socialism and individualism were of the nature 'of two antagonistic but indispensable forces evolving social progress by

---

[115] Ibid. ix.   [116] Id., 'Economic Socialism', 210.
[117] Id., *Elements of Politics*, 163.
[118] G. J. Goschen, *An Address on Laissez Faire and Government Interference* (London, 1883), 34.
[119] A. V. Dicey, *Letters to a Friend on Votes for Women* (2nd edn., London, 1912), 32.
[120] Id., 'Lord Pembroke', *National Review*, 28 (1897), 623.

their continual collision.'[121] To carry socialism to its logical end would 'at once stop the growth of the healthiest nation in existence' while the principle of liberty alone would rapidly result in the dissolution of society. Consequently a 'compromise' had to be found between these 'inharmonious' forces because 'to talk of eliminating either is really nonsense.'[122] The basis for this compromise was a careful consideration of the expediency of any proposed measure, and in accordance with this recognition he was prepared to support, for example, national education, the Factory Acts, and sanitary legislation.[123] Pembroke was echoed by that arch anti-socialist the Earl of Wemyss who believed that 'the compromise that will approximately fix what are the proper limits of the rights and duties of the state' would be found 'somewhere between the poles of Socialism and Individualism' although he was of no doubt that 'this point will finally be found a long way on the Individualistic side of the division between the two extremes.'[124]

Even among the Spencerian Individualists, the limits of legitimate State action were often not drawn as narrowly as by Spencer himself. Bruce Smith, for example, admitted several important extensions of the equal liberties principle. In accordance with his belief that the greatest happiness required the State merely to protect the principle of equal liberties, Smith objected to it becoming involved in the housing of the poor, the provision of 'free' education (although he expressed support for the 1870 Act which had compelled parents to educate their children), the building of railways, or the provision of work for the unemployed. On the other hand, he also believed that sanitary measures were justified on the grounds that they were a defence against a certain sort of aggression, the difference being that the aggressors were diseases rather than members of our own species. Similarly, the State was justified in 'taxing citizens for the purpose of affording aid to the severely distressed portion of our population.' Because such measures provided a safety-valve against rebellion, which was simply a form of internal invasion, Smith, unlike Spencer, regarded the Poor Law as being consistent with the principles of Individualism. Nor was Smith

---

[121] G. R. C. Herbert, 13th Earl of Pembroke, 'Liberty and Socialism', in id., *Political Letters and Speeches* (London, 1896), 199. Pembroke's claim that there was no simple principle which could establish in all cases when the State should interfere and when it should not was the essence of empirical Individualism; for a criticism of Pembroke see anon., 'Socialism and Legislation', *Westminster Review*, 69 (1886), 9 ff.

[122] Pembroke, 'Liberty and Socialism', 195–6.   [123] Ibid. 197, 213.

[124] F. Wemyss-Charteris-Douglas, 9th Earl of Wemyss, *Socialism at St. Stephens in 1883* (London, 1884), 10.

alone among the Spencerians in drawing the boundaries of the State more broadly than did his mentor; H. S. Constable, for example, considered the Poor Law a '*necessary* evil to prevent completely intolerable ones.'[125]

The empirical Individualists' position on issues like the Poor Law, State education, and assistance to emigration had a long and distinguished pedigree. Of all the nineteenth-century proponents of *laissez-faire*, Spencer had been the only philosopher of any note to press the principle to its utmost. By contrast, when confronted by questions like public education, the regulation of hours and conditions of work, the problems of sanitation and public health, the passenger emigration trade, and so on, the classical economists frequently responded by assigning a significant role to government. In the 1870s, for example, Henry Fawcett, then the Professor of Political Economy at Cambridge, was insisting that although his main object was to 'point out the evils resulting from an undue reliance on the State', it was scarcely less erroneous to condemn government interference in all circumstances 'without enquiring into the nature of the particular instance to which it is to be applied.'[126] He supported, *inter alia*, the Poor Law, the payment of 'passage money' to emigrants, and had been an early enthusiast for universal education. Furthermore, almost half a century before the publication of Sidgwick's book, Mill's *Principles of Political Economy* had supported *laissez-faire* as 'the general practice', while elaborating a series of exceptions to it. These had included State-assisted emigration, involvement in education, the protection of children against exploitation, legislation on the hours of labour, and in the relief of poverty.[127]

In the context of the mid-nineteenth century these ideas had been radical, but by the 1880s, and certainly by 1891, they had ceased to be so, a point on which a number of the reviews of *The Elements of Politics* commented. For example, the 'advanced' Liberal *Speaker* was decidedly frosty in its response to the book, describing Sidgwick's empirical Individualism as nothing more than 'laissez faire with the chill off',[128] while D. G. Ritchie noted the absence from the book of Bentham's

---

[125] H. S. Constable, *The Fallacies and Follies of Socialist Radicalism Exposed* (London, 1895), 35.

[126] H. Fawcett, 'General Aspects of State Intervention', in id. and M. G. Fawcett, *Essays and Lectures on Social and Political Subjects* (London, 1872), 33.

[127] J. S. Mill, 'The Grounds and Limits of the Non-Interference Principle', *Principles of Political Economy*, bk. v, Ch. 11.

[128] Anon., 'Review of Sidgwick's *Elements of Politics*', *Speaker*, 4 (1891), 327.

'strong critical antagonism to the institutions of his time',[129] an absence on which the Whiggish *Saturday Review* commented with approval:

[Sidgwick] has kept marvellously few of his prejudices of origin, and for a child . . . of Mill and Bentham he exhibits hardly any of the idola of that curious creed, or no creed, the Liberalism of the second quarter of the century.[130]

The *Saturday* continued: 'Mr. Sidgwick may almost be taken as a typical example of the *centre gauche* mind, which has as little as possible of the *gauche* and as much as possible of the *centre* in it.'

Rather than being a textbook for social reformers, Sidgwick's *Elements of Politics* was the most closely reasoned statement of the outlook of the empirical Individualists, those former University Radicals who had since entered late middle age. The fact that the most significant exceptions Sidgwick had made to the rule of non-interference had been accepted long before by political economists like Mill and Fawcett, and that they were also recognized by leading lights in the Liberty and Property Defence League, suggests that there was little that was radical, either in Sidgwick's thought or that of the empirical Individualists in general.

VI. Conclusion

In conclusion, it has been shown that the late Victorian Individualists transformed utilitarianism into a doctrine which exhibited the same combination of liberalism and conservatism which, it is contended, was characteristic of their arguments in general. Whatever the differences between Spencer and Sidgwick on the status which a utilitarian could accord to the rules necessary for practical decision, and whatever their subsequent differences on the legitimate functions of the State, they both agreed that the principle of utility was not to be applied directly to particular measures but was to be mediated by the Law of Equal Freedom, considered either as a scientifically discoverable condition for happiness or as a utilitarian middle axiom. This insistence that the principle of utility had to be mediated was a means of reinforcing the traditional liberal emphasis on the free market and minimal State, while also defusing the statist tendencies of the utilitarian doctrine.[131]

[129] D. G. Ritchie, 'Review of *The Elements of Politics*', *International Journal of Ethics*, 2 (1892), 255.

[130] Anon., 'A Review of the *Elements of Politics*', *Saturday Review*, 72 (1891), 251.

[131] Another Individualist whose attempt to rework utilitarianism had much in common

Secondly, the versions of the utilitarian doctrine expounded by Spencer and Sidgwick were, in their different ways, also examples of conservatism. Spencer's distinction between absolute and relative ethics had the consequence of robbing his theory of its critical leverage with regard to late Victorian society: the radicalism of the *Social Statics* in respect of private property in land, of universal suffrage, and equal rights for women was negated by this distinction between what was 'relatively right' given the existing condition of society and what was right for a 'completely-evolved' humanity.

Commenting on the substantial correspondence between Spencer's moral philosophy and accepted ethical notions, Sidgwick wryly remarked that it had been scarcely necessary to 'have surveyed the process of the world from the nebula to the nineteenth century' to have gained such a degree of insight.[132] However, Sidgwick's own moral and political philosophy with its elaborate deductions and carefully phrased conclusions hardly escaped the same charge. His methodological claims about the impossibility of constructing an ideal code of utilitarian ethics, and his identification of existing morality and the social order with that prescribed by utilitarianism had obviously conservative implications. As Ritchie remarked of the *Elements of Politics*, it was 'much what we might expect from the end of the nineteenth century Blackstone, or from an English Hegel, showing the rationality of the existing order of things with only a few modest proposals for reform.'[133] In Sidgwick's hands the principle of utility had been brought full circle, so that the critical instrument of the Philosophic Radicals had been transformed back into a Humean descriptive law of the behaviour of people in communities. Bentham might have been referring to Sidgwick rather than to Hume when he wrote: 'The difference between Hume and me is this, the use which he made of [the principle of utility], was to account for that which is, I to show what ought to be.'[134]

---

with those discussed in this ch. was Leslie Stephen, most notably in his book *The Science of Ethics* (London, 1882). Like Spencer, Stephen endeavoured to ground morality on evolution, although he did so in a very different way. Abstractly considered, he argued, the function of morality is to further the health and vitality of the social organism. Historically considered, moral principles undergo a process of natural selection, in which those which are most effective in furthering the good of the social organism are the most successful. Stephen believed that utilitarianism was the 'fittest' moral theory, although, like Sidgwick and Spencer, he rejected the notion of a Benthamite felicific calculus. However, because he did not develop the political implications of his views, Stephen's theory has not been discussed in this ch.   [132] H. Sidgwick, *Lectures on Ethics*, 311.

[133] Ritchie, 'Review', 255.

[134] Bentham, quoted in R. Harrison, *Bentham* (London, 1983), 110.

7

JUSTICE, PROPERTY, AND NATURAL RIGHT

I. Introduction

One of the most profound tensions between the liberal principles and conservative intentions of Individualist thought is found in its account of justice, and in particular the doctrine of natural rights. Basing their claims variously on the principle of desert or on a pre-social natural right to property, the Individualists argued that each individual had a moral right to the produce of his labour power. This doctrine has a long history as part of the liberal tradition; as Ryan has pointed out, it 'has been a commonplace of political and economic radicalism for three hundred years.'[1] The Individualists were accordingly committed to a theory of justice the revolutionary implications of which 'conservatism has had a continuous struggle to defuse.'[2] At the same time, however, the Individualists also wished to turn this doctrine to the conservative purpose of providing an intellectual justification for the established distribution of property in late Victorian Britain. Despite the vast gulf between the extremes of opulence and poverty, despite the 'unearned' income derived from inherited wealth, the Individualists wished to contend that any interference with the rights of property would constitute an injustice. The present chapter will explore this tension between the Individualists' conceptions of justice and their defence of the existing social order, and in particular it will examine their attempts to escape the radical implications of their own principles.[3]

Spencer provided two separate but related principles of justice. The first of these, which may be termed the Law of Conduct and Consequence, was a desert-based principle of justice. It affirmed that just

---

[1] A. Ryan, *Property and Political Theory* (Oxford, 1984), 1.   [2] Ibid.
[3] It should be noted, however, that by the end of the 19th cent. much radical thought had moved beyond an insistence on the natural rights of property to the idea that property must serve a social function. For an example of this argument see L. T. Hobhouse, *The Labour Movement* (1893; 3rd edn., London, 1912).

distributions of property were those in which 'each man should receive benefits proportionate to his efforts', and from this it followed that 'he may properly keep possession of all which his labour has produced, leaving the less capable in possession of all which their labours have produced.' Spencer was able to reconcile the desert-based theory with his defence of the existing distribution of property only if it was assumed that the 'natural returns' accruing to the labourer under a system of free contract would be equivalent to his 'deserts'. As Sidgwick pointed out in a forceful criticism of this view, the contention that market value could be identified with desert was unsustainable, while the principle of distribution according to desert appeared to require outcomes fundamentally at odds with those existing in late Victorian Britain. Therefore, on this first formulation of the principle of justice, Spencer appeared to have undermined the very institutions he was concerned to defend.

The same problem afflicted Spencer's attempt to derive a theory of justice from the mutual limitation of the natural right to freedom. Apart from the fact that Spencer failed to produce a convincing argument for the existence of the natural right to liberty, he was also unable to give a satisfactory account of how the appropriation of natural resources could be justified while respecting the like freedom of all other individuals. As Sidgwick again pointed out, the existence of property rights necessarily restricted the freedom of other individuals, and the problem was particularly acute in the case of land. If the appropriation of a natural resource which, like land, was fixed in supply resulted in the limitation of the freedom and a denial of the equal opportunities of the landless, then it was clearly unjust. In his youth Spencer had been aware of this point and was a trenchant opponent of private property in land; in later life, by contrast, he was concerned to defend the existing distribution of rights, including those to property, and was led to repudiate the logical consequences of his own theory. To more radical critics, like Hobson, the incompatibility of private property in land with the right-based theory of justice merely demonstrated that the Individualists had succeeded in undermining their own principles.[4]

Sidgwick was at pains to point out that the Individualist theory of justice, in either its desert-based or rights-based forms, was particularly weak as a defence of the institution of private property as it existed in late Victorian Britain, and it often appeared to offer hostages to fortune in providing a better statement of the socialist case than it did a justification

[4] This argument is examined in greater detail in a later part of this ch.

for the free-market, competitive system. Sidgwick's criticisms of Spencer have been frequently misinterpreted, since in consequence of these remarks he has been assumed to be an advocate of the socialist cause. This was far from his intention, which was not to advocate radical change in the system of property rights, but to propose an alternative defence of private property. Rather than basing the case for private property on a principle of justice which threatened to undermine Individualism, Sidgwick proposed an orthodox utilitarian defence in terms of the necessity of providing security in the enjoyment of the fruits of one's labours as an incentive to further exertion. Even in this case, however, Sidgwick was forced to downplay the radical implications of his own principles. In particular, he accorded security greater weight than the diminishing marginal utility derived from wealth and he was also unable to produce a satisfactory solution to the problem of justifying the appropriation of natural resources. While contending that those whose freedom was restricted ought to be compensated, in fact his conception of the form which this compensation should take was also limited by a concern with defending incentives and the security of private property.

II. The Law of Conduct and Consequence

Spencer gave two different formulations of his principle of justice, both of which he considered to be derived from his evolutionary theory. The first formulation was founded on the recognition that the 'survival of the fittest, and spread of the most adapted varieties' depended upon the operation of the law that 'among adults the individuals best adapted to the conditions of their existence shall prosper most, and that individuals least adapted to the conditions of their existence shall prosper least.'[5] Ethically considered, this law become the Law of Conduct and Consequence, which Spencer often referred to as the 'positive' formulation of justice. It demanded the apportionment of benefits to deserts:

Each individual shall receive the benefits and the evils of its own consequent conduct: neither being prevented from having what his good actions normally bring to him, nor allowed to shoulder off on to other persons whatever ill is brought to him by his actions.[6]

---

[5] H. Spencer, *The Principles of Ethics*, ii (London, 1893), p. 17.

[6] Ibid. It should be noted, however, that Spencer limited the application of this principle to the social sphere. Within the family unit the ruling principle was one of

Spencer contended that any degree of State action more extensive that the minimal State would create injustices since it would 'abstract from some men advantages they have earned' while awarding other men 'advantages they have not earned.'[7] In other words, justice required that each member of society should get 'benefit in proportion to merit— reward in proportion to desert: merit and desert in each case being understood as the ability to fulfil all the requirements of life.'[8] Yet despite the quasi-biological sound of Spencer's definition of desert and merit, his practical employment of the principle was indistinguishable from the common-sense notion that rewards should be apportioned to effort. This was in evidence, for example, in the deduction of the right to private property from the Law of Conduct and Consequence: from the principle that 'each man should receive benefits proportionate to his efforts' it followed that 'he may properly keep possession of all which his labour has produced, leaving the less capable in possession of all which their labours have produced.'[9] The recognition of the right of property, Spencer affirmed, was 'originally recognition of the relation between effort and benefit' and even in the earliest forms of human society it was 'tacitly' acknowledged that 'labour must bring to the labourer something like its equivalent in produce.'[10]

It is significant that Spencer did not consider the radical implications of the doctrine that the labourer has a moral title to the product of his labour; he certainly did not entertain the view that the free-market economy systematically exploits the worker by denying him the whole produce of his labour.[11] Instead, Spencer simply assumed that a market economy was the social institution which would afford the closest approximation to the ideally just state of affairs:

altruism: children were nurtured irrespective of desert or merit. The crucial point was that the principles of distribution appropriate to the two spheres of society and family had to be kept distinct: 'even a partial intrusion of the family regime into the regime of the state, will be slowly followed by fatal results.' (Id., *The Man versus the State*, ed. D. G. Macrae (1884; Harmondsworth, 1969), 137.)

[7] Id., *The Principles of Sociology*, ii (London, 1882), 700.

[8] Id., *The Man versus the State*, 136.

[9] Id., *Principles of Ethics*, ii. 100. [10] Ibid. 99.

[11] For an excellent discussion of these theories see A. Menger, *The Right to the Whole Produce of Labour* (London, 1899), 2–3: 'Our actual law of property . . . does not guarantee the labourer the whole product of his labour. By assigning the existing objects of wealth, and especially the instruments of production, to individuals to use at their pleasure, our law of property invests such individuals with an ascendancy by virtue of which without any labour of their own, they draw an unearned income which they can apply to the satisfaction of their wants.'

Under this universal relation of contract when equitably administered, there arises that adjustment of benefit to effort which the arrangements of the industrial society have to achieve. If each producer, distributor, manager, adviser, teacher, or aider of other kinds, obtains from his fellows such payment for his service as its value, determined by the demand, warrants; then there results that correct apportioning of reward to merit which ensures the prosperity of the superior.[12]

He thus believed both that wealth ought to be distributed according to desert, and that the market does distribute according to desert. Accordingly, an extensive sphere of State interference with the market was excluded on the grounds that it would undermine the mechanism which correctly apportioned benefit to desert.

Nevertheless, as Sidgwick pointed out, Spencer's attempt to defend the institution of the free market on the basis that it apportioned benefits to deserts was flawed in a number of respects. According to this theory, an individual's deserts were measured by the market value of his labour as determined by free and fair competition. But, Sidgwick argued, this claim was vitiated by the ignorance of the majority of people, who are 'not properly qualified to decide on the value of many important kinds of services, from imperfect knowledge of their nature and effects; so that, as far as these are concerned, the true judgement will not be represented in the market-place.'[13] Even in those cases in which it is possible to form a general estimate of value, in any particular instance an individual's ignorance of the real utility of the thing he exchanges may prevent him from obtaining its true market value.

Moreover, in those cases in which an individual or combination of individuals obtain a monopoly over certain goods and services they will be able to drive up the market price 'but it is absurd to say that the social Desert of those rendering the service is thereby increased'.[14] Since (given constant demand) the increase in the supply of a service drives down its price, this would seem to imply that an individual's social desert would be lessened by the increased number or willingness of others rendering the same service; but this is also absurd.[15] The increasingly international nature of trade also serves to increase the 'fluctuation and uncertainty in the relations of the demand and supply of commodities' and hence 'the complexity of the causes affecting any worker's re-

[12] Spencer, *Principles of Sociology*, ii. 701.
[13] H. Sidgwick, *The Methods of Ethics* (1874; 7th edn., London, 1907), 287.
[14] Ibid 288. Compare id., *The Principles of Political Economy* (London, 1883), 507.
[15] Id., *Methods of Ethics*, 288.

numeration tends to increase in a far greater ratio than his intellectual resources for forecasting their effects; so that the element of desert in his gains and losses of income tends to become continually less instead of greater.'[16] Finally, it would appear strange to suggest that an individual's desert is increased merely by rendering a service to those who can afford to pay lavishly for it.[17] Spencer's assumption that market value was an accurate measure of desert was therefore unsustainable.

Furthermore, Sidgwick argued, once the assumption that the free market did apportion benefits to deserts was abandoned, the principle that there should be a correspondence between the effort put forth by an individual and the advantages he received pointed to conclusions which were the very opposite of those which Spencer wished to draw. In fact, he had committed himself to the same ideal as Edward Bellamy, who had described a 'communistic Utopia' in which 'each shall make the same effort, and if by that same effort, bodily or mental, one produces twice as much as another, he is not to be advantaged by the difference.'[18] In other words, justice would appear to require 'a mode of distributing payment for services, entirely different from that at present effected by free competition: and that all labourers ought to be paid according to the intrinsic value of their labour as estimated by enlightened and competent judges.'[19] Although Spencer attacked as a violation of the rights of property the 'communist' doctrine that there should be 'equal division of unequal earnings',[20] it was, in fact, a legitimate extension of his own principle of justice.

It was an equally plausible extension of the principle that benefits ought to be proportionate to effort to contend that 'unearned' income ought to be abolished; as Hobson forcefully pointed out, the acquisition of wealth by capital gains in the share market had very little to do with an individual's industriousness or exertion: 'Can anything be more miraculous than that I should wake up to-morrow and find certain shares which to-day are worth £100 are then risen to £105?'[21] It is significant that although Spencer was prepared to make a distinction between the deserving and undeserving poor, he made no such distinction with regard to the rich.

---

[16] Id., *Principles of Political Economy*, 508.   [17] Id., *Methods of Ethics*, 289.
[18] Id., *Lectures on the Ethics of T. H. Green, H. Spencer, and J. Martineau* (London, 1902), 262.   [19] Id., *Methods of Ethics*, 288–9.
[20] Spencer, *Principles of Ethics*, ii. 100.
[21] J. A. Hobson, *The Crisis of Liberalism: New Issues of Democracy* (London, 1909), 197. Although the passage was written as a criticism of Bosanquet, the point applies with equal force against the theory of property propounded by Spencer.

A further problem arose over the right of gift and bequest, which Spencer was at pains to defend on the grounds that 'complete ownership of anything implies power to make over the ownership to another'.[22] Yet he did not pause to consider the matter from the point of view of the recipient of the bequest, who cannot be said to deserve it in the sense that it was the product of his own efforts. If eleemosynary grants, like those resulting from the Poor Law, were unjust because they gave some men advantages which they had not earned, so were the results of gift and bequest. The biologist and proponent of land nationalization Alfred Russel Wallace expressed opposition to inherited wealth on the grounds that since the Law of Conduct and Consequences decreed 'no one shall receive throughout life, that which is not the result of his own nature and actions' it forbade 'such bequests to children or others as will render them independent of all personal exertion, enabling them to live idle lives on the labour of others.'[23]

Those passages in which Spencer had contended that justice required that rewards should be proportionate to deserts had undermined his own defence of the market order: only if it was assumed that the market did distribute according to desert could Spencer's position be sustained, but this assumption appeared to be untenable.[24] Even if this assumption was granted it still did not serve to justify wealth which is acquired as a result of inheritance. Spencer's conservatism was manifested in a reluctance to explore the implications of his own principle of justice in those circumstances in which it appeared to demand social institutions of a very different nature to those existing in late Victorian Britain.

III. The Law of Equal Freedom

Contrary to Spencer's design, therefore, his principle of justice implied that the distributions produced by the free market were often unjust, and he exhibited an unjustified reluctance to explore the potentially radical implications of the Law of Conduct and Consequence; but his 'negative' formulation of the principle of justice, the Law of Equal

---

[22] Spencer, *Principles of Ethics*, ii. 118.

[23] A. R. Wallace, 'Spencer on the Land Question', 341–2.

[24] For further discussion of this point see D. L. Miller, *Social Justice* (Oxford, 1976), 185 ff.

Freedom, was beset by even greater difficulties. In the first place, Spencer was unable to give an adequate defence of the natural rights according to which the justice of distributions were to be assessed; while secondly, like its desert-based counterpart, the Law of Equal Freedom seemed to decree that a number of fundamental institutions of the late Victorian social order, and especially private property in land, could not be defended on the strict principles of justice. In the present section Spencer's attempts to justify the Law of Equal Freedom will be examined, while the following section will explore his attempts to avoid the radical implications of the Law of Equal Freedom formulation.

Spencer himself regarded the Law of Equal Freedom and the Law of Conduct and Consequence as alternative formulations of the principle of justice.[25] Had human beings lived solitary existences, the Law of Conduct and Consequence would have exhausted the subject of justice. Since human individuals were destined to exist as members of a society, another formulation was also necessary which would specify the conditions under which the Law of Conduct and Consequence could apply in the associated state, and this he referred to as the Law of Equal Freedom, which we encountered in the previous chapter.

Summarizing Spencer's theory, Sidgwick wrote that all natural rights 'may be summed up in the Right to Freedom; so that the complete and universal establishment of this right would be the complete realisation of Justice—the Equality at which Justice is thought to aim being interpreted as Equality of Freedom.'[26] By presenting his theory in these terms, Spencer was at odds with the intellectual climate at the end of the nineteenth century, which was unfavourable to the doctrine of natural rights; as Morley succinctly remarked, its 'naked appearance' in a piece of platform oratory 'gave me as much surprise and dismay as if I were this afternoon to meet a Deinotherium shambling down Parliament Street.'[27] This scepticism extended even to many Individualists who, like Bruce Smith, thought that the doctrine of natural rights would lead 'to great practical inconvenience in many matters of every-day life.'[28] Donisthorpe also attacked the tendency of Spencer and his disciple Auberon Herbert to 'hang most of their conclusions on capital letters'

---

[25] Compare ibid. 190, which misreads the Law of Equal Freedom as a principle of justice which is 'secondary' to the desert-based formulation. In fact, Spencer's most frequent references are to the rights-based principle.

[26] H. Sidgwick, *Methods of Ethics*, 274.

[27] J. Morley, *Studies in Literature* (London, 1897), 174–5.

[28] [A.] B. Smith, *Liberty and Liberalism* (London, 1887), 444.

like Justice, Liberty, or Rights. He believed that, like the 'a priori vapourings' common to Locke, Rousseau, and Henry George, such abstractions could not give rise to a 'practical working doctrine' from which to delimit the functions of the State.[29]

Yet despite the importance to Spencer's argument of the justification of the natural right to freedom, he encountered substantial difficulties in formulating this defence, and these are illustrated by the uneven quality of the arguments he deployed in *The Man versus the State*. The first such argument, in typical Spencerian fashion, attempted to establish a positive conclusion by showing the incoherence of its negative. Bentham had held that the government was the sole generator of rights and that consequently there could be no rights antecedent to the law; Spencer summarized what he took to be his argument as follows:

> The sovereign people jointly appoint representatives, and so create a government: the government thus created, creates rights; and then, having created rights, it confers them on the separate members of the sovereign people by which it was itself created.[30]

Such a view is surely nonsense, he claimed, for 'among the metaphysical absurdities the most shadowy is this which supposes a thing to be obtained by creating an agent, which creates the thing, and then confers the thing on its own creator!'[31] Ritchie pointed out, however, that either deliberately or inadvertently Spencer had failed to grasp the point of Bentham's argument. A government can create rights in a clear and unproblematical sense. It does so in the same way as a committee created to draw up the rules for a society, which in the course of enacting them thereby confers duties (and rights) on its members.[32]

Spencer also tried to derive natural rights a posteriori from the customs of ancient and primitive societies. Since these societies recognized private property before law existed, he believed that this proved that property must rest on a natural right. This argument also struck Ritchie as singularly thin and unconvincing. Spencer's references to rights recognized by the customs of ancient societies proved only that 'all rights cannot arise in an explicit contract or through a statute made by a definite legislature' but not that there are rights antecedent to, and independent of, society.[33] Furthermore, the property rights recognized

---

[29] W. Donisthorpe, 'The Limits of Liberty', in T. D. Mackay (ed.), *A Plea For Liberty* (London, 1891), 66.

[30] Spencer, *The Man versus the State*, 162. [31] Ibid. 163.

[32] D. G. Ritchie, *Principles of State Interference* (London, 1891), 33.

[33] Ibid. 36.

in primitive societies were not of the absolute variety Spencer was seeking to prove, since property was often held in common, belonging to the village, family, or the tribe.[34] Spencer had also invoked in his support the argument that since all governments have tended to recognize the same rights in different times and different places, a correspondence which could only be explained by an appeal to the doctrine of natural rights. Ritchie replied by pointing out that a more convincing explanation was that there are 'certain conditions necessary for the life of any society' and which are therefore recognized by the government of every state.

Spencer also claimed that influential Victorian thinkers like Jevons and Matthew Arnold might have been less ready 'dogmatically' to reject the existence of natural rights had they been aware that

a whole school of legists on the Continent maintains a belief diametrically opposed to that maintained by the English school. The idea of *Naturrecht* is the root-idea of German jurisprudence . . . A doctrine current among a people distinguished above all others as labourious enquirers, and certainly not to be classed with superficial thinkers, should not be dimissed as though it were nothing more than a popular delusion.'[35]

Ritchie, well familiar with German thought as a former pupil of T. H. Green, delightedly pointed out *Naturrecht* meant an ideal code of law and was not to be translated as 'Natural Rights'; this point apart, Spencer's argument could be parodied by replacing the term *Naturrecht* by the phrase 'State action', thus standing the entire argument on its head.[36]

Nevertheless, Spencer's most important argument for the existence of the natural right to liberty was derived from the 'laws of life'. He claimed that certain activities are necessary for the maintenance of life, and if we hold life to be valuable, it follows that men ought not to be prevented from carrying on their life-sustaining activities. 'Clearly, the conception of "natural rights" originates in recognition of the truth that if life is justifiable, there must be a justification for the performance of acts essential to its preservation; and, therefore, a justification for those liberties and claims which make such acts possible.'[37] Spencer's point was apparently that, life being justified on the optimistic assumption that

[34] Ibid. 39.
[35] Spencer, *The Man versus the State*, 87.
[36] Ritchie, *State Interference*, 33.
[37] Spencer, *The Man versus the State*, 171.

it involves a surplus of pleasure over pain, activities necessary for the preservation of life were also justified. The preservation of life requires the acquisition of food, which in turn demands the use of faculties of prehension and locomotion. These faculties cannot be exercised without freedom, and if it is right that these life-sustaining operations be carried on, it follows that the individual has 'a right' to the requisite freedom. Clearly, as one recent critic has noted, this 'seems to be little more than a facile verbal play on two meanings of "right".'[38] Furthermore, even if Spencer's attempted derivation of the natural right to freedom from the 'laws of life' was valid, it was true of other creatures as well as of man.

Spencer himself recognized the latter point and claimed that the distinctively *ethical* character of the right to freedom was specific to human beings, since with man there was an additional recognition of limits to what an individual may or may not do in the performance of life-sustaining acts. The natural right to liberty which this argument generates imposes on others only the negative duty that they forbear from interfering with the actions of the bearer of rights, and there arises the 'mutual limitation of spheres of action' which is Spencerian justice.[39]

Therefore, according to the Law of Equal Freedom, the formula of justice was that 'every man is free to do that which he wills, provided he infringes not the equal freedom of any other man.'[40] Spencer noted that this formula combined both positive and negative elements. It was positive in so far as it asserted that for each person 'since he is to receive and suffer the good and evil results of his actions, he must be allowed to act.' It was negative since it implied that 'each can be allowed to act only under the restraint imposed by the presence of others having like claims to act.'[41] This formula was employed by many other Individualists as the fundamental statement of their creed. For example, on M. D. O'Brien's formulation, Individualism was the expression of 'the conviction of equality'—not the socialistic equality of 'share and share alike'

---

[38] E. F. Paul, 'The Time-Frame Theory of Governmental Legitimacy', in J. Paul (ed.), *Reading Nozick* (Oxford, 1982). E. F. Paul's paper, which contains a detailed criticism of Spencer's argument for natural rights, is an attempt to reconstruct it in a more sustainable form.   [39] Spencer, *The Man versus the State*, 172.

[40] Id., *Principles of Ethics*, ii. 46. Spencer's equation of justice with 'equal liberties' had a long ancestry in British political thought. In his slim vol. on *Burke*, John Morley quoted one of his subject's letters in which he had written: 'The liberty I mean is social freedom. It is that state of things in which liberty is secured by equality of restraint. This kind of liberty is, indeed, but another name for justice.' (Morley, *Burke* (London, 1879), 146.)

[41] Spencer, *Principles of Ethics*, ii. 45.

but the conviction 'that we are all logically entitled to the same freedom for expressing our motives in action, that is, for doing as we like.'[42]

A similar account of justice was offered by Auberon Herbert, although without Spencer's evolutionary and quasi-biological trappings. The difference between Herbert's approach and that of his intellectual mentor was well summed up by Sir Roland Wilson when he wrote that 'while Spencer approached political problems, and ethical problems generally, in the scientific spirit, and from the starting point of biology, Auberon Herbert approaches them as an intuitive moralist, his starting point being the sentiment of personal dignity and responsibility.'[43] The core of Herbert's doctrine was the belief that man is by right the master of his own faculties and energies, and hence that each man is to be regarded as the 'owner and possessor of his own self' dependent 'in everything on himself and his own exertions.'[44] Herbert identified self-ownership in this sense with liberty, which was itself a natural right. Moreover, all ideas 'of justice and morality are bound up with the parent idea of liberty—that is with the right of man to direct his own faculties and energies—and that where this idea is not acknowledged and obeyed, justice and morality cannot be said to exist.'[45] Yet this natural right had to be limited in order that it could be made compatible with the enjoyment of an equal liberty for all. By this reasoning Herbert arrived at the Spencerian formula of justice, that

each man and woman is free to direct their faculties and their energies, according to their own sense of what is right and wise, in every direction except one. They are not free to use their faculties for the purpose of forcibly restraining their neighbour from the same free use of his faculties.[46]

From the mutual limitation of the natural right to liberty Spencer deduced a number of other more specific rights. Two 'self-evident corollaries' of the principle of justice were that each man has a claim to his life, 'for without it he can do nothing he has willed', and to his personal liberty, 'for the withdrawal of it partially, if not wholly, restrains him from the fulfillment of his will.'[47] The Law of Equal Freedom could in like manner be made to yield many other rights. For example, it allegedly justified the right of property, the right of exchange, the right

---

[42] M. D. O'Brien, *The Natural Right to Freedom* (London, 1893), 2.
[43] Sir R. K. Wilson, *The Province of the State* (London, 1911), 272.
[44] A. Herbert, *The Right and Wrong of Compulsion by the State* (London, 1885), 5.
[45] Ibid. 4.   [46] Ibid. 3.
[47] Spencer, *Social Statics* (1851; 2nd edn., London, 1868), 130.

of free speech, patent law ('the right of property in ideas'), and the law of libel and slander ('the right of property in character').

Spencer and his followers insisted that the natural right to freedom generated a right to private property and that, in Levy's phrase, 'liberty and property are inseparable.'[48] The justification for property rights stemmed from each person's moral right to that which he had produced by the free exercise of his faculties. As Herbert remarked, 'we claim that the individual is not only the true owner of his faculties, but also of his property, because property is directly or indirectly the product of faculties, is inseparable from faculties, and therefore must rest on the same moral basis, and fall under the same moral law, as faculties.'[49] In this he was echoed by O'Brien, who asked 'On what ground should a man defend himself and his property?' His reply was forthright:

On the ground that his life, his faculties, and what he gets for those faculties, either through the open market, or through applying them to the raw substances of nature (without aggressing on the liberty and property of others), belongs to himself, and neither to the external many or the external few. Personal right is the foundation of all right; for the biggest crowd is but a multiplication of persons.[50]

In generating proprietary right from personal right, it followed that to forcibly deprive a person of his or her property was to deny them their personhood. As Levy insisted:

Rights of property are the outcome of rights of person. A violation of proprietory rights is an indirect violation of personal rights and, so far as it goes, a reduction of the individual to a state of bondage. When we are forcibly deprived of that

[48] J. H. Levy, 'Individualism', in E. B. Bax and J. H. Levy, *Socialism and Individualism*, (London, n.d. [1904]), 97.

[49] A. Herbert, 'The Principles of Voluntaryism and Free Life', in id., *The Right and Wrong of Compulsion by the State and Other Essays*, ed. E. Mack (Indianapolis, 1978), 369. In Herbert's theory the natural right to property was so absolute that it precluded the State from raising finance by taxation, even for the purpose of maintaining order and security. Instead, Herbert proposed a scheme of 'voluntary taxation'. According to his detailed plans for the operation of this scheme, the collection of voluntary contributions would take place during certain specially dedicated national holidays. Contributions could be made for specified purposes and wherever the State fell short of a required sum it would circulate all citizens with a notice of the deficiency which it would be up to them to remedy or not, as the case may be. Remarking on this proposal, Ritchie found himself unable to determine 'whether Mr. Auberon Herbert is to be classed among the Anarchists or among the reactionaries.' (D. G. Ritchie, *Natural Rights* (London, 1894), 15.)

[50] M. D. O'Brien, *Socialism Tested by the Facts* (London, 1892), 29.

which is the fruition of our faculties, or prevented from enjoying it un-aggressively, we are to that extent robbed of the use of those faculties.[51]

Nevertheless, the Individualists resisted an apparent corollary of this link between property and personality: although property might be essential to individual personhood, it did not follow that everyone should have the right to the same basic goods. As Spencer argued, this justification of the right to private property did not require that 'all shall have like shares of the things which minister to the gratification of the faculties, but that all shall have like freedom to pursue those things—shall have like scope.'[52] If, as a result of this equality of opportunity, one individual obtains

by his greater strength, greater ingenuity, or greater application, more gratifica-tions or sources of gratification than the rest, and does this without in any way trenching upon the equal freedom of the rest, the moral law assigns him an exclusive right to those extra gratifications and sources of gratification; nor can the rest take from him without claiming greater liberty of action that he claims, and thereby violating that law.[53]

The most powerful criticism of the link between the right to private property and the natural right to freedom was made by the empirical Individualist Sidgwick. He argued that although Spencer believed that the Law of Equal Freedom could be used to generate property rights, it could justify no more than the

right to non-interference while actually using such things as can only be used by one person at once: the right to prevent others from using at any future time anything that an individual has once seized seems an interference with the free action of others beyond what is needed to secure the freedom, strictly speaking, of the appropriator.[54]

In other words, on Spencer's account, property in a thing could be said to exist only while it was actually being used, and hence property in the sense of *exclusive* ownership over an *extended* period of time was not justified by the Law of Equal Freedom. Although it might be argued that in appropriating a particular thing a person does not interfere with the freedom of others because the rest of the world is still open to them, it is possible that others might want the very thing which has been appropriated. They may be unable to find anything else as good at all, or

[51] J. H. Levy, 'Individualism', 98.   [52] Spencer, *Social Statics*, 149.
[53] Id., *Principles of Ethics*, ii. 100. (The same passage appears in id., *Social Statics*, 150.)
[54] H. Sidgwick, *Methods of Ethics*, 276.

only may be able to do so after much labour and searching. In addition, basing the right to appropriation on first use begged the question of what was to count as 'usage' in this context. For instance, would an individual be justified in excluding others from pasturing sheep on any part of the land over which his hunting expeditions might extend? The problem here was that 'the use of land by any individual may vary almost indefinitely in extent, while diminishing proportionately in intensity.'[55] There was also the final problem that on Spencer's principle it would appear to be impossible to justify an individual's right to control the disposal of his possessions after his death. If Spencer entertained the conservative objective of generating a defence of the existing rights of property, he had failed to fulfil his purpose.

Sidgwick also pointed out that in other areas there were considerable 'divergences between the colloraries from this formula and the actually established rules of law.'[56] Spencer's definition of justice was formally bad because common sense—and Spencer himself—applied the notion in cases where the Law of Equal Freedom was inapplicable. This was true, for example, of the cases of compensation due for infringment of equal freedom; of the rights and duties of husbands and wives, or of parents and children; and even of fundamental institutions of the existing social order, like marriage. In the case of the marriage laws, for instance, Spencer failed to consider the question of 'why and how far freedom of contract is to be limited?' In fact his principle seemed to demand 'perfect freedom of contract in determining the conjugal relations of men and women' and hence, Sidgwick noted with Victorian disapproval, Spencer had set himself in opposition 'to the law and custom of civilised societies.'[57] In this case Spencer's Law of Equal Freedom formulation appeared to demand a radical restructuring of the Victorian social order, and in failing to recognize this he had allowed his later conservatism to override the strict logic of his principles.

IV. Equal Rights and Private Property in Land

Nevertheless, the most fundamental divergence between the recommendations of the Law of Equal Freedom and the Individualists'

---

[55] Ibid. 277.   [56] Id., *Lectures on Ethics*, 279.

[57] Ibid. 296. Reform of the marriage laws was something of a bone of contention among the Spencerian Individualists. Free divorce was supported e.g. by Auberon Herbert but his proposal met with opposition from Donisthorpe.

intended political conclusions occurred over the problem of justifying private property in land. In the early editions of the *Social Statics*, Spencer himself had advocated the nationalization of the land, since he thought that private ownership violated the Law of Equal Freedom, but by the time that he published the last volume of *The Principles of Ethics* in the early 1890s he had recanted his views on land nationalization.[58] David Wiltshire has observed that 'Spencer's reconsideration of the . . . land question reflects a significant modification of his view of personal . . . rights in which private property has come, by 1891, to outweigh the strict logic of the derivation of the original catalogue of "natural rights" from the "law of equal freedom".'[59] On this issue he was at one with the majority of other Individualists. In its review of the 'abridged and revised' edition of the *Social Statics*, from which the land-nationalization argument had been dropped, *The Liberty Annual* commented:

> We believed that the generality of Individualists are in entire agreement with Mr. Spencer's present opinions on this subject; and, except in one or two unimportant instances, we are not aware that any professed adherents of Individualism have any sympathy with the views on land originally set forth in 'Social Statics'.[60]

The case of private property in land reveals more clearly than any other the degree to which the Individualists were concerned to resist the radical implications of their conception of justice.

In the *Social Statics* Spencer had argued that if 'one portion of the earth's surface may justly become the possession of an individual . . . then other portions of the earth's surface may be so held', so that eventually the whole of the earth's surface may lapse into private hands.[61] Once the entire globe had been enclosed those who were not landowners could 'exist on the earth by sufferance only. They are all trespassers.' There would arise an inequality between the landowners and the rest of mankind, since the latter 'can then exercise their faculties—can then exist even—only by consent of the landowners' and this would constitute an infringement of the law of equal freedom.[62] The argument was summed up by Levy:

> To be free, we require, not only the use of our faculties, but also something on which to use them; and they are mocked . . . who are told they have freedom

<hr/>

[58] This issue is examined in Wiltshire, *Herbert Spencer*, 120 ff.   [59] Ibid. 131.

[60] W. S. Crawshay and F. Millar (eds.), *The Liberty Annual* (London, 1893), 47. A rare exception to this generalization was Sir R. K. Wilson. See his *Province of the State*, and his contribution to id. and J. H. Levy (eds.), *Individualism and the Land Question* (London, 1912), esp. 18 f.   [61] Spencer, *Social Statics*, 132.   [62] Ibid.

while access to the raw material, without which they can produce nothing, is barred to them by a privileged few.[63]

In other words, the demand for the equitable right of property appeared to be a logical extension of the Law of Equal Freedom. For this reason, as Sidgwick suggested, Spencer's defence of Individualism was 'surprisingly weak' against the attacks of 'the modern Socialist who claims that an equitable right of property . . . can only be secured by common ownership of the land and the instruments of production.'[64]

An example of a 'modern socialist' who made just such a transition from the equality of rights to the demand for land nationalization was J. A. Hobson, whose arguments were strikingly similar to those originally used by Spencer in the early editions of the *Social Statics*. He pointed out in the course of criticizing the ideas of Auberon Herbert that the transition from self-ownership to ownership of the land was not justified on the principle of equal rights, which though it may justify an individual 'in retaining property in the labour or personal energy bestowed upon land and its products, by no means justifies him in claiming ownership of the materials furnished by nature.'[65] The doctrine of individual rights might generate property in labour power, but not in the material in which it was invested. The difficulty stemmed from the fact that the 'best' land was not available in unlimited quantities, and 'by allowing first comers to monopolise without restriction the best natural supplies' Herbert would enable them 'to thwart and restrict the similar freedom of those who come after.'[66] Hobson urged his readers to consider the 'extreme instance' of an island, 'the whole of which is annexed by a few individuals, who use the rights of exclusive property and transmission . . . to establish primogeniture.' In such a situation, the bulk of their descendants and other outsiders would be denied the right to exercise their faculties or to enjoy the fruits of their labour, which Herbert stated to be the inalienable rights of all. 'It is thus that the "freedom" of a few (in Mr. Herbert's sense) involves the "slavery" of the many.'[67] If the opportunity for everyone to enjoy the

---

[63] Levy, 'Individualism', 140   [64] H. Sidgwick, *Lectures on Ethics*, 287.

[65] J. A. Hobson, 'A Rich Man's Anarchism', the *Humanitarian*, 12 (1898), 390–7.

[66] Ibid. 394.

[67] Ibid. Compare F. W. Maitland, 'Mr. Herbert Spencer's Theory of Society', *Mind*, 8 (1883), 517: 'If we are going to be really serious about our law of equal liberty, and think it capable of a "strictly scientific development", we must prepare some scheme which will equalise the advantages of all children hereafter to be born.' Unlike Hobson, however, Maitland regarded this as a 'ridiculous' proposal, and hence a *reductio ad absurdum* of Spencer's defence of private property.

'largest aggregate of freedom or "self-ownership"' was to be secured in the face of the 'niggardliness' of nature, Hobson argued, it was necessary to employ the instrument of 'the State guided by considerations of social right or expediency.'[68] Of all the points Hobson raised in 'A Rich Man's Anarchism', this argument was his most effective, and Herbert was unable to provide a satisfactory response.[69]

It was clearly necessary for the Spencerian Individualists to attempt to defuse the apparently radical implications of the Law of Equal Freedom, at least with respect to the ownership of the land, and the wide variety of different responses which they made is indicative of their confusion on this issue. One group of Individualists attempted directly to challenge the inference that was drawn from the Law of Equal Freedom to the illegitimacy of private property in land. This was the approach taken by Auberon Herbert in an article for the *Liberty Annual*, which was the closest he came to attempting to answer the kinds of criticisms made by Hobson. Although Herbert made use of several different arguments, the one on which he placed most weight was that 'freedom in the use of faculties not only means free labour in the widest sense, but it means free exchange.' When applied to the case of land, this principle meant that

no man or body of men have the moral right to prevent any fellow man from buying in an open market such land as he wishes to buy. The open market for land is a human right just as sacred as the open market for bread or corn, and no persons have the right to close it against their fellow men.[70]

By contrast, J. C. Spence, a naval architect and associate of Donisthorpe's, argued that Spencer's difficulties on the land question were the result of combining the Law of Equal Freedom with the assumption that the earth was common to all mankind. The solution, Spence thought, was simply to dispense with this assumption: the land was 'common to all mankind' only in the sense that 'unappropriated land is owned by no one, but could be honestly appropriated by anyone.'[71] He concluded that private property in land was not illegitimate:

It is ... evident that ancient law, modern customs, and ordinary ethical conceptions, all agree that unoccupied land may be taken possession of by

---

[68] Hobson, 'Rich Man's Anarchism', 395.

[69] Cf. A. Herbert, 'Lost in the Region of Phrases', *Humanitarian*, 14 (1899), 320–30.

[70] Id., 'Liberty in Land', in W. S. Crawshay and F. Millar (eds.), *The Liberty Annual* (London, 1892), 8–9.

[71] J. C. Spence, *Property in Land: A Defence of Individual Ownership* (London, 1892), 16.

anyone. They also agree that after it has been taken possession of, it is no longer common, but private property. He who takes away the private property of another is, according to ancient law, modern customs, and ordinary ethical conceptions, classed as a thief.[72]

Obviously, however, neither of these contributions to the debate successfully addressed the fundamental theoretical problem. Spence and Herbert both ignored the point of the radical argument for the nationalization of the land, namely that land differed from other forms of property in that its appropriation curtailed the equal rights of others. There could be no such thing as its 'honest' appropriation, and it could be argued, contra Herbert, that land nationalization was a legitimate infringement of individual liberty, since its objective was to preserve the equal freedom of other individuals. Although Herbert also tried to argue that agricultural land was as much a human artefact as other products which an individual might own without question, it was clear that neither his nor Spence's argument constituted a solution to the difficulty.

A second Individualist response was to claim that, although the land-nationalization proposal might be theoretically valid, what was correct in theory did not always apply in practice since the rectification of the 'injustice' of private land ownership could only be achieved by the creation of other, and greater, injustices. Levy, for example, continued to insist that in theory 'private property in land is essentially inconsistent with Individualism', but he immediately drew back from the radical implications of this observation by insisting that the injustice arising from private land ownership 'cannot and ought not to be rectified by expropriation.' Instead he expressed faith in 'the vivifying effect of a great moral principle' and hoped that under its influence 'the large landowners would voluntarily turn their permanent ownership into a terminable one.'[73] Unless Levy's objective is interpreted as the conservative one of protecting the rights of all property owners, his refusal to countenance coercive redress in this case appears strange: it is not 'expropriation' to deprive someone of something to which he does not possess legitimate title.

Spencer's own response in the *Principles of Ethics* was similar. While continuing to recognize the theoretical validity of the argument he had made in the *Social Statics*, he banished it to the realm of absolute ethics and therefore to his distant (and perhaps never-to-be-achieved) Utopia. Although it remained true, from the standpoint of absolute ethics, that 'the aggregate of men forming the community are the supreme owners

---

[72] Ibid. 12.   [73] Levy, 'Individualism', 147–8.

of the land' he had now come to believe, as the result of 'a fuller consideration of the matter', that, in the realm of relative ethics, 'individual ownership, subject to State-suzerainity, should be maintained.'[74] Spencer could only prevent the Law of Equal Freedom from undermining the system of private property by abandoning any pretence of a commitment to deductive utilitarianism; his arguments against land nationalization were those of a full-blooded empirical utilitarian. In the first place, Spencer argued, 'it suffices to remember the inferiority of public administration to private administration, to see that the ownership of the State would work ill.'[75] Whereas under a system of private ownership those who manage the land enjoy a direct connection between effort and benefit, the officials of a State bureaucracy would experience no such direct connection with the consequence that their administration would be inefficient.

Spencer's most important reason for resisting land nationalization was that

the landless have not an equitable claim to the land in its present state—cleared, drained, fenced, fertilized, and furnished with farm-building & c.—but only to the land in its primitive state, here stony, there marshy, covered with forest, gorse, heather, & c.[76]

Nearly all of the value of the land had been created by its owners in the course of 'clearing, breaking up, prolonged culture, fencing, draining, making roads, farm buildings & c.' and on this portion of its value the community had no claim. In comparison to the 'gigantic robbery' which the expropriation of this value from the landowners would involve, the undoubted injustices in the history of land ownership paled into insignificance.[77] Spencer also contended that, since the landless were entitled only to the 'prairie value' of the land, they had been adequately compensated during the course of the previous three centuries. In this period the land had contributed an estimated £500,000,000 in poor rates to the support of the landless, and it was probably the case that 'the land-owners would contend that for the land in its primitive, unsubdued state, furnishing nothing but wild animals and wild fruits, £500,000,000 would be a high price.'[78]

---

[74] Spencer, *Principles of Ethics*, ii. 444, app. B.   [75] Ibid.
[76] Ibid. 443, app. B.
[77] Ibid. 92. Spencer conveniently ignored the fact that many of these improvements were the work of tenants, who received no share of the associated rise in capital values which accrued to the landlords.
[78] Ibid. 443, app. B.

This argument was flawed on a number of grounds. As F. B. Jevons pointed out in a critical notice of *The Principles of Ethics* for the *Economic Review*, Spencer had attempted to justify the injustice of private land ownership by stressing the compensation provided by the Poor Law. But, according to Spencer, the latter also involved an injustice since it had been 'administered so as to enable the individual to shoulder off some of the evil consequences of his own actions on to somebody else.' In other words,

to spend £500,000,000 in demoralizing people whom you have previously pauperized, by robbing them of £500,000,000, doubles the injury rather than gives 'a valid basis to the right of private property.'[79]

As Sidgwick also argued, a socialist might reply to Spencer's defence of private property in land by claiming that the poor rates paid in the past were 'rather a compensation to the past poor', and an inadequate one at that, and were irrelevant to the '"equal claims" of existing human beings.'[80] Spencer's estimate of the value of land ignored the 'unearned increment' exclusively due to the increase of population, yet it also seemed to be a legitimate extension of his principle that this increment, not being the result of productive labour, 'should be regarded as due to the poor.'[81]

Clearly, the doctrine of the 'unearned increment' presented the Individualists with a challenge almost as formidable as Spencer's early writings on land nationalization. It had played a pivotal role in J. S. Mill's later thoughts on the land question, and in subsequent radical proposals like those associated with Henry George or included in *The Radical Programme*; consequently the doctrine was subjected to repeated criticism in Individualist publications. For example, O'Brien insisted that the compulsory confiscation of the 'unearned increment' would not be an instance of securing justice for the underprivileged, but rather a case of 'the political abuse of power . . . Justice only exists as long as we allow our neighbours to possess whatever comes to them through the free and non-aggressive use of our own faculties.'[82] A further element of this argument was to deny that it was possible to distinguish between the 'earned' and 'unearned' value of a commodity: as O'Brien also remarked, 'the Individualist denies . . . it is . . . possible to separate what is due to exertion from what is due to fortune or to nature. This operation would require an omniscient deity, not a cumbersome and

---

[79] F. B. Jevons, 'A Review of Spencer's *Justice*', *Economic Review*, 2 (1892), 138.
[80] H. Sidgwick, *Lectures on Ethics*, 287.   [81] Ibid. 288.
[82] O'Brien, *Socialism Tested by the Facts*, 192–3.

blundering State made up of selfish time-servers and dishonest mob-bribers.'[83] Mackay also adopted this line of argument, claiming that 'increments of value are never earned by their owners.' This was because 'value is created only when, and if, effort has been directed to meet a commensurate demand . . . if this demand is not present, the product is valueless.'[84] Therefore the problem was not 'how best to appropriate one particular form of "unearned increment"', but rather, 'how best to distribute the unearned increment and decrement which must arise in all products of industry by reason of the variations of demand and supply.'[85] Mackay believed that the 'unanimous verdict of civilized society' was that the solution to this problem resided in the institution of private property.[86] Nevertheless, while this response might be unassailable from the standpoint of political economy, it presented obvious difficulties for the Spencerians. In attempting to defeat the doctrine of the 'unearned increment' they were forced into an admission that the rewards of the market were never 'deserved'; not only was this indirect contradiction with the theory of justice propounded by their mentor, but it also seemed to lend considerable weight to the empirical Individualist case urged against Spencer by Sidgwick.

V. Utility and Property

It is clear from the preceding sections that Sidgwick was a forceful and perceptive critic of Spencer's natural-rights defence of private property. Such a response is only to be expected from this careful and consistently utilitarian thinker, but some commentators have further alleged that Sidgwick is to be regarded as an advocate of policies like land nationalization and taxation of the 'unearned' increment. This is the position maintained, for example, by H. B. Acton who attributes to Sidgwick the assumption 'that originally all men had a right to exert their faculties on the whole environment in which they live' and the corollary that property

---

[83] Ibid. 189.

[84] T. D. Mackay, 'Empiricism in Politics', *National Review*, 25 (1895), 795.

[85] Ibid.

[86] Ibid. For other examples of Individualists who were critical of the doctrine of the 'unearned increment' see Spence, *Private Property in Land*; H. Fawcett, *State Socialism and the Nationalisation of Land* (London, 1883); Sir L. Mallet, *Free Exchange* (London, 1891), 291 ff.

in land was a 'usurpation'.[87] Similarly, after quoting some of Sidgwick's remarks on property rights, J. T. Kloppenberg contends that 'Sidgwick shared [T. H.] Green's conception of effective rights' and argued for the limitation of property rights in a direct challenge to 'the liberal conception of freedom.'[88] These accounts might seem to gain further plausibility from the perennial tension between the respective claims of equality and security in utilitarian thinking about property rights; the argument might be that in considering inequalities of wealth and income Sidgwick had accorded priority to the diminishing marginal utility of property owners rather than the utility they derived from security of possession.[89] Contrary to this interpretation, I shall demonstrate that although Sidgwick was aware of the aspects of utilitarianism which appeared to demand a more equal distribution of wealth, he resolved the tension between equality and security decisively in favour of the latter. Moreover, while recognizing the infringement of the principle of equal opportunities represented by private ownership of the land, he also refused to sanction land nationalization or taxation of the 'unearned increment'. Sidgwick's utilitarianism gave rise to conservative conclusions about the rights of property which were the counterpart of his conservative conclusions about the functions of the State.

It is crucial for an understanding of Sidgwick's argument that he divided justice into 'Conservative' and 'Ideal' forms. The former was realized '(1) in the observance of law or contracts and definite understandings, and in the enforcement of such penalties for the violation of these as have been legally determined and announced; and (2) in the fulfilment of natural and normal expectations.'[90] Since it was conceivable some laws were unjust, it appeared necessary to supplement conservative justice with ideal justice, which might take either desert-based or rights-based forms. As we have already observed, Sidgwick considered unsatisfactory the rights-based Law of Equal Freedom formulation because it failed to provide an adequate systematization of the principles underlying actually established rules of law (*supra*). The alternative to this conception of ideal justice was the socialistic ideal of requiting desert. But although Sidgwick acknowledged that this would

---

[87] H. B. Acton, introd. to S. Webb, *Socialism in England*, (1889; London, Gower edn., 1987), p. xlv.

[88] J. T. Kloppenberg, *Uncertain Victory: Social Democracy and Progressivism in European and American Thought 1870–1920* (Oxford, 1986), 182.

[89] For an excellent discussion of the tension between equality and security in utilitarian theories of property see Ryan, *Property and Political Theory*, ch. 4.

[90] H. Sidgwick, *Methods of Ethics*, 293.

'seem to give a nearer approximation to what we conceive as Divine Justice than the present state of society affords',[91] he shared Spencer's unwillingness to depart from the distributive mechanism of the free market.

Spencer had assumed both that benefits ought to be distributed according to desert and that, as a matter of fact, the market did distribute according to desert. Sidgwick had demonstrated that the latter assumption was unsound and, recognizing the socialistic consequences of this argument, he abandoned the first assumption as well. In the first place, he argued, it was extremely doubtful that some 'rational method of determining value', which the Socialistic ideal presupposed, could be found. For instance, it would seem impossible to discover any means of comparing the value of the different services which must necessarily be combined to produce a happy life: how were the relative values of necessities and luxuries to be assessed or how could the value of the contributions of different kinds of labour to the same product be determined?[92] In suggesting that the socialistic ideal took the form 'of a conception of Divine rather than human justice', Sidgwick appears to have effectively ruled out its realization on this side of the grave.[93]

Since distribution according to desert could not be realized by social institutions, it followed that the construction of 'an ideally just social order in which all services are rewarded in exact proportion to their intrinsic value' had to be abandoned as impractical, and this conclusion was confirmed by the fact that 'ordinarily the only kind of justice we try to realise is that which consists in the fulfillment of contracts and definite expectations [i.e. conservative justice]; leaving the general fairness of Distribution by Bargaining to take care of itself.'[94] In other words, the question was no longer that of discovering the intrinsic worth of different services but, rather, 'what reward can procure them and whether the rest of society gain by the services more than the equivalent reward.'[95] As Schneewind has pointed out, this involves a utilitarian mode of calculation,[96] and in effect Sidgwick had rejected the possibility

---

[91] Ibid. 289.   [92] Ibid.

[93] It is to be doubted whether his involvement with the Society for Psychical Research much alters the argument.

[94] H. Sidgwick, *Methods of Ethics*, 290. Compare Sidgwick's discussion of the difficulties attendant on rewarding desert in id., *Principles of Political Economy*, 504–6. There he admitted that although 'the principles of necessarianism' demanded that the attempt be abandoned as futile it was nevertheless a conclusion 'not in harmony with our common notions of Justice.' (p. 506.)

[95] Id., *Methods of Ethics*, 289.   [96] Schneewind, *Sidgwick's Ethics*, 276.

of the rectification of the existing legal system by reference to some standard of ideal justice; instead the promotion of the general utility was the only relevant criterion. If there were grounds for rectifying the competitive system and the existing distribution of private property, they would be utilitarian grounds.

Sidgwick recognized that there were utilitarian reasons for seeking greater equality of incomes. He invoked the authority of common sense in favour of Bentham's view 'that any given quantum of wealth is generally likely to be less useful to its owner, the greater total of private wealth of which it forms a part', and held that it was 'indubitable that the attainment of greater equality in the distribution of the means and opportunities of enjoyment is in itself a desirable thing.' But, as so often with Sidgwick's writings, the formulation is carefully phrased: the greater equalization of incomes is made conditional on its being 'attained without any material sacrifices of the advantages of freedom.'[97] And, as Sidgwick made abundantly clear, the diminution of the 'advantages of freedom' was precisely the result to be expected from the pursuit of the goal of equality:

Any great equalisation of wealth would probably diminish the accumulation of capital, on which the progress of industry depends; and would deteriorate the administration of the capital accumulated; since the most economic organisation of industry . . . requires capital in large masses under single management . . . Moreover, the effective maintenance and progress of intellectual culture . . . seems to require the existence of a numerous group of persons enjoying complete leisure and the means of ample expenditure.[98]

The equalitarian ideal could provide no effective substitute for the stimulus to 'industry and thrift' provided by the competitive system, and hence 'the realisation of the collectivist idea at the present time or in the proximate future would arrest industrial progress; and . . . the comparative equality of incomes which it would bring about would be an equality in poverty.'[99] The 'overwhelming majority' of political economists were in favour of the 'private competitive management of industry', he wrote,

as securing an intensity of energy and vigilance, an eager inventiveness in turning new knowledge and new opportunities to account, a freedom and flexibility in adapting industrial methods to new needs and conditions, a salutary continual expurgation of indolence and unthrift, which public management cannot be expected to rival in the present state of social morality.[100]

[97] H. Sidgwick, *Elements of Politics*, 160.   [98] Ibid. 161.   [99] Ibid. 159.
[100] Ibid.

Sidgwick's argument on this score had much in common with that of J. S. Mill's posthumously published 'Chapters on Socialism', in which the latter had recognized the theoretical attractiveness of the socialist ideal, but at the same time had declared that the moral and intellectual demands it placed on mankind were beyond its present capacities. Consequently, he argued, 'personal interest will for a long time be a more effective stimulus to the most vigourous and careful conduct of the industrial business of society than motives of a higher character.'[101] Sidgwick appears to have shared this view, although even Mill's evolutionary optimism was lacking from his version of the argument. His primary concern, as both a moralist and a political theorist, was for the present, and he was certain that for the foreseeable future the realization of the ideal of socialism was impracticable, and that to attempt to attain it would be nothing short of disastrous.

Sidgwick's utilitarian defence of the sanctity of private property was part of this general defence of the competitive system. From the point of view of empirical utilitarianism, he wrote, 'the protection of exclusive use is obviously required in order that individuals may have adequate inducement to labour in adapting matter to the satisfaction of their needs and desires', and without the full enjoyment of the utility resulting from labour 'we could not expect much of the labour to be performed.'[102] This view was echoed by a number of other Individualists. Goldwin Smith, for example, made the same point with greater literary flourish: the 'economical foundation' of property was that 'it is the only known motive power of production. Slavery has its whip; but, saving this, no general incentive to labour other than property has yet been devised.'[103] In a characteristically forthright contribution to the land-nationalization debate, Lord Bramwell declared 'without doubt or misgiving that the institution of private property is good for the community, and should exist in everything that is the product of labour, and in everything which is capable of improvement.' The reason was simply 'that if a man is entitled to the result of his labour, he will work harder and better, and be happier at his work, than if he works for the community.'[104] George Brooks concisely expressed this utilitarian

101 J. S. Mill, *Chapters on Socialism*, in *John Stuart Mill on Politics and Society*, ed. G. Williams (Glasgow, 1976), 340.
102 H. Sidgwick, *The Elements of Politics* (London, 1891), 49.
103 G. Smith, 'Social and Industrial Revolution', in id., *Essays on Questions of the Day*, 7.
104 Lord Bramwell, 'Property', *Nineteenth Century*, 27 (1890), 443.

argument that security of property rights was an essential condition for the attainment of maximum prosperity:

> Accumulations and exchanges are absolutely dependent upon the principle that there shall be private property, and private property shall be inviolable. No security, no exchange; no exchange, no accumulations; no accumulations, no capital; no capital, no labour; no labour, no production; no production, and the earth would be a desert and a marsh, and mankind a race of savages.[105]

This line of argument also found favour with a number of Spencerian Individualists, for example Bruce Smith, who, as we have already seen, was something of a sceptic with regard to the doctrine of natural rights.[106]

The incentive argument also could be used to justify the rights of inheritance and bequest. Considering Mill's proposal that the right of bequest should be limited to a 'certain maximum, which should be fixed sufficiently high to afford the means of comfortable independence', Sidgwick argued that interference of this kind with free bequest 'would dangerously diminish the motives to industry, and—what is here, perhaps, more important—thrift, in the latter part of the lives of the persons who came under the restrictions.'[107] In view of these considerations, he concluded, 'the law ought clearly to aim at securing each individual from the interference of others with his enjoyment of the results of his labour: and, in fact, the provision of this security is often simply stated as the end by reference to which private property is to be justified.'[108]

Sidgwick also recognized, however, that the security argument only justified an individual retaining the products of his labour-power; it was silent on the question of whether the initial appropriation of material resources was itself right. He offered as a solution to this problem— with which Spencer had wrestled so unsuccessfully—the following disjunctive justification:

> either (1) that the thing appropriated would not practically have been available for human use, if the appropriator had not laboured in seeking it; or (2) that his appropriation does not materially diminish the opportunities open to other

---

[105] G. Brooks, *Industry and Property* (London, 1895), 126.
[106] [A.] B. Smith, *Liberty and Liberalism*, 222.
[107] H. Sidgwick, *Elements of Politics*, 104–5.
[108] Ibid. 49. Like Spencer, Sidgwick did not explore the radical implications of the doctrine that the labourer should be entitled to enjoy the product of his labour.

persons of obtaining similar things, owing to the natural abundance of such opportunities.[109]

This formula provided an adequate justification for the appropriation 'of such things as fish caught in the open sea, or wild animals, plants, or even minerals found in large tracts of uncultivated country.' Nevertheless, Sidgwick had not managed to avoid the serious shortcomings which afflicted Spencer's proposed justification of property in natural resources, since on this formula the appropriation of the land clearly did 'materially diminish the opportunities' of the landless. This gave rise to a dilemma: on the one hand, for landless individuals, 'private property in land involved a substantial encroachment on the opportunities of applying labour productively' while appropriation is 'manifestly required by utilitarian Individualism, to stimulate and reward the most energetic and enlightened application of labour to land.'[110]

Sidgwick's solution to this dilemma was to 'allow the requisite appropriation but to secure adequate compensation for it', and this was part of the justification for the limited socialistic interference, in such spheres as education and assisted emigration, which we examined in the previous chapter. Yet, as these examples demonstrate, the conception of 'adequate compensation' entertained by Sidgwick was very restricted, and as Ryan has observed, the lengths to which the State could go in securing compensation was 'limited by the need not to disturb security and incentive so much that the general welfare is lessened.'[111] Furthermore, contrary to Acton's claim, Sidgwick did not conclude that private property in land was a 'usurpation'. Like Spencer he resisted the apparent logical consequences of his own principles when they threatened to disturb the existing distribution of property, and he contended that the 'economic disadvantages' of a change in the system of land ownership would more than outweigh its advantages 'at the present stage of social and political development.'[112]

Sidgwick's arguments against land nationalization were almost identical to those employed by Spencer, and he particularly emphasized the 'inertness and jobbery incident to public management' as well as 'the loss of special satisfactions, and any special stimulus to labour and care, which individuals derive from the sense of ownership'. Although, as a good utilitarian, Sidgwick refused to pronounce an absolute prohibition

[109] Ibid. 50.   [110] Ibid. 73.

[111] Ryan, *Property and Political Theory*, 117.

[112] H. Sidgwick, *Elements of Politics*, 148–9 n.

on the nationalization of the land, he was convinced that 'in reference to most existing communities at the present time' the 'diminuation in production' thus resulting was likely to 'outweigh any gain in equity of distribution.'[113]

Despite Sidgwick's awareness of the way in which the property rights of owners curtailed the freedom of non-owners, and despite his recognition of the principle of diminishing marginal utility, he can be seen to have resisted the radical and equalitarian implications of his own 'utilitarian Individualism'. He did so by stressing the importance of the security and incentives derived from property rights. Interpretations like those offered by Kloppenberg and Acton have missed the distinction between the logical implications of Sidgwick's arguments and his own attempts to escape these implications. That Sidgwick failed to be convincing in his attempt to remove the radical sting from his principles attests to the difficulty of the task in which he was engaged; that he undertook the project at all attests to the conservatism of his version of the utilitarian doctrine.

VI. Conclusion

In his work on *Natural Rights* published in 1894 David Ritchie observed that although Tom Paine had 'not yet been made a saint by the Knights and Dames of the Primrose League' his ghost would have taken a grim delight 'in hearing the "Rights of Man" preached by a Tory Lord Chancellor.' Ritchie offered this observation in the course of examining the way in which the once revolutionary doctrine of natural rights had become, by the end of the nineteenth century, one of the cornerstones of conservatism and reaction. He explained this apparent contradiction by pointing out that

all abstract theories about human society admit of divergent and conflicting application. Thus the theory of social contract is used by Hobbes to condemn rebellion, and by Locke to justify it. The conception of social organism is used by Plato to justify the extremest interference with individual liberty, and by Mr Herbert Spencer to condemn a very moderate amount of state control. And so the theory of natural rights is used by Anarchists to condemn the existing inequalities of social conditions, and by Conservatives to check attempts on the part of government to remedy these inequalities.[114]

[113] Id., *Principles of Political Economy*, 511.
[114] Ritchie, *Natural Rights*, 14–15.

As this chapter has suggested, the natural-rights defence of Individualism was ill-suited to the conservative purpose of defending the inequalities of property in late nineteenth-century Britain. From their intellectual ancestors the Individualists had inherited a theory of justice the radical implications of which they laboured to remove. But the task was never satisfactorily accomplished. The doctrine that each individual possessed a moral right to the products of his labour sat uneasily with a social system in which great inequalities of wealth were clearly not founded on unequal labour. Whether the defence was in terms of the desert-based or rights-based interpretations of the principle of justice, the result was the same: the theory could not perform the function which the Individualists demanded of it.

Furthermore, if justice required that the equal rights or equal opportunities of all individuals were respected, the appropriation of limited natural resources was evidently unjust since it amounted to a denial of the rights of those who were excluded from the resource. Once more, the Individualists were confronted with a conflict between their principles and their desire to mount an effective defence of the late Victorian social order; their conservatism was revealed in their readiness to resolve the conflict in favour of the latter. They might have appealed to principles of justice in order to condemn government interference which aimed at rectifying extremes of inequality, but often the best defence of the policies they abhorred were the principles they espoused.

EPILOGUE
INDIVIDUALISM AND CONSERVATISM

Individualism was a conservative political theory in the sense that it attempted to articulate an intellectual defence of the late Victorian social order against the attacks made on it by the New Radicalism. While some Individualists were clearly of the opinion that existing society fell some way short of their ideal, they nevertheless considered that the status quo was unquestionably preferable to the socialistic schemes for social reform with which the Liberal party had become increasingly identified. In this sense their conservatism was like that of Hume or Alexander Hamilton both of whom 'could be conservative because both had something—namely liberty—to conserve.'[1] Their political aim was primarily negative and defensive, to ensure that the boundaries of the mid-Victorian State were not expanded; only secondarily did they demand the further elimination of governmental interference. Consequently the Individualists were able to make common cause with mainstream Conservatives against an enemy which appeared to threaten vested interests and dreams of a distant anarchistic Utopia alike. Since this alliance was founded on common fears rather than shared ideals, the relationship between Individualism and Conservatism was under constant strain throughout the late Victorian and Edwardian eras, and the Individualists never succeeded in establishing themselves as part of the Conservative mainstream.

By the final decades of the nineteenth century the alienation of the Radicals of the 1860s from the Liberal party was complete. Against this background, it is not altogether surprising to find many Individualists expressing qualified support for the Conservatives. Although, as was pointed out in an earlier chapter, the Individualists were deeply opposed to the historical policies of 'Toryism', in *The Man versus the State* Spencer noted with approval the rise of 'a new species of Tory' committed to the defence of liberties against State interference and commended the Liberty and Property Defence League, 'largely consisting of Conservatives', for its role in promoting the cause of

---

[1] M. Cranston, *Philosophers and Pamphleteers* (Oxford, 1986), 8.

Individualism.[2] Similarly, Bruce Smith observed that while liberalism had come to mean 'liberality with the public revenue', the term conservative was now used to describe someone 'opposed to such liberality'.[3] Donisthorpe argued that a realignment in British politics had become necessary since the crucial issue of the future would be the function of the State and 'it is entirely upon difference of opinion concerning state structure that the existing party divisions are based.'[4] He noted that politicians were 'slowly and unconsciously regrouping themselves according to principles as fundamental and important as the old ones, but having little in common with them' and thought it was essential that those who 'are opposed in principle to legislation of a socialistic character' should form themselves into a party to uphold Individualism against socialism.[5] Several years prior to the Liberal party split over Home Rule, he exhorted the moderate Liberals to 'come forward boldly and to speak out for the ancient rights and liberties of all classes on the time-honoured lines of property and freedom' and if necessary to 'join hands with those who would bolster up effete institutions.'[6]

In addition, empirical Individualists were drawn into an involvement with Conservative party politics as a result of their membership of the Oxford and Cambridge Liberal Unionist Associations. Yet even before the Home Rule crisis, Henry Sidgwick found himself becoming increasingly sympathetic to the Conservative party. In January 1885, having spent some time in the company of Conservatives at Whittinghame, the country house of his brother-in-law A. J. Balfour, he noted in his journal that 'their criticism of the present phase of Radicalism seems to be unanswerable.'[7] So strongly did he feel this that in the following year he returned home early from Switzerland in order to vote for a Conservative candidate in the general election. His friend Dicey became even more closely identified with the Conservative party: unlike most of the other Individualists he lived long enough to see, and denounce, Lloyd George's budget of 1909 and was a leading figure in the British Constitution Association which also counted Conservative

[2] Spencer, *The Man versus The State*, ed. D. G. Macrae (1884; Harmondsworth, 1969), 81. He was at pains to emphasize, however, that he was not arguing that Liberals and Conservatives had 'changed places' with regard to their views on State interference.

[3] [A.] B. Smith, *Liberty and Liberalism* (London, 1887), 8.

[4] Donisthorpe, *Individualism: A System of Politics* (London, 1889), 61.

[5] Id., *Law in a Free State* (London, 1895), 2.

[6] Id., *Liberty or Law?* (London, 1884), 11.

[7] Quoted in A. S[idgwick] and E. M. S[idgwick], *Henry Sidgwick: A Memoir* (London, 1906), 398–9.

politicians like Lord Hugh Cecil and Balfour of Burleigh among its leaders.

Nevertheless, the dominant strands of late Victorian and Edwardian Conservatism contained significant statist elements which were not unwilling to countenance a measure of social reform on their own account, although they were always careful to distinguish this from socialism, to which they shared the Individualists' antipathy. While it was true that some voices within the Conservative party, like the Earl of Pembroke, were arguing that the contest between Individualism and socialism afforded the opportunity for their party to become clearly identified as the champion of the former, they never became more than a small minority.[8]

Conservatives in the 1890s and 1900s may be divided into two broad categories: those who may be termed the 'traditionalists', and the 'Radical Right' or 'Collectivists'. The former included the Conservative leadership—Salisbury and Balfour—who adhered to the traditional view of the function of the Conservative party 'as being that of preserving "national" institutions and putting a break on reckless or ill-considered change.'[9] The Collectivists, by contrast, were represented by Chamberlain, Milner, and other advocates of 'national efficiency'. This group were acutely aware of Britain's declining influence in the world, and believed that national energies should be directed into preparing British society for economic and military survival in an international environment which would increasingly witness competition between great empires.[10]

The collectivists paid respectful attention to Germany's machinery of government and political traditions, since that country had emerged as Britain's most formidable commercial competitor, not to mention her most likely military opponent. Thus when Benjamin Kidd, the

---

[8] G. R. C. Herbert, 13th Earl of Pembroke, 'An Address to the Liberty and Property Defence League with a word to the Conservative party', *National Review*, 5 (1885), 787–800.

[9] G. R. Searle, 'Critics of Edwardian Society: The Case of the Radical Right', in A. O'Day (ed.), *The Edwardian Age: Conflict and Stability 1900–1914* (London, 1979), 82.

[10] Ibid. Searle distinguishes between two strands of Collectivism: the national-efficiency movement identified with Chamberlain and Milner, and the 'Radical Right' which shared many of the aims of the former, but which sought to realize them by populist mass politics rather than by the élite consensus favoured by the 'Co-efficients'. However, since Searle's distinction is based primarily on differences concerning political tactics rather than the legitimate province of the State, it may be safely disregarded for present purposes, and the labels 'Collectivist' and 'Radical Right' will be employed interchangeably.

Edwardian Age's most popular philosopher and a close associate of the group of intellectuals around Chamberlain, prophesied that the 'next age will probably be . . . the age of the Germanization of the world' he was merely expressing the Collectivists' view that

> those lessons of which the first stage have been displayed in the history of modern Prussia . . . are likely to be worked out in their fuller applications by successful States in the future.[11]

Yet Germany,

> with its centralised bureaucracy, its conscription, its tariffs and subsidies and authoritarian regime, stood very far apart from . . . the laissez faire state of traditional liberal aspiration.[12]

Backed by academic arguments formulated by economists deeply influenced by the German Historical School, like W. J. Ashley and William Cunningham, the Collectivists argued for the formation of a British Imperial *Zollverein*.[13] Imperial preference thus became the central plank of their programme, since not only would it transform the Empire into a more closely integrated, and therefore more efficient, economic unit, but it would also generate the revenues necessary to pursue social reform at home. Recruitment of troops for the Boer War had acutely revealed the consequences for the mass of the population of poor housing, health, and sanitary conditions, and it was thought a nation could not long survive in the new world order if the physical resources of its people were inadequate for its commercial and military needs. Social reform was necessary, on this view, not to secure justice between classes, but to increase the efficiency of the nation. As Ernest Barker remarked, 'Collectivism had wrought to exhalt the province of the State: Nationalism seems to have entered and reaped the crop which it had sown.'[14]

---

[11] B. Kidd, *Individualism and After* (Oxford, 1908), 31. For Kidd's close association with the group of intellectuals around Chamberlain, see D. P. Crook, *Benjamin Kidd: Portrait of a Social Darwinist* (Cambridge, 1984), 221 ff. For Kidd's support for tariff reform see, id., 'The Larger Basis of Colonial Preference', *Nineteenth Century and After*, 55 (1904), 12–29. Kidd's superior at the Inland Revenue, where he had worked as a clerk prior to the publication of *Social Evolution*, had been Visc. Milner who had assisted in securing the book's publication.

[12] G. R. Searle, *The Quest for National Efficiency* (Oxford, 1971), 29–30. Even in the 1880s 'Germany was coming to be regarded as the alternative model, the seed-bed for the future.' (H. C. G. Matthew, introd. to *The Gladstone Diaries*, vols. x and xi (Oxford, 1990), pp. xxx–xxxi.

[13] The ideas of Ashley and Cunningham, as well as those of the social imperialists more generally, are examined in B. Semmel, *Imperialism and Social Reform* (London, 1960).

[14] E. Barker, *Political Thought in England 1848 to the Present Day* (London, 1915), 22.

Clearly there was little common ground between the Individualists and the social imperialists of the Radical Right. Leaving aside the obvious differences between the Collectivists' aggressive imperialism, and the Individualists' preference for a Gladstonian or even Cobdenite foreign policy, the conception of the State at the heart of the two political theories differed profoundly. Indeed, from the standpoint of the Collectivists, the continued hold which Individualism exercised over the national consciousness was itself part of the problem; adherence to *laissez-faire* long after it had ceased to serve Britain's commercial interests had, in their view, contributed significantly to the nation's decline. Furthermore, at a theoretical level, political writers associated with the Radical Right explicitly attacked the fundamental assumptions of utilitarianism and Individualism in arguing for a wider conception of the duties of the State. Cunningham, an Anglican archdeacon and (like Sidgwick) a Fellow of Trinity College, Cambridge, claimed:

Though for many purposes the utilitarian State seems to secure excellent results, and a community may flourish in strength and wealth and maintain a high standard of culture and comfort under its control, occasions may yet arise when political action is taken that lies outside the ordinary canons and that cannot be justified on purely utilitarian grounds. These offer an unconscious testimony to the truth that there is a right, and a duty to the State, which is above all considerations of interest.[15]

Thus, argued Cunningham, there was a common good which transcended that which emerged from a 'perfectly free play of personal ambitions and tastes and proclivities': 'As individual lives are shorter than the life of the community, the aggregate of personal interest, at any one time, can never be identical with that of the community as a whole.'[16] Similarly, Benjamin Kidd explicitly attacked Spencer's conception of the social organism on the grounds that it did not recognize a collective interest transcending the interests of particular individuals:

It will be apparent, on reflection, that Spencer's conception of a corporate life subordinate to the interests of the units comprising it, is in the nature of things invalid. . . . It is evident that it is impossible to conceive society in any scientific sense as a mere mob of units of this kind whose individual interests could be paramount over the corporate interests.[17]

Granted that the common good could not be realized by the free play of individual self-interest, it followed that there was much that the State

[15] W. Cunningham, *Christianity and the Social Order* (London, 1910), 55–6.
[16] Ibid. 53.   [17] Kidd, *Individualism and After*, 24.

would be justified in doing as the representative of the 'national interest'. As Kidd observed, 'the State, under the direction of a more organic social consciousness, can carry forms of co-operative activity to results in the public interest which are beyond the powers of voluntary competitive enterprise.'[18] This idea was given a more concrete expression by Cunningham:

The economic life of a community is so important, that it is desirable that the government should have a policy, and co-ordinate the energies of the nation in such a way as to secure the best result. The free play of private capital brings about a development of different sides of economic life in a haphazard fashion; but if a careful forecast is made of the requirements of the country as a whole, it is possible to introduce a conscious co-operation that shall secure the result with less friction and waste.[19]

Indeed, the Collectivists believed that 'the old antithesis' of Individualism and socialism 'which Herbert Spencer in his *Man v. The State* exaggerated into an antagonism' had been rendered obsolete by the conditions of modern society.[20] Instead, as Ashley wrote, they anticipated the creation of 'a corporate organisation of industry on the side alike of employers and employed . . . with the State alert and intelligent in the background to protect the interests of the community.'[21] In contrast to the Individualists' zealous defence of the rights of private property, Cunningham believed that 'the State, which has given the title to enjoy private property, may be justified in modifying the exercise of these rights, or even in resuming them altogether.'[22] The potentially radical implications of these ideas were moderated by his repeated insistence that a healthy competitive system was an essential element in any successful nation; but it is evident that the Collectivists and the Individualists were poles apart.

The Conservative traditionalists were closer in spirit to the Individualists, in the sense that both were opposed to 'any policy which undermines the foundations on which society in England now rests.'[23] Nevertheless, this cannot disguise the fact that a considerable gulf also separated traditionalist Conservatism from Individualism. The important theoretical and practical issues which were at stake are best

[18] Ibid. 34.   [19] Cunningham, *Christianity and the Social Order*, 89.
[20] Sir W. J. Ashley, *The Economic Organisation of England* (London, 1914), 191.
[21] Ibid. 190–1.   [22] Cunningham, *Christianity and the Social Order*, 85.
[23] A. V. Dicey, 'Lord Pembroke', *National Review*, 28 (1897), 622.

illustrated by considering Lord Hugh Cecil's political philosophy, and in particular his slim volume on *Conservatism*.[24]

On first acquaintance, Cecil's thought might appear to have much in common with that of the Individualists: according to W. H. Greenleaf, for example, *Conservatism* was the work of 'a fervent believer in the limited state, an extreme individualist who . . . would have been quite at home in the Manchester School.'[25] Certainly there are elements in Cecil's political philosophy which can bear this interpretation, and these led the *Contemporary Review* to the conclusion that Cecil's sympathies were with the mid-nineteenth-century insistence 'on the all-powerful character of economic laws, on the ultimate uselessness of State intervention, and . . . on the liberty of the individual.'[26] Cecil argued, for example, that 'we must always give as much liberty as possible' for he believed that whenever liberty is restricted there results a destruction of the virtues of character:

If we enfeeble human nature by removing from it the discipline of liberty, then certainly we shall be wandering astray; and while we use the machinery of the State to get, as we think, somewhat nearer the solution of this problem or that, we shall all the time be destroying that on which the State itself depends, that from which alone real and permanent good can come—the individual character.[27]

This was language which the Individualists themselves had used, and in his 1907 Presidential Address to the British Constitution Association— which included Spencerians like Thomas Mackay and Hugh Elliot among its membership—Cecil also attacked socialism in terms Spencer could have recognized. He warned against a movement towards an oppressive regime in which the conditions of labour were all regulated by a central authority, and expressed a preference for voluntary forms of action over regulation by the State. Cecil also warned that the expansion of State-run industry threatened a flight of private capital, would inflate the number of public functionaries, strain public finances making the

---

[24] I have been greatly assisted in this discussion of Cecil by an unpublished paper kindly shown to me by J. R. Meadowcroft.

[25] W. H. Greenleaf, *The British Political Tradition*, ii. *The Ideological Heritage* (London, 1983), 288. See also N. O'Sullivan *Conservatism* (London, 1976), 124, which claims that Cecil identified 'conservatism with the old liberal view of all state intervention as a threat to liberty.'

[26] Anon., 'Lord Hugh Cecil on Conservatism', *Contemporary Review*, 101 (1912), 891.

[27] Lord H. Cecil, *Liberty and Authority* (London, 1910), 64–5.

tax burden unbearable, and erode personal liberty and responsibility.[28] In other respects, too, Cecil was as zealous in the defence of the rights of property as were the Individualists, and like them he attacked the doctrine of the 'unearned increment' and proposals for 'confiscatory' taxation which would become 'in reality only the transference of property from one set of people to another.'[29]

These points illustrate that the Individualists and the Conservative traditionalists were largely in agreement over that to which they were opposed. But when Cecil turned his hand to a constructive account of the State's duties, a divergence of opinion rapidly became apparent. First of all, in contrast to the predominantly agnostic Individualists, Cecil based his political theory on 'Christian morals as revealed in the New Testament' and assigned the individual primacy over the State because, for a Christian, individuals possessed ultimate moral worth.[30] Cecil argued that the 'championship of religion is therefore the most important of the functions of Conservatism. It is the keystone of the arch upon which the whole fabric rests.' Accordingly, a Conservative was duty-bound to resist Church disestablishment and disendowment:

The recognition of religion implied in establishment and the defence of endowments against confiscation are essential parts of Conservatism, characteristic of the typical Conservative reverence both for religion and for property.[31]

In decided contrast to the Individualists, the British State was for Cecil a confessional State: it was not merely the monopoly of legitimate coercive force in society, but was a locus of reverence and authority to which the individual owed obedience in both secular and religious life.

When Cecil turned to consider the duties of the State with regard to economic and social policy, a number of further disagreements with the Individualists began to emerge. The State was in the position of a 'trustee of the interests of the whole community', and had a responsibility to uphold the interests of all those whom it represented; like the Collectivists, he believed that the national interest was more than a mere sum of its parts. The common good was the standard by which government policy had to be judged, subject to the requirement that it did not commit an injustice against individuals or classes:

[28] Id., 'Presidential Address to the British Constitution Association', in M. H. Judge (ed.), *Political Socialism: A Remonstrance* (London, 1908), 43–8.
[29] Lord H. Cecil, *Conservatism* (London, 1912), 152.
[30] Ibid. 163–4.　　　[31] Ibid. 114.

The State as a trustee acting for others may, and indeed must, prefer the good of the community to the good of any individual or minority. But it may not, any more than an honest trustee, inflict injustice in the interests of those for whom it acts.[32]

Injustice in this context meant interference with the existing distribution of entitlements, not a violation of the Spencerian Law of Equal Freedom. Furthermore, although on Cecil's definition of justice the poor, unemployed, and elderly had no claim on the State's assistance, his conception of the duties of the State did permit the provision of public welfare on the grounds that it promoted the common good. His reason for supporting institutions like the Poor Law, as well as for advocating schemes for national insurance and old age pensions, was that social stability, order, and the authority of the law would be undermined by widespread destitution, and hence that State relief was 'expedient and therefore on the same footing as national defence or any other kind of public expenditure.'[33] Therefore, Cecil argued, while Conservatives insisted that the State scrupulously avoided wronging individuals, and preferred to 'develop what exists rather than to demolish and reconstruct', they had 'no difficulty welcoming the social activity of the State' and he emphasized that 'a policy of State interference is not, as such, alien from Conservatism.'[34]

Whereas the powers of the State were regarded with loathing by the Spencerians, they could hold no terrors for the Cecils since they were, after all, a family heirloom. There were considerable similarities between the conception of the duties of the State propounded by Cecil in 1912, and that which had been expressed over thirty years earlier by his father the third Marquis of Salisbury. Despite the latter's low view of human nature and consequent pessimism about the possibility of sweeping social improvement, he was never an advocate of the *laissez-faire* State as Spencer would have understood it:

Salisbury was far from seeing the role of government in relation to society as one merely of police and administration. There were areas and contingencies in which the positive intervention of government for social ends was not only permissible but might be essential, circumstances in which the government could and should act as an agent of change and reform.[35]

Salisbury may have believed in freedom of trade, enterprise, and contract, financial prudence, and respect for the rights of property

---

[32] Ibid. 165.   [33] Ibid. 177.   [34] Ibid. 195–6.
[35] P. Smith, *Lord Salisbury on Politics* (Cambridge, 1972), 48–9.

(especially those of the landed class) but there was also 'a tinge of old-fashioned Tory paternalism in his outlook' which was 'ready to endorse a degree of cautious and practical intervention by government in the name of social betterment.'[36] Indeed, it should not be forgotten that it was not a piece of Liberal legislation which provoked Spencer into writing *The Man versus the State*, but an article of Salisbury's on 'Labourers' and Artisans' Dwellings'.[37] Distressed by the 'terrible shadow' of 'misery and degradation' cast over Britain's prosperity by the poor standard of working-class housing, Salisbury had argued for the provision of government loans to purchase and clear away unhealthy tenements and to replace them by 'wholesome dwellings'. To Spencer this was simply additional evidence of 'the way in which things are drifting towards Communism with increasing velocity' and he was later to castigate Salisbury as an empiricist who had repudiated the idea that society was governed by scientific laws.[38]

There might appear to be a closer approximation between the pragmatic approach to the role of the State adopted by the Cecils and the outlook of the empirical Individualists. Nevertheless, as Cecil's volume on *Conservatism* illustrates, the intellectual framework which defined the outlook of the Conservative traditionalists, with its emphasis on Church and Empire, and its Burkean conception of the nation as an organic unity, had little in common with the political theory of the former University Radicals.[39] Although the empirical Individualists' views on social policy may not have differed significantly from those of the Conservative traditionalists, their reasons for arriving at the same conclusions were radically contrasting, and this had ramifications for their views on a wide range of other aspects of state policy.

In addition to these theoretical differences, and the policy differences which flowed from them, the failure of Individualism to enter the mainstream of Conservative party politics may be explained by a further

---

[36] Ibid. 49.

[37] R. Cecil, 3rd Marquis of Salisbury, 'Labourers' and Artisans' Dwellings', *National Review*, 2 (1883), 301–16. For the impact of this article on Spencer see D. Duncan, *The Life and Letters of Herbert Spencer* (London, 1908), 238. Donisthorpe also attacked this article: see id., *Liberty or Law?*, 26 f.

[38] H. Spencer, *The Principles of Ethics*, ii. (London, 1893), 260 ff. The same speech referred to by Spencer in this passage was also taken as the text of T. D. Mackay's attack on 'Empiricism in Politics', *National Review*, 25 (1895), 790–803.

[39] An exception to this generalization was A. J. Balfour, who was one of Sidgwick's former pupils. The lecture delivered by Balfour to the Manchester Athenaeum in 1885 (published as 'Politics and Political Economy', *National Review*, 5 (1885), 361–7) betrays a strong Sidgwickian influence.

factor: its ideals simply lacked the broad social basis required for success in a democratic age. As J. D. Y. Peel has stressed, Spencer's political theory was 'traceable back to a time and a place well before the ideological battle-lines of mature industrial society were drawn', and his ideals were those of 'townsmen within a traditional society rapidly moving towards industrialisation.'[40] But by the end of the nineteenth century the social and political battle-lines had been drawn in a recognizably modern form, and party politicians were forced to respond, in their different ways, to the demands of the new democracy. Both the traditionalists and the Collectivists in the Conservative party were practical politicians, aware of the realities of power, and they recognized that they were confronted by the need to discover an electorally viable alternative to what they saw as socialism. Indeed, the Radical Right argued for their proposals on the grounds that they armed the Conservative party with a positive programme with which to appeal to the newly enfranchized electorate, and that by satisfying working-class demands with social reform they would stave off the much greater menace of socialism. From this point of view, and organization like the Liberty and Property Defence League was regarded as 'a dangerous reactionary group which engenders more socialism in one week than it prevents in a year by its wholesale opposition to all proposals that make for the people's welfare.'[41]

It was in this context that Ernest Barker summed up the state of party competition in the first decade of the twentieth century: 'It matters little that one party has espoused the cause of protection, and the other the cause of social reform. Both parties are "interventionists" in domestic, as both parties, in a greater or less degree, are interventionists in foreign policy.'[42] But as the Collectivists gained the ascendancy in the Conservative party, the dwindling band of Individualists increasingly came to despair of the prospects of finding a political vehicle for their ideas. From their perspective, as Sir Roland Wilson complained in 1911, the choice between Conservatism and Liberalism appeared to come down to a choice 'between the plutocratic and democratic forms of

---

[40] J. D. Y. Peel, *Herbert Spencer: The Evolution of a Socialist* (London, 971), 220, 222.

[41] Claude Lowther, letter to the *Times*, 3 Apr. 1911, quoted in K. D. Brown, 'The Anti-Socialist Union, 1908–1949' in id. (ed.), *Essays in Anti-Labour History* (London, 1974), 239. Lowther, a former Unionist MP, was chairman of the Anti-Socialist Union, a pressure group which advocated social reform to stave off socialism, and which contained many Tariff Reformers among its sympathizers.

[42] Barker, *Political Thought in England*, 22–3.

"Etatisme".'[43] Nevertheless, while practical politicians may have been denounced by the Individualists for their 'dishonesty' in sacrificing what they knew to be right and just for a brief measure of popularity, Individualism had nothing to contribute as an alternative. Once having 'Shot Niagara' (in Carlyle's famous phrase), there was little point in merely saying one preferred the view from the top.

The failure of the Individualists to establish their doctrine as part of the Edwardian Conservative mainstream suggests that sweeping generalizations about the emergence of a new form of 'liberal conservatism' in the late nineteenth century need to be treated with a degree of caution. It has been argued, for example by W. H. Greenleaf, that the British Conservative tradition in the twentieth century has been characterized by a contest between a 'Collectivist' and a 'Libertarian' strain, and that the latter owes its origin to the migration of disillusioned Liberals into the Conservative party at the end of the nineteenth century. Although Greenleaf acknowledges that hostility to State intervention was 'firmly established in Tory circles well before the influx of Liberal Unionists and others in the late nineteenth century', he nevertheless claims that 'the ideological influence most important in the development of the libertarian theme was undoubtedly that of Herbert Spencer . . . [T]he form and tone of Spencer's ideas were predominant in the formation of Conservative libertarianism.'[44] However, given the obvious tensions between Individualism and Conservatism, Spencer's infuence was nothing like as great or as lasting as this account would seem to imply.

In the first place, as we have seen, there were fundamental theoretical and practical differences between the Individualists and the Conservative traditionalists. From the distance of over a century, these might appear slight compared to the undoubted common ground which existed between Spencer and Salisbury, and thus it is tempting to classify both of them as upholders of 'the *laissez-faire* state'. But this is to ignore that they were divided by issues which, although they might now have lost their political saliency, were of monumental importance for the participants in the debates. In an age in which the government accounts for almost half of the national wealth, a dispute over the question of whether or not it is legitimate for the State to provide loans to build working-class housing may seem trivial. But this was not how Spencer

---

[43] Sir R. K. Wilson, *The Province of the State* (London, 1911), pref., p. xiii.

[44] Greenleaf, *The Ideological Heritage*, 264. See also O'Sullivan, *Conservatism*, and P. Norton and A. Aughey, *Conservatives and Conservatism* (London, 1981), 65–6.

and Salisbury saw the matter, and once we endeavour to understand the debate in their own terms, it is evident that ideological distance between Individualism and Conservatism, even in a 'traditionalist', Salisburian form, remained considerable.

Secondly, as this chapter has also demonstrated, from the perspective of the Collectivists the Individualists remained too deeply rooted in the assumptions and preconceptions of the mid-Victorian era to confront the political issues of greatest moment in the new century. Cobdenite anti-expansionism appeared outmoded in a world where the decree of a handful of powerful empires held sway; freedom of contract, *laissez-faire*, and the absolute right of the individual to 'do what he will with his own' simply seemed irrelevancies in an industrial system increasingly dominated by trusts and monopolies on the one hand, and trade unions on the other. In their opinion, Britain must either learn to adapt to her new environment or perish, and survival required the abandonment of most of the Individualists' key tenets.

Individualism was alienated from both of the dominant elements within Edwardian Conservatism, and did not even succeed in establishing itself as a minority viewpoint within the party. Instead the theory remained the exclusive province of a particular generation of disillusioned Liberal theorists, for whom the 1860s were forever a paradise lost.

SELECT BIBLIOGRAPHY

A. *Primary Sources*

ALLEN, G., 'Individualism and Socialism', *Contemporary Review*, 55 (1889), 730–41.

ANON., 'Lord Hugh Cecil on Conservatism', *Contemporary Review*, 101 (1912), 889–93.

ANON., '*The Man versus the State* by Herbert Spencer', *Spectator*, 58 (1885), 421–2.

ANON., 'Thomas Mackay' [Obituary Notice], *Charity Organisation Review*, 31 (1912), 174–82.

ANON., 'A Review of the *Elements of Politics*', *Saturday Review*, 72 (1891), 251–2.

ANON., 'Review of *Popular Government*', *Saturday Review*, 60 (1885), 782–3.

ANON., 'Review of Sidgwick's *Elements of Politics*', *Speaker*, 4 (1891), 326–7.

ANON., 'Socialism and Legislation', *Westminster Review*, 69 (1886), 1–25.

ANON., 'H. Spencer's *The Man versus the State*', *Westminster Review*, 66 (1884), 553–5.

ASHLEY, W. J., Sir, *The Economic Organisation of England* (London, 1914).

AUSTIN, J., *A Plea for the Constitution* (1859; 2nd edn., London, 1859).

BALFOUR, A. J., 'Politics and Political Economy', *National Review*, 5 (1885), 361–7.

BALL, S., *The Moral Aspects of Socialism* (Fabian Tract no. 72; London, 1896).

——'A Plea For Liberty: A Criticism', *Economic Review*, 1 (1891), 327–47.

BAX, E. B., and LEVY, J. H., *Socialism and Individualism* (London, n.d. [1904]).

BENTHAM, J., *Economic Writings*, ed. W. Stark (3 vols., London, 1954).

BLISS, W. P. D. (ed.) *The Encyclopedia of Social Reform* (1897; 2nd edn., London, 1907).

BONAR, J., *Philosophy and Political Economy in some of their Historical Relations* (London, 1893).

BOSANQUET, B., *The Philosophical Theory of the State* (London, 1899).

BRAMWELL, G. W. W., Lord, *Laissez Faire* (London, 1884).

BRODRICK, G. C., 'Democracy and Socialism', *Nineteenth Century*, 15 (1884), 626–44.

——*Literary Fragments* (London, 1891).

——'What are Liberal Principles?', *Fortnightly Review*, 19 (1876), 174–93.

BROOKS, G., *Industry and Property* (London, 1895).

CECIL, H., Lord *Conservatism* (London, 1912).

——*Liberty and Authority* (London, 1910).

CECIL, R., 3rd Marquis of Salisbury, 'Labourers' and Artisans' Dwellings', *National Review*, 2 (1883), 301–16.

CHAMBERLAIN, J., *Collected Speeches* (London, 1914).

——'Favorable Aspects of State Socialism', *North American Review*, 152 (1891), 534–48.

——'The Labour Question', *Nineteenth Century*, 32 (1892), 677–710.

CONSTABLE, H. S., *The Fallacies and Follies of Socialist Radicalism Exposed* (London, 1895).

——*Radicalism and its Stupidities* (London, 1896).

CUNNINGHAM, W., *Christianity and the Social Order* (London, 1910).

DAWSON, W. H., *Bismarck and State Socialism* (London, 1891).

DE LAVELEYE, É., 'The State versus the Man: A Criticism of Mr. Herbert Spencer', *Contemporary Review*, 47 (1885), 485–504.

DICEY, A. V., 'Address to the British Constitution Association', *Constitution Papers*, 14 (1908), 117–18.

——'Democratic Assumptions V: Conclusions', *Nation*, (NY), 53 (1891), 83–4.

——'Democracy in Switzerland', *Nation* (NY), 42 (1886), 494–6.

——*Lectures on the Relation of Law and Public Opinion in England during the Nineteenth Century* (London, 1905).

——*Letters to a Friend on Votes for Women* (1909, 2nd edn., London, 1912).

——'Lord Pembroke', *National Review*, 28 (1897), 616–29.

——'Mill "On Liberty"', *Workingman's College Journal*, 7 (1901), 17–21, 35–9, 58–62, 81–6.

DICEY, E., MP, 'The Plea of a Malcontent Liberal', *Fortnightly Review*, 44 (1885), 463–77.

DONISTHORPE, W., *Individualism: A System of Politics* (London, 1889).

——*Law in a Free State* (London, 1895).

——*Liberty or Law?* (London, 1884).

[DONISTHORPE, W.], 'The Basis of Individualism', *Westminster Review*, 70 (1886), 118–56.

EASTWOOD, A., 'A Review of M. D. O'Brien, *The Natural Right to Freedom*, *International Journal of Ethics*, 4 (1893–4), 412.

FAWCETT, H., *State Socialism and the Nationalisation of the Land* (London, 1883).

——and FAWCETT, M. G., *Essays and Lectures on Social and Political Subjects* (London, 1872).

FISKE, J., *An Outline of the Cosmic Philosophy, based on the Doctrine of Evolution* (London, 1874).

FLINT, R., *Socialism* (London, 1894).

GEORGE, H., *A Perplexed Philosopher* (London, 1893).

GILMAN, N. P., *Socialism and the American Spirit* (London, 1893).

GOSCHEN, G. J., *An Address on Laissez Faire and Government Interference* (London, 1883).

——'Since 1880', *Nineteenth Century*, 17 (1885), 723–32.

GREEN, T. H., *Collected Works*, ed. R. L. Nettleship (3 vols., London, 1885–8).

——*The Principles of Political Obligation and Other Writings*, ed. P. Harris and J. Morrow, (Cambridge, 1986).

HAKE, A. E., and WESSLAU, O. E., *The Coming Individualism* (London, 1895).

HERBERT, A., 'Liberty in Land', in W. S. Crawshay and F. Millar (eds.), *The Liberty Annual* (London, 1892), 5–11.

——'Lost in the Region of Phrases', *Humanitarian*, 14 (1899), 320–30.

——*The Right and Wrong of Compulsion by the State* (London, 1885); repr. in *The Right and Wrong of Compulsion by the State and Other Essays*, ed. E. Mack, (Indianapolis, 1978).

——*The Rights of Property: An Address* (London, 1889).

——*The Voluntaryist Creed* (London, 1908).

HERBERT, G. R. C., 13th Earl of Pembroke, 'An Address to the Liberty and Property Defence League with a word to the Conservative Party', *National Review*, 5 (1885), 787–800.

——*Political Letters and Speeches* (London, 1896).

HOBHOUSE, L. T., *Democracy and Reaction* (1904; 2nd edn., London, 1909).

——*Development and Purpose* (London, 1913).

——*The Labour Movement* (1893; 3rd edn., London, 1912).

——*Liberalism* (London, 1911).

——*Social Evolution and Political Theory* (New York, 1911).

HOBSON, J. A., 'A Rich Man's Anarchism', *Humanitarian*, 12 (1898), 390–7.

——*The Crisis of Liberalism: New Issues of Democracy* (London, 1909).

——'Herbert Spencer', *South Place Magazine*, 9 (1904), 49–55, repr. in *J. A. Hobson: A Reader*, ed. M. S. Freeden, (London, 1988), 60–4.

——*The Social Problem* (London, 1901).

HUXLEY, T. H., 'Government: Anarchy or Regulation?', *Nineteenth Century*, 27 (1890), 843–66.

HYNDMAN, H. M., *Socialism and Slavery* (London, 1884).

JEVONS, F. B., 'A Review of Spencer's *Justice*', *Economic Review*, 2 (1892), 133–8.

JUDGE, M. H. (ed.), *Political Socialism: A Remonstrance* (London, 1908).

KIDD, B., *Individualism and After* (Oxford, 1908).

——*Social Evolution* (London, 1894).

LECKY, W. E. H., *Democracy and Liberty* (London, 1896; 2nd edn., London, 1898).

——*A History of England in the Eighteenth Century* (4th edn., London, 1890).

——*Historical and Political Essays* (London, 1903).

Liberty and Property Defence League, *Report of Proceedings and Speeches of the Twelfth Annual Meeting* (London, 1894).

[LOWE, R.], 'Reform Essays', *Quarterly Review*, 123 (1867), 244–77.

MACKAY, T. D., 'Empiricism in Politics', *National Review*, 25 (1895), 790–803.

——*The English Poor* (London, 1889).

——'The Joining of Issues', *Economic Review*, 1 (1891), 194–202.

——*Methods of Social Reform: Essays Critical and Constructive* (London, 1896).

——'Old Age Pensions', *Quarterly Review*, 182 (1895), 254–80.

MACKAY, T. D., 'People's Banks', *National Review*, 22 (1894), 636–47.

——*Public Relief of the Poor: Six Lectures* (London, 1901).

——*The State and Charity* (London, 1898).

—— (ed.) *A Plea for Liberty* (London, 1891).

MCKECHNIE, W. S., *The State and the Individual* (Glasgow, 1896).

MACKINTOSH, R., *From Comte to Benjamin Kidd: The Appeal to Biology or Evolution for Human Guidance* (London, 1899).

MAINE, H. S., Sir, *Ancient Law* (1861; London, 1917).

——*The Effects of the Observation of India in Modern European Thought* (London, 1875).

——*Popular Government: Four Essays* (London, 1885).

[MAINE, Henry, Sir] 'Hares and Rabbits', *St. James's Gazette*, 1 (1880), 76.

——'Irish Land and English Justice', *St. James's Gazette*, 1 (1880), 430.

——'Malthusianism and Modern Politics', *St. James's Gazette*, 1 (1880), 524–5.

——'Mr. Godkin on Popular Government', *Nineteenth Century*, 19 (1886), 366–79.

——'Patriarchal Radicalism', *St. James's Gazette*, 2 (1881), 1467–8.

——'The Projected Economic Revolution in Ireland', *St. James's Gazette*, 2 (1881), 1379–80.

——'Radical Patriarchalism', *St. James's Gazette*, 1 (1880), 259–60.

MAITLAND, F. W., 'Mr. Herbert Spencer's Theory of Society', *Mind*, 8 (1883), 354–71, 506–24.

MALLOCK, W. H., *Aristocracy and Evolution* (London, 1898).

MARETT, R. R., 'Review of *Law in a Free State* by Wordsworth Donisthorpe', *Economic Review*, 5 (1895), 274–5.

MILL, J. S., *Auguste Comte and Positivism*, (1865), in id., *Utilitarianism, Liberty, and Representative Government*, ed. H. R. Acton (Everyman edn., London, 1972).

——*Autobiography* (1873), in id., *Collected Works*, i.

——*Chapters on Socialism* (1879), *John Stuart Mill on Politics and Society*, ed. G. Williams (Glasgow, 1976).

——*Collected Works*, ed. J. M. Robson *et al.* (Toronto, 1963–).

——*The Letters of J. S. Mill*, ed. H. S. R. Elliot (2 vols., London, 1910).

——*On Liberty* (1859); in id., *Utilitarianism, Liberty*, ed. Acton.

——*The Principles of Political Economy* (1848), in id., *Collected Works*, ii, iii.

——*The Subjection of Women* (London, 1867).

——*A System of Logic* (1843; London, 1919).

——*Utilitarianism and Other Writings*, ed. M. Warnock (London, 1979).

MORLEY, J., *Burke* (London, 1879).

——*Studies in Literature* (London, 1897).

O'BRIEN, M. D., *The Natural Right to Freedom* (London, 1893).

——*Socialism Tested by the Facts* (London, 1892).

PLEYDELL-BOUVERIE, E., *The Province of Government* (London, 1884).

The Radical Programme (London, 1885).

RITCHIE, D. G., *Darwin and Hegel* (London, 1893).

——*Darwinism and Politics* (London, 1889).

——*Natural Rights* (London, 1894).

——*Principles of State Interference* (London, 1891).

——'Review of *The Elements of Politics*', *International Journal of Ethics*, 2 (1892), 254–7.

——*Studies in Political and Social Ethics* (London, 1902).

ROBERTSON, G. C., 'Associationism', in *The Encyclopaedia Britannica*, (9th edn., London, 1875), ii. 730–4.

SALEEBY, C. W., *Sociology* (London, n.d. [1906]).

SHAW, G. B. (ed.), *Fabian Essays in Socialism* (London, 1889).

SIDGWICK, H., 'Critical Notice of *Justice* by Mr. H. Spencer, *Mind*, NS 1 (1892), 107–18.

——*The Development of European Polity* (London, 1903).

——*The Elements of Politics* (London, 1891).

——*Lectures on the Ethics of T. H. Green, H. Spencer, and J. Martineau* (London, 1902).

——*The Methods of Ethics* (1874; 7th edn., London, 1907).

——*Miscellaneous Essays and Addresses* (London, 1904).

——'Mr Spencer's Ethical System', *Mind*, 5 (1880), 216–26.

——*Outlines of the History of Ethics for English Readers* (1886; 2nd edn. London, 1888).

——Preface to P. F. Aschrott, *The English Poor Law System* (London, 1888).

——*The Principles of Political Economy* (London, 1883).

——'Review of James Fitzjames Stephen's *Liberty, Equality, Fraternity*', *Academy*, 4 (1873), 292–4.

SLOAN, J. M., *For Freedom: Three Addresses on the Fallacies of State Socialism* (London, n.d. [1894]).

SMITH, [A.] B., *Liberty and Liberalism* (London, 1887).

SMITH, G., *Essays on Questions of the Day, Political and Social* (New York, 1893).

——*False Hopes: Or Fallacies Socialistic and Semi-Socialistic Briefly Answered* (London, 1886).

——'Has Science a New Basis for Morality?', *Contemporary Review*, 41 (1882), 335–8.

——'The Manchester School', *Contemporary Review*, 67 (1895), 377–89.

——'The Organization of Democracy', *Contemporary Review*, 47 (1885), 315–33.

SPENCE, J. C., *The Conscience of the King* (London, 1899).

——*Private Property in Land: A Defence of Individual Ownership* (London, 1892).

SPENCER, H., Synthetic Philosophy:

An Epitome of the Synthetic Philosophy, ed. F. H. Collins (4th edn., London, 1897).

First Principles (3rd edn. London, 1875).

The Principles of Biology (2 vols., London, 1864–7).

The Principles of Psychology (London, 1855: 2nd edn., 2 vols, London, 1870–2).

The Principles of Sociology (3 vols., London, 1876–96).

The Principles of Ethics (2 vols., London, 1892–3). (Part 1 separately published as *Data of Ethics* (London, 1879)).

——Other Writings:

Autobiography (London, 1904).

Education: Intellectual, Moral, and Physical (1861; Thinker's Library edn., London, 1929).

Essays: Scientific, Political and Speculative (3 vols., London, 1868–74; enlarged edn. London, 1891).

Facts and Comments (London, 1902).

Social Statics (1851; 2nd edn. London, 1868; abridged and revised edn., London, 1892).

The Man versus the State, ed. D. G. Macrae (London, 1884, Harmondsworth, 1969).

The Study of Sociology (1873; 15th edn., London, 1889).

Various Fragments (enlarged edn., London, 1900).

STEPHEN, L., *The English Utilitarians* (London, 1900).

——'The Good Old Cause', *Nineteenth Century*, 51 (1902), 11–23.

——*Hobbes* (London, 1904).

——*The Life of Henry Fawcett* (1885; 3rd edn., London, 1886).

——*Social Rights and Duties* (London, 1896).

TOYNBEE, A., *Lectures on the Industrial Revolution of the Eighteenth Century in England* (London, 1884).

WALLACE, A. R., *Studies Scientific and Social* (London, 1900).

WEBB, S., *The Difficulties of Individualism* (Fabian Tract no. 69; London, 1896).

——*Socialism in England* (London, 1889).

——*Socialism: True and False* (Fabian Tract no. 51: London, 1894).

WEMYSS-CHARTERIS-DOUGLAS, F., 9th Earl of Wemyss, *Socialism at St. Stephens in 1883* (London, 1884).

WILSON, R. K., Sir, *The Province of the State* (London, 1911).

——and LEVY, J. H. (eds.), *Individualism and the Land Question* (London, 1912).

B. Secondary Sources

ACTON, H. B., Introduction to S. Webb, *Socialism in England* (London, Gower edn., 1987).

ANDRESKI, S., *Herbert Spencer: Structure, Function and Evolution* (London, 1972).

ARBLASTER, A., *The Rise and Decline of Western Liberalism* (Oxford, 1984).

ATIYAH, P. S., *The Rise and Fall of Freedom of Contract* (Oxford, 1979).

BALDWIN, J. M., *A History of Psychology* (London, 1913).

BALL, T., *Transforming Political Discourse* (Oxford, 1988).

BANNISTER, R. C., *Social Darwinism: Science and Myth in Anglo-American Social Thought* (Philadelphia, 1979).

BARKER, E., *Political Thought in England 1848 to the Present Day* (London, 1915).

BARKER, R., *Political Ideas in Modern Britain* (London, 1978).

BARRY, N. P., *On Classical Liberalism and Libertarianism* (London, 1986).

BLEASE, W. L., *A Short History of English Liberalism* (London, 1913).

BOWLER, P. J., 'Malthus, Darwin, and the Concept of Struggle,' *Journal of the History of Ideas*, 37 (1976), 631–50.

BRADLEY, F. H., *Ethical Studies* (1876; 2nd edn., Oxford, 1927).

BRADLEY, I., *The Optimists* (London, 1980).

BREBNER, J. B., 'Laissez Faire and State Intervention in Nineteenth Century Britain', *Journal of Economic History*, suppl. 8 (1948), 59–73.

BRINTON, C., *English Political Thought in the Nineteenth Century* (London, 1933).

BRISTOW, E., 'The Liberty and Property Defence League and Individualism', *Historical Journal*, 18 (1975), 761–89.

BROWN, K. D., (ed.), *Essays in Anti-Labour History* (London, 1974).

BRYCE, J., *Essays in Contemporary Biography* (London, 1903).

BULLOCK, A., and SHOCK, M., *The Liberal Tradition from Fox to Keynes* (London, 1956).

BURROW, J. W., *Evolution and Society* (Cambridge, 1966).

——*Whigs and Liberals* (Oxford, 1988).

CLARKE, P. F., *Liberals and Social Democrats* (Cambridge, 1978).

COHEN, G. A., *Karl Marx's Theory of History: A Defence* (Oxford, 1978).

COLLINI, S., 'The Idea of "Character" in Victorian Political Thought', *Transactions of the Royal Historical Societys*, 35 (1985), 31–50.

——'Idealism and "Cambridge Idealism",' *Historical Journal*, 18 (1975), 171–7.

——'Liberalism and the Legacy of Mill', *Historical Journal*, 20 (1977), 237–54.

——*Liberalism and Sociology: L. T. Hobhouse and Political Argument in England 1880–1914* (Cambridge, 1978).

——BURROW, J. W., and WINCH, D., *That Noble Science of Politics* (Cambridge, 1983).

COSER, L. A., *The Masters of Sociological Thought* (2nd edn., New York, 1977).

COSGROVE, R. A., *The Rule of Law: Albert Venn Dicey, Victorian Jurist* (London, 1980).

CRANSTON, M., *Philosophers and Pamphleteers* (Oxford, 1986).

CROOK, D. P., *Benjamin Kidd: The Portrait of a Social Darwinist* (Cambridge, 1984).

DEWEY, C. J., '"Cambridge Idealism": Utilitarian Revisionists in Late Nineteenth Century Cambridge', *Historical Journal*, 17 (1974), 63–78.

DUNCAN, D., *The Life and Letters of Herbert Spencer* (London, 1908).

ELLIOT, H., *Herbert Spencer* (London, 1917).

FAIRFIELD, C., *Some Account of George William Wilshere, Baron Bramwell of Hever* (London, 1898).

FEAVER, G., *From Status to Contract: A Biography of Sir Henry Maine, 1822–1888* (London, 1969).

FLUGEL, J. C., *One Hundred Years of Psychology* (London, 1933).

FORD, D. J., 'W. H. Mallock and Socialism in England 1880–1918', in Brown (ed.), *Essays in Anti-Labour History*, 317–42.

FRANCIS, M., 'Herbert Spencer and the Myth of Laissez Faire', *Journal of the History of Ideas*, 39 (1978) 317–28.

FREEDEN, M. S., *The New Liberalism: An Ideology of Social Reform* (Oxford, 1978).

GLICKMAN, H., 'The Toryness of English Conservatism', *Journal of British Studies*, 1 (1961), 111–43.

GOODWIN, C. D., 'Evolution Theory in Australian Social Thought', *Journal of the History of Ideas*, 25 (1964), 393–416.

GRANT-DUFF, M. E., *Sir Henry Maine: A Brief Memoir of His Life* (London, 1892).

GRAY, J. N., 'Spencer on the Ethics of Liberty and State Interference', *History of Political Thought*, 3 (1982), 465–81.

GRAY, T. S., 'Herbert Spencer: Individualist or Organicist?', *Political Studies*, 33 (1985), 236–53.

GREENLEAF, W. H., *The British Political Tradition*, i. *The Rise of Collectivism*; ii. *The Ideological Heritage* (London, 1983).

HALÉVY, E., *The Growth of Philosophic Radicalism* (London, 1972).

HALLIDAY, R. J., 'Social Darwinism: A Definition', *Victorian Studies*, 14 (1971), 389–405.

HARRIS, S. H., *Auberon Herbert: Crusader for Liberty* (London, 1943).

——*The Doctrine of Personal Right* (Barcelona, 1935).

HARRISON, R., *Bentham* (London, 1983).

HARVIE, C., *The Lights of Liberalism: University Liberals and the Challenge of Democracy 1860–1886* (London, 1976).

HAVARD, W. C., *Henry Sidgwick and Later Utilitarian Political Philosophy* (Gainesville, Fla., 1959).

HAWTHORN, G., *Enlightenment and Despair: A History of Social Theory* (1976; 2nd end., Cambridge, 1987).

HEARNSHAW, F. J. C., *Conservatism in England* (London, 1933).

HOFSTADTER, R., *Social Darwinism in American Thought* (New York, 1944; 2nd edn., Boston, 1955).

HUDSON, W. H., *An Introduction to the Philosophy of Herbert Spencer* (London, 1897).

HUME, L. J., *Bentham and Bureaucracy* (Cambridge, 1983).

JONES, G., *Social Darwinism and English Thought: The Interaction between Biological and Social Theory* (Brighton, 1980).

KEYNES, J. M., *Essays in Persuasion* (Cambridge, 1972).

KLOPPENBERG, J. T., *Uncertain Victory: Social Democracy and Progressivism in European and American Thought 1870–1920* (Oxford, 1986).

LECKY, E., *A Memoir of the Rt. Hon. W. E. H. Lecky by his Wife* (London, 1909).

LUKES, S., *Individualism* (Oxford, 1973).

LYONS, D., *The Forms and Limits of Utilitarianism* (Oxford, 1965).

MACPHERSON, H., *Herbert Spencer: The Man and his Work* (London, 1900).

MALCOLM, N., *Wittgenstein: Nothing is Hidden* (Oxford, 1986).

MATTHEW, H. C. G., *The Liberal Imperialists* (Oxford, 1973).

——(ed.), *The Gladstone Diaries*, x and xi (Oxford, 1990).

MEADOWCROFT, J., and TAYLOR, M. W., 'Liberalism and the Referendum in British Political Thought 1880–1914', *Twentieth Century British History*, I (1990), 35–57.

MEDAWAR, P. B., *The Art of the Soluble* (London, 1967).

MENGER, A., *The Right to the Whole Produce of Labour* (London, 1899).

MILLER, D. L., *Social Justice* (Oxford, 1976).

MILLER, W. L., 'Herbert Spencer's Drift to Conservatism', *History of Political Thought*, 3 (1982), 482–97.

MOORE, G. E., *Principia Ethica* (Cambridge, 1959).

NORTON, P., and AUGHEY, A., *Conservatives and Conservatism* (London, 1981).

OAKESHOTT, M., *On Human Conduct* (Oxford, 1975).

O'SULLIVAN, N., *Conservatism* (London, 1976).

PARRIS, H., 'The Nineteenth Century Revolution in Government: A Reappraisal Reappraised', *Historical Journal*, 3 (1960), 17–37.

PASSMORE, J., *The Perfectability of Man* (London, 1970).

PAUL, E. F., 'Herbert Spencer: The Historicist as Failed Prophet', *Journal of the History of Ideas*, 64 (1983), 619–38.

——'Liberalism, Unintended Orders and Evolutionism', *Political Studies*, 36 (1988), 251–72.

——'The Time-Frame Theory of Governmental Legitimacy', in J. Paul (ed.), *Reading Nozick* (Oxford, 1982).

PEEL, J. D. Y., *Herbert Spencer: The Evolution of a Sociologist* (London, 1971).

POLANYI, K., *The Great Transformation* (Boston, 1957).

QUINTON, A. M., *The Politics of Imperfection* (London, 1978).

RAIT, R. S., *Memorials of Albert Venn Dicey* (London, 1925).

REES, J. C., *John Stuart Mill's On Liberty* (Oxford, 1985).

RICHTER, M., *The Politics of Conscience: T. H. Green and his Age* (London, 1964).

ROACH, J., 'Liberalism and the Victorian Intelligentsia', *Cambridge Historical Journal*, 13 (1957), 58–81.

ROBERTSON, J. M., *Modern Humanists Reconsidered* (London, 1927).

ROLT, L. T. C., *Isambard Kingdom Brunel* (Harmondsworth, 1970).

ROSEN, F., *Jeremy Bentham and Representative Democracy* (Oxford, 1983).

ROYLANCE-KENT, C. B., *The English Radicals* (London, 1900).

RUSSELL, G. W. E., *Portraits of the Seventies* (London, 1916).

RYAN, A., *J. S. Mill* (London, 1974).

——*The Philosophy of John Stuart Mill* (London, 1970).

——*Property and Political Theory* (Oxford, 1984).

SABINE, G. H., and THORSON, T. L., *A History of Political Theory*, (4th edn., Hinsdale, Ill., 1973).

SCHNEEWIND, J. B., *Sidgwick's Ethics and Victorian Moral Philosophy* (Oxford, 1977).

SEARLE, G. R., 'Critics of Edwardian Society: The Case of the Radical Right', in A. O'Day (ed.), *The Edwardian Age: Conflict and Stability 1900–1914* (London, 1979), 79–96.

——*The Quest for National Efficiency* (Oxford, 1971).

SEMMEL, B., *Imperialism and Social Reform* (London, 1960).

SHANNON, R., *The Crisis of Imperialism* (London, 1976).

S[IDGWICK], A., and S[IDGWICK], E. M., *Henry Sidgwick: A Memoir* (London, 1906).

SIMON W. M., 'Herbert Spencer and the "Social Organism",' *Journal of the History of Ideas*, 21 (1960), 294–9.

SKINNER, Q., 'Meaning and Understanding in the History of Ideas', *History and Theory*, 8 (1969), 3–53.

SMELLIE, K. B., 'Sir Henry Maine', *Economica*, 8 (1928), 64–94.

SOLDON, N. C., 'Individualist Periodicals: The Crisis of Late Victorian Liberalism', *Victorian Periodicals Newsletter*, 6 (1973), 17–26.

——'Laissez Faire as Dogma: The Liberty and Property Defence League 1882–1914', in Brown (ed.), *Essays in Anti-Labour History*, 208–33.

STEINTRAGER J., *Bentham* (London, 1977).

SUGARMAN, D., 'The Legal Boundaries of Liberty: Dicey, Liberalism and Legal Science', *Modern Law Review*, 46 (1983), 102–11.

TULLOCH, H. A., 'Changing British Attitudes to the United States in the 1880s', *Historical Journal*, 20 (1977), 825–40.

TURNER, J. H., *Herbert Spencer: A Renewed Appreciation* (Beverly Hills, Calif., 1985).

VINCENT, A. W., and PLANT, R., *Philosophy, Politics and Citizenship: The Life and Thought of the British Idealists* (Oxford, 1984).

VINER, J., 'The Intellectual History of Laissez Faire', *Journal of Law and Economics*, 3 (1960), 45–69.

WARREN, H. C., *A History of the Association Psychology* (London, 1921).

WEBB, B., *My Apprenticeship* (1926; Cambridge, 1979).

WEILER, P., *The New Liberalism* (New York, 1982).

WEINSTEIN, W. L., 'The Concept of Liberty in Nineteenth Century English Political Thought,' *Political Studies*, 13 (1965), 145–62.

WILTSHIRE, D., *The Social and Political Thought of Herbert Spencer* (Oxford, 1978).

WINCH, D., *Adam Smith's Politics* (Cambridge, 1978).

WOOD, A., *Karl Marx* (London, 1981).

YOUNG, R. M., 'Malthus and the Evolutionists: The Common Context of Biological and Social Theory', *Past and Present*, 43 (1969), 104–45.

——*Mind, Brain, and Adaptation in the Nineteenth Century* (Oxford, 1970).

INDEX